As one of the world's longest established and best-known travel brands, Thomas Cook are the experts in travel.

For more than 135 years our guidebooks have unlocked the secrets of destinations around the world, sharing with travellers a wealth of experience and a passion for travel.

**Rely on Thomas Cook as your travelling companion on your next trip and benefit from our unique heritage.**

Thomas Cook **driving** guides

# IRELAND

## Donna Dailey

D0846588

Thomas Cook

Your travelling companion since 1873

Written, researched and updated by Donna Dailey

**Published by Thomas Cook Publishing**
A division of Thomas Cook Tour Operations Limited
Company registration no. 3772199 England
The Thomas Cook Business Park, Unit 9, Coningsby Road,
Peterborough PE3 8SB, United Kingdom
Email: books@thomascook.com, Tel: + 44 (0) 1733 416477
www.thomascookpublishing.com

**Produced by Cambridge Publishing Management Limited**
Burr Elm Court, Main Street, Caldecote CB23 7NU
www.cambridgepm.co.uk

ISBN: 978-1-84848-378-1

Series Editor: Karen Beaulah
Production/DTP: Steven Collins

Printed and bound in India by Replika Press Pvt Ltd

Cover photography © IIC

# About the author

Donna Dailey is a writer and photographer who has written numerous travel books, including *driving guides Scotland*. She has a keen interest in Celtic history and mythology, and is presently on the trail of ancestors in counties Westmeath and Clare.

## Acknowledgements

The author would like to thank the following people for their invaluable help in researching this guide: Pat Dooley, Dan Dooley, Rent-A-Car; Katrina Flanagan, Bord Fáilte (Irish Tourist Board), London; Colette Reynolds, Northern Ireland Tourist Board; Sarah Wallace, BGB & Associates; Catherine McCluskey and Linda Mulligan, Dublin Tourism; Norman Black, Kathleen Murtagh and Róisín Burns, Midlands East Tourism; Alison Russell, Michael Brady and Fiona Henshaw, East Coast & Midlands Tourism; Pat Nolan and Gary Breen, South East Tourism; Monica Leech and Carol Hutcheson, Waterford Tourism; Frank

Donaldson and Lillian Cox, Cork & Kerry Tourism; Nandi O'Sullivan, Mark Wrafter and Chris Meehan, Shannon Development; Fionnuala O'Malley and Fiona Burns, Ireland West Tourism; Róisín Sorahan and Gemma Shannon, North West Tourism. The author would also like to thank Eithne and Tony Healy of Fore, County Westmeath; Patrick Walsh of Dublin; Catherine O'Grady and Paddy O'Donoghue of Mungret, County Limerick; and all her hosts at the following establishments who provided such a warm welcome and splendid hospitality: Ferrycarrig Hotel, Wexford; Richmond Country House, Cappoquin; The Hibernian, Kilkenny; St Gobnaits, Drogheda; Hounslow House, Fore; Spinners Town House, Birr; Garnish House, Cork; Sceilig Bed & Breakfast, Kinsale; Westlodge Hotel, Bantry; Kenmare Bay Hotel, Kenmare; Muckross Park Hotel, Killarney; Brook Manor Lodge, Tralee; Baunacloka House, Mungret, Limerick; Glenomra House, Ennis; Tuar Beag B&B, Spiddal; Mal Dua Guest House, Clifden; Brooklodge B&B, Westport; Ardtarmon House, Sligo; Rossahilly House, Enniskillen; Bay View Country House, Ardara; Mount Errigal Hotel, Letterkenny; Beech Hill Country House Hotel, Derry; The Bushmills Inn, Bushmills; Madison's, Belfast; Burrendale Hotel & Country Club, Newcastle.

# Contents

# About driving guides

Thomas Cook's driving guides are designed to provide you with a comprehensive but flexible reference source to guide you as you tour a country or region by car. This guide divides Ireland into touring areas – one per chapter. Major cultural centres or cities form chapters in their own right. Each chapter contains enough attractions to provide at least a day's worth of activities – often more.

### Ratings

To make it easier for you to plan your time and decide what to see, every area is rated according to its attractions in categories such as Architecture, Entertainment and Children.

### Chapter contents

Every chapter has an introduction summing up the main attractions of the area, and a ratings box, which will highlight the area's strengths and weaknesses – some areas may be more attractive to families travelling with children, others to plant lovers visiting gardens, and others to people interested in finding castles, churches, museums, nature reserves or good beaches.

Each chapter is then divided into an alphabetical gazetteer, and a suggested tour. You can select whether you just want to visit a particular sight or attraction, choosing from those described in the gazetteer, or whether you want to tour the area comprehensively. If the latter, you can construct your own itinerary, or follow the author's suggested tour, which comes at the end of every area chapter.

### The gazetteer

The gazetteer section describes all the major attractions in the area – the villages, towns, historic sites, nature reserves, parks or museums that you are most likely to want to see. Maps of the area highlight all the places mentioned in the text. Using this comprehensive overview of the area, you may choose just to visit one or two sights.

One way to use the guide is simply to find individual sights that interest you, using the index or overview map, and read what our author has to say about them. This will help you decide whether to visit the sight. If you do, you will find plenty of practical information, such as the street address, the telephone number for enquiries and opening times.

Alternatively, you can choose a hotel, perhaps with the help of the accommodation recommendations contained in this guide. You can then turn to the overall map on *pages 8–9* to help you work out which chapters in the book describe those cities and regions that lie closest to your chosen touring base.

## Symbol key

- ❶ Tourist Information Centre
- ❷ Advice on arriving or departing
- ❷ Parking locations
- ❷ Advice on getting around
- ❷ Directions
- ❷ Sights and attractions
- ❷ Accommodation
- ❷ Eating
- ❷ Shopping
- ❷ Sport
- ❷ Entertainment

## Practical information

The practical information in the page margins, or sidebars, will help you locate the services you need as an independent traveller – including the tourist information centre, car parks and public transport facilities. You will also find the opening times of sights, museums, churches and other attractions, as well as useful tips on shopping, market days, cultural events, entertainment, festivals and sports facilities. Some attractions have OPW at the end of their entries – this is the Office of Public Works in Ireland.

## Driving tours

The suggested tour is just that – a suggestion, with plenty of optional detours and one or two ideas for making your own discoveries, under the heading *Also worth exploring*. The routes are designed to link the attractions described in the gazetteer section, and to cover outstandingly scenic coastal, mountain and rural landscapes. The total distance is given for each tour, as is the time it will take you to drive the complete route, but bear in mind that this indication is just for the driving time: you will need to add on extra time for visiting attractions along the way.

Many of the routes are circular, so that you can join them at any point. Where the nature of the terrain dictates that the route has to be linear, the route can either be followed there and back, or you can use it as a link route, to get from one area in the book to another.

As you follow the route descriptions, you will find names picked out in bold capital letters – this means that the place is described fully in the gazetteer. Other names picked out in bold indicate additional villages or attractions worth a brief stop along the route.

## Accommodation and food

In every chapter you will find lodging and eating recommendations for individual towns, or for the area as a whole. These are designed to cover a range of price brackets and concentrate on more characterful small or individualistic hotels and restaurants. In addition, you will find information in the *Travel facts* chapter (*see page 12*) on chain hotels, with an address to which you can write for a guide, map or directory. The price indications used in the guide have the following meanings:

€/£     budget level
€€/££   typical/average prices
€€€/£££ de luxe

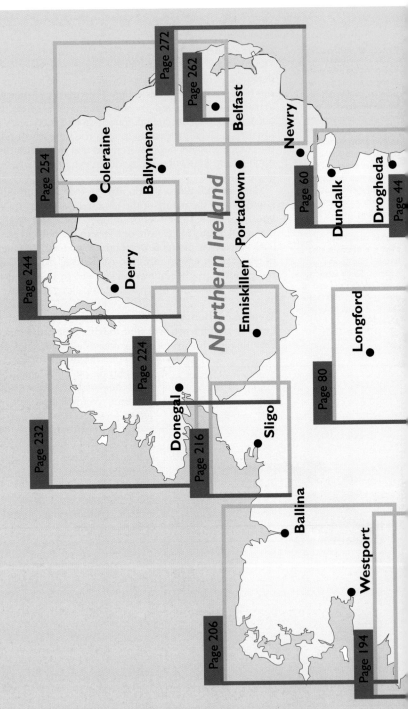

Page 272

Page 262

Belfast

Newry

Coleraine

Ballymena

Page 254

Northern Ireland

Portadown

Page 60

Dundalk

Drogheda

Page 44

Derry

Page 244

Enniskillen

Longford

Page 224

Page 80

Donegal

Sligo

Page 232

Page 216

Ballina

Westport

Page 206

Page 194

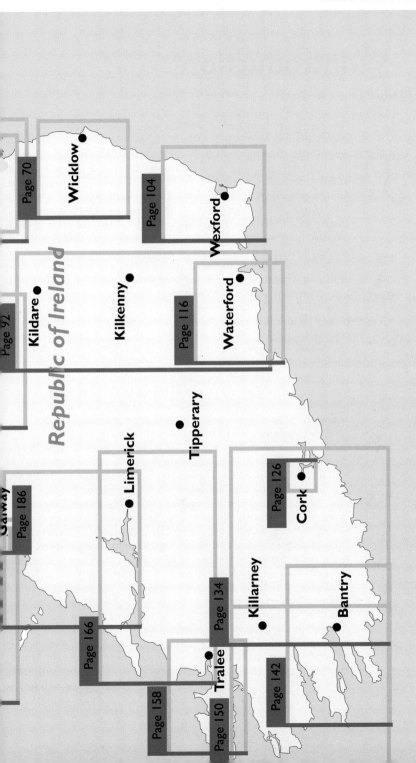

Republic of Ireland

Page 70 — Wicklow ●

Page 104 — Wexford ●

Page 92 — Kildare ●

Kilkenny ●

Page 116 — Waterford ●

Tipperary ●

Galway
Page 186 — Limerick ●

Page 126 — Cork ●

Page 166

Page 134 — Killarney ●

Bantry ●

Page 158

Page 150 — Tralee ●

Page 142

# Introduction

Few people arrive in Ireland without some preconceived notions, for the reputation of this small island nation in the North Atlantic is surprisingly strong around the world. Some visitors come on retreat, seeking relaxation in the quiet country lanes and timeless seaside villages, others on a trendy weekend break in the bustling capital. Some come on pilgrimage to the ancient holy places of Christian saints, still others on a quest for the homeland of their ancestors. Whatever its image, it is certainly not detached, for Ireland is an emotive place with as many facets of culture and history as the 40 shades of green in its landscape.

This island, which is 303 miles (488km) long and 189 miles (304km) at its widest point, has an amazing diversity of terrain. Geographically, it is somewhat like a basin, with mountains rising up around the rim and a limestone plain in the centre which is alternately flat and rolling, broken by low hills, called drumlins, and numerous lakes. Much of the land is agricultural, fed by meandering rivers and divided by thick hedgerows or drystone walls. The most unique feature of Ireland's landscape is the vast stretches of blanket bog that cover much of the central and northwestern counties, a sight all the more startling when you learn that this country was once covered in thick oak forests. Ireland has both the longest river, the Shannon, and the largest lake, Lough Neagh, in the British Isles, as well as the highest sea cliffs in Europe.

It's not, however, the turquoise blue of the lakes, the purple grey of the mountains or the tawny gold pelt of the boglands at sunset that is most frequently used to describe Ireland. This is, after all, the Emerald Isle, and it is the spectrum of greens you most remember, from dark and lush to shimmering with an almost electric brightness. The price to be paid for all this green is rain, and you should be prepared for sudden changes in the weather. However, the climate is moderated by the Gulf Stream, allowing fuchsias and even palms to flourish in sheltered spots.

The 'four green fields' of Irish ballads refer to its four provinces: Ulster in the north, Leinster in the east, Munster in the south and Connacht in the west. They are based on the country's ancient kingdoms, and while they have no political significance today, they still hold cultural and historical importance. Ireland comprises 32 counties, 26 in the Republic and 6 in Northern Ireland. The biggest division, in all respects, is the partition of the country into separate states. With the Northern Ireland peace agreement in place, the Troubles of the past 30 years seem to be at an end. Tourists have nothing to fear – and much to gain – by visiting Northern Ireland. The border checkpoints are a thing of the past, and in most places the only sign that you've crossed the border will be the name of the road and the price of petrol.

The population of the Republic is over 4.3 million. More than one million people live in Dublin. Cork, the second-largest city, has less than half that number. About 1.7 million people live in Northern Ireland. And it is 'the people' that most visitors will mention first when asked what they liked best about the country.

Irish humour and wit are legendary, and ordinary people express themselves with great imagination and insight. No place in Ireland is without a story, and a lyrical one at that. People know and respect their history, for the sense of place and belonging to the land is inherent in the Irish character, a fact that makes the tragedies of the past all the more poignant. 'You are very welcome' is the greeting you'll receive in an Irish home, for their hospitality is second to none, a custom that dates back to Celtic times when such behaviour to travellers was a matter of honour.

Over the centuries, religion has been both a uniting and dividing force in Ireland. It is palpable in the South, not just in the ornate churches, sculpted crosses and ruined abbeys but also in the holy medals and the invocations used in everyday speech. There is a greater spirituality here, too, that encompasses more than mere religion – a love and appreciation of nature that is Celtic to the core and celebrated in poetry and literature. Ireland's literary greatness today is simply a continuation of its ancient bardic tradition. There's no doubt that Ireland is 'hot' – especially when it comes to the arts – as the world enjoys a love affair with all things Celtic, from rock stars to Riverdance.

Ireland's economy has had plenty of ups and downs in recent decades. During the 1990s and early 2000s, spurred on by investment from the European Union and foreign multinationals, Ireland was one of the greatest success stories in the industrialised world. It was christened the Celtic Tiger, with computer software and services, along with tourism and agriculture, at the forefront of the economy. However, the Irish financial crisis, which began during the global recession in 2008, took its toll. Unemployment rose steeply, and the country is still struggling to recover from banking scandals and industrial unrest.

Ireland is an easy place to travel – it's informal, friendly, with all the comforts of home. Because the country is small, it's tempting to try to cover as much ground as possible. You might see a lot that way, but you'll miss much more, for Ireland's greatest rewards lie in the chance encounters and unexpected charms you'll discover when you match its pace.

A word about the leprechauns... If they do exist, they only come out at night to tamper with the road signs. When driving the back roads you often get the feeling that they're sitting in the field sniggering as they watch you drive off in the opposite direction from where you want to go. But apart from this bit of mischief, you'll find Ireland a delightful place for a touring holiday and it's likely that your first trip here will not be your last.

**Below**
Street performer

# Travel facts

## Accommodation

Accommodation in Ireland ranges from luxurious castles to horse-drawn caravans. You'll find large purpose-built hotels as well as renovated historic buildings with modern amenities. Many hotels also function as a social centre for the community, with food, entertainment, sports and leisure facilities on the premises. 'You're very welcome' is a greeting you'll hear at most guesthouses and bed-and-breakfast accommodation; it's a heartfelt sentiment. This is where you'll experience Ireland's legendary hospitality and get to know its people, often over a tray of tea and home-made scones.

Properties that belong to organisations such as the **Irish Hotels Federation** or the **Northern Ireland Hotels Federation** have been inspected by the Irish Tourist Board or the Northern Ireland Tourist Board. Look for the green shamrock enclosed in a circle, their sign of approval.

Hotels are classified from one to five stars. Five-star hotels are luxurious world-class establishments; all four- and three-star hotels and most two-star hotels have en-suite facilities, as well as restaurants; one-star hotels may also have some rooms with a private bath or shower.

Guesthouses are rated separately, from one to four stars. All rooms in three- and four-star guesthouses have en-suite facilities and dinner may be served. Some rooms in one- and two-star guesthouses may also have en-suite rooms.

Almost all accommodation in every category offers breakfast.

### Booking

It is always wise to book ahead, especially in high season (July and August) or during local festivals and school or public holidays. It is also a good idea to check with the Dublin tourist office when you are making plans to visit the city, as conventions or other major events can make last-minute accommodation scarce.

In all categories, prices are quoted either as a room rate, which specifies the cost of a room per night and excludes breakfast, or as B&B (bed and breakfast) per person, which is based on two people sharing a twin or double room. Single supplements are often charged for one person occupying a double room. There may be restrictions on the number of persons allowed to share a room. In the Republic, rates are quoted in euros; in Northern Ireland they are quoted in STG£ (see *Currency, page 15*).

When booking, be sure to ask about special offers, such as weekend or midweek specials, which may be available at certain times of the year.

## Types of accommodation

**Hotels** range from atmospheric village inns to modern city properties, from stately country houses to grand castles. Rates vary based on location, time of year and the attributes of the individual properties. The average price for a three-star hotel starts at around €50 B&B per person (from £40 in Northern Ireland).

**Guesthouses** offer an informal atmosphere in Victorian and Georgian houses, large family homes, or modern buildings. The average price for a two-star guesthouse starts at around €35 (£30 in NI) per person.

**Irish Homes and Farmhouses** accommodation (B&B) gives you a chance to experience Irish family life, in traditional cottages, bungalows, farmhouses and other homes located in towns, villages and the countryside. Prices start at around €30 (£24 in NI) per person.

## Gulliver

The Gulliver tourism information and reservations system features all officially approved accommodation in Ireland. *Tel: 066 979 2030 or 066 979 1804; email: reservations@ gulliver.ie.* You can book online at *www.goireland.com* or *www.gulliver.ie*

## Travellers with disabilities

More and more hotels and guesthouses are providing facilities for travellers with disabilities. You can request a fact sheet that lists suitable establishments by county from the **National Disability Authority**, *Access Dept, 25 Clyde Road, Dublin 4; tel: 01 608 0400; fax: 01 660 9935; email: nda@nda.ie; www.nda.ie.* In Northern Ireland, contact **Disability Action** *on 028 9029 7880; email: information@disabilityaction. org; www.disabilityaction.org*

If you are taking your car to Ireland by ferry, please see *Drivers with disabilities* in the *Driver's guide* section, page 26.

## Camping and caravanning

For information on camping in Ireland, contact the **Irish Caravan and Camping Council**, *PO Box 4443, Dublin 2; fax: 098 28237; email: admin@camping-ireland.ie; www.camping-ireland.ie*

**Self-catering** accommodation is available in cottages, houses, apartments and other properties, which are often located in scenic areas. You can even splash out on an Irish castle or manor house, complete with butler and housekeeping staff!

**Hostels** throughout Ireland, in both the cities and the countryside, provide cheap dormitory-style accommodation, with fees between €10 and €30 (£10–24 in NI). There are also self-catering holiday hostels with a limited number of single, twin and family rooms from €10 to €60 (£10–50 in NI) per night.

There is a good network of **camping and caravanning sites** throughout Ireland. All approved camping and caravan parks are inspected regularly and provide a range of facilities, including showers, laundry rooms, shops, cafés and children's play areas. Many sites have modern mobile homes that can be rented by the week.

If you want to experience the old spirit of the Irish countryside, you can hire a **horse-drawn caravan** equipped for four to five people, and you'll be shown how to care for the horse. Nightly 'parking' costs apply. Check *www.irishhorsedrawncaravans.com* for more information.

## Be our guest

The **Irish Hotels Federation**, *13 Northbrook Road, Dublin 6; tel: 01 808 4419; fax: 01 497 4613*, provides information and publishes the useful *Be Our Guest* guide to hotels and guesthouses throughout the Republic. If you are moving around from region to region, the proprietors of these establishments will help you select and book your next accommodation from the guide. You can also make bookings through the Gulliver service *(see sidebar)*. You can book online at *www.irelandhotels.com* or send an email to *info@ihf.ie*

Ireland's tourist information offices operate a nationwide accommodation booking service for visitors. There is a small charge to cover the cost of the telephone calls, and a non-refundable 10 per cent booking deposit is required.

**Ireland's Blue Book** is an association of charming country-house and restaurant accommodation. Contact *Ireland's Blue Book, 8 Mount Street Crescent, Dublin 2; tel: 01 676 9914; fax: 01 631 4990; email: enquiry@irelandsbluebook.com; www.irelands-blue-book.ie*

**The Hidden Ireland** is a collection of private heritage houses, most surrounded by attractive parks or gardens, that offer a unique experience of Irish country life. Contact *The Hidden Ireland, PO Box 31, Westport, Co. Mayo; tel: 98 66650 or 01 662 7166 (Dublin); email: info@hiddenireland.com; www.hiddenireland.com*

**Other useful contacts:**

**Northern Ireland Hotels Federation** *The McCune Building, 1 Shore Road, Belfast BT15 3PG; tel: 028 9077 6635, fax: 028 9077 1899; email: office@nihf.co.uk; www.nihf.co.uk.*

**Premier Guesthouses of Ireland** *Bracken Court, Bracken Road, Sandyford, Dublin 18; tel: 01 205 2826; fax: 01 293 3027; email: premier@ premierguesthouses.com; www.premierguesthouses.com*

**B&B Ireland** *Belleek Road, Ballyshannon, Co Donegal; tel: 071 982 2222; fax: 071 982 2207; email: admin@bandbireland.com; www.bandbireland.com*

**Irish Farm Holidays** *B&B Ireland, Belleek Road, Ballyshannon, Co Donegal; tel: 071 982 2222; fax: 071 982 2207; email: info@bandbireland.com; www.irishfarmholidays.com*

**Irish Cottage Holiday Homes** *Central Reservations Office, Bracken Court, Bracken Road, Sandyford, Dublin 18; tel: 01 205 2777; fax: 01 293 3025; email: cottage@ irishcottageholidays.com; www.irishcottageholidays.com*

**Independent Holiday Hostels of Ireland** *57 Lower Gardiner Street, Dublin 1; tel: 01 836 4700; fax: 01 836 4710; email: info@hostels-ireland.com; www.hostels-ireland.com*

**Left**
St Kevin Church in the Wicklow Mountains

**Friendly Homes of Ireland** is a collection of charming family homes, small hotels and guesthouses that have historic interest or special attractions. Contact *Adams & Butler, PO Box 2281, Dublin 4; tel: 01 288 9355; fax: 01 288 9282; email: info@irishluxury.com; www. tourismresources.ie/fh*

## Children

With over 50 per cent of Ireland's population under the age of 30, children won't lack for company. The Irish love children and welcome them in hotels and restaurants, with few exceptions. Most hotels can provide a cot for infants, with advance notice, and many can arrange babysitting services. Restaurants often have children's menus. Children are allowed to enter pubs until around 1730 (sometimes a bit later if the pub isn't busy), although they cannot drink alcohol until the age of 18. Theme parks and other attractions geared for children are mentioned throughout the guidebook; many places offer family tickets. When booking hotels and public transport, be sure to ask about any children's discounts and the age limit; these can add up to considerable savings.

## Climate

The flip side of enjoying Ireland's emerald green landscape is enduring the rain that creates it. Ireland is one of the wettest countries in Europe, with the west receiving the most rainfall. April is generally the driest month, though rainfall figures are fairly steady throughout the year, but even when it rains, rarely is it wet the entire day. One of the amazing things about this climate is how quickly it changes. You can get soaked in a downpour one minute and have bright blue sky the next, so be prepared for anything when you set out from your hotel. In areas such as the Ring of Kerry, where clear skies make all the difference to the scenery, it's a good idea to build 'rain' days into your schedule so you can wait out any storms. The southeast gets the most sunshine, Northern Ireland the least. Even in high summer, it's never unbearably hot. Winter is mild throughout the country, although the high mountains will get snow.

## Currency

The Republic of Ireland's national currency is the euro. There are 8 coin denominations: 2-euro and 1-euro coins (silver and gold); 50-, 20- and 10-cents (gold); 5-, 2- and 1-cent (bronze). Euro notes are in denominations of 5 (grey), 10 (pink), 20 (blue), 50 (orange), 100 (green), 200 (yellow) and 500 (purple). In Northern Ireland, the currency is the pound sterling, as in the rest of the United Kingdom. It is divided into 100 pence; and comes in denominations of £50, £20,

### Entry formalities

British citizens born in the United Kingdom do not require a passport to enter Ireland. However, it is a good idea to carry identification. Airlines and ferry companies may require a passport or driving licence, so check with your carrier or travel agent. Citizens of the European Union should carry passports for identification, as some National ID cards are not accepted. All other visitors will need a passport, which must have a minimum of six months' validity. Citizens of Australia, Canada, New Zealand, South Africa and the United States do not need a visa. Citizens of other countries may require an entry visa. Check with the Irish Embassy in your country.

**The Irish Embassy**
*17 Grosvenor Place, London SW1X 7HR; tel: 020 7235 2171; fax: 020 7201 2515; www.embassyofireland.co.uk*

£10 and £5 notes; and coins of £2, £1, 50p, 20p, 10p, 5p, 2p and 1p. The euro is not on a par with sterling, so you need to exchange money when crossing the border.

The best exchange rates for foreign currency can be found at banks and bureaux de change. There are foreign-exchange counters at all the main airports. Automated Teller Machines (cashpoints) accept cards with the 'Plus' and 'Cirrus' symbols. Most major credit cards, including cards with the Eurocard symbol, are accepted in hotels, restaurants, petrol stations and larger shops; you will need cash for small hotels and farmhouse stays. Personal cheques from British banks are generally accepted in Northern Ireland when backed with a bank card, but they are not accepted in the Republic of Ireland.

## Customs regulations

Duty-free allowances for bringing goods into Ireland from outside the EU are: 200 cigarettes or 100 cigarillos or 50 cigars or 250g tobacco; 4 litres table wine; 1 litre spirits or 2 litres fortified or sparkling wine or 2 litres additional still table wine; 16 litres beer; other dutiable goods to the value of €430 (£390 in Northern Ireland). Travellers under the age of 17 may not claim tobacco or alcohol allowances.

Duty-free goods are not available when travelling between the Republic and Northern Ireland. Duty-free sales for inter-community (EU) travellers were abolished in 1999. Limits on duty-paid goods have been increased, as long as they are for personal use. A number of items, including meat and meat products, plants, vegetables, firearms and ammunitions, are prohibited.

For bringing goods home, duty-free allowances vary from country to country. Check with your travel agent or customs authority.

## Drinking

Ireland's most famous beer is Guinness®, a dark, heavy stout with a thick creamy head. The taste and texture of stout depends on how it is stored – and poured. A good pint can't be hurried, so enjoy the ritual. Other Irish beers include Murphy's, which is a slightly sweeter stout, Beamish and Smithwick's. Stout is often drunk with Ireland's other famous drink, whiskey (note the 'e' in the spelling), and in country pubs you'll hear the locals ordering 'a pint and a drop' or 'a bottle and a half 'un'.

Bushmills in Northern Ireland claims to be the world's oldest legal whiskey distillery. Other leading brands include Jamesons and Powers. Irish whiskey must be matured in wooden casks for at least seven years before it is bottled, and its flavour is distinct from its Scottish, American and Canadian counterparts. You might also want to try the whiskey-based liqueurs, Irish Mist and Bailey's Irish Cream.

## Food guides

The *Taste of Ulster* and the *Belfast Restaurant Guide* are two useful Northern Irish publications listing restaurants, cafés, pubs and hotels, price brackets and type of food served. They are sold at newsagents and tourist information offices.

## Tipping

If service is not already included in your bill, the standard tip in restaurants is 10 per cent (up to 15 per cent for particularly good service). Tip taxi drivers by rounding up the fare to the nearest euro or pound, but hackney cabs who drive for prearranged sums do not expect tips. Tipping is not expected by bar staff in pubs, or for hotel services such as serving a drink or carrying bags to your room – if in doubt, a small tip of 20–50 cents will suffice.

Fine wines are widely available in restaurants and bars. And although Ireland's climate is generally not thought suitable for grape growing, there are in fact a handful of vineyards that produce small quantities of local wines.

## Eating out

You will find meals to suit all tastes and budgets in Ireland, from superb *table d'hôte* dining in country-house hotels to simple but filling café fare. Though the tradition of eating a large meal at midday is shifting with the times, big breakfasts such as the Ulster fry (bacon, sausage, egg, grilled tomato, black pudding, potato cake and soda farl) are still the norm. Pub lunches are excellent value, with tasty dishes that range from soup and sandwiches to full meals or a carvery. Many pubs also serve evening meals. In Northern Ireland, families tend to have high tea – a light cooked meal – around 1800. Ethnic restaurants serving a variety of cuisine, and pizza, pasta and fast-food chains, are on the rise. Fish and chips, an Irish favourite, is also a good budget option.

## Electricity

The standard electrical current in Ireland is 220 volts AC (50 cycles). You will need to bring a converter for appliances from abroad, as well as a plug adaptor to fit the 3-pin flat or 2-pin round wall sockets.

## Food

Ireland's unpolluted waters and fertile farmlands produce top-quality beef, lamb, pork, fish, seafood and vegetables. It comes as no surprise, therefore, that gourmet restaurants are springing up around the country, presided over by some of Europe's best chefs, whose modern Irish cuisine is an imaginative variation on traditional ingredients. The country's top restaurants are found not only in Dublin and Belfast but also in County Galway, West Cork and especially in Kinsale – which has been called the Gourmet Capital of Ireland. In the north, a mark of quality to look out for is the 'Taste of Ulster' designation.

Ireland is the place to indulge yourself with seafood – it's fresh, plentiful and reasonably priced. Fresh and smoked salmon is usually on the menu; mussels and oysters are specialities around Bantry and Galway bays; and creamy chowders are served with fresh brown bread. Beef from the Midlands and tender lamb cutlets will please the pickiest carnivore.

Among the traditional dishes to try are Irish stew, a thick lamb or mutton casserole topped with potatoes; Dublin coddle, a supper dish made with chopped sausages, ham or bacon cooked in a stock with potatoes and onions; and boxty, a potato pancake stuffed with marinated beef, chicken or other fillings. Ireland is also renowned for

**Above**
Kylemore Abbey

its fine cheeses, some of which have been produced at monasteries and farms for centuries. Durrus, Carrigaline and Cashel Blue are among the favourites. Irish breads and sweets, including scones, barm brack (a fruity bread) and porter cake (made with dried fruit and stout), are also delicious.

## Health

There are no unusual health hazards in Ireland – except perhaps the midge, a tiny nasty biting fly that goes on the warpath in cloudy, calm and moist weather. Midges don't carry disease but their bites can cause spots on sensitive people. Insect repellent is useful, particularly in boggy areas. Apart from the usual over-the-counter remedies, you will need a doctor's prescription to obtain medicines, so it is best to bring what you need from home.

EU citizens are eligible for medical treatment in Ireland under the EU's social security regulations, provided you see a general practitioner who has an agreement with the Health Board. Take identification and clarify your eligibility. Visitors from EU countries are advised to bring a European Health Insurance Card (EHIC); forms are available from post offices. Fees are charged for visits to the doctor's surgery in Ireland.

## Heritage organisations

The Office of Public Works (OPW) cares for many of Ireland's national monuments, historic sites, inland waterways, parks, gardens and

## Festivals

Festivals and fairs are held year-round throughout the country, with most taking place between March and October. Many are dedicated to music, dancing, literature and the arts, such as Dublin's theatre festival or Wexford's opera festival; others are local harvest festivals or livestock fairs, such as Clarenbridge's oyster festival and Killorglin's Puck Fair. Other famous gatherings include the matchmaking festival at Lisdoonvarna and the Rose of Tralee festival. The regional and national tourist boards publish a Calendar of Events.

## Museums

In the larger cities and towns, museums are open year-round. Some of the smaller, rural museums, as well as historic houses and castles, have reduced opening hours or may be closed altogether in the winter.

nature reserves. The Heritage of Ireland website, *www.heritageireland.ie*, contains information on many heritage sites throughout the country in state care.

If you plan to visit a number of heritage sites, you can purchase a heritage card that allows unlimited admission to their properties for one year. They can be obtained at most sites, and you should buy one at the first OPW site you visit. Adult, senior, child/student and family heritage cards are available. For more information on the heritage card, *tel: 01 647 6592; fax: 094 937 3395; email: heritagecard@opw.ie. Phone lines are open Mon–Fri 1000–1700.*

The National Trust in Northern Ireland cares for historic properties in Northern Ireland. For membership information contact *The National Trust, Membership Department, PO Box 39, Warrington WA5 7WD, UK; tel: 0844 800 1895; fax: 0844 800 4642; email: enquiries@nationaltrust.org.uk; www.ntni.org.uk*

## Information

There are separate national tourist information offices for the Republic of Ireland and Northern Ireland.

**The Irish Tourist Board**, or Bord Fáilte (pronounced 'Fawl-cha'), operates local and regional offices throughout the Republic and Northern Ireland. Local offices are listed in each chapter. For information on planning your trip, contact the Irish Tourist Board offices in your country or the following regional offices. For website information visit *www.discoverireland.com*

In the Republic: **Fáilte Ireland** *Baggot Street Bridge, Dublin 2; tel: 1850 230 230 or 01 602 4000; www.discoverireland.ie*

In Northern Ireland: **Northern Ireland Tourist Board** *St Anne's Courts, 59 North Street, Belfast BT1 1NB; tel: 028 9023 1221; email: info@nitb.com; www.discovernorthernireland.com*

**The Northern Ireland Tourist Information Centre** *47 Donegall Place, Belfast BT1 5AD; tel: 028 9024 6609; fax: 028 9031 2424; email: info@belfastvisitor.com; www.gotobelfast.com, www.discovernorthernireland.com*

### Regional offices (Republic)
**Cork Kerry Tourism** *Avas Fáilte, Grand Parade, Cork; tel: 021 425 5100; fax: 021 425 5199; email: corkkerryinfo@failteireland.ie; www.discoverireland.ie/southwest* – for Cork City and County and South Kerry.
**Dublin Tourism** *Dublin Tourism Centre, Suffolk Street, Dublin 2; tel: 1850 230 230; email: information@dublintourism.ie; www.visitdublin.com* – for Dublin City and County.
**East Coast & Midlands Tourism** *Clonard House, Dublin Road, Mullingar, Co Westmeath; tel: 044 934 8761; fax: 044 934 0413; email: eastandmidlandsinfo@failteireland.ie; www.discoverireland.ie/eastcoast* – for counties Kildare, Laois, Longford, Louth, Meath, North Offaly, Westmeath and Wicklow.

**Ireland West Tourism** *Aras Fáilte, Forster Street, Galway; tel: 091 537700; fax: 091 537733; email: irelandwestinfo@failteireland.ie; www. discoverireland.ie/west* – for counties Galway, Mayo and Roscommon.
**North West Tourism** *Aras Reddan, Temple Street, Sligo; tel: 071 916 1201; fax: 071 916 0360; email: northwestinfo@failteireland.ie; www. discoverireland.ie/northwest* – for counties Cavan, Donegal, Leitrim, Monaghan and Sligo.
**Shannon Development** *Shannon Town Centre, Co Clare; tel: 061 361555; fax: 061 361903; email: tourisminfo@shannondev.ie; www.discoverireland. ie/shannon* – for counties Clare, Limerick, North Kerry, North Tipperary and South Offaly.
**South East Tourism** *4th floor, Wallace House, Maritana Gate, Canada Street, Waterford; tel: 051 312700; fax: 051 312710; email: southeastinfo@failteireland.ie; www.discoverireland.ie/southeast* – for counties Wexford, Waterford, Kilkenny, Carlow and South Tipperary.

Regional offices (Northern Ireland)
**Armagh Tourist Information Centre** *40 English Street, Armagh BT61 7BA; tel: 028 3752 1800; fax: 028 3752 8329; email: tic@armagh.gov.uk; www.armagh.co.uk*
**Belfast Visitor and Convention Bureau** *47 Donegall Place, Belfast BT1 5AD; tel: 028 9024 6609; fax: 028 9031 2424; email: welcomecentre@belfastvisitor.com; www.gotobelfast.com*
**Causeway Coast and Glens** *11 Lodge Road, Coleraine, Co Londonderry BT52 1LU; tel: 028 7032 7720; fax: 028 7032 7719; email: mail@causewaycoastandglens.com; www.causewaycoastandglens.com*
**Derry Visitor and Convention Bureau** *44 Foyle Street, Londonderry BT48 6AT; tel: 028 7126 7284; fax: 028 7137 7992; email: info@derryvisitor.com; www.derryvisitor.com*
**Fermanagh Lakeland Tourism** *Wellington Road, Enniskillen, Co Fermanagh BT74 7EF; tel: 028 6632 3110; fax: 028 6632 5511; email: info@fermanaghlakelands.com; www.fermanaghlakelands.com*
**Newcastle Tourist Information Centre** *10–14 Central Promenade, Newcastle, Co Down BT33 0AA; tel: 028 4372 2222; fax: 028 4372 2400; email: newcastle.tic@downdc.gov.uk; www.downdc.gov.uk*
**Sperrins Tourism** *30 High Street, Moneymore, Co Londonderry, BT45 7PD; tel: 028 8674 7700; fax: 028 8674 7754; email: info@sperrinstourism.com; www.sperrinstourism.com*

Overseas offices
Irish Tourist Board offices abroad include:
**UK:** Tourism Ireland, *Nations House, 103 Wigmore Street, London W1U 1QS; tel: 0800 039 7000; fax: 020 7493 9065; email: info.gb@ tourismireland.com; www.discoverireland.com/gb*; Britain Visitor Centre, *12 Regent Street, London SW1 (personal callers only); 98 West George Street, 7th Floor, Glasgow G2 1PJ; tel: 0800 039 7000; fax: 0141 572 4033; email: info.glasgow@tourismireland.com*

**Australia:** *Level 5, 36 Carrington Street, Sydney NSW 2000; tel: 02 9299 6177; fax: 02 9299 6323; email: info@tourismireland.com.au; www.discoverireland.com.au*
**Canada:** *2 Bloor St West, Suite 3403, Toronto M4W 3E2; tel: 1 800 223 6470 or 416 925 6368; fax: 416 925 6033; email: info.ca@tourismireland. com; www.discoverireland.com/ca-en*
**New Zealand:** *7th Floor, 23 Customs Street East, Auckland 1; tel: 09 977 2255; fax: 09 977 2256; email: info.nz@tourismireland.com; www. discoverireland.com/nz*
**USA:** *345 Park Avenue, New York, NY 10154; tel: 800 223 6470 or 212 418 0800; fax: 212 371 9052; email: info.us@tourismireland.com/us; www.discoverireland.com/us*

## Insurance

Unless you are a UK or EU citizen, you are advised to take out medical insurance, as you will be expected to pay for treatment if you fall ill. Travel insurance covering theft or loss of luggage, travel delays, etc, is always a good idea. Check your home contents policy to see if you are covered while travelling abroad.

## Maps

Unless you plan to stick to the main national roads, it is advisable to have a detailed map. The *Ordnance Survey Road Atlas of Ireland* is recommended. You can buy it in the Dublin Tourism Centre, which has a good selection of maps of all regions of the country, or at major booksellers. Many of the larger local tourist offices also have a selection of maps. Another good source is the SouthWest Walks Ireland, *28 The Anchorage, Tralee; tel: 066 712 8733; www.southwestwalksireland.com*

## Opening times

General opening times are as follows:
**Banks** In the Republic, banking hours are *Mon–Fri 0930* or *1000–1630*. In small towns and rural areas, they close for lunch *1230–1330*. Banks in Dublin stay open until *1700* on *Thursdays*, and those outside the capital until *1700* one day a week. In Northern Ireland, banking hours are *Mon–Fri 0930–1630*, with some city banks opening longer or on *Saturdays*. In villages, banks may not open every day.
**Shops and businesses** *Mon–Sat 0900–1730* or *1800*. Smaller towns may close early on one day. Many towns and most shopping centres have late-night shopping until *2000* or *2100* on *Thursdays*. *Sunday* opening hours are generally *1200–1700* or *1800* in the Republic, *1200* or *1300–1700* or *1800* in Northern Ireland.
**Tourist offices** Tourist offices are generally open from *0900* or *1000–1730*, with longer hours in summer. Most are closed on *Sunday*,

**Above**
Local post office, Northern
Ireland

except for high season. Many of the smaller local tourist information offices are seasonal and are only open from *Apr* or *May* to *Sept*.
**Pubs and bars** In the Republic, *Mon–Sat 1030–2330* (some are open until *0030 Fri–Sat*); *Sun 1230–2300*. In Northern Ireland, *Mon–Sat 1100–2300, Sun 1230–2200*. Some pubs that provide food or entertainment may stay open until *0100*.
**Restaurants** Lunch is generally served *1200–1430* and dinner *1830–2200*. Many ethnic and city-centre restaurants stay open later.
**Heritage sites** Last admission to OPW sites is approximately one hour before closing (30 minutes to National Trust sites) unless otherwise stated.

## Postal services

Most post offices are open *Mon–Fri 0900–1730*. Main post offices are also open on *Saturday, 0900–1700* in the Republic and *0900–1230* in Northern Ireland.

In the Republic, letter boxes are painted green and you must use Irish stamps. British stamps are used in Northern Ireland, and letter boxes are painted red.

To receive post in Ireland, it should be addressed to the recipient, *c/o Poste Restante, Town and Postcode*. In Dublin, poste restante mail should be sent to the *General Post Office, O'Connell Street, Dublin 1*. You should bring identification when collecting your post.

## Public holidays

New Year's Day (1 January), St Patrick's Day (17 March), Christmas Day (25 December) and St Stephen's Day (26 December) are public holidays. If they fall on a weekend, Monday or Tuesday are given in lieu and banks, shops and other services are generally closed. In addition, Easter Monday, the first Mondays of May, June and August and the last Monday in October are also public holidays. Although Good Friday is not an official public holiday, it is observed in most parts of Ireland.

In Northern Ireland, Easter Monday, the first and last Mondays in May, Orangeman's Day (mid-July) and the last Monday in August are observed in addition to the four main public holidays.

## Public transport

CIE is Ireland's national transportation company. It has an information desk at Dublin Airport. Its three subsidiaries provide bus and train services throughout the country.
**Irish Rail** (Iarnród Éireann*), tel: 1850 366 222; www.irishrail.ie*, operates trains to most cities and major towns. The Dublin Area Rapid Transit (DART) system reaches 30 railway stations from Malahide to Greystones. The Luas tram system, *tel: 1800 300 604; www.luas.ie*, has two lines and connects outlying areas to the city centre.

**Useful addresses**

**Go Ireland Walking and Cycling Tours** *Killorglin, Co Kerry; tel: 066 976 2094; fax: 066 976 2098; email: info@govisitireland.com; www.govisitireland.com.* Irish Cycling Safaris, *Belfield Bike Shop, UCD, Dublin 4; tel: 01 260 0749; email: info@cyclingsafaris.com; www.cyclingsafaris.com*

**SouthWest Walks Ireland** *28 The Anchorage, Tralee, Co Kerry; tel: 066 712 8733; fax: 066 712 8762; email: swwi@iol.ie; www. southwestwalksireland.com.* Mail order for maps, books and walking routes for the whole of Ireland.

For information on angling, contact Inland Fisheries Ireland via their website: *www.fishinginireland.info*

**The Irish Sailing Association** *3 Park Road, Dun Laoghaire, Co Dublin; tel: 01 280 0239; fax: 01 280 7558; email: info@sailing.ie; www.sailing.ie*

**Below**
Racehorses

**Dublin Bus** (Bus Átha Cliath), *tel: 01 873 4222; www.dublinbus.ie*, operates in the greater Dublin area. There is a range of discount tickets available from the head office at *59 Upper O'Connell Street* and at numerous bus ticket agencies.

**Irish Bus** (Bus Éireann), *tel: 01 836 6111; www.buseireann.ie*, has a nationwide network of buses serving all cities and most towns and villages outside the Dublin area. It also provides city bus services in Waterford, Cork, Limerick and Galway.

In Northern Ireland, there are four main rail routes from Belfast Central Station. The region is also well served by a good bus network. **Ulsterbus (Translink)** provides services outside Belfast. Note that Belfast has two main bus stations. City services are provided by **Citybus (Translink)**. For information on these and **Northern Ireland Railways**, *tel: 028 9066 6630; www.translink.co.uk*

## Safety and security

Ireland is generally a safe place to visit, but you should take normal precautions against petty crime. Do not carry your passport or large amounts of cash around on the street. Deposit jewellery and valuables in the hotel's safe rather than in your room – better yet, leave them at home. Mind your wallet or handbag in crowds and when having a drink or meal. Never leave cameras, bags or luggage unattended, especially in cars.

If your passport is lost or stolen, the main foreign embassies are located in Dublin, and there is an American consulate in Belfast.

## Shopping

Ireland produces a range of high-quality goods that make lasting souvenirs. These include Irish linen such as tablecloths or napkins; Carrickmacross lace; Belleek porcelain; hand-woven tweeds; and handknitted Aran sweaters (*see page 196*) and other woollens. Irish lead crystal is justly prized around the world; Waterford crystal is the best known, but it's worth considering lesser-known glassware

**Above**
Ireland's rugged landscape

produced in Galway, Cork, Dublin, Tipperary and Tyrone. Then there are the more unusual items, such as ornaments made from compressed peat, polished Mourne granite or Connemara marble. Musical instruments also make a great purchase, as do reproductions of Celtic jewellery. When in Galway, look for Claddagh friendship rings (*see page 191*). The larger tourist shops, such as the **House of Ireland** and **Blarney Woollen Mills**, sell a range of goods from around the country. **Avoca Handweavers** has several branches, as does **Quills** in western Ireland. Also look out for small local craft workshops, where you'll find unique items of pottery, ceramics and other goods. Many towns have weekly markets that can be fun places to browse.

## Sport

Horse racing is Ireland's favourite national sport, and there are 25 racecourses around the country. The two most famous meetings are the Irish Derby at the Curragh in County Kildare, and the Irish Grand National at Fairyhouse in County Meath. Information on various courses and meetings is available from the tourist information offices. Greyhound racing is also popular, with 18 tracks around the country. Contact Bord na gCon (Irish Greyhound Board), *104 Henry Street, Limerick; tel: 061 316788; fax: 061 316739; email: pr@igb.ie; www.igb.ie*

Ireland is a walker's paradise, with unspoilt forests, hills, mountains and open countryside. Information on walks for all levels of ability is available from the tourist information offices or from the Irish Sports Council, *tel: 01 860 8800; email: info@irishsportscouncil.ie; www. irishsportscouncil.ie*

With over 400 links and parkland courses, Ireland is becoming one of Europe's main golfing destinations. Top courses include Portmarnock near Dublin, Ballybunion in County Kerry and Royal County Down and Royal Portrush in Northern Ireland. The tourist information offices provide details of golf facilities in their areas.

Ireland's coastline is dotted with many Blue Flag beaches, indicating that they merit the accepted European symbol of quality. Watersports are also popular on several inland lakes. Other popular activities include cycling, angling, sailing and horse riding. Many stables offer riding lessons for all levels of ability.

## Telephones

This guide lists both the area code and telephone number; omit the area code when dialling locally. To phone or fax the Republic from abroad, dial your international access code, plus *353* (Ireland's national code), plus the area code (omitting the initial zero), then the number. The national code for Northern Ireland is *44*. When dialling Northern Ireland from the Republic, dial *048* before the local number. If you want to call abroad from Ireland, the international prefix is *00* (plus the country code, area code and local number you wish to dial). Calls are cheaper between 1800 and 0800.

It is always cheaper to dial direct, rather than using the operator. In general, it is best to avoid making calls from your hotel room as they normally add hefty surcharges. Such charges should be listed in your room information.

Card phones are widely available throughout Ireland and are cheaper than payphones. Phonecards of various denominations are sold at post offices and newsagents. You can also make calls from coin phone boxes and from payphones in bars and shops.

## Time

All of Ireland is on Greenwich Mean Time (GMT), which is the same as the United Kingdom and five hours ahead of Eastern Standard Time in the United States.

## Toilets

If you learn no other words of Irish, remember that *Fir* means 'Men' and *Mná* means 'Women'. When looking for the public toilets in Gaeltacht areas, the word is *Leithreas*. If there are no public toilets, you can generally use the facilities in a pub or hotel.

# Driver's guide

## Automobile clubs

It is a good idea to join an automobile association before your trip, as it can provide useful information and documents, as well as suggesting itineraries and routes. Contact:

UK: Automobile Association (AA), *tel: 0800 085 2721 in the UK, (+44) 161 333 0004 from outside the UK; www.theaa.com;* Royal Automobile Club (RAC), *tel: 0844 891 3111; www.rac.co.uk*

American Automobile Association (AAA), *www.aaa.com*

Australian Automobile Association, *tel: 02 6247 7311; www.aaa.asn.au*

Canadian Automobile Association, *www.caa.ca*

New Zealand Automobile Association, *tel: 0800 500 444; www.nzaa.co.nz*

AA Republic of Ireland, *tel: 01 617 9999; www.aaireland.ie*

AA Northern Ireland, *tel: 0800 085 2721.*

## Breakdowns

Try to park as safely as possible; alert other drivers with hazard lights or a warning triangle if you have one. SOS telephones are located at regular intervals on the 'hard shoulder' (verge-side lane) of motorways. This is for

## Accidents

If you have an accident, you are obliged by law to stop and give your name, address and car registration number to anyone involved. If anyone is injured, the police must be notified within 24 hours and a report filed. For fire, police or ambulance, dial *999*. Exchange insurance details with other relevant drivers, and do not admit fault or liability, or give money to any person. If you can find any independent witnesses, ask for their details. Take photographs of the accident scene and vehicles. If you are involved in an accident with a rental car, you must notify the hire company immediately. Do not carry out any repairs without the company's permission.

To avoid having accidents in the first place, keep alert by taking sensible rest breaks and don't allow yourself to be distracted by the scenery. Most roads have places to pull off which are signposted. If you are unfamiliar with driving in Ireland, take it steady, but be aware of other drivers and allow them to overtake (pass) you whenever possible. A line of frustrated motorists stuck behind a slow-moving vehicle is a recipe for disaster.

## Caravans and camper vans (trailers and RVs)

Many roads in Ireland are narrow and winding and may not be suitable for caravans. It's a good idea to check locally before you set off on the back roads. Pay heed to signs warning of dangerous bends, narrow bridges and so forth as these can be particularly hazardous for large vehicles.

Touring caravans for up to five people are available for hire. You can also rent motorhomes, some of which are equipped with sleeping bags and utensils. For information, contact the Irish Caravan and Camping Council, *PO Box 4443, Dublin 2; email: admin@camping-ireland.ie; www.camping-ireland.ie*

## Drivers with disabilities

If you are taking your own car to Ireland by ferry, you should first obtain a form from the Disabled Drivers' Association or Motor Club in Britain. Send the form to the ferry company, who may offer discounts on your car on certain sailings. The blue badge issued to drivers with disabilities in the United Kingdom is also recognised in Ireland, and should be displayed prominently when in use. For more information,

emergency use only and you should never use it for a rest stop. (Remember, it can be very dangerous to walk on the hard shoulder of any motorway. Your passengers are probably safer out of the vehicle and well up the verge away from the traffic.)

Car-hire companies will provide you with a contact number to ring if your rental car breaks down. Motoring organisations like the Automobile Association (AA) and the Royal Automobile Club (RAC) may have reciprocal arrangements with similar clubs overseas, and may provide a free rescue service or advice; check with your organisation before you leave home.

Emergency rescue services: AA: *0800 887766*; RAC: *0800 828282*.

**Documents**

All drivers will need a full driving licence or international driving permit. A provisional licence is not accepted. If you are bringing your own car, motorcycle or caravan to Ireland you will need the motor registration book, and a letter of authority if the registration is not in your name. You will also need a green card or insurance certificate that is valid for the Republic of Ireland.

If you are bringing your own vehicle, you will need to inform your insurance company, especially if you want full comprehensive

contact the Disabled Drivers' Association of Ireland, *Ballindine, Co Mayo; tel: 094 936 4054; fax: 094 936 4336; email: info@ddai.ie; www.ddai.ie*

## Driving in Ireland

Most cars in Ireland have manual transmissions. A limited number of cars with automatic transmission are available, but you must specify if you want this when reserving a rental car.

Roads are good and well maintained throughout the country. There are three main classes of road in Ireland. Motorways are designated by the prefix 'M'. In the Republic, the old 'T' (Trunk) and 'L' (Link) routes have been renumbered as 'N' (National) and 'R' (Regional) routes. You will see both old and new signs and map designations. However, the road number is often not given at all, and local people rarely refer to roads by a number, rather, it's 'the Cork road' or similar. It is more useful to know the name of the next town you're heading for. At unmarked intersections, a general rule is to carry on straight ahead unless a sign directs you otherwise.

Several roads in Ireland impose a toll, including the East Link Bridge and M50 in Dublin, the M1 Toll (Drogheda Bypass) and the N25 Waterford City Bypass.

In Northern Ireland, major roads have 'A' and minor roads have 'B' designations, with 'M' for motorways.

Driving may be less aggressive in Ireland than in some other countries, but that doesn't mean it is stress-free. Sharing the narrow, winding roads with lorries, pedestrians, and huge trucks and tour buses that bear down towards you at high speeds and take up your share of the road can make for very anxious moments. Dangerous bends and accident black spots are usually signposted – heed them – but beware those charming stone bridges, which are usually approached suddenly round a sharp curve that obscures oncoming traffic until you meet head on. Many town centres are clogged with traffic. Farm vehicles and an inordinate number of roadworks also add to delays, so don't expect to get anywhere quickly. And, it has to be said, in rural areas there are some amazingly poor, often elderly, drivers, so be prepared for anything.

Sheep, cows and other livestock are put out to graze on roadside verges. This is a time-honoured tradition throughout rural Ireland, called 'grazing the long acre', so be prepared for animals to wander on to the road. Be especially careful on roads with blind curves.

You may notice some cars with red 'R' plates, which means 'Restricted'. This identifies inexperienced drivers who have held their licences for less than a year and must keep to low speeds.

## Driving rules

In Ireland, drive on the left and overtake (pass) on the right. A number of accidents are caused each year by visitors straying on to the wrong

coverage. Note that the vehicle may not be driven by an Irish resident, except for a garage mechanic with your written permission.

Before taking out additional insurance on your rental car, check to see what coverage you already have on your own car insurance policy or credit card, as this can sometimes include rental cars.

**Drinking and driving**

Penalties are severe for driving with more than the legal limit of blood alcohol, currently .50mg% (50mg/100ml), or driving while under the influence of any drugs. If you have an accident while in such a condition, you will automatically be considered at fault. Police have the right to administer a breathalyser test at any time, and if you refuse to take it you are likely to be prosecuted. The strong penalties apply to visitors as well as residents. The safest thing is not to drink and drive.

side of the road after a momentary lapse in concentration; arrows have been painted on the roads in some places as a reminder. Be particularly vigilant when starting off from the side of the road, when turning from one road to another and when driving on a road with little traffic.

Cars on roundabouts have priority, and at unmarked road junctions the vehicle to the right has right of way. A continuous white line down the centre of the road means overtaking is prohibited. Crash helmets are a legal requirement for motorcyclists.

In Ireland, flashed headlights are habitually used both as a warning (an alternative to the horn), and as an invitation to take priority over another driver. You will simply have to use your judgement to decide what is meant – flashed headlights do not officially form part of the Highway Code. Elementary courtesy includes raising your hand to thank a driver who has given way to you.

The rules and regulations on driving in Britain (including Northern Ireland) can be found in the current edition of *The Highway Code*, available from bookshops, newsagents and motoring organisations such as the AA and RAC.

Throughout the Republic of Ireland, the rules of the road are similar to those in Britain, with some minor differences. For further information, a booklet published by the Department of Transport, *Rules of the Road*, is available from local post offices or from the Government Publications Sales Office, *Sun Alliance House, Molesworth Street, Dublin 2*.

## Fuel

Super, unleaded, extra (leaded) and diesel fuel is available in Ireland. Some petrol stations may be closed on Sunday, or in the evening, so it is best to keep your tank topped up. Petrol can be more expensive in Northern Ireland, so fill up before you cross the border.

## Information

It is useful to have an up-to-date map. Free tourist maps are often available from the tourist offices, but you may want to buy a more detailed map or road atlas. These are available at bookshops and newsagents, as well as many of the larger tourist information centres. The *Ordnance Survey Complete Road Atlas of Ireland* is very good.

## Parking

A round sign with a red 'P' indicates parking is permitted; if crossed by a diagonal line, parking is prohibited. Obey the signs, as wheel clamping is time-consuming and fines are expensive. A blue 'P' sign indicates a car park or a lay-by. Car parks are free or have a nominal charge in most towns, and it is best to use them. You can also park on the street, unless there is a no-parking sign. Many towns operate disc

## Fines

Speed cameras are widely in use and fines are automatic. If you are caught speeding by a speed camera, a ticket will be sent to the address of the car registration. If you are driving a rental car, the ticket will be sent to the car-hire company and they will pass it on to you, usually with an additional administration charge. An unpaid parking ticket will also be passed on to the car-hire company and they will bill it to your credit card. If you are stopped by a police officer, he or she will take your licence and car registration details and any fine will be processed through the courts and sent to the address on the registration. If the address is overseas, it may not be enforced at present.

In the Republic of Ireland, traffic wardens and the police can impose on-the-spot fines for parking offences. The police can also issue on-the-spot fines for speeding offences and using a mobile phone while driving; failure to pay will result in an increased fine.

It is an offence to use a speed camera detector in Ireland, and such equipment will be confiscated.

## Lights

Dipped headlights should be used in rain or whenever weather conditions reduce light levels, as well as after the official 'lighting-up' time, when street lamps are switched on. Use fog lights when visibility falls below

parking schemes which use scratch cards available from nearby shops and newsagents. Pay and Display is another common parking scheme. Clearways are indicated by a red circle with an 'X' through the middle. You may not stop in the Clearway during the hours indicated.

The police have published *A Short Guide to Tourist Security*, available free at major tourist offices. It shows the locations of car parks in Dublin, Cork, Limerick and other cities.

In villages and rural areas, parking space is limited and you may need to use a car park (generally free) at the edge of town. When visiting small archaeological sites in the countryside, there is often only parking space for one or two cars and you may have to park on the verge. Respect the needs of local farmers and do not block gates and private drives. Never, ever park in designated passing places – it is dangerous to obstruct traffic on single-track roads.

Whenever you park and leave your car, remove all valuables from sight or you may return to find a smashed window and your possessions missing.

## Security

Car theft is all too common, especially in the larger cities and at tourist attractions. Always lock your car if you leave it, even for a moment or two, and never leave cameras or other valuables on view inside, in the glove compartment or on a roof rack. Keep luggage in the boot (trunk) out of sight.

If you break down or need roadside assistance, take special care when getting out of your vehicle. Throughout Ireland and Northern Ireland, the emergency number for the police (garda) is *999*. Drivers unfortunate enough to find the police contacting them (via flashing blue lights or wailing sirens) should pull over as soon as it's safe to do so.

## Speed limits

Keep to the following speed limits unless otherwise posted:

Motorways and dual carriageways: 120kph (70mph in Northern Ireland)
Single carriageways: 80kph (60mph in NI)
Towns and built-up areas: 50kph (30mph in NI)

Camper vans or cars towing caravans are restricted to 80kph (50mph) unless otherwise stated. On single-track roads you should drive with care according to road conditions. Always make allowances for adverse conditions (rain, fog, ice, etc), when braking distances increase dramatically.

## Essentials

It is recommended (but not required) to carry a first-aid kit, spare bulbs, torch (flashlight) and petrol container. A warning triangle is only compulsory for vehicles with an unladen weight exceeding 1.5 tonnes (1524kg). Horns must not be used between 2330 and 0700.

328 ft (100m). If you are driving a left-hand-drive vehicle, don't forget that your headlights will need to be adjusted. Simple beam adjusters are available at ferry terminals, or from motoring organisations.

## Mobile phones

The use of a hand-held phone or similar device while driving is prohibited and carries a penalty. Drivers can still be prosecuted for using a hands-free phone when driving, for failure to have proper control of the vehicle.

## Seat belts

The use of seat belts is compulsory in Ireland for drivers and passengers, including those in the rear seats if they are fitted. Babies and small children should not sit in the front seats, but should be properly restrained at all times in a child seat or carrier in the back of the vehicle. Children under 12 are not allowed in front seats. Be sure to request a car seat for young children when making your car-hire reservation.

## Irish miles

The old granite milestones along road verges, especially in County Down, are marked in Irish miles. An Irish mile measures 2,240 yards, which is 480 yards longer than an English mile. All modern road signs, however, give distances in standard English miles or kilometres.

# Road signs

Most regions of Ireland conform to the standard style of road signage used in the rest of the EU. Generally, signing is clear, though city suburbs can be confusing. Distances are given in miles in Northern Ireland, and in kilometres in the Republic of Ireland. Also note that the Republic uses the 'Yield' sign, which means the same as the 'Give Way' sign in the UK.

Motorways are marked in blue, major trunk routes in green, minor routes in white. Advisory or warning signs are usually yellow diamond-shaped (in the Republic) or triangular in red and white (in Northern Ireland). Watch out for overhead electronic messages on motorways indicating roadworks, accidents, fog or other hazards, and the advised speed limit. Level crossings over railway lines have manually operated gates or more often automatic barriers. If the lights flash you must stop to let a train pass.

Visitor information is indicated on brown signs with white lettering. These signs indicate attractions, accommodation, tourist information centres, recreational facilities, natural attractions and picnic areas, as well as scenic drives. Archaeological sites are indicated by smaller white signs with blue lettering.

Ireland's small country roads are scenic, but they can also be frustrating to navigate. Road signs are notoriously poor or misleading in rural areas, if they exist at all (many end up in the pubs). Others may be broken off or purposely twisted in the wrong direction. A detailed map is essential.

The old black-on-white fingerpost road signs give distances between towns in miles, but as Ireland has gradually converted to metric, the new white signs and all of the green signs give the distances in kilometres. In Northern Ireland, all distances are given in miles.

In most parts of the country, place names are written in both English and Irish (Dublin, for example, is 'Baile Atha Cliath'), but in the Gaeltacht areas such as Connemara, the Dingle Peninsula and Donegal, signs are only in Irish. A map that gives both names is useful. Don't be afraid to ask a local for directions if you get lost. Important phrases worth remembering are 'GÉIL SLÍ' (yield) and 'MALL' or 'GO MALL' (slow). Other commonly used legends on information road signs are:

| English | Irish |
|---|---|
| Caution Children Crossing | Aire – Leanaí ag Trasnú |
| Concealed Entrance | Oscailt Cheilte |
| Except Buses and Taxis | Ach Amháin Busanna agus Tacsaithe |
| Except for Access | Act Amháin Rochtain |
| Loose Chippings | Cloichíní Scaoilte |
| Pedestrian Zone | Coisithe Amháin |
| Ramp Ahead | Rampa Romhat |
| Road Closed | Bóthar Dúnta |
| Road Liable to Flooding | Baol Tuilte |
| School Patrol Ahead | Patról Scoile Romhat |
| Signal Controlled Roundabout Ahead | Timpeallán Soilse Romhat |
| Single Line Traffic | Trácht Aon Líne |
| Temporary Road Surface | Dromchla Sealadach |
| Toll Bridge | Dola-Dhroichead |
| Toll Plaza | Dola-Phlás |
| Tree/Hedge Cutting | Bearradh Crann/Fáil |

## UK ROAD SIGNS

Maximum Speed
Limit (MPH)

No Entry for
Vehicular Traffic

National Speed
Limit

Left Turn Ahead
(right if reversed)

Priority over
approaching
traffic

Roundabout

Give Way to traffic
on major road

On approaches
to junctions

## REPUBLIC OF IRELAND ROAD SIGNS

Series of bends

Crossroads
(no Priority shown)

Crossroads
(give Priority)

Crossroads
(your Priority)

Yield at end
(Give Way)

Junctions on
bend

Keep Left

No Entry

# Getting to Ireland

## By air

Most international flights arrive at Dublin, Belfast and Shannon airports. In addition, there are regional airports at Cork, Kerry, Waterford, Galway, Knock, Sligo, Derry and Carrickfinn. Most airports handle direct flights from London, as well as from other cities and regional airports in the United Kingdom. The main operators are Aer Lingus, British Airways, British Midland and Ryanair.

There are several flights daily to Dublin and Belfast from London Heathrow. Flights to Ireland from airports throughout Britain take about an hour. Advance booking is essential at peak commuter times. Fares may be cheaper outside the peak flight times, and some airlines offer discounted fares, subject to availability, though you generally need to book well ahead to get these rates. Taxes are added on all return flights from the UK to Ireland.

There are direct services from many European cities to Dublin and Belfast. Major airlines operate services from the US and Canada to Dublin and Shannon airports in the Irish Republic, and to Belfast International Airport via London and Glasgow. Charter flights are also available from many cities.

There are good internal flight connections from Dublin to other regions. For flights to Cork, Kerry, Shannon, Galway and Sligo, contact **Aer Lingus**, *tel: 0818 365 000* in Ireland, *0871 718 5000* in the UK; *www.aerlingus.com*. For flights to Donegal and the Aran Islands, contact **Aer Arann**, *tel: 0818 210 210* in Ireland, *0870 876 7676* in the UK; *www.aerarann.com*

### Airports

**Dublin Airport**, *tel: 01 814 1111*, is 6 miles (10km) north of the city centre. The Airlink is the Dublin bus service that runs between the airport and the city centre, with stops at the central bus station (Busaras), Connolly Rail station and Heuston Rail station. It runs every 10–15 minutes *Mon–Sat 0545–2330*, and less frequently on *Sun 0700–2300*, fare €5. Taxi fares to the city centre are about €20–22.

**Aircoach**, *tel: 01 844 7118; www.aircoach.ie*, runs a luxury coach service to Dublin and further afield. **Shannon Airport**, *tel: 061 712 000*, is 16 miles (26km) west of Limerick. Irish Bus operates regular connections to Limerick, Ennis and Galway. Smaller airlines land at **Cork Airport**, *tel: 021 431 3131*, and several regional airports.

**Below**
There are numerous direct flights to Ireland

**Ferry operators**

**Stena Line** Tel: 0870 570 7070; www.stenaline.com. Service from Holyhead to Dublin and Dun Laoghaire, from Fishguard to Rosslare and from Stranraer to Belfast.

**Irish Ferries** Tel: 0871 730 0400 (call charges apply); www.irishferries.com. Service from Holyhead to Dublin and Pembroke to Rosslare.

**Fastnet Line** Tel: 0844 576 8831; www.fastnetline. com. Service from Swansea to Cork.

**P & O Irish Sea Ferries** Tel: 0871 664 4 999 (call charges apply); www.poirishsea.com. Service from Liverpool to Dublin and Cairnryan to Larne.

**Norfolkline Irish Sea Ferries** Tel: 0844 499 0007; www.norfolkline.com/ ferry. Services from Liverpool to Dublin and Belfast.

**Steam Packet Company** Tel: 0871 222 1333 (call charges apply); www.steam-packet.com. Service from the Isle of Man to Dublin and Belfast.

**Stena Line** offers holiday and Rail & Sail packages to Ireland. For brochures, tel: 0870 727 0444.

For up-to-date details of long-distance bus, ferry and rail services, consult the Thomas Cook European Rail Timetable.

**Belfast International Airport**, tel: 028 9448 4848, is 15 miles (24km) outside the city at Aldergrove. There is a regular Airbus service into the city centre. Smaller airlines land at **George Best Belfast City Airport**, tel: 028 9093 9093, and the **City of Derry (Eglinton) Airport**, tel: 028 7181 0784.

## By coach

There are many coach services between Britain and Ireland, but they can involve long hours on the road and possible delays. Coaches use the Holyhead–Dublin or the Fishguard/Pembroke–Rosslare ferry crossings. The main companies include **Eurolines/National Express** and **Bus Éireann**, which operate a joint service; contact **Bus Éireann**, tel: 01 836 6111, or any of their offices or agents for booking and more information. In the UK (including Northern Ireland), contact **Eurolines**, tel: 0871 781 8181 (call charges apply).

## By ferry

Several ferry companies operate car and passenger ferry services between Britain and Ireland. The principal ferry routes are from Holyhead on the Isle of Anglesey to Dublin or Dun Laoghaire harbours (2½ miles/4km south of the city centre); from Fishguard or Pembroke in Wales to Rosslare Harbour; and from Stranraer or Cairnryan in Scotland to Belfast or Larne. Crossings between other ports are less frequent. Taxis wait at the ferry ports, and from Dun Laoghaire you can take a DART train or bus to the city centre.

Departure times and prices vary according to the season; there can be a big difference in the cost of the journey, so spend some time comparing prices. During the busy summer season, you will need to book your crossing well ahead. At peak holiday times, a sailing/regulation ticket is required as well as the travel ticket; check when booking. It is best to book your return crossing at the same time. Most companies have several sailings per day. Average sailing times vary between 1½ and 4 hours.

**Fastnet Line** operates a ferry service between Swansea in Wales and Cork, with six crossings per week from March to November, and nine per week in July and August. The crossing takes 10 hours, but good road access to both ports makes this a viable option if your main destination is the southwest of Ireland.

## By rail

For information on train services to British ports for onward ferry connections to Ireland, contact National Rail enquiries, tel: 0845 748 4950; www.nationalrail.co.uk. For information on rail and bus connections to ferry ports in Ireland, contact CIE, www.cie.ie

**Above**
Government Buildings,
Merrion Street, Dublin

# Setting the scene

## History

At the end of the Ice Age, land bridges connected Ireland to continental Europe, enabling the first hunter-gatherers to reach it around 8000 BC. Within a few hundred years, the rising sea had cut off this thickly forested island, and subsequent settlers arrived in crude boats, first across the channel from Scotland, later from Neolithic settlements in northern Europe and the Mediterranean. Between 3000 and 2000 BC, these early Irish settlers established the first agricultural communities, and built the dolmens and other megalithic tombs that are scattered throughout the countryside in their hundreds. During the Bronze Age, the Irish became skilled at copper and bronze working, and as goldsmiths, and their swords, axes and jewellery were highly prized along a trading circuit that stretched to the eastern Mediterranean. Another group of migrants, known as the Beaker Folk, produced exquisite pottery.

The people who made the most indelible impression on the Irish character, however, were the Celts, who, from their origins on the western Russian steppes, came to dominate much of Europe in pre-Roman times. They were an inventive and cultured people, fierce and skilful in battle. Despite – or perhaps because of – their verbal eloquence and love of poetry, they had no written language, save for a crude script of chiselled lines, called Ogham, which developed around the 4th century AD (*see also page 146*). Their laws and customs were passed down orally, and with great accuracy, from one generation to the next. In the 6th century BC, a branch of the Celts called the Gaels arrived in Ireland. Intermixing with the native Irish, they established cultural and legal systems which became the basis for Irish society and lasted into the 17th century. The Celts also possessed iron tools, which they used to build forts and circular enclosures of stone or earth to protect themselves and their cattle – their symbol of wealth – from enemies. Thousands of these so-called 'fairy rings' still exist throughout the land. While the Roman armies conquered the Celts throughout the rest of Europe, they never crossed the sea to Ireland, where the Gaels flourished as the last outpost of Celtic society.

### The coming of Christianity

The first Christian missionaries arrived in Ireland in the 3rd century, cleverly incorporating the country's pagan mythology into the doctrine they preached. It was partly because of the Celts' tribal organisation into petty kingdoms, called *tuaths*, that Christianity easily gained a foothold;

when a chieftain was converted, the whole clan followed. With the coming of St Patrick in AD 432, Christianity soon became the dominant faith of the land. Because of Ireland's distance from Rome, however, it took a less rigid approach and blended with local custom. While the rest of Christian Europe floundered during the Dark Ages, Ireland's monasteries blossomed as centres of art and learning. With the introduction of Latin, literature also flourished. During Ireland's Golden Age of the 7th to 9th centuries, some of the country's most magnificent treasures were produced: beautifully illustrated religious and historical manuscripts, such as the *Book of Kells*, and the exquisitely carved high crosses that brought the Word to the illiterate.

But God could not deliver Ireland from the Vikings, who landed in 795 and plundered the country over the next two centuries. Another form took shape on the Irish landscape: the tall round towers with a single doorway, where the monks took refuge from the invaders. The Norsemen established the country's first large towns, Dublin, Limerick, Wexford and Cork among them. In 1014, they were finally defeated by Ireland's first high king, Brian Ború.

### The English Ascension

Ireland's greatest conqueror did not invade but was invited in. In 1169, the King of Leinster, Dermot MacMurrough, exiled to England after a long-standing feud, sought help from Anglo-Norman mercenaries to regain his lands. Their leader was the Earl of Pembroke, known as Strongbow, who, following his success in battle, married MacMurrough's daughter. When the old king died, Strongbow succeeded to the Leinster throne and began to expand his power. In eight short decades, the Anglo-Normans gained control of three-quarters of Ireland. Although they owed allegiance to England, they gradually adopted the Irish language and customs and saw to their own interests.

At the beginning of the 16th century, only a fortified area around Dublin – called the Pale – was controlled by the Crown (*see page 67*). But later, in the throes of the Protestant Reformation, England viewed the upstart Norman and Irish lords as more of a threat. It was feared that Ireland would be used as a stepping stone by England's Catholic enemies, France and Spain. Henry VIII sparked insurgence by the Irish nobles when he demanded that they surrender their lands to the Crown, promising to return them as English fiefdoms. His successor, Elizabeth I, ruthlessly suppressed their rebellions, which intensified over the next two centuries as England tightened her grip. In 1601, two Ulster noblemen, Hugh O'Donnell and Hugh O'Neill, along with their Spanish allies, were defeated at the Battle of Kinsale. O'Donnell chose exile on the Continent and, five years later, O'Neill and other nobles followed. The 'Flight of the Earls' robbed Ireland of its Gaelic leadership, while the forfeiture of their lands opened the way for English 'plantations'.

In 1610, the first boundaries for Northern Ireland were staked out and the seeds of bitterness sown when the earls' substantial holdings in Derry, Donegal, Tyrone, Armagh, Fermanagh and Cavan were divided up and given to loyal English and Scottish settlers; only a few poor plots were reserved for the Irish. These usurpers were well funded, well organised and industrious, and they prospered. Their success led to more plantations in other provinces. Irish resentment erupted into violence in 1641, when thousands of settlers were killed or driven out. But the rebel alliance could not hold, especially in the face of the avenging fury of Oliver Cromwell and a 12,000-strong army that launched barbarous attacks on Drogheda and Wexford in 1649. Within four years, all Ireland was defeated, its lands confiscated and its landowning families banished west of the Shannon. Thousands were deported to the colonies as slaves.

This marked the beginning of the so-called Protestant Ascendancy – the domination of the British ruling class over the native Irish Catholics. Hopes were briefly raised by the crowning of the Catholic English king, James II, in 1685, but three years later he was driven to exile in France. He landed at Kinsale to raise Irish support, but in 1690 was defeated by William of Orange, who had assumed the Crown, at the Battle of the Boyne.

### Famine and rebellion

English oppression culminated in a series of measures enacted between 1702 and 1715, known as the Penal Laws, which lasted to the end of the century. Catholics were forbidden to vote, buy land, hold public office or practise law, attend university or possess firearms. Any clergyman more senior than a parish priest was banished. The Irish conducted Masses and their education in secret, and Catholicism survived.

**Below**
Part of Edward Delaney's memorial to the Great Famine, Dublin

In the late 18th century, secret Catholic societies were formed, largely to defend peasant farmers against abuses by their landlords. By now, even the Protestant settlers were becoming resentful of English patronage. Both sides supported this common cause when Theobald Wolfe Tone, a Protestant lawyer, founded the Society of United Irishmen in 1791. He enlisted the aid of a French fleet in the rebellions of 1796 and 1798, which met with defeat.

It was hoped that the joining of Ireland and England as a United Kingdom, on 1 January, 1801, would bring stability, but calls for Irish sovereignty were soon revived, especially when King George III reneged on a pledge to repeal the Penal Laws. A new leader arose in Catholic lawyer Daniel O'Connell, 'the Liberator'. He swept to victory in the elections of 1828, despite the law forbidding Catholics to hold office, and the government, fearing a rebellion, was forced to rescind the hated statutes and allow him to take his seat in Parliament.

Within a few years, however, Ireland was devastated by a greater blow than even the English could muster. In 1845, a potato blight wiped out the crop that was the staple – and often the only – diet for the majority of Irish peasants. It struck again the following year, and in 1848 and 1849. More than a million people starved or died of disease, and nearly twice their number were forced to emigrate. Government response to the crisis was abominable, as too little assistance came far too late, and landlords evicted starving tenants for non-payment of their rents. The appalling truth was that there was no shortage of other foods during the so-called 'famine' years; Irish-produced eggs, beef, bacon and flour continued to be exported as usual. Meanwhile, other ships sailed from the western ports laden with Ireland's greatest resource, its people.

Underground groups such as the Irish Republican Brotherhood and the Fenian Brotherhood, whose uprisings were quelled in 1867, kept the drive for independence alive. During the next two decades, the banner was carried by a Protestant landowner, Charles Stewart Parnell, who fought for tenants' land rights in Parliament and won several reforms. However, his efforts to achieve legislative independence from Britain, known as Home Rule, were blocked by northern Protestants, who feared Catholic domination.

The turn of the century saw the reawakening of Gaelic culture. The Irish language was taught in schools, and the Irish gift for literature flourished in writers such as W B Yeats. In 1905, Arthur Griffith founded the nationalist party Sinn Féin, which means 'We Ourselves'.

## Civil War and Independence
The Home Rule bill finally passed in 1914, but the Orange Order, a militant Protestant group, pushed through an amendment that gave the six counties of Ulster the option to remain part of Great Britain. World War I further delayed implementation of the bill.

The resurrected Irish Republican Brotherhood and the Irish Volunteers planned a nationwide uprising for Easter Monday, 24 April, 1916. Confusion in the chain of command meant that it was largely confined to Dublin, where the rebels seized the General Post Office, and their leader, Patrick Pearse, read out the Proclamation of the Republic of Ireland from atop the steps. The rebels held out for five days before surrendering, and the 15 who had signed the proclamation were executed. Public opinion, which had been against the uprising, swung fervently in favour of these new martyrs.

In the general election of 1918, 73 Sinn Féin candidates won a landslide victory. They refused to take their seats at Westminster, and formed the Dáil Éireann (Assembly of Ireland) in Dublin, with Eamon de Valera, a survivor of the Easter Rising, at its head. A year later, the Dáil proclaimed Irish independence. Britain swiftly gaoled its leaders, setting the two countries at war.

The Irish Volunteers re-formed as the Irish Republican Army (IRA) and, led by Michael Collins, waged an effective guerrilla campaign against the British armed forces. After two years of bitter fighting, Britain proposed the division of the country under the Government of

Ireland Act, giving domestic powers to each while keeping them under Britain's wing. The six counties of Ulster with Protestant majorities readily accepted, but the South was staunchly divided. After long negotiations, in 1922 the Dáil narrowly ratified the Anglo-Irish Treaty, which made Ireland a dominion in the Commonwealth and created the Irish Free State in the South. Collins saw this as a step towards a united Ireland, but de Valera and a wing of the IRA rejected it. A year of civil war between pro- and anti-Treaty factions ensued, which claimed thousands of lives, including Collins'. But the Treaty held.

In 1937, with de Valera as prime minister, the government drafted a new constitution and, 12 years later, on 18 April, 1949, the Republic of Ireland, or Eire, at last broke free from the Commonwealth.

### The way forward
The division of Northern Ireland continued to plague the new Republic, which had asserted a claim to the Ulster counties in its constitution. The Ulster Protestants opposed assimilation, fearing the loss of economic and political power. In the late 1960s, peaceful demonstrations by Catholics against discrimination they suffered in the region met with violent reprisals by the police and paramilitary groups. In 1972, after the British Army killed 13 Civil Rights marchers in Derry on Bloody Sunday, the parliament of Northern Ireland was suspended and rule by Westminster was reinstated in the province. A revived IRA, bent on driving out the British and achieving a united Ireland, launched a terrorist campaign of bombings and shootings that spread to England.

More than 20,000 people were injured or killed in the 30 years of violence that followed. Yet the desire for peace among the majority of Irish people, North and South, triumphed in May 1998. The people voted for the setting-up of a new Northern Ireland Assembly in which all sections of the community would be represented. This assumed power in December 1999 but continuing disputes led to its suspension in October 2002. New elections were held and full power was restored in May 2007. The transfer of policing and justice powers to the Assembly marked a new milestone in April 2010.

**Right**
A popular evening out

## Irish mythology

Ireland is rich in folklore and mythology, from the fairy people to the Celtic gods and heroes. Reading just a few of these tales will add greatly to the atmosphere of any journey through Ireland. The fairy people, who are said to be fallen angels, redundant gods or an ancient race lost in the mists of time, make love, war and beautiful music. Their most famous member is the leprechaun, a grouchy old shoemaker, who buries the riches of his trade at the end of the rainbow. Numerous customs have sprung from the need to placate the fairies; for example, ash was placed on the threshold to protect an unattended child in a cradle from fairy abductions.

The gods and heroes of Celtic lore are related to those of Scotland, Wales and Celtic Europe. Because the Celts had an oral rather than a written tradition, their stories were only recorded by scribes in Christian times. Sadly, many of these early manuscripts were destroyed by Viking raiders, but what remains comprises the earliest examples of Irish literature. Scholars have categorised the sagas into four cycles, whose two greatest heroes are Cú Chulainn and Fionn MacCumhail (Finn MacCool).

## The pub

The pub is the centre of Irish social life, much more than a mere venue for downing a pint. In days gone by, marriage agreements and business deals were sealed here, and it's still the place for courting, singing, playing music and, most of all, enjoying the *craic* (pronounced 'crack'), an Irish word meaning fun and entertainment. 'Singing pubs' are simply places where impromptu music sessions break out and everyone joins in; don't worry if you don't know the words to the Irish ballads – contemporary folk and country tunes are part of the standard repertoire. Some of the best *craic* can be had at small, local hangouts where visitors are welcome but not catered for. Large tourist-oriented venues exist in the main centres. In cities, seek out the old-style Victorian pubs with ornate décor and 'snugs', private booths designed to afford privacy to genteel womenfolk. In rural areas, you'll still find pubs that function as a sort of general store. There's no better place for people-watching, and you don't have to drink alcohol to enjoy the atmosphere. Many pubs now serve food at lunchtime, or coffee and tea during the day. In 2004, a nationwide ban on smoking in the workplace has rendered pubs smoke-free.

## Irish music and dance

Music is such an integral part of Ireland's culture that the harp is its national emblem. Traditional music can be heard throughout the country, and small towns such as Doolin and Dingle are as famed for their music pubs as cities such as Galway and Sligo. There are music festivals, called *fleadhs* (pronounced 'fla'), and dances, called *céili* (pronounced 'kay-lee'), where you can enjoy jigs, reels, airs and laments that are centuries old, as well as revivals of the *Sean-Nós*, sung *a cappella* in Irish, a form that nearly died out in the 1940s. Set dancing, a paired group dance, is also popular in pubs and village halls.

Traditional instruments include the fiddle, harp, flute, tin whistle (or penny whistle), melodeon, *uillean* pipes (pronounced 'ill-un'), similar to bagpipes, and the *bodhrán* (pronounced bow-ráwn), a goat-skin drum shaped like a large tambourine and played with a 'tipper', or beater.

Music in Ireland is more about participation than performance. *Seisiúins* (sessions) are impromptu evenings of music and song, which usually take place in pubs. One person may begin playing a guitar, another brings out a fiddle or *bodhrán*, and soon everyone joins in. Even when the music is organised by the establishment, the audience is encouraged to participate.

Bands such as The Chieftains and Clannad, and singers such as Mary Black and Enya, have brought Irish music to the forefront of the modern music scene, as have top bands such as U2, The Pogues, The Corrs and The Cranberries and artists such as Van Morrison, Kirsty MacColl and Sinead O'Connor. Irish-American Michael Flatley caused

## Literature

Irish poetry and stories, like the Irish soul, are forever linked to the land. A love of nature and an awareness of mankind's place in it is ever-present and imbues the spirit of Irish eloquence. Classic Irish literature includes poetry by W B Yeats and Louis MacNeice; *Dubliners*, *Ulysses* and *Finnegans Wake* by James Joyce; *Waiting for Godot* by the playwright Samuel Beckett; and short stories by Frank O'Connor, Elizabeth Bowen and Sean O'Faolain. Anthologies such as *The Field Day Anthology of Irish Writing*, a three-volume tome edited by Seamus Dean, and collections of Irish verse provide an overview of the wealth of talent. Works by J M Synge are wonderfully evocative of Irish life in the early 1900s. Bernadette Devlin's *The Price of My Soul* and Dervla Murphy's *A Place Apart* give heartfelt insights into Northern Ireland. In 1996, poet Seamus Heaney became the fourth Irish winner of the Nobel Prize for Literature. Contemporary Irish novels include Frank McCourt's *Angela's Ashes*, and Roddy Doyle's *The Van* and *Paddy Clark Ha Ha Ha*.

a sensation around the world in the 1990s with his spectacular Irish dance productions, 'Riverdance' and 'Lord of the Dance'.

## Art and architecture

Ireland's rich architectural history begins in ancient times, with the megalithic portal tombs (or dolmens), passage tombs and court cairns erected between 3000 and 2000 BC. They are often decorated with carved spirals, diamonds, suns and other symbols. The early Irish had no cities, but lived in scattered family farmsteads throughout the countryside. Their dwellings consisted of ring forts – round enclosures encircled by earthen banks and built of wood or stone – and *crannogs*, which were platforms built on artificial islands in the lakes and enclosed by a wooden palisade. In the west, small stone *clochans*, or beehive huts, still dot the rocky hillsides.

The early Christian era saw the birth of Ireland's most outstanding architecture. The tall, slim, round towers with their pointed caps are unique to Ireland and were built on monastic sites between 900 and 1200. Their Irish name, *cloigtheach*, means 'bell house', and they served as watchtowers and storehouses for manuscripts and treasures. The doors were built some 12ft (3.5m) from the ground and were reached by ladders which could be drawn up inside; thus they also served as refuges in times of attack. The monasteries also produced the exquisite carved stone high crosses that are the symbol of Ireland. From the 12th century, churches, previously unadorned, began to display carved ornamental decoration in the Romanesque style on doorways, windows and chancel arches; this was probably introduced by the English. Gothic architecture developed from the 13th century.

Irish castles, built by the gentry from the early 15th century, most frequently took the form of a fortified tower house, often surrounded by a bawn wall which also protected residents of nearby farmsteads and livestock in times of danger. By contrast, the traditional Irish dwelling was a single-storey, rectangular cottage with one to three rooms and a thatched or slate roof. Between 1714 and 1820, Georgian architecture reached its glory in neoclassical country manor houses such as Russborough House, Castle Coole and Emo Court. Dublin is known for the Georgian elegance of its red-brick, four-storey town houses, whose plain, well-proportioned façades are decorated with wrought-iron balconies, classical door frames and fanlights above the doors. These were generally built in terraces surrounding a central park or square. Towns such as Birr and Westport, with their tree-lined malls, are also fine examples of Georgian design.

## Sport

*'Rugby is a game for ruffians played by gentlemen*
*Soccer is a game for gentlemen played by ruffians*

**Above**
Dublin's Anna Livia Fountain celebrates James Joyce's personification of the River Liffey. She is known locally as the 'Floozy in the Jacuzzi®'

*Gaelic football is a game for ruffians played by ruffians But Hurling is a game for gentlemen played by gentlemen.'*

So goes an old saw about Ireland's national sport. **Hurling** is similar to hockey and is played on turf. Each team has 15 players who use a flat stick with a wide base, called a hurley, or *camán*, to carry or handle a hard leather ball, called a *sliothár*; the aim is to score points by getting the ball inside the goal or over the crossbar. Because it demands great strength and skill, it is one of the most exciting field sports.

**Gaelic football**, a cross between football and rugby, is another highly popular team sport. The Gaelic Athletic Association (GAA) was founded in 1884 to boost the national identity through these sports, which had been played in Ireland's towns and parishes down the centuries. Ireland also lays claim to inventing the game of **rugby**, first played in universities and public schools in the 1860s.

The first steeplechase was run in Ireland in 1752, so called because it took place between two church steeples. Since then **horse racing** has become the nation's favourite spectator sport. There are 25 major racecourses (*see Sport, page 24*).

When it comes to **golf courses**, Ireland has some beauties. There are over 400 courses of varying sizes and difficulties around the country, many of them challenging links courses set alongside the sea, making Ireland second only to Scotland in the amount of golf greens per square mile (*see Sport, page 25*).

## Tracing your ancestry

With so many descendants of Irish emigrants touring the homeland of their forebears, ancestor hunting is one of the most popular visitor activities in Ireland. Every county has a heritage or genealogical centre that can help you gain access to parish records and other data from that region. The extent of information available and the level of facilities varies from one centre to the next; some are computerised. Fees are generally charged for professional assistance, so always enquire before you begin a search. The names of some genealogical centres are given in the respective chapters; otherwise, enquire at the tourist information office in the area your ancestors are from. Another good starting point is the Genealogy Advisory Service at the National Library in Dublin (*see page 51*).

Before you can begin a search, you will need to find out as much as possible about your ancestors (not simply your family name) from family records: civil records of births, deaths and marriages, church records, immigration records and the like.

# Highlights

## Castles

Malahide Castle (*see page 50*)
Trim Castle (*see page 66*)
Tullynally Castle and Gardens (*see page 84*)
Kilkenny Castle (*see page 98*)
Cahir Castle (*see page 117*)
Ormonde Castle (*see page 119*)
Blarney Castle (*see page 134*)
Bunratty Castle (*see page 167*)
Knappogue Castle (*see page 169*)
Castle Ward (*see page 276*)

## Stately homes

Newman House, Dublin (*see page 52*)
Russborough House (*see page 74*)
Bantry House (*see page 142*)
Muckross House and Abbey (*see page 154*)
Kylemore Abbey (*see page 199*)
Lissadell House and Gardens (*see page 218*)
Castle Coole (*see page 227*)
Florence Court (*see page 228*)

## Cities

Dublin (*see pages 44–59*)
Cork (*see pages 126–33*)
Limerick (*see pages 169–70*)
Galway (*see pages 186–93*)
Derry (*see pages 244–7*)
Belfast (*see pages 262–71*)

## Towns

Drogheda (*see page 62*)
Birr (*see page 82*)
Kilkenny (*see page 98*)
Enniscorthy (*see page 106*)
Wexford (*see page 110*)
Waterford (*see page 122*)
Kenmare (*see page 152*)
Killarney (*see page 152*)
Westport (*see page 210*)

## Villages

Dalkey (*see page 48*)
Skerries (*see page 68*)
Fethard, Tipperary (*see page 96*)

Kilmore Quay (*see page 109*)
Lismore (*see page 120*)
Youghal (*see page 122*)
Kinsale (*see page 136*)
Adare (*see page 166*)
Clifden (*see page 197*)
Roundstone (*see page 200*)
Ardara (*see page 232*)
Ballycastle (*see page 254*)
Cushendall (*see page 260*)
Cushendun (*see page 260*)
Portaferry (*see page 276*)
Strangford (*see page 276*)

## Traditional music towns

Dungarvan (*see page 120*)
Dingle (*see page 159*)
Ennis (*see page 179*)
Milltown Malbay (*see page 183*)
Doolin (*see page 183*)

## Churches

Christ Church Cathedral, Dublin (*see page 47*)
St Canice's Cathedral, Kilkenny (*see page 98*)
Christ Church Cathedral, Waterford (*see page 122*)
St Anne's Church (Bells of Shandon), Cork (*see page 128*)
St Finbarre's Cathedral, Cork (*see page 128*)
St Coleman's Cathedral, Cobh (*see page 136*)
Down Cathedral (*see page 272*)

## Monastic sites and religious monuments

Monasterboice (*see page 65*)
Glendalough (*see page 72*)
Clonmacnoise (*see page 84*)
Rock of Cashel (*see page 94*)
Jerpoint Abbey (*see page 96*)
Dunbrody Abbey (*see page 104*)
Ardmore monastery (*see page 116*)
Gallarus Oratory (*see page 160*)
Quin Abbey (*see page 173*)
Cong Abbey (*see page 197*)

## Architecture

Custom House, Dublin (*see page 47*)
General Post Office, Dublin (*see page 49*)
National Library, Dublin (*see page 51*)
Dublin's Georgian squares (*see page 55*)
City Hall, Belfast (*see page 265*)
Grand Opera House, Belfast (*see page 265*)

## Art galleries
Dublin City Gallery The Hugh Lane (*see page 48*)
National Gallery of Ireland, Dublin (*see page 51*)
Crawford Municipal Art Gallery, Cork (*see page 127*)
The Model Arts and Niland Gallery, Sligo (*see page 220*)
Glebe House and Gallery (*see page 236*)

## Museums and exhibitions
Dublin Writers Museum (*see page 48*)
National Museum of Ireland Archaeology and History, Dublin (*see page 51*)
Trinity College Library, Dublin (*see page 54*)
Famine Museum, Strokestown Park House (*see page 88*)
Kerry County Museum (*see page 162*)
Hunt Museum, Limerick (*see page 169*)
Whowhatwherewhenwhy – W5, Belfast (*see page 266*)

## Parks and gardens
Merrion Square, Dublin (*see page 51*)
St Stephen's Green, Dublin (*see page 53*)
Mount Usher Gardens (*see page 73*)
Powerscourt Gardens (*see page 73*)
Belvedere House, Gardens and Park (*see page 82*)
John F Kennedy Park and Arboretum and Homestead (*see page 108*)
Glenveagh Castle Gardens (*see page 238*)
Botanic Gardens, Belfast (*see page 265*)
Mount Stewart Gardens (*see page 275*)

## Folk parks and attractions
Guinness Storehouse® (*see page 49*)
Irish National Heritage Park (*see page 107*)
Bunratty Folk Park (*see page 167*)
Craggaunowen (*see page 168*)
Connemara Heritage and History Centre (*see page 198*)
An Clachan, Glencolumbkille (*see page 237*)
Ulster American Folk Park (*see page 249*)
Ulster Folk and Transport Museum (*see page 277*)

## Prehistoric sights
Brú na Bóinne (*see page 60*)
Hill of Tara (*see page 63*)
Loughcrew Cairns (*see page 86*)
Staigue Fort (*see page 155*)
Dunbeg Fort (*see page 160*)

Fahan Beehive Huts (*see page 160*)
Dun Aengus, Aran (*see page 194*)
Céide Fields (*see page 208*)
Carrowmore Megalithic Tombs (*see page 216*)
Grianán of Aileach (*see page 248*)

## Scenic drives
Across the Wicklow Mountains via Sally Gap (*see pages 75–9*)
Blackwater Valley Drive, Waterford (*see page 124*)
Lee Valley, County Cork (*see page 140*)
Mizen Head (*see pages 145, 149*)
Sheep's Head Peninsula (*see pages 145, 149*)
Beara Peninsula (*see pages 146–9*)
The Ring of Kerry (*see pages 155–7*)
The Dingle Peninsula (*see pages 163–5*)
The Burren (*see pages 182–5*)
Connemara (*see pages 202–205*)
Atlantic Drive, Achill Island (*see page 206*)
Donegal Coast & Glengesh Pass (*see pages 240–43*)
Glens of Leitrim (*see pages 258*)
Antrim Coast Road (*see pages 259–61*)
Mourne Mountains (*see page 278*)

## Beauty spots
Vale of Avoca (*see page 75*)
Gougane Barra Forest Park (*see page 136*)
Killarney National Park (*see page 153*)
Slea Head (*see page 164*)
Cliffs of Moher (*see page 178*)
Connemara National Park (*see page 198*)
Leenane (*see page 199*)
Castle Caldwell Forest (*see page 226*)
Lower Lough Erne (*see page 230*)
Bunglas Cliffs (*see page 235*)
Glenveagh National Park (*see page 238*)
Giant's Causeway (*see page 257*)
Glenariff Forest Park (*see page 258*)

## Beaches
Courtown (*see page 104*)
Rosslare (*see page 110*)
Ardmore (*see page 116*)
Tramore (*see page 122*)
Inch Strand (*see page 163*)
Portstewart Strand (*see page 259*)
Newcastle (*see page 275*)
Tyrella (*see page 275*)

# Dublin and environs

## Ratings

Architecture ●●●●●

Art ●●●●●

Entertainment ●●●●●

Literary connections ●●●●●

Museums ●●●●●

Shopping ●●●●●

Food and drink ●●●●○

Cathedrals/ churches ●●●○○

Dublin is one of the hottest destinations in Europe. The Celtic Tiger has set the city roaring, generating restaurants and a lively nightlife in such areas as Temple Bar. Dublin is no less fashionable as a centre for the arts. The Vikings founded the city around 837 beside the black pool, or *dubh linn*, for which it is named. It was the centre of the Pale in Norman times, and reached its golden age in the 18th century, when the city's handsome public buildings and elegant Georgian squares were built. Despite a wealth of attractions, Dublin is a compact city, bisected by the River Liffey. After you've explored the attractive streets, river quays, superb museums and atmospheric pubs, the Dublin environs are easily reached by train. Do take a DART journey south to Bray, if only to enjoy the splendid coastal scenery.

## Getting there and getting around

**Dublin Airport** is 6 miles (10km) north of the city centre. Airlink is the Dublin bus service that runs between the airport and the city centre, with stops at the central bus station (Busaras), Connolly Rail station and Heuston Rail station. It runs every 10–15 minutes *Mon–Sat 0545–2330*, and less frequently on *Sun 0700–2300*, fare €5. Aircoach is a private bus service departing every 15 minutes from *0445 to 0045* calling at numerous city-centre locations, *tel: 01 844 7118*. Public buses also stop at the airport. Taxi fares are about €20–22. *Tel: 01 814 1111; www.dublinairport.com*

**Ferry**
The ferry ports for Dublin are Dublin Port and Dun Laoghaire (pronounced 'Dun-Leary'), 6 miles (10km) south of the city centre. Buses and taxis serve both ports and the DART stops at Dun Laoghaire.

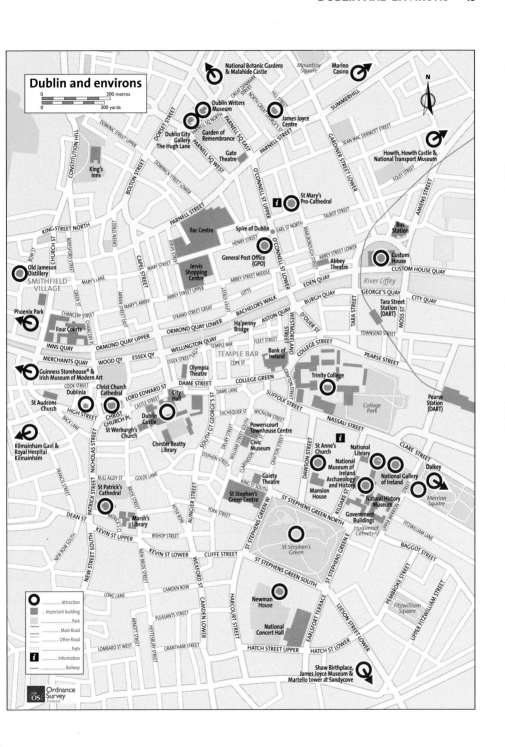

# Dublin and environs

0 ——————— 300 metres
0 ——————— 300 yards

N

National Botanic Gardens & Malahide Castle
Mountjoy Square
Marino Casino

Dublin Writers Museum

James Joyce Centre

Dublin City Gallery The Hugh Lane
Garden of Remembrance

Gate Theatre

Howth, Howth Castle & National Transport Museum

King's Inns

St Mary's Pro-Cathedral

SMITHFIELD VILLAGE

Ilac Centre
Spire of Dublin
Bus Station

Old Jameson Distillery

Jervis Shopping Centre
General Post Office (GPO)
Abbey Theatre
Custom House

River Liffey

Phoenix Park

GEORGE'S QUAY
CITY QUAY

Four Courts

Ha'penny Bridge
Tara Street Station (DART)

Guinness Storehouse® & Irish Museum of Modern Art

Olympia Theatre
Bank of Ireland
Trinity College

TEMPLE BAR

St Audeons Church
Christ Church Cathedral
Dublinia

City Hall

Pearse Station (DART)

Kilmainham Gaol & Royal Hospital Kilmainham

St Werburgh's Church
Dublin Castle
Chester Beatty Library
Civic Museum

St Anne's Church
National Library

Dalkey

St Patrick's Cathedral
Gaiety Theatre
St Stephen's Green Centre

National Museum of Ireland Archaeology and History

Mansion House

National Gallery of Ireland

Natural History Museum

Marsh's Library

Government Buildings

Huguenot Cemetery

St Stephen's Green

Newman House

National Concert Hall

Shaw Birthplace, James Joyce Museum & Martello tower at Sandycove

○ .............. Attraction
▨ .... Important building
.......... Park
══ ........... Main Road
── ........... Other Road
∷∷ ........... Path
𝒊 ........... Information
── ........... Railway

Ordnance Survey Ireland

### Driving

Dublin traffic is becoming as legendary as its pubs. The city centre is so compact that a car is unnecessary; you can take a city bus to any outlying attractions, and the DART to nearby villages such as Howth and Dalkey. It's best to arrange for car hire when you start your tour beyond the city.

### Parking

There are signboards on all the main streets directing you to the car parks and indicating how many spaces are available. On-street parking has numbered bays and you pay for your spot at a nearby meter; the time is limited. Pay and Display and disc parking are also available.

### Public transport

There is a good network of buses running on main routes throughout the city centre and suburbs. The Dublin Area Rapid Transit (DART) is a train service that runs from Malahide in the north to Greystones in the south, with stops in the city centre, as well as Dun Laoghaire.

### Maps

Good touring maps of Ireland are woefully scant; the scale on most is usually too small to be of much use off the main highways, or the colours are garish and distracting. Your best bet for serious touring is the *Ordnance Survey Road Atlas of Ireland*, which can be found at the tourist office shop or at **Hodges & Figgis**, *56–58 Dawson Street.*

### Information

Dublin Tourist Information Office is housed in the deconsecrated St Andrew's Church on Suffolk Street, where you can book tickets, tours and hotels, as well as pick up information and purchase maps and books. *Tel: 1850 230 330 (within Ireland), 0800 039 7000 (UK), 00 353 66 979 2083 (from elsewhere); email: information@dublintourism.ie; reservations@dublintourism.ie; www.visitdublin.com*

There are additional tourist information offices at the arrivals hall in Dublin Airport, the terminal building at Dun Laoghaire Harbour, and on Upper O'Connell Street.

Dublin Tourism publishes several booklets that can enhance your enjoyment of the city, including the Heritage Trails signposted walking tours and the Rock 'n' Stroll music trail. There are also guides to activities in the area, such as golfing.

### Tours

There are several walking tours of Dublin. Highly recommended is the **Literary Pub Crawl**, a very entertaining evening whether you're a book lover or not. The guides are actors who perform sketches outside the drinking haunts of such literary greats as Oscar Wilde, James Plunkett and Mary Lavin. Tours start from The Duke pub on Duke Street; booking is advised to ensure a place. *Tel: 01 670 5602; www.dublinpubcrawl.com*

## Sights

**Christid Church Cathedral €€** *Christ Church Place; tel: 01 677 8099. Open Jun–Aug daily 0900–1800; Sept–May daily 0945–1700 (last admission 45 mins before closing). Access limited during services.*

**Custom House €** *Custom House Quay; tel: 01 888 2538. Open mid-Mar– Oct Mon–Fri 1000–1230, Sat & Sun 1400–1700; Nov– mid-Mar Wed–Fri 1000– 1230, Sun 1400–1700.*

**Above**
Custom House

### Christ Church Cathedral

Founded by the Vikings in 1038, Christ Church Cathedral is Dublin's oldest building, though the magnificent stone edifice that stands today was built in 1169 by the Anglo-Norman conqueror, Strongbow, who is buried here. It was built for Laurence O'Toole, Archbishop of Dublin, who became Dublin's patron saint. The Great Nave, 68ft (25m) high, has some fine early Gothic arches. The crypt is nearly as large as the upper church and houses many unusual relics, including a mummified cat and rat, discovered in an organ pipe.

### Custom House

The Custom House, designed by the master architect James Gandon and completed in 1791, is Dublin's finest Georgian public building. Its gleaming façade of Portland stone stretches 374ft (114m) from end to end. A copper dome rises behind the central portico, crowned by a statue of Commerce. The interior was badly damaged when Republicans

**Chester Beatty Library** *Dublin Castle; tel: 01 407 0750; www.cbl.ie. Open May–Sept Mon–Fri 1000–1700, Sat 1100–1700, Sun 1300–1700; Oct–Apr closed Mon. Admission free.* Set in a new building behind Dublin Castle, this magnificent collection includes rare illustrated medieval manuscripts, Arabic texts and exquisite artworks. It was amassed by Sir Alfred Chester Beatty, an American mining entrepreneur who retired to Ireland in 1950 and left his collection to his adoptive nation. Among the treasures are 2nd-century gospel texts written on papyrus and copies of the Koran produced by master calligraphers.

**Dublin Castle** *€€ off Dame Street; tel: 01 645 8813. Open Mon–Fri 1000–1645, Sat, Sun & bank holidays 1400–1645.*

**Dublin City Gallery The Hugh Lane** *Charlemont House, Parnell Square North; tel: 01 222 5550; www.hughlane.ie. Open Tue–Thur 1000–1800, Fri–Sat 1000–1700, Sun 1100–1700. Free.*

**Dublin Writers Museum** *€€ 18 Parnell Square North; tel: 01 872 2077; www.writersmuseum. com. Open Mon–Sat 1000–1700 (till 1800 weekdays Jun–Aug); Sun & holidays 1100–1700.*

**Dublinia** *€€ Christ Church pl; tel: 01 679 4611. Open Apr–Sept daily 1000–1700; Oct–Mar daily 1000–1630.*

set fire to the building in 1921, and it only reopened in the 1990s. It now houses government offices, and a visitor centre with exhibits on the building and its architect. The best view of the building is from the south side of the Liffey, particularly at night when it is lit.

## Dalkey

This picturesque fishing village, home to many rock and film stars, makes a pleasant excursion from the city. It has narrow, winding streets lined with attractive shopfronts and several pubs and restaurants. Its name comes from an Irish word meaning 'thorn island', and the little island offshore was inhabited in 3500 BC. At the end of the 17th century, Dalkey was a walled town and an important port, with at least seven castles. Only two survive: Goat's Castle, which is now the town hall; and Archibold's Castle, a tower house three storeys high, dating to the 15th or 16th century.

## Dublin Castle

The Vikings built a fortress on this strategic site, on a ridge at the confluence of the River Liffey and its tributary, the Poddle. Here they formed a black pool, or *dubh linn* in Irish, which gave the city its name. The present castle was built by the Normans in the early 13th century, and it was the seat of English power until 1922. Little of that early structure remains beyond the Record Tower. Highlights include the lavish State Apartments where the English viceroys lived, the Undercroft ruins of the Viking fortress and the Gothic Revival Chapel Royal.

## Dublin City Gallery The Hugh Lane

The grand Georgian interior of Charlemont House forms the backdrop for the gallery's collection of 20th-century Irish art. The works of Roderic O'Conor, Jack B Yeats, Walter Osborne and John Lavery are displayed alongside contemporary artists such as Kathy Prendergast, Dorothy Cross and Willie Doherty. The international collection includes Impressionist works and those of late 20th-century artists. Some of the paintings are exchanged with others in London's National Gallery every few years. There is also a sculpture hall and stained-glass work by Harry Clarke and Evie Hone. The studio of Francis Bacon, the gallery's special bequest, opened in 2001.

## Dublin Writers Museum

Housed in a splendid Georgian mansion on the north side of Parnell Square, this museum commemorates the lives and works of the *crème de la crème* of Dublin's literary world. You can peruse the letters, diaries, photographs and mementos left behind by Swift, Wilde, Beckett, Joyce and Shaw, to name a few. The house, former home of John Jameson (the whiskey producer), is elegantly restored, particularly the Gallery of Writers, and features magnificent plasterwork and stained-glass windows. Readings are sometimes held here; *see website for details.*

**General Post Office (GPO)**
*O'Connell Street; tel: 01 705 7000. Open Mon–Sat 0800–2000, Sun & bank holidays 1030–1830. Free.*

**Guinness Storehouse®**
*€€€ St James Gate; tel: 01 408 4800; www.guinness-storehouse.com. Open daily 0930–1700; Jul–Aug 0930–1900.*

**Howth Castle Gardens**
*€ Tel: 01 847 5623. Open daily 0800–dusk.*

**National Transport Museum** *€ Howth Castle, Howth; tel: 01 832 0427. Open Jun–Aug Mon–Sat 1000–1700; Sept–May Sat, Sun & bank holidays 1400–1700.*

## Dublinia

Dublin's medieval heritage centre traces the development of the city from the arrival of the Anglo-Normans to Tudor times in the 16th century. Ten scenes from Dublin's medieval history are re-created in sets and tableaux. In the museum area are artefacts from the Wood Quay excavations where the Norsemen founded their first settlement in 841. A panoramic view over Dublin can be had from atop St Michael's Tower, and a pedestrian bridge connects Dublinia with the grounds of Christ Church Cathedral.

## General Post Office (GPO)

This striking public building, designed by the neoclassical architect Francis Johnston and built between 1814 and 1818, is famous in Irish history as the headquarters of the Republican rebels during the 1916 Easter Rising. From its steps, Patrick Pearse read out the Proclamation of the Republic of Ireland (*see page 37*). Most of the original building was destroyed in the subsequent shelling, though the façade survived. After restoration, it reopened in 1929 and it remains the city's main post office today. Step inside for a look at the handsome interior.

## Guinness Storehouse®

The Brewery, home of the world's most famous stout, was established by Arthur Guinness in 1759 at James Gate, west of Christ Church Cathedral. The Guinness Storehouse® opened in December 2000 and is housed in a 1904 listed building that covers around 170,000sq feet (15,800sq m). The Guinness® Experience shows visitors what goes into making a pint of Guinness®, the ingredients and the brewing process. You can follow the history of Guinness® and its export to 150 countries and see an exhibition of the company's famous campaign posters. The tour ends on the roof of this six-floor building with the perfect pint pulled for you in the Gravity Bar.

## Howth

This attractive harbour town on Dublin Bay is a favourite excursion, about half an hour from the city by DART. The name Howth (pronounced 'Hoath') is derived from the Norse word 'hoved', meaning head; in the early 19th century it was the port for sea crossings from Wales. There are several good walks here, the easiest leading out along the sea wall, with fine views of the boats in the harbour and the rock island offshore known as 'Ireland's Eye'. Local boatmen can take you there in good weather to see the old stone church and Martello tower. A 1½-mile (2.5km) cliff walk takes you around the headland to the Baily Lighthouse, where there are splendid views. You can visit the grounds of **Howth Castle**, which have beautiful rhododendron gardens, a ruined 16th-century castle and a Neolithic dolmen. The **National Transport Museum** is also here. The steep winding streets of the village have good restaurants and pubs.

**James Joyce Centre**
€€ 35 North Great George's Street; tel: 01 878 8547. Open Tue–Sat 1000–1700, Sun 1200–1700.

**James Joyce Museum**
€€ The Martello Tower, Sandycove; tel: 01 280 9265. Open Apr–Aug Tue–Sat 1000–1300, 1400–1700, Sun 1400–1800.

**Malahide Castle** €€
Tel: 01 846 2184. Open Apr–Sept daily 1000–1700; Oct–Mar Mon–Sat 1000–1700, Sun 1100–1700 (closed for tours 1245–1400 in winter).

## James Joyce Centre

Housed in a restored Georgian town house, the James Joyce Centre focuses on the life and works of one of Ireland's greatest authors. Along with the reference library and exhibition rooms, there are tours of the house and walks through Joyce's old stomping grounds in this north section of the inner city. Joyce fans can also pick up the *Ulysses* Map of Dublin from the tourist information office, which points out related sights of interest. The **James Joyce Museum** is located 8 miles (13km) south of Dublin in the Martello tower at Sandycove, which formed the setting for the opening chapter of his great novel, *Ulysses*.

## Malahide Castle

Set in 250 acres (100 hectares) of parkland in the seaside town of Malahide, the castle makes a good day trip from the city. The fortress, built in 1185, was the home of the Talbot family for nearly 800 years. Its mix of architectural styles includes the medieval Great Hall, the Tudor Oak Room and rococo plasterwork in the reception rooms. It contains beautiful period furnishings and a collection of portraits from

**Natural History Museum** € *Merrion Street; tel: 01 677 7444. Open Tue–Sat 1000–1700, Sun 1400–1700.*

**Government Buildings** € *Upper Merrion Street; tel: 01 662 4888; tours on Sat 1030, 1130, 1230, 1330.*

**National Gallery of Ireland** *Merrion Square West; tel: 01 661 5133. Open Mon–Sat 0930–1730 (Thur till 2030), Sun 1200–1730.*

**National Library** *Kildare Street; tel: 01 603 0200. Open Mon–Wed 0930–2100, Thur–Fri 0930–1700, Sat 0930–1300.*

**National Museum of Ireland Archaeology and History** € *Kildare Street; tel: 01 677 7444. Open Tue–Sat 1000–1700, Sun 1400–1700.*

**National Museum of Ireland Decorative Arts & History** € *Collins Barracks, Benburb Street; tel: 01 677 7444. Open Tue–Sat 1000–1700, Sun 1400–1700.*

**Opposite**
Georgian Dublin

the National Gallery. The Botanic Garden, with over 5,000 species, is open from May to September, and there is also the Fry Model Railway Museum in the castle.

### Merrion Square

This peaceful Georgian square, laid out in the 1760s, is one of Dublin's finest. Winding paths dotted with monuments lead to a central green with lovely flower gardens. Plaques bearing the names of famous former residents are dotted around the perimeter. Number 1, on the north side, was the childhood home of Oscar Wilde from 1855 to 1878; it is now the American College in Dublin and is being restored. The 'Liberator' Daniel O'Connell lived at No 58, and W B Yeats resided at No 52 and later No 82. Opposite the west side of the square is the green lawn of **Leinster House**, with an obelisk commemorating the founders of the Irish State. Built in the mid-18th century, Leinster House is now the seat of the Irish Parliament, the Dáil, and the Seanad (Senate). To the left is the **Natural History Museum** and **Government Buildings**, a neoclassical edifice built in the early 1900s which now houses the offices of the *taoiseach* (pronounced 'tea-shook'), the Irish prime minister. Tours of the lovely interior are given on Saturdays. To the right is the National Gallery of Ireland (*see below*).

### National Gallery of Ireland

Founded in 1854, the National Gallery houses an extensive collection of paintings, drawings, prints and sculpture. Every major European school of painting is represented, including a major collection of Irish art. The **Yeats Museum**, dedicated to the works of Jack B Yeats and his family, opened here in 1999. Among the highlights are Caravaggio's *The Taking of Christ*, Vermeer's *Lady Writing a Letter* and Gainsborough's *The Cottage Girl*. The handsome building was designed by Francis Fowke, architect of London's Victoria and Albert Museum. A new Millennium Wing adjoining the building (entrance on Clare Street) opened in 2001.

### National Library

The National Library, designed by Sir Thomas Deane, opened in 1890 and houses a copy of every book ever printed in Ireland, including first editions by all the major literary figures. You can obtain a visitor's pass to see the great domed Reading Room where the likes of James Joyce and W B Yeats researched their material and no doubt gained inspiration. The library now contains the excellent **Genealogy Room**, moved here from No 2 Kildare Street, which offers advice, references and computer searches for tracing your Irish ancestry.

### National Museum of Ireland Archaeology and History

Opened in 1890, this magnificent building designed by Sir Thomas Deane, with its classical domed rotunda, marble pillars and zodiac

**Newman House**
€€ 85 & 86 St Stephen's Green; tel: 01 716 7422. Open Jun–Aug Tue–Fri tours at 1400, 1500, 1600.

mosaic floor, is a splendid storehouse for the collection of Ireland's antiquities, dating from 7000 BC to the 20th century. The stunning gold jewellery, carved stones and iron and bronze weaponry comprises the world's largest group of Celtic artefacts. Some of the most famous pieces are kept in the Treasury, including the Tara brooch, the Ardagh chalice, St Patrick's Bell and the Cross of Cong. Exhibitions on Prehistoric Ireland, Viking Ireland and the Road to Independence put the many artefacts into historical perspective. There is also a collection of ancient Egyptian artefacts. Another branch of the National Museum at Collins Barracks houses the collection of **decorative arts**, including furniture, silver, ceramics, glassware and costume.

### Newman House

Comprising Nos 85 and 86 St Stephen's Green, Newman House contains one of the finest Georgian interiors in the city. It is noted for its sumptuous plasterwork, particularly the late Baroque Apollo Room decorated by the La Franchini brothers from Switzerland. The houses were joined in the mid-19th century when Cardinal John Newman

**Right**
St Patrick's Cathedral

**Old Jameson Distillery €€€** Bow Street, Smithfield Village; tel: 01 807 2355. Open daily 0900–1800 (last tour 1730).

**St Anne's Church** Dawson Street. Open Mon–Fri 1000–1600.

**St Patrick's Cathedral** €€ Patrick's Close; tel: 01 475 4817. Open Mar–Oct daily 0900–1730; Nov–Feb Mon–Fri 0900–1730, Sat & Sun 0900–1500. No tours admitted during services.

founded the Catholic University of Ireland here. James Joyce and Flann O'Brien were former students, and the great Jesuit poet Gerard Manley Hopkins taught here towards the end of his life; the room where he lived has been restored in his honour. The house is accessible on a guided tour.

## Old Jameson Distillery

This distillery produced one of Ireland's most famous whiskeys from its beginnings in 1791 until 1966, when operations moved to County Cork. It was then turned into a museum, and now you can follow the craft of whiskey making on a guided tour. You will see the working mash tun, original copper pot stills and wooden fermentation casks, followed by a tasting in the Jameson bar.

## St Anne's Church

The pretty interior of this church was completed in 1720, though the sombre neo-Romanesque façade was the work of Sir Thomas Deane in 1868. Notice the shelf near the altar, put up in 1723 by Lord Newton for the distribution of bread to the poor. Oscar Wilde, Bram Stoker and Wolfe Tone are among the famous people who worshipped here. Lunchtime recitals are often held.

## St Patrick's Cathedral

A church beside the well where St Patrick is said to have baptised early converts has stood here since 450, making this the oldest Christian site in Dublin. The present edifice, the largest church in Ireland, was built in 1191, and the first University of Ireland was founded here in 1320. Jonathan Swift served as dean of St Patrick's from 1713 until 1745. Among the highlights of the cathedral are the medieval brasses, tiles and chapterhouse, the choir with the banners and stalls of the Knights of St Patrick, and the West Tower, which dates from 1370 and contains the largest set of ringing bells in Ireland. There are also memorials to many famous people, including Carolan, the last of the Irish bards, and Douglas Hyde, the country's first president.

## St Stephen's Green

The city's most famous park covers 27 acres (11 hectares), a verdant space with formal lawns, flower gardens, an ornamental lake and a Victorian bandstand. It was an open common until 1663. During the latter part of the 18th century, the north side was known as Beaux' Walk, after the aristocratic gentlemen who strolled there. In 1880, Sir Arthur Guinness paid for the landscaping that gave the green its present shape. Along its shady paths are many monuments, including memorials to the writers Yeats and Joyce, the patriots Robert Emmet and Wolfe Tone, the moving Famine memorial and the bronze statue group, the *Three Fates*.

**Trinity College Library** €€ *College Street, tel: 01 896 1127. Old Library open Mon–Sat 0930–1700; Oct–Apr also Sun 1200–1630; May–Sept also Sun 0930–1630.* Try to visit Trinity College Library early in the day, when it is less crowded with tour bus groups.

## Trinity College

Trinity College, set in 40 acres (16 hectares) in the heart of Dublin, was founded by Queen Elizabeth I in 1592. Its most famous building is **Trinity College Library**, which contains the magnificent medieval manuscript the *Book of Kells*, thought to have been produced by the monks of Iona in the early 9th century. Its intricate, interlacing Celtic patterns and symbolic motifs depict the four gospels and it is considered to be the finest illuminated manuscript in existence. An excellent exhibition, 'Turning Darkness into Light', introduces this treasure and provides a fascinating look at how these lavishly

## Georgian Dublin

Dublin is famous for its splendid Georgian architecture, from its handsome public buildings to its well-proportioned town houses. These are best seen around the city's five elegant squares: Merrion, Fitzwilliam, Parnell and Mountjoy squares and St Stephen's Green. The town houses were typically built of red brick, standing four storeys high above a basement and three bays wide. The plain façades are enlivened by simple, semicircular wrought-iron balconies on the second-storey windows. Their finest decorative feature are the doors, which are framed with classical-style pillars and architraves, panelled and painted in bright reds, blues and yellows, adorned with heavy brass knockers and crowned by decorative fanlights.

decorated gospels were produced in medieval times, from the preparation of the vellum (calfskin) and inks to the symbolic drawing and lettering with quill pens and brushes. Also on view are other fine manuscripts, including the *Book of Durrow* and the *Shrine Book of Dimma*, a 'pocket gospel' carried by missionaries in a leather pouch around the neck.

Adjoining the *Book of Kells* display room is the **Long Room**, the impressive main chamber of the Old Library, which measures nearly 213ft (65m) in length and houses some 200,000 volumes on high wooden shelves. The barrel-vaulted ceiling was raised in 1860 to create more storage capacity when the original shelves became full. The central aisle is lined with marble busts of distinguished scholars and statesmen, and contains one of the few remaining copies of the 1916 Proclamation of the Irish Republic.

Wander through the campus, where other fine buildings include the **Museum Building**, home to the geography department. Its Venetian-style exterior is a clue to the rich architectural detail in the lobby, including exquisite Irish marbles, finely carved capitals, arches and mosaic skylights. In the foyer are the skeletons of a pair of extinct Giant Irish Deer. Around the cobblestoned quadrangle, Parliament Square, are the classical West Front, campanile, chapel and ornate Examination Hall. The modern Arts and Social Sciences Building houses the Douglas Hyde Gallery of Modern Art.

### Also worth exploring

Dublin has many more sights that are worth seeking out if you have more time to explore the city. The best of the rest include **Four Courts**, home of the Irish law courts, designed by James Gandon and completed in 1802; **City Hall**, a domed classical building (1769–79), seat of the city's governing body, the Dublin Corporation; **King's Inns** (1795–1817), home of the legal profession; and **Marsh's Library**, Ireland's oldest public library, built in 1701. Interesting churches include **St Michan's Church, St Mary's Pro-Cathedral** and **St Werburgh's Church**. To the south of the city centre is the **Shaw Birthplace**, Victorian home of the playwright George Bernard Shaw. In west Dublin, the **Royal Hospital Kilmainham**, considered the finest 17th-century building in the country, houses the **Irish Museum of Modern Art**. The enormous **Kilmainham Gaol** held the leaders of Irish rebellions between 1796 and 1924 and is an insight into the country's turbulent history. The vast **Phoenix Park**, covering some 1,752 acres (710 hectares), contains the People's Garden and **Dublin Zoo**. In the north of the city are the **National Botanic Gardens** at Glasnevin and the delightful villa **Marino Casino**, designed by Sir William Chambers between 1762 and 1771.

**Opposite**
Trinity College

# Suggested walk

## Irish wood

In 1962, five ships were discovered submerged in Roskilde fjord in Denmark. They had been deliberately sunk across a channel around €€1100 to form a barricade to protect Roskilde, an important medieval city. One warship measured 98ft (30m) – the largest Viking longboat ever found. With a crew of between 60 and 100 warriors at the oars, it could reach speeds of 5 knots; under sail in favourable winds it would have been much faster. Tree-ring analysis of the wood showed that the boat had been built in Ireland in the 1060s, probably in a Dublin shipyard.

🏛 **Bank of Ireland**
*2 College Green; tel: 01 677 6801. Open Mon–Fri 1000–1600 (Thur 1700); House of Lords tours: Tue 1030, 1130, 1345; Arts Centre (€) Tue–Fri 1000–1600.*

🍷 **O'Neill's Pub**
*2 Suffolk Street,* is an atmospheric old Dublin pub with the best pub carvery in the city. Food served *daily 1030–2230.*

**Time:** You could complete the main route in under 2 hours, with an additional hour for the detour, but why rush? Take half a day or more and allow yourself to linger over unexpected discoveries. For sightseeing, those with little time should concentrate on Trinity College Library, St Stephen's Green, the National Museum, Merrion Square and the Custom House.

**Links:** Dublin is the starting point for tours of several adjoining regions, including the Boyne Valley (*see page 60*), the Wicklow Mountains (*see page 70*) and Kildare (*see page 97*).

Begin at **TRINITY COLLEGE**. Exit through the main entrance on College Green opposite the **Bank of Ireland**, built in 1729 to house the Irish Parliament. You can view the splendid chambers of the House of Lords, with beautiful tapestries, woodwork and crystal chandeliers. Turn left and walk down Grafton Street, turning right on to Suffolk Street past the statue of the legendary street trader Molly Malone. Just beyond, on your left, is **St Andrew's Church**, now converted into the tourist information office. Opposite is **O'Neill's Pub**, a Victorian gem with several bars to explore. Continue south on William Street past the **Old Stand**, another traditional pub. On the left is the **Powerscourt Townhouse Centre**, a delightful shopping complex set around the courtyard of a converted Georgian mansion. Exit the centre on the opposite side of the building, and follow the narrow lane called Johnson's Court through to **Grafton Street**. This pedestrianised thoroughfare, with Dublin's best shops and department stores, is a mecca for locals and visitors alike. The acoustics of this brick-lined street are such that the buskers actually sound good! Just beside the lane is **Bewley's Grafton Street Café**, a Dublin landmark and one of several branches in the city. Turn right and proceed down Grafton Street to **ST STEPHEN'S GREEN**.

**Detour:** The pedestrian lane opposite the William Street entrance to the Powerscourt Townhouse Centre leads to the **George's Street Market Arcade**, a charming covered market. Walk through to **South Great George's Street**, with many fun shops for browsing. The **Long Hall Pub** at No 51 is another Victorian gem, with chandeliers, mirrors and plasterwork ceilings. Turn left out of the arcade, then left again at Stephen Street, which veers right into King Street South. Continue straight ahead to rejoin the main tour at St Stephen's Green.

Exit the green on the south side, and cross over the road to **NEWMAN HOUSE**. Continue east, and at the end of the green carry on straight ahead into Leeson Street. Turn left on Pembroke Street which leads past Fitzwilliam Square, the smallest of Dublin's Georgian squares. The park is not open to the public. Turn right and continue along the north side of the square, which has fine houses and

🛈 **Number Twenty-
Nine €** *Lower
Fitzwilliam Street; tel: 01
702 6165. Open Tue–Sat
1000–1700, Sun
1200–1700; closed two
weeks prior to Christmas.*

doorways; at its end turn left on to Upper Fitzwilliam Street. This road
once boasted the longest unbroken line of Georgian town houses in
Europe. Just before you reach Merrion Square, on your right is
**Number Twenty-Nine**, which has been restored as a middle-class
house of the late 18th century. Turn left at the corner; about halfway
along is the entrance to lovely **MERRION SQUARE**. On the west side
of the square is the **NATIONAL GALLERY OF IRELAND**.

Continue west along Clare Street. Turn left at Kildare Street. About
halfway along on the left is the **NATIONAL LIBRARY**. Just beyond is
the **NATIONAL MUSEUM OF IRELAND ARCHAEOLOGY AND
HISTORY**. Number 30 Kildare Street, across from the museum, was the
home of Bram Stoker, author of *Dracula*; it is now a solicitors' office. At
the end of Kildare Street is the **Shelbourne Hotel**. On its eastern side is
the **Huguenot Cemetery**, used in the late 17th century. Turn right
along St Stephen's Green North, and right again into Dawson Street.
On the right is **Mansion House**, residence of the Lord Mayor of
Dublin. Beyond on the right is **ST ANNE'S CHURCH**. Continue up
Dawson Street to Nassau Street, on the south side of Trinity College.

**Detour:** To continue the walk north of the Liffey, turn right at
Grafton Street and walk up College Green past the Bank of Ireland;
turn left on Fleet Street. This leads into **Temple Bar**, Dublin's liveliest
area for pubs and restaurants. It is also a centre for the arts, with
many galleries and studios centred around Meeting House Square.
Walk through Merchant's Arch to Aston Quay, alongside
the River Liffey. The charming footbridge ahead of you is the
**Ha'penny Bridge**; up until the early 20th century, there was a half-
penny toll to cross it. It's free today, so cross over and admire the
views to the west. If shopping is on your mind, carry on straight
ahead along Liffey Street, with dozens of small speciality shops, pubs
and cafés. This will bring you to the shopping thoroughfares of Mary
and Henry streets. Otherwise, turn right over the bridge and walk
along Bachelors Walk to **O'Connell Street**, a broad boulevard lined
with shops and hotels; a monument to Daniel O'Connell, the
'Liberator', stands at the end of the bridge. Turn left. The handsome
building on the left is the **GENERAL POST OFFICE**. In the centre of
the boulevard is the **Spire of Dublin**, erected in 2003 and standing
394ft (120m) high, with a time capsule underneath. Just beyond is
the famous statue of James Joyce on Earl Street North. At the top of
O'Connell Street is the Parnell Monument. Continue up the hill
along Parnell Square East. Past the Gate Theatre, an entrance into the
square leads to the **Garden of Remembrance**, dedicated to those who
died in the pursuit of Irish freedom. On the north side of Parnell
Square are the **DUBLIN WRITERS MUSEUM** and the **DUBLIN CITY
GALLERY THE HUGH LANE**. Turn right into Great Denmark Street.
On the right, North Great George's Street leads to the **JAMES JOYCE
CENTRE**. Continue along Great Denmark Street into Gardiner's Place,

**Dublin coffee houses**

If you don't want to
queue for coffee at the
famous **Bewley's**, try
the **Metro Café**, off
the beaten Grafton
Street track on South
William Street. This
mellow café is a popular
hangout for young
Dubliners and serves a
great cappuccino. There
are also a couple of
cafés on Anne Street,
such as the trendy
**Gotham**.

**ⓘ** For arts and entertainment listings, *The Irish Times* and the *Evening Herald* have guides to theatres, cinemas, live music and other events. *In Dublin* and *The Event Guide* are two free fortnightly guides distributed in pubs and cafés around town; they also have dance club listings.

which leads to **Mountjoy Square**. Parts of this Georgian square have seen better days, but the northern side has some fine houses. Turn right along the west side of the square, and carry straight on along Gardiner Street back towards the city centre. The street ends at the back of the **CUSTOM HOUSE**. Turn left and follow the road around to the river, turning right to view this magnificent building from all sides. Continue west along the quays to the O'Connell Street Bridge; cross over and Westmoreland Street leads back to Trinity College.

## Shopping

Dublin's famous department store, **Brown Thomas**, along with **Marks & Spencer**, can be found on Grafton Street. Many shops, particularly bookshops, are located on the parallel Dawson Street and on Duke and Anne streets, which run between them. Here, too, is the **Royal Hibernian Way**, a small stylish shopping complex. If you're looking for traditional Irish goods such as Belleek china, Waterford crystal, tweeds and knitwear, try **Blarney Woollen Mills, House of Ireland** and the **Kilkenny Shop**, all located on Nassau Street. **Tower Design Centre**, east of the city centre, has numerous craft workshops, many of which sell to visitors. Dublin's largest shopping mall is **St Stephen's Green Centre**, on the northwest corner of the green. Nearby is the **Powerscourt Townhouse Centre**, with upmarket shops and an antiques row. There are more antiques' dealers located on Francis Street and the surrounding area. South Great George's Street and Exchequer Street have small speciality shops that are fun to browse through, including **Waltons**, a good place to buy Irish instruments. The George's Street covered market is good for bargains, as is **Mother Redcap's Market** (*Fri–Sun*) on High Street. North of the Liffey, the main shopping streets are Henry Street and Mary Street, where you will find the **Ilac Centre** and **Jervis Shopping Centre**.

## Entertainment

Dublin's pubs are legendary. There are more than 900, from Victorian gems such as **O'Neill's** and **Ryan's** near Phoenix Park, to crowded Temple Bar favourites such as **Oliver St John Gogarty's** and authentic watering holes such as **Mulligan's** and **Doyle's**. There are numerous nightclubs in the city centre, with some of the trendiest located on the quays on the north side of the Liffey.

Two of the best places to hear traditional music are south of the city centre. **Johnnie Fox's** (*tel: 01 295 5647*) is a characterful pub at Glencullen, in the Dublin mountains off the Enniskerry road. **Comhaltas Ceoltóirí Eireann**, the association for the promotion of traditional music and culture, has its headquarters in Belgrave Square,

Monkstown, where it organises nightly entertainment from June to September. It also holds a *céilí* on Friday nights year-round. *Tel: 01 280 0295 for information.*

The **Abbey** (*tel: 01 878 7222*) and its sister, the **Peacock**, are the two theatres of the National Theatre Society, founded by W B Yeats, Lady Gregory and J M Synge. Since its birth, the Society has premiered the work of every leading Irish playwright, and continues to promote new writing and acting talent in its productions today. The **Gate Theatre** (*tel: 01 874 4045*) is also renowned for productions of the classics and contemporary Irish plays.

## Accommodation and food in Dublin

**Gallagher's Boxty House** € *20–21 Temple Bar; tel: 01 677 2762; www.boxtyhouse.ie.* Either book or come early to this popular restaurant serving traditional Irish favourites. Boxty is a potato pancake stuffed with marinated beef, chicken or other fillings. Irish stew, coddle and steaks, lamb and vegetarian dishes are also on the menu. Pleasant country-cottage-style décor, with stone walls, wooden beams and panelling. *Open daily for lunch and dinner.*

**Kilkenny Café and Restaurant** € *6 Nassau Street; tel: 01 677 7075.* Salmon plait, quiche, Irish stew and casserole, accompanied by a choice of fresh salads, are among the items served at this large, smart cafeteria occupying the top floor of the Kilkenny Shop overlooking Trinity College Green. Fresh-baked scones, cakes and desserts complement the traditional home cooking. *Open Mon–Sat 0830–1700 (1900 Thur), Sun 1100–1700.*

**Number 31** €€ *31 Leeson Close; tel: 01 676 5011; fax: 01 676 2929; email: info@number31.ie; www.number31.ie.* Four-star guesthouse in two renovated Georgian mews houses, formerly the home of architect Sam Stephenson, just off St Stephen's Green. Peaceful setting with garden and contemporary-style sitting room. *Open year-round.*

**Central Hotel** €€–€€€ *1–5 Exchequer Street; tel: 01 679 7302; fax: 01 679 7303; email: reservations@centralhotel.ie; www.centralhotel.ie.* Old-style hotel with a great location in the heart of the city. Rooms have pleasant décor and high ceilings. First-floor restaurant and Library Bar; traditional music Friday and Saturday nights at the adjacent pub. *Open year-round.*

**Restaurant Patrick Guilbaud** €€€ *21 Upper Merrion Street; tel: 01 676 4192; www.restaurantpatrickguilbaud.ie.* Arguably the best restaurant in Ireland, with two Michelin stars to its name, Restaurant Patrick Guilbaud has been in business since 1981. It occupies an 18th-century Georgian town house, but the food and the feeling is French throughout. A starter alone can cost €40, while main courses are elaborate creations such as a fillet of Irish beef and roast *foie gras* with Madeira and truffle jus. *Open Tue–Sat for lunch and dinner.*

# The Boyne Valley

## Ratings

| | |
|---|---|
| Historical sights | ●●●●● |
| Monastic sites | ●●●●● |
| Prehistoric sites | ●●●●● |
| Castles | ●●●●○ |
| Scenery | ●●●●○ |
| Beaches | ●●●○○ |
| Cathedrals/ churches | ●●●○○ |
| Coastal towns/ villages | ●●●○○ |

The wide, slow-moving River Boyne weaves a twisting path through the counties north of Dublin, and among these green and scenic rolling hills lie some of Ireland's greatest historical sites. This land is the very cradle of Irish civilisation, where Neolithic farmers with a mysterious but sophisticated culture built enormous passage tombs (*see page 68*). The prehistoric remains at Brú na Bóinne are some of the world's most important archaeological remains. The Celts considered the Boyne a sacred river, and for centuries crowned their high kings on the Hill of Tara. On the nearby Hill of Slane, St Patrick lit the paschal fire that signalled the arrival of Christianity in Ireland, and great monasteries were founded at Monasterboice and Mellifont. Military campaigns were waged here, too: Cromwell's vicious slaughter in the medieval town of Drogheda, and the great turning point in Irish history, the Battle of the Boyne.

## BRÚ NA BÓINNE / NEWGRANGE

🏛 **Brú na Bóinne**
€€–€€€ *Donore;*
*tel: 041 988 0300;*
*www.heritageireland.ie.*
*Newgrange and visitor centre open daily: Feb–Apr 0930–1730; May 0900–1830; Jun–mid-Sept 0900–1900; mid–end-Sept 0900–1830; Oct 0930–1730; Nov–Jan 0900–1700. Very busy in summer when early arrival is advised.*

**Brú na Bóinne**, the 'dwelling place of the Boyne', is an area that lies between Drogheda and Slane, surrounded on three sides by a winding stretch of the river. The series of remarkable passage tombs here, built by Neolithic farmers more than 5,000 years ago, is one of the world's most important archaeological sites. It is often known by the name of the most famous tomb, Newgrange, but in fact there are some 50 monuments within the area, all on private land. The other two main sites are Knowth and Dowth (both closed to visitors due to ongoing excavations). The tombs can only be visited on a guided tour from the visitor centre, where there are excellent exhibits and a film about the site. You then cross the footbridge over the River Boyne where shuttle buses take you on the respective tours.

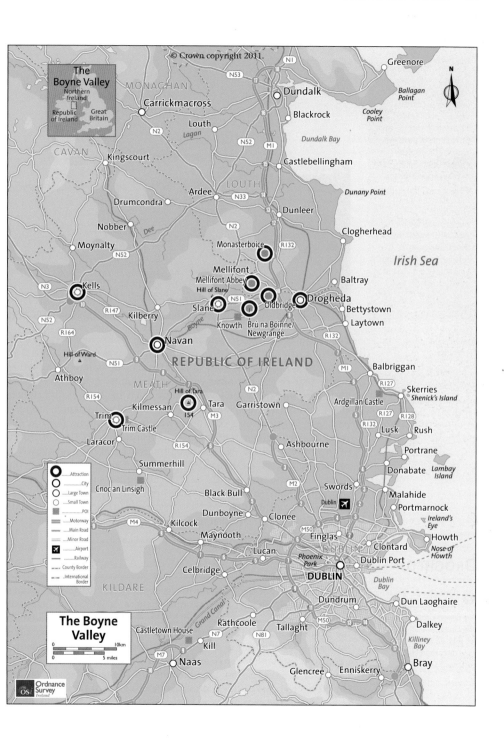

The Boyne Valley

© Crown copyright 2011.

Northern Ireland
Republic of Ireland
Great Britain

MONAGHAN

Carrickmacross

Louth
Lagan

CAVAN

Kingscourt

Drumcondra

Ardee

LOUTH

Nobber

Dee

Moynalty

Monasterboice

Mellifont
Mellifont Abbey
Hill of Slane

Kells

Kilberry

Slane

Knowth  Brú na Bóinne/
Newgrange

Navan

Hill of Ward

Athboy

MEATH

Hill of Tara

Kilmessan  Tara  Garristown

Trim

Trim Castle

Laracor

Summerhill

Cnoc an Linsigh

Black Bull

Dunboyne  Clonee

Kilcock

Maynooth

Lucan

Celbridge

KILDARE

Castletown House

Rathcoole  Tallaght

Kill

Naas

Glencree  Enniskerry

Greenore

Dundalk

Blackrock

Ballagan Point
Cooley Point

Dundalk Bay

Castlebellingham

Dunany Point

Dunleer

Clogherhead

Irish Sea

Baltray

Drogheda
Oldbridge
Bettystown
Laytown

Balbriggan

Skerries
Shenick's Island

Ardgillan Castle

Lusk  Rush

Portrane

Donabate  Lambay Island

Swords

Dublin ✈

Malahide

Portmarnock

Ireland's Eye

Finglas  Howth

Clontarf  Nose of Howth

Phoenix Park  Dublin Port

DUBLIN

Dublin Bay

Dundrum  Dun Laoghaire

Dalkey

Killiney Bay

Bray

REPUBLIC OF IRELAND

Attraction
City
Large Town
Small Town
POI
Motorway
Main Road
Minor Road
Airport
Railway
County Border
International Border

The Boyne Valley

0          10km
0        5 miles

Ordnance Survey
Ireland

## Knowth

This is a larger site than Newgrange, with an enormous central mound surrounded by 17 satellite tombs, each of which is a passage grave. The central mound is complex, with two separate passages leading to distinct and unconnected burial chambers. It is outstanding for its rich display of megalithic art. The Celts built fortifications here, and Knowth was a seat of power for Irish high kings in early Christian times.

**Above right**
Newgrange

The enormous passage tomb at **Newgrange**, built from over 200,000 tons of earth and stone, covers more than an acre and stands 36ft (11m) high, and is the only tomb that can be entered. The white quartz that covers the front comes from County Wicklow, 44 miles (70km) south, and is believed to have been hauled here by coracle along the coast and river. Behind the decorated entrance stone, a passage 62ft (19m) long and lined with standing stones leads to the inner burial chamber. An outstanding feature here is the 20ft (6m)-high corbelled roof, which has remained waterproof over five millennia. The greatest wonder of Newgrange's construction is the 'roof box': at dawn on the day of the winter solstice, a shaft of sunlight beams through this small opening above the door and penetrates the passage to the very back of the chamber. This undoubtedly had great ritual significance for the Neolithic farmers.

# DROGHEDA

 **Drogheda Tourist Information Office**
Bus Eireann station, N 1 and Donore Road;
tel: 041 983 7070;
www.discoverireland.ie/ eastcoast. Open year-round.

Set on the banks of the River Boyne, its skyline punctuated by the spires of three cathedrals, Drogheda is one of the most attractive medieval towns in the Midlands. It was founded by the Vikings and captured by the Norman Hugh de Lacy, Lord of Trim; by the early 15th century, the walled and fortified town was the largest English town in the country. Cromwell launched a savage attack on Drogheda in 1649, and **St Lawrence Gate** is the only sizeable remnant of the medieval defences. On West Street, the Gothic Catholic **St Peter's Church** houses a sad and rather gruesome relic: the head of the martyred saint, Oliver Plunkett.

**Millmount Museum and Martello Tower €€** *Tel: 041 983 3097; www.millmount.net. Open Mon–Sat 0930–1730, Sun 1400–1700.*

Born of a prominent Meath family, he became the Archbishop of Armagh, but was falsely convicted of instigating a 'Popish Plot' and was hanged, drawn and quartered in 1681. The mummified head is displayed in a side chapel. The church also has a beautiful high altar of Carrara marble. The old **Tholsel** on West and Shop streets, now a bank, is topped by a cupola whose clock chimes every quarter hour. Off Narrow West Street, the Gothic tower – a remnant of the Abbey of St Mary d'Urso – which bridges Abbey Lane is dubbed the 'drive-in friary'. The **Millmount Museum** on the outskirts of town has a wonderful collection of guild parade banners, richly coloured and embroidered with slogans and insignia. Craft workshops occupy the buildings around the square. There are magnificent views from the newly restored **Martello Tower**.

### Accommodation and food in Drogheda

**St Gobnaits €** *Dublin Road; tel: 041 983 7844.* You'll receive a friendly welcome at this pleasant B&B, situated in an attractive modern home just outside the town centre. The comfortable bedrooms are all en-suite and have TV. There's also a private car park.

**Sorrento's Ristorante €** *41 Shop Street; tel: 041 984 5734.* Cheerful Italian restaurant in the town centre serving a good selection of pizzas, pasta, steak and other dishes. Takeaway also available. *Open daily for lunch and dinner.*

**Bru Restaurant and Bar €€** *Haymarket, Dyer Street; tel: 041 987 2784; email: info@bru.ie; www.bru.ie.* Overlooking the River Boyne, Drogheda's newest restaurant has won rave reviews for its superb food and fresh, bright atmosphere. The fare ranges from light salads, pizza and pasta dishes to outstanding grills featuring salmon, sea bass, barbary duck breast and Angus beef. *Open Sun–Thur 1200–2200, Fri & Sat 1230–2230.*

# HILL OF TARA

**Hill of Tara Interpretative Centre €** *Tel: 046 902 5903. Open May–mid-Sept daily 1000–1800.*

Rising more than 300ft (91m), the Hill of Tara is the legendary seat of the High Kings of Ireland. All that remains is a series of earthworks dating from the Iron Age, so the glory of Tara is left largely to the imagination. It reached its height around the 3rd century AD, during the reign of Cormac MacArt, when five royal roads led to the site where sacred rituals and political affairs were conducted. Until its decline in the 11th century, great triennial feasts, called *feis*, were held at Tara in which all the tribal leaders gathered to pass laws and settle disputes. Given that the bells of Christianity were Tara's death knell, the statue of St Patrick that stands here today alongside a pillar thought to be the coronation stone of the kings seems somewhat disrespectful of its ancient history. In 1843, Daniel O'Connell held a mass rally here for the nationalist cause which was attended by a million people. Later in the 19th century, the great green mound was dug up by religious fanatics searching for the Ark of the Covenant, destroying much archaeological data. A visit to the **Interpretative Centre** is recommended to help make sense of the site. Excavation and research work is ongoing. The views are stupendous, and on a clear day you can see across the central plain to the mountains of Galway.

# KELLS

**Kells Tourist Information Point**
Kells Civic Offices, Headfort Place; tel: 046 924 8856; email: kellstouristoffice@ meathcoco.ie. Open Mon–Fri 0930–1700.

Kells, or Ceanannus Mór, is famed for the monastery founded by St Colmcille in the 6th century. Monks from the island of Iona fled here in the 9th century, and it is thought that they were the creators of the *Book of Kells*, which can be seen at Trinity College in Dublin (*see page 54*). The remains of the monastery lie west of town. A 9th-century round tower stands in the graveyard of the church. The scriptural high cross of St Patrick and Columba is the finest of four carved crosses. In town is a fifth cross with a broken top, removed from the churchyard for use as a gallows in the 1798 rebellion. St Columba's House, a small 7th-century stone oratory with a steep roof, is just north of the ruins.

**Right**
Medieval stonework at Kells

# MELLIFONT ABBEY

**Mellifont Abbey €**
Tel: 041 982 6459.
Open May–Sept daily 1000–1800.

Founded by St Malachy in 1142, Mellifont Abbey was the first Cistercian monastery in Ireland. It marked the introduction of the European monastic system in a country where independent, less hierarchical monastic settlements were the rule. When it was dissolved in 1539, Mellifont ranked as the second-wealthiest Cistercian house in the country (after St Mary's Abbey in Dublin). The property was

**Right**
Mellifont Abbey

subsequently converted into a fortified house, and during the Battle of the Boyne William of Orange made his headquarters here. Mellifont's ruins are more fragmentary than other sites. Its finest feature is the octagonal Romanesque lavabo, where the monks washed before entering the refectory, built in the early 13th century. There is a small architectural museum on the site.

# MONASTERBOICE

Two of Ireland's finest high crosses stand in this charming cemetery amid the ruins of a monastery founded in the 6th century by St Buite. Monasterboice was a renowned centre of learning in the 11th century, and one of the country's most distinguished masters, Flann, taught here, but it fell into decline with the establishment of nearby Mellifont Abbey. Muiredach's Cross, named after the 10th-century abbot for whom it was made, stands over 17ft (5m) high; the shaft and head were carved from a single block of sandstone. The scriptural carvings, with great detail of dress, accoutrement and gesture, are outstanding and depict such scenes as Cain killing Abel, and David slaying Goliath. The West Cross, at 23ft (7m) high, is the tallest in Ireland. It has a unique carving of Jesus walking on the water and saving Peter from drowning. The third, less notable North Cross was also carved in the 10th century. The round tower, minus its top, once held a great monastic library and other treasures, which were destroyed in 1097 when it burnt down.

# NAVAN

This busy town at the confluence of the Boyne and Blackwater rivers, fortified by Hugh de Lacy in the 12th century, was another stalwart of the Pale. **St Mary's Catholic Church**, built in 1839, has a late 18th-century woodcarving of the Crucifixion by Edward Smyth, the greatest Irish sculptor of his day. A Friday market is held on the green beside the church. Look out for the stocks outside the town hall.

## OLDBRIDGE

Oldbridge is the place on the River Boyne where the deposed Catholic monarch of England, James II, challenged the new king, William of Orange, in an attempt to regain his crown. The Battle of the Boyne, which took place on 1 July, 1690, was a turning point in Irish history. The Catholic force of Irish and French soldiers, poorly trained and greatly outnumbered, were soundly defeated by the English allies. In the aftermath, Catholic lands were confiscated and discriminatory laws were passed, setting the division of Ireland in motion. A signposted route takes you past significant sites of the battle on a pretty riverside drive.

## SLANE

The **Hill of Slane** (signposted off the N2) is the site where St Patrick allegedly lit the paschal fire in 433 to celebrate the arrival of Christianity in Ireland. In doing so, he unknowingly disobeyed King Laoghaire at nearby Tara, for this was a night when, according to the Druidic religion, no fires could be lit. When Patrick's fire was seen, one of the Druid leaders prophesied that if the flames were not quenched now they would burn forever and consume Tara – which, figuratively, they did. The Easter fire is still lit here each year. The remains of Slane Abbey stand on the site of a 5th-century monastery, a short walk across the field from the statue of St Patrick. There are panoramic views across the Boyne Valley.

## TRIM

**Trim Tourist Information Office**
Castle Street; tel: 046 943 7227. Seasonal.

**Trim Castle €**
Tel: 046 943 8619.
Open Easter–Sept daily 1000–1800; Oct daily 0930–1730; Nov–Jan Sat & Sun 0900–1700; Feb–Easter Sat & Sun 0930–1730.

Situated on the River Boyne at a boundary of the Pale, this attractive town has some of the best medieval ruins in Ireland. **Trim Castle**, built in 1176, is the largest of its era in the country, covering 2 acres (0.8 hectares). Its formidable turreted keep, towers, long curtain wall and drawbridge made an impressive setting in the film *Braveheart*. The central stronghold of Trim Castle, the three-storey keep, took 30 years to build. Access is by guided tour only, so arrive early as the site gets very busy. Nearby are the ruins of the medieval Royal Mint and a 13th-century Augustinian abbey. St Patrick's Cathedral, built in the 19th century, incorporates a 15th-century tower. The visitor centre has an exhibition on medieval Trim.

# Suggested tour

**Total distance:** The main route is 128 miles (206km). The detour is 11 miles (18km).

## The Pale

The Pale was a term that defined the territory under English control from the time of the Norman settlement until the early 17th century. The boundaries fluctuated, but its most extensive reach was from Dundalk in County Louth to Waterford city. Those within the Pale upheld English values, customs and interests. In Elizabethan times, Gaelic chieftains outside the area were allowed to keep their lands if they agreed to raise their heirs within the Pale. The expression 'beyond the Pale' still denotes those who operate on the fringes of society.

**☰ Tracing your ancestry** If you are ancestor hunting in County Meath, a helpful contact is the **Meath Heritage and Genealogy Centre**, *Castle Street, Trim; tel: 046 943 6633; fax: 046 943 7502; email: meathhc@iol.ie; www.meathroots.com*

**Time:** Allow a minimum of half a day for the main route, as driving on the minor roads will be slower. You are also likely to encounter traffic delays in Drogheda. Brú na Bóinne can take up half a day, so an overnight stay in Drogheda is advisable if you want to spend time exploring the other sights. Those with little time should concentrate on Brú na Bóinne and Monasterboice.

**Links:** This route adjoins the tour of the Midlands (*see page 88*), and the Loughcrew Cairns (*see page 86*) can be approached from Kells.

Leave Dublin on the N3 and, at Black Bull, take the R154 towards Trim. At Pike's Corner, turn right and continue on minor roads through the hamlet of Kilmessan, following signs for the **HILL OF TARA ❶**. Return to the R154 and continue west, where the moated ruins and towers along the Boyne make for an atmospheric entry into **TRIM ❷**.

Continue northwest on the R154, passing the ruins of **Trimblestown Castle**, a stronghold during the Cromwellian wars. Athboy, about 7 miles (11km) along, was a stronghold of the Pale, founded by the Plunketts, a Norman family and ancestors of St Oliver Plunkett (*see pages 62–3*). Nearby are the ruins of the 15th-century **Rathmore Church**, with some fine stone carving and monuments. Take the N51 towards Navan; the mound on your right is the **Hill of Ward**, site of an ancient palace and Celtic festival. Turn left on to the R164 which heads north to **KELLS ❸**. Take the R147 southeast to **NAVAN ❹**, and from there join the N51 to **SLANE ❺**.

Continue east on the N51 towards Drogheda. About 6 miles (10km) along, you will see a big sign on your right for **OLDBRIDGE ❻**, the Battle of the Boyne site. Opposite, there is a left-hand turn for **MELLIFONT ABBEY ❼**, which is signposted off the Drogheda–Collon road, the R168. (If you're approaching Mellifont from Drogheda, take Trinity Street from the town centre.) Return on the same road to **DROGHEDA ❽**. To visit **BRÚ NA BÓINNE/NEWGRANGE ❾**, take the Donore road from the tourist information office. The visitor centre, on the south side of the Boyne, is signposted 5 miles (8km) from town. The archaeological sites lie on the north side of the river and are not accessible by car; they can only be visited on a guided tour from the visitor centre.

To see the splendid high crosses at **MONASTERBOICE ❿**, take the N1 north towards Dundalk from Drogheda for about 6 miles (10km). Immediately beyond the Monasterboice Inn, take the slip road exiting off to your left (badly signposted if at all); this is the exit for the R132 to Dunleer and Boyne Drive, though you won't go that far. Instead, at the end of the slip road (the *second* turning), turn to your left. Only then will you see a sign welcoming you to Monasterboice. Take the next turn on your left, signposted by a tiny, faded, dirty white sign for Monasterboice Round Tower. Keep to the left-hand fork, and as you come around the bend you will see the round tower and a car park on your left. If you have not already visited Mellifont Abbey, you may be tempted to follow the sign for Old Mellifont Abbey beside the cemetery (*see Driving tip*). Should you decide to take this back route, follow the very narrow curving road carefully to its end at an unsignposted T-junction. Turn to your right. At the intersection with the main road, R168, continue straight ahead (signposted towards Drogheda). About a mile (1.6km) beyond, Mellifont Abbey is signposted off to the right. Return to Drogheda.

From Drogheda, take the R132 south to **Balbriggan**, with its fine sandy beach. Continue on the R132 through **Swords**, where there are the ruins of a round tower and 12th-century castle, to return to Dublin.

**Detour:** From Balbriggan, continue south along the coast on the R127. Just north of Skerries is **Ardgillan Castle**, an 18th-century manor house furnished in Victorian style and set in woodland and gardens. It has superb views southeast to the Rockabill lighthouse and Lambay Island, and north to the Mourne Mountains. This coast road is the best approach to **Skerries**, as you get a splendid view of the picturesque harbour. It is a lovely village with a long sandy beach, boating and sailing, and a fine thatched house at No 17 Church Street. **Shenick's Island**, one of three just offshore, has a Martello tower and is accessible by foot at low tide. The R128 runs south to **Rush**, another coastal resort with good beaches. Continue inland to **Lusk**. Its **heritage centre** is an unusual 16th-century belfry that incorporates a 6th-century round tower, with three later towers built to match; they are attached to a church with some lovely medieval tombs. The belfry contains an exhibition on the medieval churches of north County Dublin. Take the R127 south to rejoin the R132. On your left is the turn for the R126, which leads to good beaches at **Donabate** and **Portrane**. On the outskirts of Donabate is the 18th-century **Newbridge House**, with a splendid Georgian interior. Rejoin the main tour at Swords, where you can take another detour on the R106 to **Malahide**.

## Also worth exploring

The pretty country lanes just south and east of Trim offer some delightful drives. About a mile (1.6km) downstream from Trim Castle is **Newtown Trim**, with the ruins of an abbey built in 1206 by Simon de Rochfort, first Anglo-Norman bishop of Meath; its large cathedral served as the see of Meath for over 300 years. **Laracor**, 2 miles (3km) south of Trim, is the village where Jonathan Swift was rector from 1699 to 1714. **Summerhill**, an attractive village, has a ruined castle nearby. **Cnoc an Linsigh** is a forested area with pleasant walking paths and picnic sites. The area to the south of the Boyne estuary has some fine sandy beaches at **Bettystown** and **Laytown**, where the Strand races are held; to the north are the fishing villages of **Baltray** and **Clogherhead**, where there are superb views from the top of the headland.

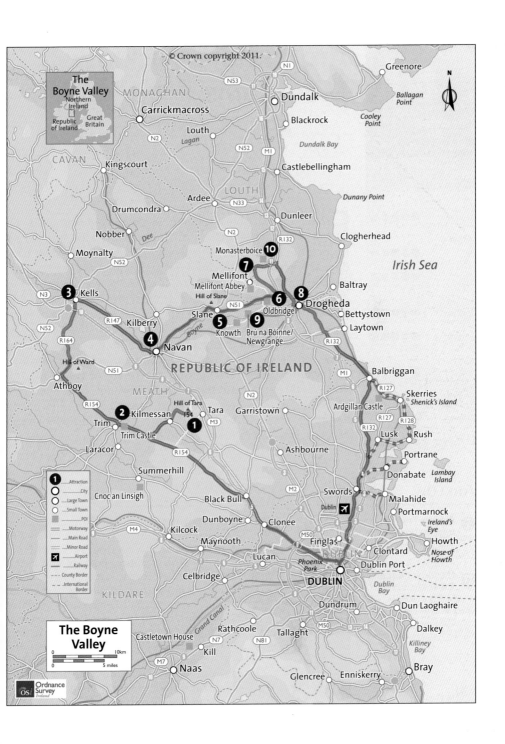

The Boyne Valley
Northern Ireland
Republic of Ireland
Great Britain

© Crown copyright 2011

MONAGHAN
Carrickmacross
Louth
Lagan
CAVAN
Kingscourt
Drumcondra
Nobber
Dee
Moynalty
Kells
Kilberry
Navan
Hill of Ward
Athboy
MEATH
Kilmessan
Trim
Trim Castle
Laracor
Summerhill
Cnoc an Linsigh
KILDARE
Castletown House
Kill
Naas

N1
N53
Dundalk
Blackrock
Cooley Point
Ballagan Point
Greenore
N2
N52
M1
Dundalk Bay
Castlebellingham
Ardee
N33
LOUTH
Dunleer
Dunany Point
N2
R132
Clogherhead
Monasterboice
Mellifont
Mellifont Abbey
Hill of Slane
Slane
N51
Oldbridge
Drogheda
Baltray
Irish Sea
Bettystown
Knowth
Brú na Bóinne/
Newgrange
Laytown
R132
Boyne
REPUBLIC OF IRELAND
M1
Balbriggan
R127
Skerries
Shenick's Island
Hill of Tara
Tara
154
M3
Garristown
Ardgillan Castle
R127
R128
R132
Lusk
Rush
Ashbourne
Portrane
Donabate
Lambay Island
M2
Swords
Black Bull
Dunboyne
Clonee
M50
Finglas
Malahide
Portmarnock
Ireland's Eye
Kilcock
Maynooth
Lucan
Celbridge
Phoenix Park
DUBLIN
Clontard
Dublin Port
Howth
Nose of Howth
Dublin Bay
Dundrum
Dun Laoghaire
Rathcoole
Tallaght
M50
Dalkey
Killiney Bay
Glencree
Enniskerry
Bray

N3
N52
R164
R147
N51
R154
M4
M7
Dublin ✈
Grand Canal
N7
N81

Key:
① Attraction
○ City
○ Large Town
○ Small Town
■ POI
Motorway
Main Road
Minor Road
✈ Airport
Railway
County Border
International Border

The Boyne Valley
0      10km
0      5 miles

Ordnance Survey Ireland

N

① ② ③ ④ ⑤ ⑥ ⑦ ⑧ ⑨ ⑩

# Around the Wicklow Mountains

## Ratings

| | |
|---|---|
| Gardens | ●●●●● |
| Monastic sites | ●●●●● |
| Mountains | ●●●●● |
| Outdoor activities | ●●●●● |
| Scenery | ●●●●● |
| Stately homes | ●●●●○ |
| Beaches | ●●●○○ |
| Children | ●●●○○ |

From the south Dublin suburbs, an old military road snakes up into the wild landscape of the Wicklow Mountains. Few major cities are blessed with an outdoor paradise at their back doorstep, teeming with dark forests, tranquil lakes, sunny vales, magnificent waterfalls and vast stretches of windswept moor. Amid the purple silhouette cast by these granite mountains, the distinctive peak of the Great Sugar Loaf Mountain is a well-loved landmark. County Wicklow is called 'The Garden of Ireland', rather fitting as you drive through the idyllic vales of Clara and Avoca, while man-made gardens such as Powerscourt and Mount Usher rank among the finest in the land. The Wicklow Mountains also shelter one of Ireland's most important early Christian monastic sites at Glendalough. The grand Palladian mansion of Russborough House, the white-sand beaches and seaside towns round out this glorious playground, just a few miles but a world away from the bustle of city life.

## ARKLOW

ℹ **Arklow Tourist Information Office**
*The Coach House; tel: 0402 32484. Seasonal.*

🅜 **Maritime Museum**
€€ *St Mary's Road; tel: 086 384 3283; www.arklowmaritimemuseum. com. Open Jun–Sept Tue–Sat 1000–1300, 1400–1700.*

**Right**
Maritime Museum

The Vikings founded a settlement here at the mouth of the River Avoca in the 9th century, and today Arklow is a popular resort with beaches, boating and a golf course. The town sprawls along its long, narrow main street, dominated by the spire of St Saviour's Church. The 1798 Memorial honours the memory of Father Michael Murphy, who died here leading the county's United Irishmen in battle against the English. Arklow's seafaring history is recalled in the **Maritime Museum**. Exhibits include some original boats, logs from historic journeys and old photographs.

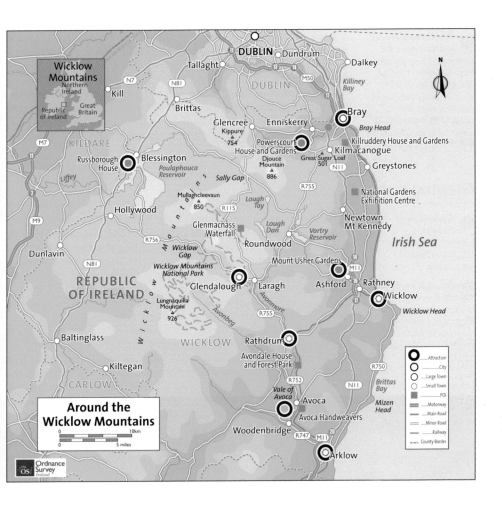

# BRAY

**Bray Tourist Information Office**
Tel: 01 286 7128. Open year-round Mon–Sat.

**National Sealife Centre** €€ Strand Road; tel: 01 286 6939. Open Mar–Oct daily 1000–1700; Nov–Feb Mon–Fri 1100–1600, Sat & Sun 1000–1700.

Bray is one of Ireland's oldest seaside towns, and its location on the DART line from Dublin ensures that its popularity – unlike its Victorian ambience – never fades. The safe sand-and-shingle beach stretches for over a mile (1.6km), backed by an oceanfront promenade and various amusement centres. Children may enjoy the **National Sealife Centre**. The **Bray Tourist Information Office and Heritage Centre** are housed in the old courthouse on Main Street. A recent revamping of the Heritage Centre provides a re-created castle on the ground floor, celebrating 100 years of Bray, and a model of the railways on the first floor. The house at **No 1 Martello Terrace** (*not open to the public*) was the home of the writer James Joyce from 1887 to 1891.

**ℹ Killruddery House and Gardens €€**
*South end of Bray, just off the Bray– Greystones road; tel: 087 419 8674; www.killruddery.com. Gardens open May–Sept daily 1230–1700, weekends only in Apr; house open May, Jun & Sept daily 1300–1700.*

A scenic cliff walk carries on from the end of the boardwalk around the eastern flank of Bray Head to the fishing village of **Greystones**, about 3 miles (5km) away. South of town, there are splendid views of the mountains and the sea from the Eagle's Nest pathway leading to the top of **Bray Head**, which rises 791ft (241m) high. Nearby, the French-style **Killruddery House and Gardens**, with twin canals and high beech hedges, were laid out in the 17th century and are a rare survivor of early, large-scale formal landscaping.

# GLENDALOUGH

**ℹ Glendalough Tourist Information Office**
*Tel: 0404 45688. Summer only.*

**Glendalough Visitor Centre** € *for exhibition,* € *to visit the ruins. Tel: 0404 45325. Open daily mid-Mar–mid-Oct 0930–1800; till 1700 rest of the year.*

Glendalough is one of Ireland's most important monastic sites. It was founded by St Kevin, a descendant of one of Leinster's ruling families, in the 6th century. Although he preferred the life of a hermit, retreating to the cave above the Upper Lake known as St Kevin's Bed, his reputation as a holy man grew and he attracted many followers. He became abbot of the monastery in 570, and the settlement flourished for more than six centuries after his death in 618, despite repeated raids and rebuilding. English forces reduced it to ruins in 1398, but Glendalough remained a great pilgrimage site well into the 19th century.

The ruins of Glendalough, the 'valley of two lakes', are spread along 2 miles (3km) of a peaceful wooded valley that is part of the Wicklow Mountains National Park. The cathedral, St Kevin's Church and several smaller churches are approached through the granite arched gateway behind the visitor centre. Here, too, is the famous round tower, built of mica-slate and granite and rising some 98ft (30m). The visitor centre has exhibits and a good audiovisual programme. St Kevin's Cell, Reefert Church and other sites are set around the Upper Lake. They are accessible from a separate car park or on foot from the visitor centre, making a lovely walk on a fine day.

**Left**
Glendalough

# Mount Usher Gardens

**Mount Usher Gardens €€**
Ashford; tel: 0404 40205;
www.mountushergardens.ie.
Open Mar–Oct daily
1030–1720.

These beautiful gardens, spreading over 20 acres (8 hectares) alongside the River Varty, were originally laid out by Edward Walpole, a Dublin businessman, in 1868. The natural terrain enhances their wild, romantic style, and suspension bridges span the winding waterway with its mesmerising cascades. Over the years, the Walpole family introduced many exotic species from around the world, which flourished in the sheltered environment. Today there are about 5,000 species, including eucalyptus, magnolias, camellias and giant rhododendrons. There are craft shops and a tearoom on-site.

# Powerscourt House and Gardens

**Powerscourt House and Gardens €€** Enniskerry;
tel: 01 204 6000;
www.powerscourt.ie. Open
year-round, daily 0930–
1730 (till dusk in winter).

**Below**
Powerscourt House and
Gardens

Powerscourt, one of the finest estates in Ireland, takes its name from the Le Poer (Power) family, who built a castle here in 1300. In 1603, the lands were granted to the Englishman Richard Wingfield, whose descendants remained here for over 350 years. Between 1731 and 1740, Richard Castle, the architect of Russborough House, converted the castle into an impressive Palladian mansion, which once boasted the grandest ballroom in the country. However, a tragic fire in 1974 gutted the building, and the interior now houses speciality shops, a terrace café and an exhibition on the history of the estate, showing its former glory. There are long-term plans to restore the ballroom. A large new garden centre has recently been added to the site.

The magnificent Powerscourt Gardens are the real attraction. A monumental terrace sweeps down to the lake, where graceful winged horses frame the Triton fountain spurting a high stream against the backdrop of the Great Sugar Loaf Mountain. Much of the credit goes to the landscape architect Daniel Robertson, who drew up garden designs for the 6th Viscount Powerscourt in the 1840s and directed the work from a wheelbarrow, staving off his gout pains with a bottle of sherry. Later generations continued to enhance the grounds, and today the 47-acre (19-hectare) demesne is adorned with leafy avenues, specimen trees, ponds, fine statuary and ironwork, a pepper-pot tower and Italianate, Japanese and walled gardens.

# RATHDRUM

**Avondale House and Forest Park**
€€ Tel: 0404 46111.
Open Jul–Aug daily;
Sept–Oct Tue–Sun.

Rathdrum, with its attractive pastel-coloured houses, is the birthplace of Charles Stewart Parnell (1846–91). Although Parnell was a Protestant landowner, he fought passionately for tenants' land rights and Home Rule for Ireland from his seat at Westminster. His shining political career was brought down by the scandal surrounding his affair with a married woman, Mrs Kitty O'Shea. A bronze statue of the great politician stands in Parnell National Memorial Park, a restful town park with walks, streams and ponds.

One mile (1.6km) south of town is **Avondale House and Forest Park**, where Parnell was born in 1846. The house, restored to its mid-19th-century décor, is a museum filled with memorabilia of his career and personal life, including some of his love letters to Kitty O'Shea. It is set in 500 acres (200 hectares) of parkland along the River Avonmore, with miles of woodland paths to explore.

# RUSSBOROUGH HOUSE

**Russborough House** €€ 2 miles (3km) south of Blessington, off the N81; tel: 045 865239; www.russborough.ie. Open Apr & Oct Sun & bank holidays 1000–1700; May–Sept daily 1000–1700.

In 1741, Joseph Leeson, later the Earl of Milltown, decided to spend his newly acquired fortune on building one of the finest Palladian-style mansions in the country. Russborough House was designed by Richard Castle, the architect of Powerscourt House, and finished by Francis Bindon after Castle's death. The palatial façade, built of silver Wicklow granite and flanked by semicircular loggias and wings, conceals a Baroque interior with elaborate plasterwork ceilings. Sir Alfred Beit purchased Russborough in 1952 and for a time it was the home of one of Europe's finest private art collections. After two major robberies, many of the paintings were donated to the National Gallery of Ireland. Works by Rubens, Reynolds, Gainsborough, Murillo and Guardi still remain, along with displays of fine porcelain, silver and bronzes. Visitors can also wander among the extensive woodlands.

# VALE OF AVOCA

**Avoca
Handweavers**
*Tel: 0402 35105. Shop open daily 0900–1800
(0930–1730 in winter); mill open weekdays 0800–1630.*

**The Meeting of the Waters**

*There is not in this wide world a valley so sweet, as that in whose bosom the bright waters meet.*

Thomas Moore, 1807

This delightful vale, where the Avonmore and Avonbeg rivers meet, inspired the Irish Romantic poet Thomas Moore (1779–1852) to pen 'The Meeting of the Waters' in 1807. Today the spot is marked by a pub, called The Meeting, renowned for its traditional music sessions.

Avoca village, 2 miles (3km) beyond, inspires creative arts of a different sort – it is the setting for the BBC television series *Ballykissangel*; thus the Church of Sts Mary and Patrick, built in 1862, and the local pub may look familiar to some visitors. **Avoca Handweavers**, which now has shops around the country, occupies the oldest working mill in Ireland, dating from 1723. You can take a guided tour and watch the weavers creating their beautiful woven tweeds.

Northeast of the village, the Motte Stone sits on a summit 800ft (244m) high. This granite boulder, deposited on its precarious perch by glaciers, is halfway between Dublin and Wexford and was once used as a milestone for travellers.

# WICKLOW TOWN

**Wicklow Tourist
Information Office**
*Rialto House, Fitzwilliam Square; tel: 0404 69117;
fax: 0404 69118.*

**Wicklow's Historic
Gaol €€** *Kilmantin Hill; tel: 0404 61599; www.wicklowhistoricgaol.com.
Open Mon–Sat 1030–1630, Sun 1100–1630.*

**County Wicklow
Heritage and
Genealogical Research
Centre** *Wicklow's Historic Gaol. Tel: 0404 20126;
fax: 0404 61612.*

Wicklow's county town looks out over a wide crescent bay. Founded by the Vikings, its name in Danish, *Wyking alo*, meant 'Viking meadow'. The town's later history can be traced at **Wicklow's Historic Gaol**. **County Wicklow Heritage and Genealogical Research Centre**, housed in the Historic Gaol, provides a research service for people tracing their local ancestry. **St Lavinius Church**, topped by an 18th-century copper cupola, is worth a look for its carved Romanesque doorway, fine stonework and pews. To view the ruins of the 13th-century **Franciscan friary** on Main Street, enquire at the priest's house. The harbour is the town's most interesting area, home to a sailing and yacht club, while the long pebble beach, backed by Broad Lough, a wildfowl lagoon, is popular with beachcombers and fishermen. The sprawling ruins of **Black Castle**, built by the Anglo-Norman lord Maurice Fitzgerald in the 12th century, stand on a promontory to the south of the harbour. Castle buffs may find the ruins of **Dunganstown Castle**, 6 miles (9.5km) south of town on an unclassified road, more impressive.

# Suggested tour

**Total distance:** The main route is 77 miles (124km). The detour to Russborough House from Sally Gap is 37 miles (60km).

**Time:** Allow a full day to drive the main route and/or detour, including stops at your chosen attractions. Those with little time should try to see Powerscourt Gardens and Glendalough, both of which are easy day trips from Dublin.

**Links:** This route adjoins the tours of counties Wexford (*see page 112*) and Kildare (*see page 100*).

Begin the tour at the coastal town of **BRAY ❶**, some 14 miles (22km) south of Dublin. Take the N11 (M11) south for about a mile (1.6km), then take the exit for Enniskerry and follow signs to **POWERSCOURT HOUSE AND GARDENS ❷**. The spectacular **Powerscourt Waterfall**, the highest waterfall in Ireland, is well worth a visit, especially after a rainy spell. To reach it, turn right out of the gates and follow the signs for 3 miles (5km) along narrow, winding lanes to the entrance. Around the falls, there are picnic areas from which to admire this impressive torrent, made by the River Dargle as it plunges 390ft (121m) into the glen, its spray blowing into a cool mist. There are hiking paths into the surrounding woods.

Head back past Powerscourt Gardens to the pretty village of **Enniskerry**, with its clock tower and sloping central square. The Catholic church, built in 1843, was the first Gothic Revival church in the country. From here, follow the road signposted Glencree Drive, which climbs into the wooded slopes above the river valley. After

**Below**
Powerscourt Waterfall

**ⓘ Wicklow County Tourism** *Unit C23, Wicklow Enterprise Park, The Murrough, Wicklow Town; tel: 0404 20070; fax: 0404 20072; email: info@wicklowct.ie; www.visitwicklow.ie.* County Wicklow is part of the East Coast & Midlands Tourism region (*see page 19*).

**Blessington Tourist Information Office** *Tel: 045 865850; fax: 045 865870. Open year-round.*

**ⓝ Powerscourt Waterfall** €€ *Open daily, summer 0930–1900; winter 1030–dusk. Closed 12–25 Dec.*

**ⓝ** Outside Bray, near the motorway at Kilmacanogue, look for the **Avoca Handweavers** shop, set in a 19th-century arboretum that was once part of the Jameson (whiskey) family home. The lovely terrace restaurant serves delicious food. *Tel: 01 286 7466. Open 0930–1800.*

**Poppies €** *The Square, Enniskerry; tel: 01 282 8869; www.poppies.ie.* With its cosy country-kitchen décor, this is a pleasant spot for a coffee break – the cappuccino is peaked with foam like the Great Sugar Loaf itself. It's also a good place for breakfast or lunch, with delicious quiches, shepherd's pie, casserole dishes and a selection of house salads. The home-made desserts and baked goods are terrific. *Open Mon–Sat 0800–1900, Sun 0900–1900.*

## Irish monasteries

Ireland's distance from continental Europe spared it from the ravages of the Dark Ages, and during those years this small island became the vanguard of Christian culture. It was well suited to the development of rural monasteries, and thousands sought the rigid discipline of monastic life. Unlike their later European counterparts, the early Irish monasteries did not belong to large hierarchical orders but operated as isolated units. Many were tiny communities of two or three ascetics who prayed, studied and copied the gospels. Others, such as Glendalough and Clonmacnoise, grew into large settlements as word of their holy founders spread. Learning, craftsmanship and the religious arts flourished, giving birth to what became the proud symbols of Irish culture: the great Celtic stone crosses; the beautiful decorated manuscripts; intricate chalices and reliquaries; and the unique round towers, which served as bell tower, storehouse and refuge in times of siege. In the 12th century, the old Irish monasteries began to fade as continental orders such as the Cistercians established themselves, but Ireland's role in the development of Christian culture is unique.

about 5½ miles (9km), turn left at the junction on to the R115, signposted to Sally Gap. Shortly after this, ignore the turning signposted Glencree Drive, which takes you down into the valley, and continue straight ahead on the main road. The abrupt change of scenery from pretty pastureland to the vast expanse of desolate moorland at the centre of the Wicklow range is disconcerting – the next 5 miles (8km) can feel ominous on a bleak and windy day. The only sign of civilisation is the signposts at the four-way crossroads known as **Sally Gap**, which is surrounded by a vast blanket bog.

**Detour:** Turn right on the road to Blessington, 14 miles (23km) away, which leads down the western slopes and along the River Liffey. At the junction with the N81, turn left to Blessington, which sits along a northern branch of the huge **Poulaphouca Reservoir**. The building of the dam and hydroelectric power station here, which supplies the Dublin region, created the Blessington Lakes, covering 5,000 acres (2,000 hectares) and providing recreational activities. Just south of town is **RUSSBOROUGH HOUSE ❸**. Continue south on the N81 to Hollywood, and turn left on the R756 which leads back into the mountains and through the **Wicklow Gap** to rejoin the main tour at Glendalough.

The main route continues straight ahead at Sally Gap on the old military road to Laragh and Glendalough, 13 miles (21km) away. After a few miles of rough tarmac, you pass through a stretch of forest that opens up to a magnificent view of the **Glenmacnass Waterfall** tumbling into the broad valley below. The road descends to **Laragh** (pronounced 'Laura'). With little more than a petrol station, bar and woollen shop, this hamlet is a favourite spot for the many ramblers

**ⓘ Wicklow Mountains National Park** €
*Education Centre, Bolger's Cottage, Upper Lake, Glendalough; tel: 0404 45425; www.wicklowmountains nationalpark.ie. Open May–Sept daily 1000–1800; Oct–Nov & Feb–Apr Sat–Sun 1000–1730; Dec–Jan Sat–Sun 1000–1600.*

**Clara Lara Fun Park**
€€ *Tel: 0404 46161; www.claralara.com. Open May–Sept daily 1030–1830.*

**Ⓦ Guided walks in the** Wicklow Mountains are a feature of the spring and autumn walking festivals. Contact Wicklow County Tourism (see page 77).

The Wicklow Way walking route traverses the Wicklow Mountains and covers 82 miles (132km), from Marlay Park in south County Dublin to Clonegal in County Carlow. The Wicklow Way Map/Guide is available from East West Mapping; tel/fax: 053 937 7835; email: sales@ eastwestmapping.ie; http://eastwestmapping.ie

**❸ The annual Wicklow** Gardens Festival takes place from Easter–Sept throughout the county. Heritage properties and many private gardens open especially for the event. Contact Wicklow County Tourism (see page 77).

**Above right**
The ruins of Glendalough

and cyclists who pass through the area; in summer, tables are set out on the village green and some of the little cottages operate makeshift tearooms. GLENDALOUGH ❹ and the main entrance to **Wicklow Mountains National Park** is nearby. The national park covers some 49,421 acres (20,000 hectares), encompassing forests, boglands, lakes and nature reserves. The Education Centre has information on the park and offers an interesting programme of summer lectures and activities.

Return to the junction at Laragh and head south towards Rathdrum on the R755 through Clara Vale. About 2½ miles (4km) along, the **Clara Lara Fun Park** in the tiny village of Clara is a big hit with families, offering water slides, a boating lake, an adventure playground and picnic areas alongside the River Avonmore. RATHDRUM ❺ is 6 miles (9km) further. As you drive along these beautiful shady vales, you may see locals selling the tasty Wicklow honey. Continue south on the R752, which runs through the **VALE OF AVOCA** ❻, following signs to Avoca and Arklow. **Woodenbridge** marks the end of the vale, and its hotel, which dates from 1608, claims to be the oldest in the Republic. The nearby mountain of Croghan Kinsella was a rich source of gold for Celtic craftsmen in ancient times, and the finding of a nugget there in 1796 led to a minor gold rush. At the village, bear left on the R747 to ARKLOW ❼.

North of Arklow on the R750 are the undulating dunes of **Brittas Bay**, a haven for rare plants and wildlife species. The 2-mile (3km) stretch of powdery white sand is one of the most popular beaches on the east coast and consistently rates a Blue Flag for quality. The scenic stretch continues north to **WICKLOW TOWN** ❽.

MOUNT USHER GARDENS ❾ lie 3 miles (5km) inland at Ashford. The R764 takes you past the Vartry Reservoir to **Roundwood**, 9 miles (14.5km) away. At 780ft (238m), it is Ireland's highest village and is surrounded by magnificent wild scenery. Nearby are Lough Dan and Lough Tay, encircled by mountain forests. From here, head north on the R755 past the Great Sugar Loaf Mountain to Kilmacanogue, and on into Bray.

The Sunday-afternoon market (open 1500–1700) at Roundwood's Parish Hall is a good place to find handicrafts, jams and home baking.

County Wicklow offers a wealth of recreational activities, including golf, cycling, horse riding, fishing and watersports. Contact the tourist information office for details.

## Also worth exploring

**Baltinglass**, south of Blessington on the N81, has the remains of a 12th-century Cistercian Abbey and a group of Bronze Age burial chambers. The **Glen of the Downs**, west of Greystones on the N11, is a rocky gorge formed during the Ice Age, with an old oak wood. Two miles (3km) south, at Kilquade, the **National Gardens Exhibition Centre** presents a diverse collection by modern garden designers.

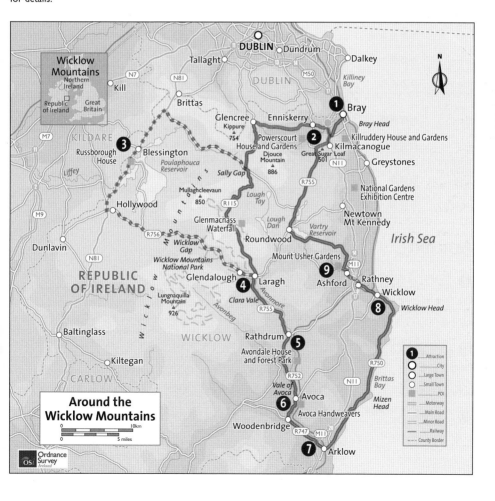

# The Midlands

## Ratings

| | |
|---|---|
| Gardens | ●●●●● |
| Monastic sites | ●●●●● |
| Castles | ●●●●○ |
| Museums | ●●●●○ |
| Prehistoric sites | ●●●●○ |
| Villages | ●●●●○ |
| Manor houses | ●●●○○ |
| Scenery | ●●●○○ |

The Midlands is often underrated as a touring destination. It may lack the dramatic vistas of the western coast, but it is an area rich in history and folklore. Its landscape is quintessential Ireland, especially in the counties of Meath and Westmeath, with peaceful loughs and prehistoric ruins tucked away in the rolling green hills. It is delightful in spring, when the hillsides are covered with clusters of bright yellow furze. This region offers busy market towns, atmospheric villages, Ireland's largest castle at Tullynally and the outstanding Famine Museum at Strokestown Park House. To the south is the Georgian jewel of Birr, with its magnificent castle gardens; to the west, on the edge of the Shannon country, is the great monastic settlement of Clonmacnoise. Nearby, the Blackwater Bog Railway trundles through a portion of the Bog of Allen, which stretches across the Midlands from Kildare to Galway.

## ATHLONE

ⓘ **Athlone Tourist Information Office**
*Civic Centre, Church Street; tel: 090 649 4630. Open Apr–Oct.*

🏰 **Athlone Castle €€**
*Tel: 090 649 2912. Currently closed for renovation but will reopen in summer 2011.*

🚲 A popular cycle route is the 5-mile (8km) Lough Ree Trail, which starts at Glasson, northeast of Athlone.

Set along the River Shannon at the base of Lough Ree, Athlone is a busy market town and road junction. Its main attraction is **Athlone Castle**, built in the 12th century to protect the strategic river crossing. The Irish retreated here in 1691 after their defeat at the Battle of the Boyne (*see Oldbridge, page 66*), and the castle suffered in the subsequent bombardment, but has now been restored. Its museum contains exhibits on the siege, the history of the town and the life of the great tenor, John McCormack (1884–1945), a native of Athlone. Behind the castle, the buildings of the 'Left Bank' date back more than 200 years. The town is also a base for pleasure cruises on the River Shannon and Lough Ree. The MV *Ross* takes passengers on a 90-minute cruise (€€€) on the River Shannon from Jolly Mariner Marina (*tel: 090 647 2892. Open Apr–Sept daily*). Viking Tours (*tel: 090 647 3383. Open May–Sept daily*) has trips along the Shannon to Clonmacnoise and entertaining cruises to Lough Ree, with tales of Viking warbands and treasure islands.

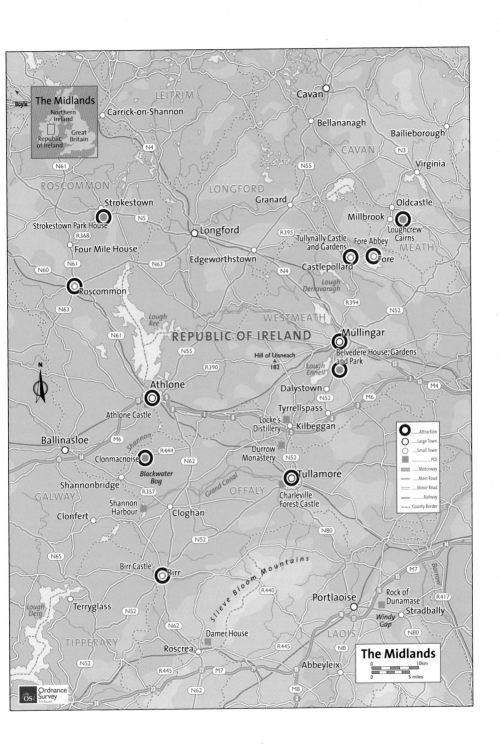

The Midlands

Northern
Ireland

Great
Republic   Britain
of Ireland

LEITRIM

Carrick-on-Shannon

Cavan

Bellananagh

Bailieborough

CAVAN    N3

Virginia

N4

N61

N55

ROSCOMMON

LONGFORD

Strokestown

Granard

Oldcastle

Millbrook

Strokestown Park House

Longford

Loughcrew
Cairns

N5

R368

Four Mile House

R395   Tullynally Castle   Fore Abbey
and Gardens

MEATH

N60   N61

N63

Edgeworthstown

Fore

N4

Castlepollard

Lough
Derravaragh

Roscommon

R394   N52

N63

Lough
Ree

N61

WESTMEATH

REPUBLIC OF IRELAND

Mullingar

N55

Hill of Uisneach

Belvedere House, Gardens
and Park

N
R390

182

Lough
Ennell

M4

Athlone

Dalystown

N52   M6

Athlone Castle

Tyrrellspass

Locke's
Distillery   Kilbeggan

Ballinasloe

M6

Shannon

R444

Durrow
Monastery   N52

Clonmacnoise

N62

Blackwater
Bog

Shannonbridge   R357

GALWAY

Grand Canal   OFFALY

Tullamore

Charleville
Forest Castle

Clonfert   Shannon
Harbour   Cloghan

N80

N52

N65

Slieve Bloom Mountains

Birr Castle   Birr

M7

Barrow

R440   Portlaoise

Rock of
Dunamase   R417

Lough
Derg   Terryglass   N52

N62

Damer House

Windy
Gap   Stradbally

LAOIS   N80

Roscrea

R445   N8

N52

Abbeyleix

R445   M7

N62   M8

○  Attraction
○  Large Town
○  Small Town
■  POI
    Motorway
    Main Road
    Minor Road
    Railway
    County Border

The Midlands
0          10km
0      5 miles

Ordnance
Survey
Ireland

## Accommodation and food in Athlone

**Hodson Bay Hotel €€–€€€** *Tel: 090 644 2000; fax: 090 644 2020; email: info@hodsonbayhotel.com; www.hodsonbayhotel.com.* Set on the scenic shores of Lough Ree, this luxurious spa hotel offers a range of stylish bedrooms and suites, many with lough views. Facilities include a steam room, sauna, gym, hydrotherapy pool and a stunning 65ft (20m) pool with picture windows looking out on to the lough. There's also a separate children's pool. Enjoy fine dining at L'Escale Restaurant, or casual dining in the Waterfront Carvery and Bar.

**Prince of Wales Hotel €€** *Church Street; tel: 090 647 6666; fax: 090 649 1750; email: info@theprinceofwales.ie; www.theprinceofwales.ie.* Though it dates back to 1810, this lovely hotel in the town centre features spacious rooms decorated in contemporary style with many amenities, including DVD players, films and complimentary Wi-Fi. The Prince Bar is one of the most popular nightspots in town, with many food and drink options. There is also a deli and a fine dining restaurant.

# BELVEDERE HOUSE, GARDENS AND PARK

🏛 **Belvedere House, Gardens and Park €€** *Tullamore Road, Mullingar; tel: 044 934 9060; www.belvedere-house.ie. Open May–Aug 1030–2000; Mar, Apr, Sept & Oct 0930–1800; Nov–Feb 1000–1630.*

This Palladian villa, built around 1740 by Richard Castle, enjoys a beautiful setting on the shores of Lough Ennell. Delightful terraces descend towards the lake, while the surrounding gardens contain a vast display of shrubs, flowers and trees. Nearly 2 miles (3km) of pathways wind through the woodlands and past architectural follies such as the Gothic Arch and the Jealous Wall. The latter was built by Robert Rochford, the first Earl of Belvedere, to block the view of his brother's grander mansion across the lake. The house has been exquisitely restored and its history is explained in the visitor centre.

# BIRR

ℹ **Birr Tourist Information Office** *Wilmer Road; tel: 509 20110. Open May–Sept.*

🏛 **Birr Castle Demesne €€€** *Ireland's Historic Science Centre; tel: 057 912 0336; www.birrcastle.com. Open mid-Mar–Oct daily 0900–1800; Nov–mid-Mar daily 1200–1600.*

Birr is a splendid example of a small-scale Georgian town. Its spacious, tree-lined malls and avenues, with their handsome squares and houses, date from the 1740s with the building of Emmet Square. Oxmantown Mall and John's Mall are especially fine, with graceful façades sporting fanlights, panelled doors and other classical Georgian features. The town is a walker's delight with myriad charming corners, from the traditional shopfronts on Connaught Street, and Mercy Convent designed by Pugin, to the riverside walk along the south bank of the Camcor.

**Birr Castle** was built in 1620 on a site fortified since Norman times, and it has been the home of the Parsons family, earls of Rosse, ever since. The magnificent demesne, the largest gardens in the country, features trees and plants collected by the family from around the world. This is a place to linger, with tranquil walks along the lake and river

The first All Ireland Hurling Final was held in Birr in 1888. The town maintains a championship hurling team, and matches are played in St Brendan's Park.

**Below**
Birr Castle Demesne

under towering oak and beech trees, a delightful fernery and impressive formal gardens. The box hedges, over 300 years old, are the world's tallest at 30ft (9m). A wrought-iron suspension bridge, built in the 1820s, spans the river near the waterfall; downstream, a turbine supplied the castle and the town with electricity until the 1950s. The Great Telescope, built by the third earl in the 1840s, was the world's largest for over 70 years; it still operates and demonstrations are given daily. In the coach house are the galleries of **Ireland's Historic Science Centre**.

## Accommodation and food near Birr

**Charlotte's Way Bed and Breakfast €** *The Hill, Banagher, Co Offaly; tel: 087 246 7411; www.charlottesway.com.* This 17th-century Georgian town house, 12km (7 miles) north of Birr on Banagher Hill, was visited by the writer Charlotte Brontë and her husband. It offers lovely views over the River Shannon and surrounding countryside, en-suite bedrooms and a hearty Irish breakfast featuring free-range eggs and home-made bread and jams.

# CASTLEPOLLARD

**Tullynally Castle and Gardens €€**
*Tel: 044 966 1159; www.tullynallycastle.com. Gardens open May–Jun weekends and holidays, Jul–Aug 1400–1800; castle open by pre-arranged booking.*

This attractive village of 19th-century houses is set around a triangular village green. Just outside is **Tullynally Castle and Gardens**. The seat of the earls of Longford since 1655, it is Ireland's largest castle still used as a family home. If you walked round the perimeter of this turreted and castellated pile you would cover nearly a quarter of a mile (0.5km). The Gothic Revival additions to the original tower house were added in the 19th century. Interior highlights include the panelled dining room and collection of family portraits, the Victorian kitchens and laundries, and the extensive library. The grounds include a woodland walk, walled gardens, a grotto and two ornamental lakes.

# CLONMACNOISE

**Clonmacnoise €€**
*Tel: 090 967 4195. Open mid-Mar–mid-May & mid-Sept–Oct daily 1000–1800; mid-May–mid-Sept daily 0900–1900; Nov–mid-Mar daily 1000–1730. Closed 25 Dec.*

One of the most important sites in early Christendom, Clonmacnoise was founded by St Ciarán in 548, along the Shannon at an ancient crossroads where the river and overland routes met. Within a year of constructing the first wooden and wattle buildings, Ciarán died of the yellow plague at the age of 33, but despite his death the monastery flourished, supported by the kings of Connacht and Royal Tara. Clonmacnoise became a great centre of Irish art and literature, producing the first known manuscript in the Irish language. The work of its craftsmen in precious metals was unsurpassed, though it is best known for its magnificent stone-carved high crosses, the Cross of the Scriptures and the South Cross. These have been moved inside the visitor centre to protect their intricate carvings from weathering, and replicas stand on the site.

At its height, Clonmacnoise covered more than 10 acres (4 hectares). But it was repeatedly raided by Vikings, Anglo-Normans and warring Irish tribes, and was finally destroyed by the English in 1552. Amazingly, much remains, including two round towers, several churches and hundreds of early grave slabs. The visitor centre has a good audiovisual programme on the history of the monastery, and exhibits about the high crosses and decorated stone slabs.

Pilgrims still walk the traditional route three times around Clonmacnoise on St Ciarán's Day, 9 September.

## Irish high crosses

Although Celtic crosses are found elsewhere in the British Isles, the art of the decorative stone high cross reached its pinnacle in Ireland. Set in a base, its four arms encircled by a wheel, and capped by a shrine, it has become one of Ireland's most distinctive symbols. The majority were carved between the 8th and 12th centuries. The early crosses had ornamental carving, with the interlacing and spiralling patterns typical of other Celtic art. In the early 10th century, figurative crosses with finely carved biblical scenes provided 'sermons in stone'. It is not known whether high crosses were once coloured, but traces of pigment on carved pieces from Europe, and the frequent use of colour in other Celtic art forms, suggests this is possible. Erected at cardinal points within the monasteries, they served as protective barriers against evil, as well as focal points for meeting and prayer. About 70 high crosses still stand around the country, many in their original positions. The finest are at Clonmacnoise, Monasterboice, Ahenny, Durrow and Kells.

# FORE

Nestled in a beautiful green valley, this tiny village keeps watch over some of Ireland's most atmospheric monastic ruins. As you approach, the remains of **Fore Abbey**, the country's largest Benedictine site, glisten in the surrounding bog. The abbey was built in the early 13th century by the Normans, on the site of an earlier monastery founded by St Feichin in the 7th century. At the start of the path that leads through the bog to the ruins, an ash tree grows over the ancient holy well. The tree was poisoned by coins driven into its bark for luck and only a single branch survives, with bits of cloth and wrappings tied round it in the old pagan tradition. On the hill opposite the abbey are the remains of **St Feichin's Church**. Legend claims the massive lintel was raised in place by the saint's prayers, one of the 'seven wonders' associated with the site. In a chapel nearby is the anchorite's cell, occupied by hermits until the 17th century. The medieval stone gateways still stand at either end of the village.

## Accommodation and food in Fore

**Hounslow House €** *Tel: 044 966 1144; fax: 044 966 1847.* Set on a hillside overlooking Fore Abbey, this 200-year-old farmhouse is a peaceful, scenic base for exploring the Midlands. Rooms are bright and comfortable in a modern extension, and have all the amenities. The spacious lounge, with its bank of windows, is a relaxing spot for surveying the green valley and enjoying the delicious breakfasts, tea and home baking. The hosts offer heartfelt Irish hospitality, and are a goldmine of information about their native region. There are swings and a games room in the grounds. Dinner available. *Open Apr–Sept.*

# LOUGHCREW CAIRNS

**Loughcrew Cairns**
*Near Oldcastle;*
*tel: 049 854 1240;*
*www.loughcrew.com. Cairn T*
*open mid-Jun–Aug daily*
*1000–1800; site accessible*
*all year.*

Ireland's largest Stone Age necropolis is spread across three peaks of the Slieve-na-Caillighe, or Loughcrew Hills. Some 30 chambered cairns dating between 2500 and 3000 BC have been excavated here, making it one of the most important archaeological sites in the country. The passage tombs were built with the same techniques as those at Knowth and Newgrange (*see page 60*), although only a few of their decorative stones remain. The finest is Cairn T on the summit of Carnbane East. It measures 115ft (35m) in diameter, with a star-shaped chamber covered by a mound of smaller stones. On the days of the spring and autumn equinox, sunlight enters the tomb at dawn and illuminates a series of patterns on the stones inside. Such orientation and the symbolic carvings emphasise the ritual nature of the site. The main cairn is surrounded by smaller tombs, and to the north is the stone seat called the 'Hag's Chair'. The views of the surrounding countryside are magnificent.

**ⓗ Loughcrew Historic Gardens**
€€ *Oldcastle; tel: 049 854 4356; www.loughcrew.com. Open Mar–Oct daily 1200–1800.* Beautiful pleasure gardens with an ancient yew walk, water garden and other features. Tearoom.

**Right**
Loughcrew passage tomb

# MULLINGAR

**ⓘ Mullingar Tourist Information Office**
*Market Square; tel: 044 934 8650. Open year-round Mon–Sat.*

**ⓗ Cathedral of Christ the King** € *tel: 044 9348338. Open daily 0900–1730.*

The twin spires of the Renaissance-style **Cathedral of Christ the King** dominate Mullingar's skyline. Inside are superb mosaics of St Patrick and St Anne by the Russian artist Boris Anrep, and an ecclesiastical museum. Mullingar is a former garrison town, and artefacts from the various conflicts in Irish history are displayed in the **Military Museum** € (*tel: 086 840 9400. Open by appointment only*) in Columb Barracks. There is an energetic, friendly feel to this market town, which has become a popular touring base for the region. Mullingar is also at the heart of Ireland's cattle-raising lands, and farmers across the country judge a good cow as 'beef to the heels, like a Mullingar heifer'.

# ROSCOMMON

**ⓘ Roscommon Tourist Information Office**
*Harrison Hall; tel: 090 662 6342. Open Jun–Aug.*

This stone-built market town lies at the heart of an agricultural district. In the centre, the old town gaol commemorates its last executioner, 'Lady Betty'. Sentenced to death for the murder of her son in 1780, she escaped her fate by agreeing to take on the unwanted job of hangwoman, which she fulfilled for 30 years. Opposite the gaol is the lovely Georgian courthouse, now the Bank of Ireland. South of the centre in Abbey Street are the ruins of **Roscommon Abbey**, a Dominican friary built in 1253 by Felim O'Connor, King of Connaught. His tomb in the church is supported by eight sculpted gallowglasses – Scottish medieval warriors hired to repel the Anglo-Norman invaders. To the north of town are the formidable ruins of **Roscommon Castle**, a Norman stronghold.

## STROKESTOWN PARK HOUSE

**Strokestown Park House €€**
Tel: 071 963 3013;
www.strokestownpark.ie.
Open mid-Mar–Oct daily
1000–1730. Museum (€€).

Strokestown's wide, attractive main street leads to the Gothic arches that mark the entrance to this Palladian mansion. Designed by Richard Castle, it was built in the 1730s for Thomas Mahon, whose descendants lived here until 1979. The present owner converted the stable yard into the outstanding **Famine Museum**. Drawing on documents from the Strokestown Park archives, this tragic chapter in Ireland's history is explained in a moving and personal manner. Two-thirds of the Strokestown tenants were evicted or dispatched to Canada on coffin ships by Major Dennis Mahon, who was later murdered for his schemes. A final exhibit looks at famine in the developing world today.

The museum can be followed by a tour of the manor, an insightful portrayal of life in the Big House, from the coffin table in the entry hall to the incredible kitchen with its unusual viewing gallery, from which the lady of the house oversaw household affairs. Side by side, the museum and the house provide one of the most striking depictions of the changing fortunes of both the Irish tenancy and aristocracy.

## TULLAMORE

**Tullamore Tourist Information Office**
in Tullamore Dew Heritage Centre; tel: 057 935 2617. Open year-round.

**Tullamore Dew Heritage Centre**
€€ Bury Quay; tel: 057 932 5015; www.tullamoredew.com/heritage-centre. Open May–Sept Mon–Sat 0900–1800 (1000–1700 rest of the year), Sun 1200–1700.

**Charleville Forest Castle €€€**
Tel: 057 932 1279;
www.charlevillecastle.com.
Phone for opening times.

Following the construction of the Grand Canal in the 18th century, Offaly's county town flourished as a milling, brewing and distilling centre, and the former warehouses and granaries add character to its busy modern appearance. The **Tullamore Dew Heritage Centre**, named after the whiskey once produced here, recounts the history of distilling and the importance of the canal transport to this manufacturing town. Today Tullamore is a popular embarkation point for narrowboat cruises on the waterway.

Just outside town is **Charleville Forest Castle**, towered, turreted and crenellated in fairy-tale style. Built in 1812, it was designed by Francis Johnston, a departure from his many Georgian buildings in the capital. The dining room was the work of William Morris and retains its original wallpaper. There are splendid woodland walks through the grounds.

## Suggested tour

**Total distance:** The main tour is 153 miles (245km). The detour to Loughcrew Cairns will add an extra 33 miles (53km) to the main route.

**Time:** It will take you a full day to cover the main route, and 2 days are recommended if you want to take in several attractions. The detour will take you about 2½ hours, including the visit to the cairns. Those with little time should try to take in Clonmacnoise and Birr.

**Links:** This route connects with tours of the Boyne Valley (*see page 66*) and Kildare to Cashel (*see page 100*) to the east and southeast.

From **MULLINGAR** ❶ take the N4 northwest for 26 miles (42km) to the county town of **Longford**. The town's major landmark, the historic 19th-century Cathedral of St Mel, was gutted in a fire on Christmas Day in December 2009. It is now in the process of being restored.

**Detour:** Take the R394 north from Mullingar to **CASTLEPOLLARD** ❷ and the nearby village of **FORE** ❸. Along the way, the turn-off for **Lough Derravaragh** leads to a pretty picnic spot on the tip of this tranquil lake. It is associated with the tragic legend of the *Children of Lir*, who were turned into swans by their wicked stepmother. From Fore, take the road signposted to Hounslow House which curves past the abbey. Just beyond this hilltop B&B, turn right at the stop sign on the road to Oldcastle. After about 6 miles (10km), the road forks to the left, but carry straight ahead on the main road. A little further on as you enter the village of Millbrook, you will see signs for the right-hand turn to **LOUGHCREW CAIRNS** ❹, which are 2½ miles (4km) on. Return to Castlepollard and take the R395 west to rejoin the main route at Edgeworthstown, 9 miles (14km) outside Longford.

## The potato

Sir Walter Raleigh is said to have planted Ireland's first potato, brought back from the New World, at his home in Youghal, County Cork in the 1580s. In celebration, the town holds a potato festival every year. Nutritious and easy to grow, the tuber spread throughout the land. By the 1840s, the Irish tenancy had become so adept at cultivating it that they produced about 6 tonnes per acre, a greater output than any other place in Europe. The average adult consumed 14lb (6kg) of potatoes per day, and often little else. Even on a small plot, enough potatoes could be produced to sustain a family for the coming year, but this dependency on a single crop led to disaster when it failed (see page 36).

From Longford, take the N5 (signposted Sligo) west to **STROKESTOWN PARK HOUSE** ❺, 14 miles (22km) away. Take the R368 southwest for 7½ miles (12km) to Four Mile House and turn left on to the N61 to **ROSCOMMON** ❻. Continue southeast on the N61 for 20 miles (32km) to **ATHLONE** ❼. As you leave town, follow signs for Dublin (N6) and at the outskirts of town take the right-hand turn signposted for Birr. Note that the turn is a bit tricky: just after the sign you'll see another right-hand turn for Clonbuny, but you want to take the more major Birr road (N62) just beyond.

About 6 miles (9km) along, turn right on the R444 for 7 miles (11km) to **CLONMACNOISE** ❽. Continue south on the R444 for 4½ miles (7km) to Shannonbridge. This road travels across the top of the eskers, the term used for the long gravel ridges deposited across Ireland during the last Ice Age. These 'highways' formed the only routes across the boglands for early Celtic travellers. From this short road you have a wonderful view of two contrasting landscapes: to the west is the broad, lush floodplain of the River Shannon; to the east is the vast, dark Blackwater Bog. At the T-junction, turn left on to the R357 and, continue southeast on the R357 to **Cloghan**, where the house and

**Cloghan Castle €€**
*Tel: 091 870102.
Pre-booked parties only.*

**Locke's Distillery €€**
*Kilbeggan; tel: 057 933 2134;
www.lockesdistillerymuseum.ie.
Open Apr–Oct daily
0900–1800; Nov–Mar daily
1000–1600.*

**MV *Goldsmith***
*Athlone; tel: 090 648
5163. The largest ship
to sail on Ireland's inland
waterways, it can carry
up to 200 passengers.*

gardens of **Cloghan Castle** are now a romantic venue for weddings. Nearby **Shannon Harbour**, where the river intersects with the Grand Canal, holds a poignant place in Irish history as the departure point for many famine emigrants heading to America. Both are signposted off the R357. Turn south on to the N62 for 11 miles (18km) to **BIRR ❾**.

Take the N52 northeast for 22 miles (35km) to **TULLAMORE ❿**. Continue north on the N52, past the site of the monastery at **Durrow**, founded by St Colmcille in the 6th century. Its great treasures – the illuminated *Book of Durrow* and an ornate crozier – are in Dublin's Trinity College Library and the National Museum respectively. All that remains here are some early gravestones and a 10th-century high cross. A couple of miles beyond, at Kilbeggan, **Locke's Distillery**, established in 1757, is Ireland's oldest licensed distillery. It closed in 1954, but later reopened as a museum. The 40-minute guided tour takes you through the age-old process of whiskey making, from the millstones to the pot stills and casks. Or you can opt for a self-guided tour and visit the Whiskey Bar, shop and restaurant. At Kilbeggan you turn right and briefly join the M6 Dublin road; at **Tyrrellspass**, turn left by the village green, encircled by a pretty crescent of Georgian houses, to continue north on the N52. The town is named after the Tyrrells, who in medieval times guarded a strategic pass through the bog from their castle, now restored. Just beyond Dalystown is the turn-off for **BELVEDERE HOUSE, GARDENS AND PARK ⓫**. From here it is 3 miles (5km) back to Mullingar.

## Also worth exploring

The R390 between Mullingar and Athlone is a scenic road that runs past the **Hill of Uisneach**, an important site of kings in ancient times. The region to the west and southwest of Clonmacnoise has much to explore, including **Ballinasloe**, the abbey at **Kilconnell** and the Romanesque church at **Clonfert**, site of St Brendan's monastic settlement. To the north, **Boyle**, with its Cistercian abbey and historical exhibits at King House, is surrounded by lakes and the Curlew Hills. **Lough Key Forest Park**, near Boyle, is also worth a visit. Southwest of Birr, there is a scenic route around **Lough Derg**, which passes through the picturesque village of Terryglass.

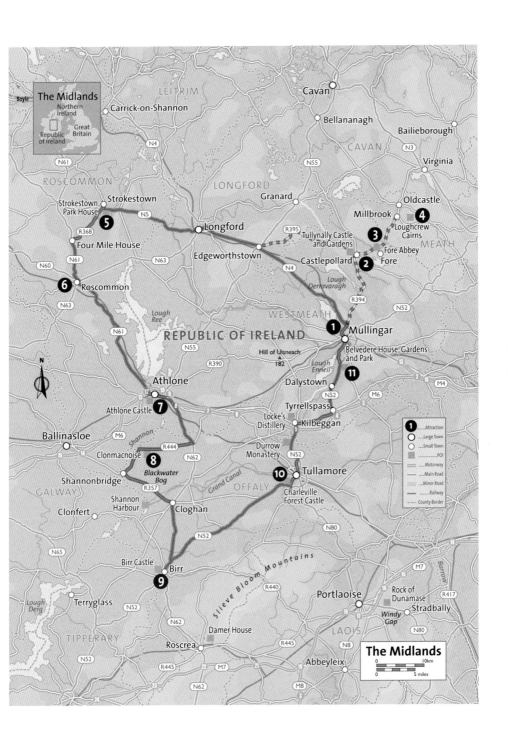

# Kildare to Cashel

## Ratings

| | |
|---|---|
| Abbeys | ●●●●● |
| Churches | ●●●●● |
| Horse racing | ●●●●● |
| Medieval towns | ●●●●● |
| Castles | ●●●○○ |
| Scenery | ●●●○○ |
| Outdoor recreation | ●●○○○ |
| Prehistoric sites | ●●○○○ |

This tour, running diagonally through the Irish heartland from the thoroughbred pastures of Kildare to the Golden Vale of Tipperary, encompasses some of the best-known sights of the Midlands. This is a region steeped in history, once a bulwark of Anglo-Norman power, though some of the most strategic towns of yesteryear are now simple riverside villages dozing amid the remnants of their past. Throughout the rolling green hills, tidy farmlands and flat stretches of field lies holy ground. The ruins of great monasteries and cathedrals abound, from St Brigid's nunnery and the sculpted cloisters of Jerpoint Abbey to the imposing ecclesiastical centre atop the Rock of Cashel. There is much to explore, and you may wish to break the journey at Kilkenny, a delightful medieval town with many atmospheric corners and one of the country's finest castles. In Kildare you can visit the National Stud and join the punters at some of Ireland's most famous racetracks.

## ATHY

**ⓘ Athy Heritage Centre Tourist Information Point**
*Tel: 059 863 3075. Open year-round Mon–Fri 1000–1700.*

**Right**
Window embrasure, White's Castle

The Anglo-Normans founded this settlement at the confluence of the Grand Canal and the River Barrow in the 12th century. It was fortified in medieval times; the 16th-century White's Castle, now a private home, still marks the river crossing on the north side of the bridge. The Georgian Court Market House and the striking, modern Dominican church, with stained glass by Irish artist George Campbell, are among the sights of interest in this market town. There is an interesting **Heritage Centre** in the 18th-century town hall.

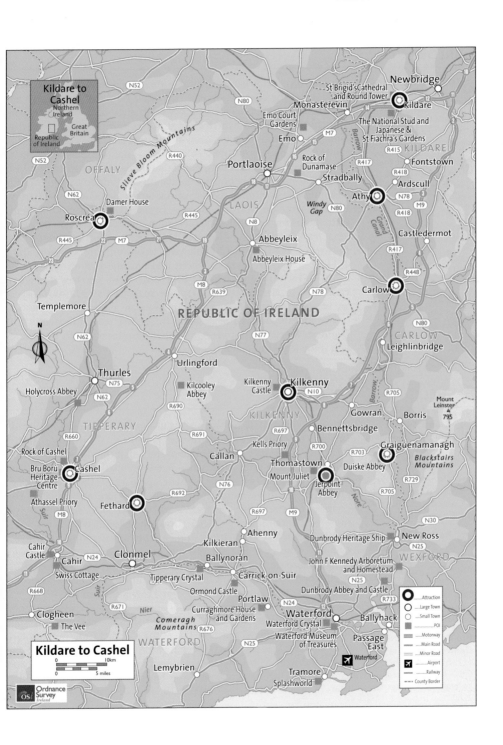

Kildare to Cashel
Northern Ireland
Great Britain
Republic of Ireland

N52
N80

Newbridge
St Brigid's Cathedral and Round Tower
Monasterevin
Kildare
Emo Court Gardens
The National Stud and Japanese & St Fiachra's Gardens
M7
Emo
N52
R440
Portlaoise
Rock of Dunamase
R417
Fontstown
OFFALY
Stradbally
R418
Ardscull
N62
Damer House
LAOIS
Windy Gap
N80
Athy
N78
M9
Roscrea
R445
N8
R418
Castledermot
R445
M7
Abbeyleix
R417
Abbeyleix House
R448
M8
R639
N78
Carlow
Templemore
REPUBLIC OF IRELAND
N80
N62
N77
CARLOW
Leighlinbridge
Thurles
Urlingford
N75
Kilcooley Abbey
Kilkenny Castle
Kilkenny
Holycross Abbey
N62
R690
N10
R705
Mount Leinster 795
TIPPERARY
KILKENNY
Gowran
Borris
R660
R691
R697
Bennettsbridge
Rock of Cashel
Kells Priory
R700
R703
Graiguenamanagh
Bru Boru Heritage Centre
Cashel
Callan
Thomastown
Duiske Abbey
Blackstairs Mountains
R729
Athassel Priory
R692
N76
Mount Juliet
Jerpoint Abbey
R705
Fethard
R697
M9
N30
Ahenny
Dunbrody Heritage Ship
New Ross
Cahir Castle
Kilkieran
N25
Cahir
N24
Clonmel
Ballynoran
John F Kennedy Arboretum and Homestead
WEXFORD
Swiss Cottage
Tipperary Crystal
Carrick-on-Suir
N25
R668
Ormond Castle
Dunbrody Abbey and Castle
R733
Portlaw
N24
Clogheen
R671
Nier
Curraghmore House and Gardens
Waterford
Ballyhack
The Vee
Comeragh Mountains
R676
Waterford Crystal
WATERFORD
Waterford Museum of Treasures
N25
Passage East
Kildare to Cashel
0    10km
0    5 miles
Lemybrien
Tramore
Splashworld
Waterford

Ordnance Survey Ireland

Attraction
Large Town
Small Town
POI
Motorway
Main Road
Minor Road
Airport
Railway
County Border

# CARLOW

**ⓘ Carlow Tourist Information Office**
Located at the junction of Tullow and College Streets; tel: 059 913 1554. Open year-round.

**ⓗ Cathedral of the Assumption €**
Tullow Street. Open daily 1000–2000.

Carlow Town dates back to Norman times, and once held a strategic position on the edge of the Pale (*see page 67*). Today it is a large but unassuming market town where cows still graze on the village green. The Gothic-Revival **Cathedral of the Assumption** with its striking lantern tower and stained-glass windows was built in 1828. Inside, the tomb of Bishop James Doyle, a champion of Catholic emancipation, is adorned with an outstanding marble monument sculpted by the Irish artist John Hogan. The former Presentation Convent on College Street is currently being restored as part of the redevelopment of the **Carlow County Museum**, whose collection contains more than 5,000 items including many archaeological finds from the area (*check with the tourist office for opening details*). Near the bridge are the ruins of 13th-century **Carlow Castle**. It survived Cromwell's troops only to be blown up in 1814 by a doctor trying to remodel it into a mental asylum.

Microbrewery enthusiasts may enjoy the **Carlow Brewing Company** in The Goods Store (*Station Road; tel: 059 913 4356*). Beers are brewed on-site and tours of the brewery are available on request.

Two miles (3km) east of town on the Tullow road is **Browne's Hill Dolmen**, a megalithic Stone Age tomb. Its capstone weighs 100 tonnes and is the largest in Ireland.

# CASHEL

**ⓘ Cashel Tourist Information Office**
Heritage Centre, Town Hall, Main Street; tel: 062 61333.

**ⓟ** There is a large car park at the top of the hill, near the entrance to the Rock of Cashel site (€).

**ⓗ Rock of Cashel €€**
Tel: 062 61437. Open daily: mid-Mar–mid-Jun 0900–1730; mid-Jun–mid-Sept 0900–1900; mid-Sept–mid-Oct 0900–1730; mid-Oct–mid-Mar 0900–1630.

**Bru Ború Heritage Centre €–€€€** Tel: 062 61122. Open Mon–Fri 0900–1700; Folk Theatre performances Jun–Sept at 2100.

Rising 200ft (61m) above the plain and topped by a cluster of historic ruins, the **Rock of Cashel** is truly an impressive sight. The kings of Munster ruled their lands from atop this limestone outcrop from around 370 until 1101, when it was granted to the Church. The Bishop's Walk makes an atmospheric approach to the Rock; it takes about 10 minutes from the town below. The entrance to the ecclesiastical site is through the **Vicar's Choral Hall**, where there is a museum containing St Patrick's Cross; the base in which it is set is reputed to be the coronation stone of the Munster kings. **Cormac's Chapel**, consecrated in 1134, is a masterpiece of medieval architecture, with its steep stone roof and decorated 11th-century stone sarcophagus. A gilt copper crozier found inside is now in the National Museum in Dublin. The first cathedral, founded in 1169, was burnt in 1495 by the Earl of Kildare. He was hauled to justice before Henry VII, who pardoned him when he explained that he 'thought the archbishop was in it'. The new cathedral suffered the same fate at the hands of Cromwell's troops, after which it was deconsecrated in 1647. Among its highlights are the north transept, with a series of sculptures depicting the Apostles and saints; the octagonal staircase turret beside the central tower, which leads to defensive passages in the walls; the round tower; and the views from atop the central tower.

**Cashel Heritage Centre** *City Hall; tel: 062 62511; www.cashel.ie. Open Mar–Oct daily 0930–1730; Nov–Feb Mon–Fri 0930–1730. Guided tours of the town can be arranged.*

**Bolton Library** €€ *John Street; tel: 062 61944. Open May–Sept; call for opening times.*

**Cashel Folk Village** € *Dominic Street; tel: 062 62525. Open daily: Mar–Apr 1000–1800; May–Oct 0930–1930.*

**Cashel Palace Hotel** €€€ *Main Street; tel: 062 62707; fax: 062 61521; email: reception@cashel-palace.ie; www.cashel-palace.ie. Open year-round.*

**Below**
Rock of Cashel

The **Bru Ború Heritage Centre** at the base of the rock is named after Brian Ború, Ireland's first high king, who was crowned here in 977. It has exhibits on Irish culture and traditional entertainment in the evenings. In Cashel Town, the **Cashel Heritage Centre**, adjacent to the tourist information office, has a scale model of the town as it was in the 1600s. The **Bolton Library**, on the grounds of St Peter the Rock Cathedral, has several exhibits from its extensive collection of rare books and manuscripts on display. **Cashel Folk Village** has replicas of 18th- to early 20th-century buildings and a range of memorabilia.

Even if you don't stay there, drop into the **Cashel Palace Hotel** for tea to see its fine interior carving and panelling. The Queen Anne-style building was designed in 1730 by Edward Lovett Pearce who also built Dublin's Houses of Parliament, and was a former archbishops' residence.

## Of devils and saints

There are many legends associated with the Rock of Cashel. It is said to have been formed when the Devil, flying across Ireland in a great hurry, took a bite out of the mountains in his path and spat it out in the Golden Vale. A gap to the north, called the Devil's Bit, is said to be a perfect match to the dimensions of the Rock.

St Patrick arrived in 450 to baptise King Aengus and his brothers. During the ceremony, the saint accidentally drove his sharp-pointed staff into the king's foot, but the king didn't flinch, thinking the pain was part of the Christian initiation rites. From that point onwards, Cashel was also called 'St Patrick's Rock'.

# FETHARD

**ⓘ Fethard Tourist Information Office**
*Tierry Centre; tel: 052 31000. Open year-round.*

You can see more of medieval Ireland in this tiny Tipperary town than in most cities twice its size. Parts of it are enclosed by sections of its 14th-century town walls, including the grounds of Holy Trinity Church (13th century), with many interesting tombs and monuments. Its west tower is one of three medieval fortress towers that still stand in the town centre. The town hall in Market Square is housed in a merchant's house dating to 1640. A well-preserved Augustinian friary, dating from the 14th century and reopened in 1823, lies at one end of town. The Presentation Convent was designed by Pugin and Ashlin in 1862.

# GRAIGUENAMANAGH

The pretty town of Graiguenamanagh, whose name means 'village of the monks', is set alongside a bend of the River Barrow beneath Brandon Hill. **Duiske Abbey**, built in the early 13th century, was the largest Cistercian church in Ireland and an important religious centre. Monks remained here long after its suppression in 1536, but by the 18th century it was in ruins and the tower collapsed. In the 1970s, extensive restoration began and parts of it now form the parish church. Among the notable features are the oak roof, the Romanesque door in the south transept and an effigy of a cross-legged knight in armour. There are two 9th-century high crosses in the graveyard.

# JERPOINT ABBEY

**ⓝ Jerpoint Abbey €€**
*1 mile (1.5km) south of Thomastown; tel: 056 772 4623. Open daily: Mar–May & mid-Sept–Oct 1000–1700; Jun–mid-Sept 1000–1800; Nov 1000–1600; rest of year groups by appointment.*

**Right**
Jerpoint Abbey ruins

Jerpoint Abbey is one of Ireland's finest monastic ruins. It was founded in 1158, but most of the existing structures date from 1180, when the Cistercians from Baltinglass colonised the site. The crossing tower was added in the 15th century. Much of the church and chapterhouse still stand. The church contains many fine 13th- to 16th-century tombs; some feature effigies of abbots and knights, others display panels with intricate stone-carved figures, attributed to the O'Tunney family of sculptors from nearby Callan. Equally outstanding is the cloister arcade, each pier finely carved with figures ranging from saints to grotesques. The visitor centre has interesting exhibits on the region's high crosses and the medieval tiles discovered in the abbey.

**Right**
Jerpoint Abbey

# KILDARE

**Kildare Tourist Information Office**
Market Square; tel: 045 521240. Open year-round.

**St Brigid's Cathedral €** and **Round Tower €€** The Square; tel: 045 521229. Open May–Sept Mon–Sat 1000–1300, 1400–1700.

**The National Stud and Japanese & St Fiachra's Gardens €€€** Tully; tel: 045 521617; www.irish-national-stud.ie. Open mid-Feb–Dec daily 0930–1700.

St Brigid, one of Ireland's patron saints, established a religious community here in 490. The 13th-century **cathedral** named in her honour stands on the site. It has some noteworthy monuments and a stained-glass window depicting Brigid with saints Patrick and Colmcille. You can climb the **round tower**, at 108ft (33m) the second highest in the country, for panoramic views. Located on the edge of the broad green pastures of the Curragh, Kildare is a major centre for breeding and training horses. **The National Stud**, just outside town at Tully, covers 1,000 acres (400 hectares). Colonel William Hall-Walker, a Scotsman, began breeding thoroughbred horses there in 1900. He believed that the fate of every creature was dictated by the stars, and so built skylights into the stables so that the heavens could exert maximum influence. These unusual ideas bore fruit with a string of winners. In 1943 he presented the grounds and horses to the state. Along with a tour of the paddocks and stables, you can visit the Horse Museum. Adjacent to the National Stud are the **Japanese Gardens**, also established by Colonel Hall-Walker and designed by Tassa Eida and his son Minoru. They symbolise stages in the life of man, from birth through to death. **St Fiachra's Garden** was opened in 1999.

# KILKENNY

**ⓘ Kilkenny Tourist Information Office**
*Located in the Shee Alms House, Rose Inn Street; tel: 056 775 1500; fax: 056 776 3955; www. discoverireland.ie/kilkenny. Open year-round.*

**ⓑ Kilkenny Castle €€**
*Tel: 056 772 1450; www.kilkennycastle.ie. Open daily: Oct–Feb 0930–1630; Mar 0930–1700; Apr, Aug & Sept 0930–1730; May–Jun 0900–1730. Admission by guided tour only; last tour 1 hour before closing.*

**St Canice's Cathedral € (Round Tower €)**
*Tel: 056 776 4971; www. stcanicescathedral.com. Open Apr, May & Sept Mon–Sat 1000–1300, 1400–1700, Sun 1400–1700; Jun–Aug Mon–Sat 0900–1800, Sun 1400–1800; Oct–Mar Mon–Sat 1000–1300, 1400–1600, Sun 1400–1600.*

Kilkenny is one of Ireland's finest cities, full of medieval treasures and lined with brightly painted Victorian-style pubs and shopfronts. St Canice founded a monastic school here in the 6th century, from which Kilkenny (Kil Cainneach or 'Church of Canice') takes its name. The powerful Anglo-Norman family, the Butlers, came to power here in the 12th century and built their formidable castle, which often served as the seat of the Irish Parliament. During their 500-year reign, walls and gates were built for segregation as well as for defence. The town is made for walking, and the main attractions are joined by picturesque streets such as High Street, with its 18th-century Tholsel and clock tower. The medieval alleyways, called 'slips', running off it are also fun to explore, such as the Butter Slip, once lined with market stalls selling butter. There is a wealth of architecture, from Georgian façades to Tudor features, much of it sporting the local black limestone called Kilkenny marble.

**Kilkenny Castle**, set in parkland and commanding a fine position along the River Nore, is one of Ireland's most impressive castles. Built in the 1190s, its Norman features have been enhanced by later Gothic Revival-style alterations. Its highlight is the Long Gallery, stretching 150ft (46m) with a magnificent oak hammer-beam ceiling and skylights. The Butler gallery, with its ornate painted ceiling, houses a modern art collection. **St Canice's Cathedral**, built in the 13th century, is the second-longest cathedral in Ireland. It, too, has a splendid hammer-beam roof with carved wood figures, ornate carved choir stalls and beautiful lancet windows. It is studded with magnificent and intricately

**(P)** The parking disc system operates around Kilkenny. Discs can be bought in shops near the car parks. The Market Cross car park is located on Parliament Street and James Street, and there is one below the castle on The Parade.

Kilkenny is a centre for crafts and design, and a great range of original work is produced here, from glass, pottery and precious metals to leather and textiles. The **Kilkenny Design Centre**, renowned throughout Ireland, carries a good range. It is located in Castle Yard on The Parade (tel: 056 772 2118. Open Mon–Sat 1000–1900, Sun 1100–1900). The **Crafts Council of Ireland** (tel: 056 776 1804), located in the building, or the tourist information office can help you seek out individual workshops.

sculpted stone tombs, under which many bishops and Butlers are laid to rest. Other treasures include the finely carved west door, the 12th-century baptismal font and the ancient stone throne, St Ciarán's Chair. You can climb the round tower for a fine view over the town.

The **Black Abbey**, another of Kilkenny's five medieval abbeys, was founded by the black-robed Dominicans in 1225. They were viewed as radicals, so when the bishop was finally persuaded to let them draw water from Kenny's Well, he stipulated that the pipe could be no larger than his episcopal ring. But the community flourished and the church has stunning stained glass, some as old as the 14th century. The Rosary Window covers 575sq ft (51sq m) and depicts the 15 decats of the rosary. More sombre features are the 13th-century stone coffins of victims of the Black Death. Among Kilkenny's other highlights are **Rothe House**, a Tudor merchant's house and small museum; the **Shee Almshouse**, one of few such buildings from Tudor times and now the home of the tourist office and an exhibition on the city; and **Grace's Castle**, now the courthouse.

Smithwick's beer has been brewed in Kilkenny since 1710, when the Smithwick family took over the medieval St Francis Abbey and converted it into a brewery. The monks had been brewing there from the 13th century.

## Accommodation and food in Kilkenny

**Café Sol €–€€** William Street; tel: 056 776 4987; email: info@cafesolkilkenny.com; www.cafesolkilkenny.com. Located in the medieval heart of Kilkenny near City Hall, this bistro-syle restaurant serves contemporary Irish cuisine with a Mediterranean flair. From simple sandwiches and lunch dishes to creative dinner menus, the chef sources local produce such as Lavistown sausage, free-range eggs and fresh fish from Dunmore East. The restaurant's yellow and terracotta tones are bright and colourful by day, but take on an intimate ambience for evening dining. There are two- and three-course value menus as well as occasional theme nights and regular wine-tasting dinners. Open Mon–Sat 1130–2130, Sun 1200–2100.

**The Hibernian Hotel €€** 1 Ormonde Street; tel: 056 777 1888; fax: 056 777 1877; email: info@kilkennyhibernianhotel.com; www.kilkennyhibernianhotel.com. You will feel like a millionaire in this richly renovated bank building, right in the heart of town, a stone's throw from Kilkenny Castle. The splendid interior retains its stained-glass windows and grand central staircase. Rooms are smart and comfortable, with sleek bathrooms and roomy showers. Those facing Patrick Street, once the bank directors' offices, have grand marble fireplaces and good views over the town; others are located in a recent extension. The panelled Victorian banking hall is now a spacious breakfast, lunch and tea room. There are two bars, the popular City Bar and Grill and on-site parking.

**Opposite**
Kilkenny High Street

**Opposite**
Cashel sculpture of dancing
musicians

### Within these walls

In Ireland, town walls often served to keep foreign invaders in, not out. Medieval cities such as Kilkenny and Youghal in County Cork were 'closed boroughs' and had separate 'Irish towns' outside the walls. The native Irish had to obtain special permission to enter the city gates or trade within. In 1366, the Crown decided that its Norman families were becoming too assimilated into Irish ways and, fearful of losing its grip, enacted the hated Statutes of Kilkenny. Under these laws, intermarriage was high treason and Norman settlers could lose their lands for speaking Irish, wearing Irish dress or giving their children Irish names. It was too late to change the natural tide, however, and after a few years of enforcement the statutes fell into decline.

# ROSCREA

**Damer House €**
*Tel: 0505 21850.*
*Open mid-Mar–Oct daily*
*1000–1800.*

Heavy traffic from the Dublin–Limerick road mars the first impression of this otherwise attractive town, which has a long religious history. The 8th-century *Book of Dimma*, now in Trinity College Library, and the Roscrea Brooch in the National Museum, are two early Christian artefacts that were found here. The ruins of **St Cronan's Monastery**, founded in the early 7th century, include a high cross, church and round tower. Nearby is the west façade of a later Romanesque church, now a gateway to a 19th-century church. In Abbey Street, the remnants of a 15th-century **Franciscan friary** adjoin **St Cronan's Churchyard**, with an early Christian stone known as the Roscrea Pillar. **Roscrea Castle**, built by the Anglo-Normans in the 13th century and surrounded by a moat, retains its gate tower, two corner towers and the curtain walls. Within them is **Damer House**, built in 1725, with a fabulous carved pine staircase. It now houses the Roscrea Heritage Centre and tourist information office.

# Suggested tour

**Total distance:** The main route is 156 miles (251km). The Castledermot detour adds only a couple of miles. The detour to Graiguenamanagh is about 8 miles (13km) longer than the main route. The detours through Fethard and Thurles/Roscrea are 5 miles (8km) and 10 miles (16km) longer respectively.

**Time:** Allow at least a day for the main tour, although two or even three days are recommended if you want to spend time savouring the many attractions. While the suggested detours are only slightly longer than the main route in miles, they can add considerable time to your journey because of the slower driving on the secondary roads, so

you should plan accordingly. Those with little time should concentrate on Kilkenny and Cashel.

**Links:** This route links up with tours of counties Waterford, Wexford, Wicklow and the Midlands. Kildare is only 32 miles (51km) southwest of Dublin on the N7 and M7.

After exploring the sights around **KILDARE ❶**, Ireland's premier horse-breeding and training centre, take the R415 south; this very narrow rural road gives glimpses of the bright green, flat pastures that are quintessential Kildare countryside. After 8 miles (13km), turn right at Fontstown on to the R418. **Ardscull**, a hamlet about 2 miles (3km) further on, contains one of the largest Norman mottes in the country. The heritage town of **ATHY ❷** lies 4 miles (6km) further south. The county town of **CARLOW ❸** is 12 miles (19km) south on the R417.

**A bewitching tale**

Kyteler's Inn on Kieran Street was once the home of Dame Alice Kyteler, a 14th-century 'witch'. She married four times: each husband was a wealthy man and each subsequently died. The witchcraft-mad bishop accused her of poisoning them. In truth, Dame Alice was a very powerful woman and much of the town was in debt to her. Perhaps this is why they so readily accepted the allegations and sentenced her to be burnt at the stake. When she mysteriously disappeared before the sentence was carried out, Petronella of Meath was burnt instead.

**Detour:** Leave Athy on the R418 to see the fine round tower and two high crosses, both dating from the 10th century, at **Castledermot**. In the village are the ruins of a 14th-century Franciscan friary. Take the R448 south to rejoin the main route at Carlow.

Continue south from Carlow, passing through the town of **Gowran**, with its famous racecourse. **Thomastown** is 7½ miles (12km) further on. This picturesque town straddles the River Nore, and there is a pleasant walk along the riverbank through woodlands and fields to the ruins of Grennan Castle (13th century). **Mount Juliet**, once one of Ireland's largest estates and now a private hotel with a championship golf course, also has extensive walled gardens, a rose garden and a rockery among its beautiful grounds. It is open to non-residents on request and is signposted from the town. Thomastown's main attraction, however, is **JERPOINT ABBEY ❹**.

**Detour:** From Leighlinbridge, take the R705 south through the valley of the River Barrow to **GRAIGUENAMANAGH ❺**. Head west on the R703 to rejoin the main route at Thomastown.

Take the R700 north for 10 miles (16km) to **KILKENNY ❻**. Leave town on the N76 south and turn right (west) on the R691 to **CASHEL ❼**.

**Abbeyleix Heritage House €**
Tel: 057 873 1653. Open year-round, Mon–Fri 1000–1700 and also May–Sept, Sat & Sun 1300–1700.

**Emo Court Gardens (House €€)** Tel: 057 862 6573. House open Easter–Sept daily 1000–1800 by guided tour; gardens open year-round during daylight hours.

**Holycross Abbey €**
Tel: 050 443124; www.holycrossabbey.ie. Open Apr–Sept daily 1000–1700; Oct–Mar Mon–Sat 1000–1100, 1530–1700, Sun 1500–1730.

**Right**
St Canice's Cathedral, Kilkenny

**Detour:** A slightly longer route to Cashel is via the R692, a right-hand turn off the N76 further south beyond Callan. It passes through the town of **FETHARD ❽**, a small but important medieval town. Continue west to rejoin the main tour at Cashel.

From Cashel, take the N8 northeast towards Portlaoise, passing through the attractive town of **Abbeyleix**, with its wide tree-lined streets and period houses. It was founded in the mid-18th century by the de Vesci family, and the lush grounds of their estate, **Abbeyleix House**, are open to visitors. You can also visit the re-created Abbeyleix Carpet Factory, which made carpets for the *Titanic*. **Portlaoise**, a road and rail junction, has little of interest in town, but just outside on the N80 Stradbally road is the **Rock of Dunamase**, a defensive fort that predated Viking times. Another sad victim of Cromwell's march, it has fine views from the top. Take the M7 north, and if the day is fine you may want to follow signs to Emo and **Emo Court Gardens**. The mansion, built in 1790, is only open in summer, but the grounds, with their sweeping lawns, woodland walks and specimen trees, are accessible. Continue northeast on the M7 through the canal town of **Monasterevin** back to Kildare.

**Detour:** Take the R660 north from Cashel. **Holycross Abbey**, 3 miles (5km) south of the busy market town of Thurles, was founded in the 12th century to house a relic of the True Cross. It was taken over by the Cistercians, who built the splendid Gothic church with its many ornate features and made the abbey a place of pilgrimage. Now restored, it is open for prayer. Continue north on the N62 to **ROSCREA ❾**. From here take the R445 Dublin road northeast to rejoin the main route at Portlaoise.

## Also worth exploring

The N80 between Carlow and Stradbally (the Portlaoise road) is a scenic drive through **Windy Gap**, with sweeping views of the East Midlands landscape. North of Kildare Town, County Kildare has several sights of interest, including **Castletown House, Celbridge Abbey** at Celbridge and more horse-racing centres at **Punchestown, Naas** and **Kill**. North of the R445, between Portlaoise and Roscrea, are the Slieve Bloom Mountains, bisected by the scenic R440. It is also worth seeking out the ruins of **Hore Abbey** and **Athassel Priory**, both near Cashel; **Kilcooley Abbey**, south of Urlingford on the R690; and **Kells Priory**, south of Kilkenny on the R697.

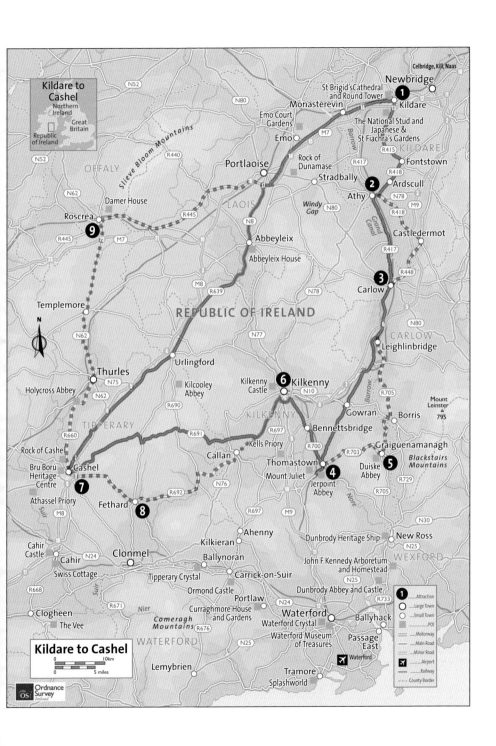

Kildare to Cashel

Northern Ireland

Great Britain

Republic of Ireland

Celbridge, Kill, Naas

Newbridge

St Brigid's Cathedral and Round Tower ❶

Kildare

Monasterevin

Emo Court Gardens

The National Stud and Japanese & St Fiachra's Gardens

Emo

Rock of Dunamase

Fontstown

Portlaoise

Stradbally

Ardscull ❷

Athy

Castledermot

Windy Gap

Abbeyleix

Abbeyleix House

Carlow ❸

Damer House

Roscrea ❾

REPUBLIC OF IRELAND

Leighlinbridge

Templemore

Urlingford

Thurles

Holycross Abbey

Kilcooley Abbey

Kilkenny Castle

Kilkenny ❻

Gowran

Borris

Mount Leinster 795

Bennettsbridge

Kells Priory

Graiguenamanagh

Rock of Cashel

Callan

Thomastown

Duiske Abbey ❺

Blackstairs Mountains

Bru Ború Heritage Centre

Cashel ❼

Mount Juliet

Jerpoint Abbey ❹

Athassel Priory

Fethard ❽

Ahenny

Dunbrody Heritage Ship

New Ross

Cahir Castle

Cahir

Clonmel

Kilkieran

Ballynoran

John F Kennedy Arboretum and Homestead

WEXFORD

Swiss Cottage

Tipperary Crystal

Carrick-on-Suir

Ormond Castle

Dunbrody Abbey and Castle

Portlaw

Curraghmore House and Gardens

Clogheen

The Vee

Comeragh Mountains

Waterford

Waterford Crystal

Ballyhack

Waterford Museum of Treasures

Passage East

Kildare to Cashel

0   10km
0   5 miles

Lemybrien

Waterford

Tramore

Splashworld

Ordnance Survey
Ireland

❶  Attraction
◯  Large Town
◯  Small Town
▪  POI
—  Motorway
—  Main Road
—  Minor Road
✈  Airport
—  Railway
- - County Border

# County Wexford

## Ratings

| | |
|---|---|
| Beaches | ●●●●● |
| Coastal villages/ towns | ●●●●● |
| History | ●●●●● |
| Wildlife | ●●●●● |
| Churches | ●●●●○ |
| Outdoor recreation | ●●●●○ |
| Abbey ruins | ●●●○○ |
| Castles | ●●○○○ |

The Normans first settled in Ireland in County Wexford, and the ferry terminal at Rosslare Harbour remains the gateway for many visitors arriving from France and Wales. The subtle charms of this quiet southeast corner, which catches more sun than any other part of the country, are often lost on those who rush through it too quickly in their quest for more well-known regions. Wexford's 125 miles (200km) of coastline are marked by long sandy beaches – four of them sporting the EU Blue Flag – golden dunes, hidden coves and mellow river estuaries that are a haven for wildlife. Watersports naturally abound, or you can spend leisurely days pottering around the historic harbours, fishing villages and seaside resorts. Inland, the River Slaney runs through the heart of the county, its tributaries, along with the Barrow, feeding the fertile green valleys and providing an idyllic setting for anglers and ramblers on the riverside trails. The Wicklow and Blackstairs mountains, rising to Mount Leinster's 2,600ft (793m) peak, form natural borders to the north and northwest.

## COURTOWN

Set on a wide bay at the mouth of the Ounavarra River, this popular family resort has a great sandy beach that stretches for 2 miles (3km). The harbour piers were built in 1847 as part of a famine relief project funded by the Earl of Courtown. The earthworks on a hill outside the village are said to be the fort of Ladhru, an ancient Celtic leader celebrated in Irish folklore. Another fine beach lies 3 miles (5km) north at Ballymoney, while Pollshone and Ardamine to the south have good swimming in secluded coves.

## DUNBRODY ABBEY

The impressive ruins of Dunbrody Abbey, founded in 1175, stand on the banks of the River Barrow. The church measures 194ft (59m), making it one of the longest Cistercian churches in the country.

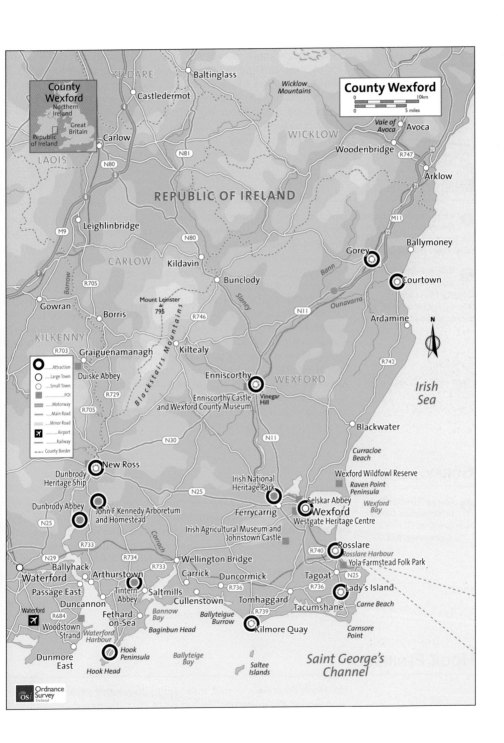

County Wexford

Baltinglass

Wicklow Mountains

Castledermot

County Wexford
Northern Ireland
Great Britain
Republic of Ireland

County Wexford
0                    10km
0          5 miles

Carlow

WICKLOW

Vale of Avoca    Avoca

Woodenbridge    R747

20

N81

N80

REPUBLIC OF IRELAND

Arklow

21

M11

Leighlinbridge

M9

N80

Ballymoney

22

Gorey

CARLOW    Kildavin

Bunclody

Bann

Courtown

R705

Barrow

Slaney

Ounavarra

Ardamine

Mount Leinster
795

R746

N11

Gowran

Borris

N

KILKENNY

R703    Graiguenamanagh    Kiltealy

R742

Attraction
Large Town
Small Town
POI
Motorway
Main Road
Minor Road
Airport
Railway
County Border

Duiske Abbey

R729

Blackstairs Mountains

Enniscorthy    WEXFORD

Enniscorthy Castle    Vinegar Hill
and Wexford County Museum

Irish Sea

R705

N30

N11

Blackwater

Curracloe Beach

New Ross

Wexford Wildfowl Reserve

Dunbrody Heritage Ship

Irish National Heritage Park

Raven Point Peninsula

N25

Dunbrody Abbey

N25

John F Kennedy Arboretum and Homestead

Ferrycarrig

Selskar Abbey    Wexford Bay

Wexford

Westgate Heritage Centre

R733

Corrach

Irish Agricultural Museum and Johnstown Castle

Rosslare
Rosslare Harbour

N29

R734

Wellington Bridge

R740

Yola Farmstead Folk Park

Ballyhack    Arthurstown

R733

Carrick

Duncormick

Tagoat

N25

Waterford

R736

R736

Lady's Island

Passage East

Tintern Abbey

Saltmills

Cullenstown

Tomhaggard

Carne Beach

Duncannon

Tacumshane

Waterford

R684

Fethard-on-Sea

Bannow Bay

Ballyteige Burrow

R739

Carnsore Point

Woodstown Strand

Waterford Harbour

Baginbun Head

Kilmore Quay

Dunmore East

Hook Peninsula

Ballyteige Bay

Saltee Islands

Saint George's Channel

Hook Head

Ordnance Survey
OSi Ireland

**Dunbrody Abbey €**
*Tel: 051 388603;*
*www.dunbrodyabbey.com.*
*Open May–mid-Sept daily*
*1000–1800.*

Outstanding features include the vaulted chapels off the transepts, the east window and the enormous crossing tower, added in the 15th century. A stairway which once led to the monks' dormitories and an abbot's residence above the chapels can also be seen in the south apse. Across from the abbey is the ruin of **Dunbrody Castle**. There is a visitor centre with a small museum here, and a hedge maze, one of only two in the country.

# ENNISCORTHY

**Enniscorthy Tourist Information Office**
*The Castle; tel: 053 923 4699. Open year-round.*

**Enniscorthy Castle and Wexford County Museum**
*Closed for refurbishment; due to open in summer 2011.*

The narrow streets of this inviting town climb up the steep banks of the River Slaney. A panoramic view of the town and the river valley can be had from the ruined windmill at the top of Vinegar Hill, a stronghold of the Irish rebels during the insurrection of 1798. The battle is commemorated in the Market Square with a bronze statue of their leader, Father Murphy, and a Wexford pikeman, and at the **Enniscorthy Castle and Wexford County Museum**. This Norman structure dates from the 13th century and was once leased by the poet Edmund Spenser, who is said to have penned some of *The Faerie Queene* here. A still for making the bootleg liquor *poteen* stands out among the myriad items portraying Wexford country life. **St Aidan's**, one of several Wexford churches designed by the English architect Augustus Welby Pugin, and **St Mary's**, with its graceful spire, also enhance the town's skyline. The area around Enniscorthy is known for its traditional pottery; the **Carleys Bridge Pottery**, Ireland's oldest, dates back to the 17th century.

# GOREY

**Gorey Tourist Information Office**
*Main Street, tel: 053 942 1248. Open year-round.*

Gorey dates from the 13th century and was a market town for the plantations of north Wexford. Now its brightly painted shops serve the area's coastal resorts. This is another town that played a key role in the 1798 rebellion; patriots camped on Gorey Hill before their attack on Arklow. Gorey boasts two of Pugin's finest works in Ireland: St Michael's Roman Catholic parish church, which was inspired by Dunbrody Abbey; and the Loreto Convent, erected between 1839 and 1842. Wellan's Church of Ireland parish church (1861) is worth a look for its exquisite stained-glass memorials.

# HOOK PENINSULA

The Hook Peninsula, dotted with small villages and ancient ruins, can be explored along the unclassified roads that criss-cross the headland.

**Tourist Information Office**
Fethard-on-Sea;
tel: 051 397502; www.
thehook-wexford.com

**Duncannon Fort**
€€ Tel: 051 389454;
www.duncannonfort.com.
Open Jun–Sept daily
1000–1730; guided tours
Apr–Sept, ring for
appointment.

**Hook Head Lighthouse**
€€ Tel: 051 397055;
www.thehook-wexford.com.
Open Mar–May & Sept–Oct
daily 1100–1700; Jun–Aug
daily 1000–1730; Nov–Feb
Sat & Sun 1100–1700.

**Fethard-on-Sea** is a quiet little resort. The village's 9th-century St Mogue's Church is still in use and has a Norman-French tombstone in the churchyard. A round tower still stands among the ruins of Fethard Castle. To the south, **Baginbun Head** was the site of an Iron Age promontory fort, a Norman stronghold and a Martello tower. Another castle towers over the pretty fishing harbour at Slade.

Continue south to **Hook Head**, where the black-and-white striped **lighthouse** is possibly the oldest in Europe. It was built in 1172, though the monks of St Dubhann's monastery tended a beacon of burning pitch to guide ships from much earlier times. It is now thoroughly modernised and guided tours are provided. There are invigorating walks along the sea-pounded headland, where there are secluded coves and beaches harbouring seals, seabirds and an abundance of fossils.

The 7-mile (11km) stretch north to Duncannon, along the scenic Hook Head Drive, passes beautiful coves at Booley Strand and Dollar Bay. The lands around Templetown were associated with the Knights Templar and the Knights Hospitallers, who built the medieval church here. **Duncannon** is a colourful resort and fishing port with a fine Blue Flag beach and 18th-century lighthouse. The present **fort** was built in the 16th century as a deterrent to the Spanish Armada.

# IRISH NATIONAL HERITAGE PARK

**Below**
Mesolithic canoe, Irish National Heritage Park

The Irish National Heritage Park presents 9,000 years of Irish history through a series of reconstructed dwellings that illustrate life from Mesolithic to Norman times. A pleasant walk through the woodlands leads you to a campsite of 7000 BC, an early Irish farmstead, a portal tomb, a ring fort (*see page 180*), a monastic settlement and horizontal

**Irish National Heritage Park €€**
*3 miles (5km) from Wexford Town at Ferrycarrig, at the junction of the N11 and N25; tel: 053 912 0733; www.inhp.com. Open daily: May–Aug 0930–1830, Sept–Apr 0930–1730 (last admission 90 minutes before closing).*

mill. The *crannog* – a homestead built on an artificial island – is very atmospheric, surrounded by its reed-filled lake. There is also a Viking boathouse, a round tower and a Norman motte and bailey. The park is extremely well done, with realistic exhibits that are informative without being overwhelming, and can be easily covered in a few hours. Children will enjoy the animals at the Celtic farm; there are optional guided tours, and special activities and demonstrations take place periodically. There is also a restaurant at the visitor centre.

**Right**
Neolithic farmstead, Irish National Heritage Park

## JOHN F KENNEDY ARBORETUM AND HOMESTEAD

**John F Kennedy Park and Arboretum € 7½ miles (12km) south of New Ross; tel: 051 388171. Open daily from 1000.**

**Kennedy Homestead €€ Tel: 051 388264; www.kennedyhomestead.com. Open May, Jun & Sept Mon–Fri 1130–1630; Jul & Aug daily 1000–1700.**

Set on a hill to the south of New Ross, the **John F Kennedy Park and Arboretum** commemorates one of Ireland's most famous descendants, the former president of the United States who was assassinated in 1963. The 623-acre (252-hectare) site contains more than 4,500 species of trees and shrubs from around the world. There are wonderful panoramic views from the hillsides, walking paths and nature trails, picnic areas, a visitor centre and, in summer, pony and trap rides. The **Kennedy Homestead** at nearby Dunganstown, where JFK's great-grandfather lived before emigrating in the 19th century, has been restored and is open to visitors. It contains a collection of memorabilia celebrating the story of five generations of the Kennedy dynasty.

# KILMORE QUAY

This picturesque village is one of the main fishing ports in the southeast. It is known for its old-world thatched cottages, unique to the area, with their thick whitewashed walls and hip and gable ends. The marina is a popular angling and boating centre and several operators here offer boat charters, sailing and fishing trips. **Ballyteigue Burrow** is an outstanding system of sand dunes that stretches for 5½ miles (9km) along the coast from Kilmore Quay to Cullenstown; the western end is a national nature reserve that protects thousands of wild flowers and butterflies. Offshore are the **Saltee Islands**, two large granite outcrops that form one of Ireland's primary bird sanctuaries. They are particularly significant for their colonies of breeding cormorants. Boat trips from Kilmore Quay operate in good weather, or ask the local fishermen at the harbour.

# LADY'S ISLAND

Like so many ancient sites in the British Isles, Lady's Island metamorphosed from a place of pagan worship to a Christian shrine. Its Celtic name translates as 'Meadow of the Women' and it is thought to have been associated with female druids. St Ibar christianised the site and dedicated it to the Blessed Virgin. Her shrine became one of the first places of pilgrimage in Ireland, and remains so today. The lake which surrounds the island dries out considerably in summer, enabling pilgrims to walk round the island from around mid-July to mid-August. Ibar's monastery was destroyed by Cromwell's forces in 1649, but the ruins of a Norman castle still stand. Lady's Island Lake supports Ireland's largest tern colony, the only known site where all five species breed together; they can be seen from pathways around the lake.

# NEW ROSS

**New Ross Tourist Information Office**
*Dunbrody Heritage Centre;*
*tel: 051 421857.*
*Open year-round.*

The River Barrow runs through the heart of this busy port town, one of the oldest in Wexford. Developed by the Normans in the 12th century and later surrounded by walls, there is still a medieval feel along some of the narrow streets. The old warehouses make a pretty façade along the river, while summer cruise boats operate from the quayside. The Tholsel on Quay Street, an old tollhouse, dates from 1749 and is now the town hall. Atop the hill, St Mary's Church was among the largest medieval churches in the country. Built in 1210–20, it is Ireland's earliest, pure Gothic building. It is now a ruin with a 19th-century church attached, but the south transept, lancet windows, medieval gravestones and other features remain.

**Dunbrody Heritage Ship €€**
Tel: 051 425239;
www.dunbrody.com. Open daily: Apr–Sept 0900–1800; Oct–Mar 0900–1700.

At the New Ross docks, the **Dunbrody Heritage Ship** is a full-size replica of the original famine ship which was built in 1845 and carried thousands of emigrants to North America. Costumed actors tell the story of the famine years and re-create the experience of sea travel. President John F Kennedy's ancestors were among those who set sail from this spot. There is also a database of over 2 million passenger records.

# ROSSLARE

George Bernard Shaw was 'lost in dreams' in this picturesque village, which lies 5 miles (8km) north of its more famous harbour. Its beautiful beach – 6 miles (10km) long and golden, with an EU Blue Flag – and the fact that it's one of the sunniest places in the country, makes it a popular resort (www.rosslareholidayresort.ie). It also has a championship golf course (www.rosslaregolf.com). Rosslare Harbour became the area's principal port when Wexford's harbour silted up and could no longer handle the big ships. Today it is a busy terminal, serving car and passenger ferries.

# TINTERN ABBEY

**Tintern Abbey €**
Saltmills, New Ross;
tel: 051 562650. Forest walks and guided tours May–Sept daily 1000–1800.

Around the year 1200, William Marshal, Earl of Pembroke, and his wife were sailing to Wexford from Britain when they were caught in a ferocious storm. He vowed that if he survived the journey he would build an abbey on the spot where he landed in safety. The ship skirted treacherous rocks before beaching itself at this pretty creek, where the earl built the abbey in thanksgiving. It was named after Tintern Abbey in Wales, which sent Cistercian monks to occupy it. It passed into residential use after the dissolution of the monasteries in 1536. Restoration is in progress, but the ruins are accessible.

# WEXFORD TOWN

**Wexford Tourist Information Office**
Crescent Quay;
tel: 053 912 3111; email: info@wexfordtourism.com; www.wexfordtourism.com

**Westgate Heritage Centre €** Spawell Road; tel: 053 914 6506. Call for opening times.

This historic county town was founded by the Vikings, who named it Waesfjord, the 'harbour of the mud flats'. It flourished as a major port until the harbour silted over in the 19th century. Wexford is one of the more atmospheric of Ireland's larger heritage towns, with its Viking street plan, and medieval alleys such as Keyser and Oyster lanes, running between Main Street and the quays. Opposite the tourist information office in the Crescent is a bronze statue of Commodore John Barry, a Wexford native who became a naval hero and father of the American Navy. The **Westgate Heritage Centre**, housed in the only surviving gateway of the old Norman town walls, combines West Gate Tower and some coach houses, and traces

Walking tours of Wexford Town (€€) and **Selskar Abbey** can be arranged at the Westgate Heritage Centre.

**Wexford Wildfowl Reserve** *Tel: 053 912 3406. Open daily 0900–1700.*

The **Wexford Opera Festival**, held annually in October, attracts international artists and opera buffs. This prestigious event stages three lesser-known operas, along with exhibitions and fringe events, over 18 days at the Theatre Royal. *Tel: 053 9122144 (booking office); www.wexfordopera.com*

**Below**
Wexford estuary

the town's history. Nearby are the ruins of **Selskar Abbey**, a 12th-century Augustinian priory where Henry II is said to have done penance for the murder of Thomas à Becket. The square known as the **Bull Ring** recalls the bull-baiting that occurred here in Norman times. On Main Street, the **Cornmarket**, a striking 18th-century market house, is now the Wexford Arts Centre. Other sights of interest include the Franciscan Friary, the Pugin-designed St Peter's College Chapel, and several town churches. Wexford also has a lively nightlife.

The mud flats to the northeast of town, known as The Wexford Slobs, contain the 250-acre (100-hectare) **Wexford Wildfowl Reserve**, wintering ground for thousands of geese and other bird species.

## Accommodation and food in Wexford

**Ferrycarrig Hotel €€–€€€** *Ferrycarrig Bridge; tel: 053 912 0999; fax; 053 912 0982; email: ferrycarrig@ferrycarrighotel.com; www.ferrycarrighotel.ie.* You'd be hard pressed to find a more comfortable place to unwind after a ferry crossing than this smart, modern hotel. Set just outside the bustle of Wexford Town, the sweeping views of the River Slaney estuary bring instant tranquillity. Rooms are large with all amenities, and guests can use the adjoining health and fitness club with its 65ft (20m) pool. The bright, casual Boathouse Bistro with its coloured sailcloth canopies is set alongside the water. The food is excellent, with a good variety of à la carte dishes – and is all reasonably priced. There is also the romantic Reeds Restaurant for more intimate dining, the lively Dry Dock Bar, and a residents' lounge that will make you think you've been whisked away to the Caribbean.

# Suggested tour

**Total distance:** The main route is 93 miles (149km). The detour to Carnsore Point is an additional 17 miles (28km), the detour around the Hook Peninsula can add up to 25 miles (40km), and the detour to Gorey and the northeast coast adds an extra 33 miles (53km).

**Time:** The main tour will take you about half a day, not counting sightseeing stops. The drives to Carnsore Point and the Hook Peninsula could take 1–2½ hours respectively, due to the nature of the small roads. The detour to the northeast coast will take an extra hour. Those with little time should visit Wexford Town, the Irish National Heritage Park and Kilmore Quay.

**Links:** This route adjoins the tours of counties Wicklow (*see page 75*), Waterford (*see page 123*) and Kildare (*see page 100*).

Leave **WEXFORD TOWN ❶** along Custom House Quay, following signs for the N25 south towards Rosslare Harbour. The turn-off to **Johnstown Castle**, 3 miles (5km) outside town, leads to the ancestral seat of the Esmondes, which dates back to Norman times. It now houses a college and research centre, but the gardens, lakes and picnic areas are accessible. The **Irish Agricultural Museum** here contains displays of Irish country furniture, along with regional farming exhibits. Continue south on the N25 and turn left on to the R740 for **ROSSLARE ❷**. The village of **Tagoat** lies roughly halfway between the village and the harbour on the N25. Its Catholic church was designed by Augustus Pugin. Near the village, **Yola Farmstead Folk Park** has displays of traditional crafts, farm buildings, old machinery and animals (*tel: 053 913 2610*). Continue west from Tagoat on the R736, and after about 5 miles (8km) turn left on the R739 for **KILMORE QUAY ❸**.

**Detour:** At Tagoat, follow signs heading south for **LADY'S ISLAND ❹**. Carry on south along the lake to **Carnsore Point**. The dunes of this tranquil strand shelter a variety of wild fauna and flora. The beach is unsafe for swimming, however, so if you fancy a dip, on your way back turn right at the Lobster Pot pub and restaurant for lovely **Carne Beach** to the east. Those with time to spare can meander the back roads to rejoin the main tour at Kilmore Quay. Return to Lady's Island, and take the first left turn after the village, signposted Broadway and Tacumshane. Turn left again for **Tacumshane**. The windmill here, built in 1846, is one of only two complete windmills in Ireland. Tacumshane Lake is an important refuge for migrating birds and attracts some rare species. Carry on with the windmill on your left; veer right at the first crossroads and turn left at the second crossroads towards Tomhaggard. From here follow signs to Kilmore Quay.

Leave Kilmore Quay on the road signposted to Wellington Bridge. Turn left at the junction with the R736. The road passes through

---

**Irish Agricultural Museum €€**
*Johnstown Castle; tel: 053 918 4671; www. irishagrimuseum.ie. Open Apr–Oct Mon–Fri 0900–1700, Sat & Sun 1100–1630; Nov–Mar Mon–Fri 0900–1300, 1400–1700. Castle grounds open year-round.*

**Mummers' the word**

Remnants of medieval life still survive in Wexford. 'Yola' was the dialect spoken by the first Norman settlers to the region, and traces of it are reflected in the local pronunciation of certain words, particularly around Wexford Town. 'Mummers', now very rare in Ireland and largely focused in this county, are entertainers who elect a king and perform a kind of medieval pageantry, with dancing, mime and the beating of wooden swords in rhythm.

## By Hook or by Crooke

As the Anglo-Normans battled for a foothold in the southeast of Ireland in 1170, their leader, Strongbow, vowed he would take Waterford 'by Hook or by Crooke'. He was referring to two heavily fortified defences at Waterford Harbour: the Tower of Hook on the Wexford side and Crooke Castle, across the water near Passage East. He succeeded and, unlike the ruined towers, his words are still in use today.

The **car ferry** (€€) from Ballyhack to Passage East, operated by Passage East Ferry Co, runs *year-round; closed 25 & 26 Dec.* First sailings are *0700 Mon–Sat, 0930 Sun.* Last sailings are *2200 Apr–Sept, 2000 Oct–Mar.* There is continuous service; the crossing time is 10 minutes. Buy tickets on board. *Tel: 051 382480 or 382488; www.passageferry.ie*

**Ballyhack Castle €** *Tel: 051 389468. Open mid-Jun–Aug daily 1000–1800.*

**Above right**
Ballyhack

Duncormick to **Carrick**, where some early Christian stone crosses mark the old church boundaries. Nearby at **Bannow Bay**, site of the first Norman landing in 1169, the village of Bannow has been buried in sand since the 17th century. All that remains is the ruined church, with some interesting tombs and gravestones. Carry on to Wellington Bridge, which spans the River Corrach, and turn left on the R733. About 5 miles (8km) along, at the junction with the R734, turn left for **TINTERN ABBEY** ❺.

**Detour:** From Tintern Abbey, continue south on the R734 to Fethard-on-Sea to explore the **HOOK PENINSULA** ❻. From Duncannon, rejoin the main tour at Arthurstown.

**Arthurstown** and **Ballyhack** are fishing villages perched side by side on Waterford Harbour. The latter is the terminus for the **car ferry** that makes the 10-minute hop to Passage East in Waterford, a great time-saver if you're heading west. Ballyhack's **castle**, built in the 15th and 16th centuries, has been partially restored and houses a heritage centre.

**Wexford Coastal Path** The Wexford Coastal Path (Sli Charman) extends for 138 miles (221km), from Kilmichael Point north of Courtown Harbour on the northeast shores of the county, to Ballyhack in Waterford Harbour. *Tel: 053 9142211.* Details are available from the tourist information office.

From Arthurstown, continue north on the R733 to **DUNBRODY ABBEY 7**. Further on, near the junction with the R734, is the **JOHN F KENNEDY ARBORETUM AND HOMESTEAD 8**. At the junction, turn left and continue north to **NEW ROSS 9**. Head northeast on the N30 to **ENNISCORTHY 10**, then take the N11 back to Wexford. Just outside town at Ferrycarrig is the **IRISH NATIONAL HERITAGE PARK 11**.

**Detour:** To explore Wexford's northeast coast, take the N11 north from Enniscorthy to **GOREY 12**. The popular beach at **COURTOWN 13** is just 4 miles (6km) away. The R742 runs south on a pretty coastal drive passing sandy beaches, pleasant villages such as **Blackwater**, and thatched countryside cottages. **Curracloe Beach**, 7 miles (11km) before Wexford Town, is a magnificent stretch of golden sand nearly 6 miles (10km) long. The World War II Normandy landing was re-created here for the film *Saving Private Ryan*. The Raven Point Peninsula between Curracloe and Wexford Harbour is a nature reserve.

## Also worth exploring

The drive north from New Ross on the R729 takes you through the valley of the River Barrow. At Borris, an attractive town at the junction of three rivers, follow signs for Kildavin and the **Mount Leinster Drive**, which is a scenic route through the Blackstairs Mountains to Mount Leinster, their highest peak. There are more fabulous views of the mountains on the R746 between Bunclody and Kiltealy.

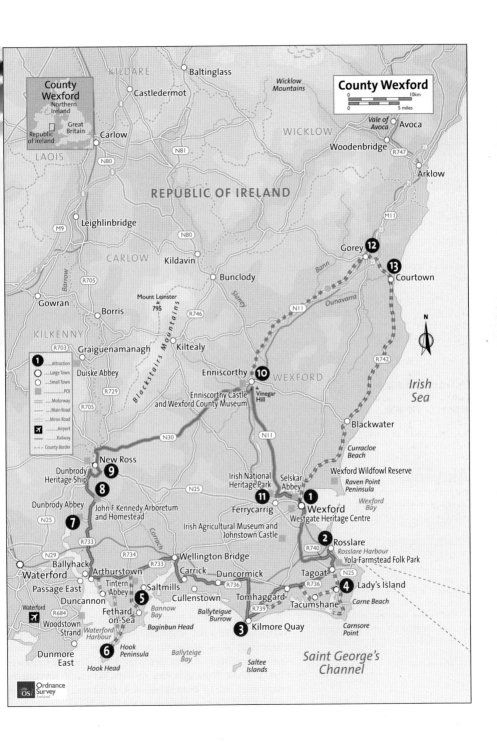

# Waterford Byways

## Ratings

| | |
|---|---|
| Beaches | ●●●●○ |
| Children | ●●●●● |
| Coastal villages/ towns | ●●●●○ |
| History | ●●●●○ |
| Outdoor recreation | ●●●●● |
| Abbeys | ●●●●○ |
| Scenery | ●●●●○ |
| Castles | ●●●○○ |

The city of Waterford, the largest in the southeast, is a fulcrum of Irish history. The Vikings landed here in 852 and established what is possibly the oldest continuous settlement in the country. The Welsh warlord Strongbow married Dermot MacMurrough's daughter Aoife here in 1170, succeeded to the Leinster throne and opened the door to English dominion. More historic towns lie inland, such as Lismore, or Cahir and Carrick-on-Suir in County Tipperary, each with a splendid castle, nestled either side of the mountains.

County Waterford's Atlantic coastline runs between two river estuaries: the Blackwater to the west and the Barrow to the east. It is marked by pleasant resort towns and picturesque fishing villages, impressive cliffs and sheltered coves, and magnificent stretches of beach at Tramore, Clonea and Ardmore, whose round tower marks one of Europe's earliest Christian sites. The county's northern border is framed by the Comeragh and Knockmealdown mountain ranges, which form a magical backdrop to its many scenic byways.

## ARDMORE

### Magic rock

Near the shore at Ardmore stands a large glacial boulder. Local legend claims it was borne across the sea from Rome in the wake of St Declan's ship, carrying a bell which the holy man had forgotten. Supposedly, it also has healing powers, and those who manage to crawl underneath it are said to be cured of the pains of rheumatism.

The resort village of Ardmore, with its magnificent golden beach, is also one of the oldest religious sites in Europe. St Declan brought Christianity to this region in 416, well before the arrival of his famous successor, St Patrick. The ruins of the monastery he founded are set on the hillside, overlooking the beach. Most of the buildings date from the 12th century. The Romanesque cathedral has some outstanding carvings of biblical scenes on the exterior of the west wall. They depict the Adoration of the Magi, the Judgement of King Solomon, and the Archangel Michael weighing the souls of the dead. In the chancel are two notched ogham stones (see page 146). The round tower beside the cathedral is one of Ireland's finest specimens, tapering up to a height of 95ft (29m). There is a spectacular cliff walk beyond the village.

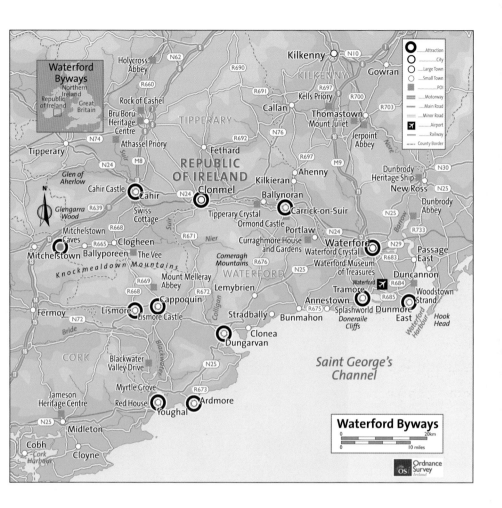

# CAHIR

**Cahir Castle €**
Tel: 052 744 1011.
Open daily: mid-Mar–mid-Jun
& Sept–mid-Oct 0930–
1730; mid-Jun–Aug 0930–
1830; mid-Oct–mid-Mar
0930–1630.

**Cahir Castle,** hulking on its island in the River Suir, dominates this attractive town. It was built by the powerful Butler family in the 15th century, on the site of an earlier Norman fortress. The highlights of the castle, which was known as the 'bulwark of Munster' in the 16th century, are its defensive features, including the curtain wall, the working portcullis and the holes for pouring boiling oil upon the enemy. In 1650, however, the threat of Cromwell's cannon proved too great and the garrison surrendered, leaving this splendid fortress intact. The Great Hall and other rooms have been restored and the interior is decorated with period furnishings.

**ⓘ Cahir Tourist
    Information Office**
*Castle car park; tel: 052 744
1453. Open Apr–Oct.*

**ⓗ Swiss Cottage €**
    *Tel: 052 744 1144.
Open Apr–Oct daily
1000–1800.*

The town of Cahir dates mainly from the 18th century; some of its best architecture can be seen in the Mall opposite the castle and in the town square. On the outskirts of town – and easily reached by a half-hour walk along the river – is the delightful **Swiss Cottage**, designed by John Nash in the early 19th century as an idyllic thatch-roofed retreat for Lord Cahir. Nash also designed St Paul's Church (1817), to the east of the square.

**Right**
Thatcher at work

# CAPPOQUIN

**Mount Melleray Abbey €**
Tel: 058 54404; www.mountmellerayabbey.org. Open daily 0900–1800.

**Glenshelane River Walk** Cappoquin. Over 6 miles (10km) of this tranquil walk feature pockets of original oak and Norway spruce. The bluebells are a stunning sight in spring.

The village of Cappoquin, with its handsome grey stone houses, sits at the top of the tidal estuary formed by the River Blackwater. Nestled in the foothills of the Knockmealdown Mountains, its peaceful wooded surroundings are a favourite with trout fishermen. **Mount Melleray Abbey**, founded by the Cistercians in 1832, lies 4 miles (6.5km) to the north on the R669. This is an active religious community, and visitors are welcome. There are several ogham stones on the grounds, and a statue of the Blessed Virgin in Melleray Grotto, at the foot of the hill on the abbey road.

## Accommodation and food in Cappoquin

**Richmond Country House and Restaurant €€** Tel: 058 54278, fax: 058 54988; email: info@richmondhouse.net; www.richmondhouse.net. This beautiful Georgian house, built in 1704, is set in wooded parkland in the Blackwater Valley. The Deevy family adds touches of home comfort to the gracious surroundings, such as tea and scones before the open log fire in the drawing room or in the cheery conservatory overlooking the garden. The large bedrooms are furnished with lovely antiques in country-house style. The restaurant is outstanding, and open to non-residents (booking is recommended). The four-course *table d'hôte* menu is superbly prepared from local ingredients – much of the fruit, vegetables and herbs are grown on the premises – and imaginatively presented. For those who have trouble deciding between the delicious starters and entrées, the last choice can be simple: a tasting plate of Richmond desserts! For an encore, handmade chocolates are served with the coffee.

# CARRICK-ON-SUIR

**Ormond Castle €€** Tel: 051 640787. Open Apr–early Oct daily 1000–1800.

**Tipperary Crystal** Ballynoran; tel: 051 641188. Visitor centre open daily year-round.

This old market town enjoys a fine setting alongside a beautiful stretch of the River Suir. Its medieval bridge and winding streets survive, though little remains of the 13th-century friary. The Tholsel (town hall) on Main Street houses an excellent **heritage centre**. The town's highlight is **Ormond Castle**, an Elizabethan mansion and the only one of its kind in Ireland. 'Black Tom' Butler, 10th Earl of Ormonde, built the graceful gabled manor house in 1565, adjoining the battlemented 15th-century keep of his ancestors. He was a supporter and cousin of Queen Elizabeth I and built the house in hopes of a royal visit, which never materialised. The interior is outstanding for its stucco decorations, particularly the Long Gallery with its heraldic ceiling crests and medallions, and elaborately carved fireplaces.

# CLONMEL

**ⓘ Clonmel Tourist Information Office**
*Town centre; tel: 052 612 2960. Open year-round.*

Clonmel, the county seat of Tipperary and one of Ireland's largest inland towns, occupies a pretty position beneath the Comeragh Mountains on the River Suir. The West Gate at the start of O'Connell Street was built in 1831 on the site of its medieval predecessor. The old mills form a pleasing façade along the quays. Nearby is the Franciscan Friary, with interesting tombs and monuments inside. The Court House, designed by Sir Richard Morrison, and St Mary's Protestant Church, partly enclosed by the old town walls, are also noteworthy. Clonmel is also a famous centre for greyhound races.

The towpath that runs along the river for 12 miles (19km) between Clonmel and Carrick-on-Suir makes for a scenic day's walk.

# DUNGARVAN

**ⓘ Dungarvan Tourist Office** *Grattan Square; tel: 058 41741; fax: 058 45020. Open all year. There are guided walking tours (€€) Jun–Sept.*

Dungarvan is a busy market town, set at the mouth of the River Colligan. St Garvan founded a monastery here in the 7th century, from which the town takes its name. Alongside the river are remnants of 12th-century Dungarvan Castle. The Augustinian priory on the outskirts of town, founded a century later, is better preserved. Dungarvan is a major centre for sea angling, and boat hire can be arranged at the tourist office. The town is also known for its traditional music, lying as it does at the top of An Rinn (The Ring), a Gaeltacht area (*see page 201*) where the Irish language and culture hold sway. It is also a good base for walking – there are walks detailed in the booklet *Come Walking Southern Style* available from the tourist office. The beautiful sandy beach at Clonea is less than 2 miles (3km) away.

# DUNMORE EAST

The picturesque fishing village of Dunmore East has become a favourite regional resort. The steep hills rising up from the harbour have a sprinkling of attractive thatched cottages, many of which are holiday homes. The harbour is busy with pleasure boats and fishing vessels. There are safe sandy beaches nearby, while the coastline in either direction is marked by red sandstone cliffs, coves and headlands that beckon with scenic paths and gorgeous views.

# LISMORE

This delightful small town on the River Blackwater has more to repay a visit than first meets the eye. Its name means 'great fort' in Irish, and

**Lismore Castle Gardens €€**
Tel: 058 54424;
www.lismorecastle.com.
Open mid-Mar–Sept daily
1100–1645.

**Lismore Heritage Centre €€**
Tel: 058 54975;
www.discoverlismore.com.
Open Nov–Apr Mon–Fri
0930–1730; May–Oct
Mon–Fri 0930–1730, Sat
1000–1730, Sun
1200–1730.

**Right**
Ancient statuary

the grey stone bulk of **Lismore Castle** towers over the village from its lofty perch. The castle, erected by King John in 1185, was rebuilt in the 19th century by the 6th Duke of Devonshire, and it remains the family's Irish home. Only the gardens are open to the public, but these lush grounds are well worth a visit, especially in late spring when the magnolias and camellias are blooming.

Lismore's luminous history is told in the **Heritage Centre** in the courthouse. From the 7th to 12th centuries it was a centre of religion and learning, renowned throughout Europe. The monastic city was destroyed by the Normans, but in 1814, two treasures – the Lismore Crozier, now in the National Museum in Dublin, and the *Book of Lismore*, a 15th-century manuscript – were discovered hidden in the castle. Not to be missed is **St Carthach's Cathedral**, approached along a path lined with ancient trees. It was built in the 17th century, incorporating parts of an earlier church. The austere nave has a fine vaulted ceiling, while that of the chancel sports brightly coloured rosettes. Two stained-glass windows in the south transept are by the Pre-Raphaelite artist, Sir Edward Burne-Jones.

# MITCHELSTOWN CAVES

**Mitchelstown Caves €€** Between Cahir and Mitchelstown.
Tel: 052 746 7246; www.mitchelstowncave.com. Open daily: Apr–Sept 1000–1730; Oct–Mar from 1000, closing times vary.

The Mitchelstown Caves are an outstanding system of limestone caverns, often used by Irish rebels as a hiding place in the 16th century. Their majesty and grandeur are reflected in such appellations as the Altar Cave or The Lords and The Commons, named after the Houses of Parliament. They are full of impressive stalactites, stalagmites, columns and other magical formations, and are home to a rare species of spider. The subterranean wonders can only be explored on a guided tour, which is entertaining as well as informative.

Nearby **Mitchelstown** was laid out in the 18th century with wide streets and grand squares. Kingston Square is of interest for its central chapel and former almshouses on the north side, which were designed by John Morrison. The early feminist Mary Wollstonecraft worked as a governess here for Lady Kingsborough in 1786.

# TRAMORE

**ⓘ Tramore Tourist Information Office**
*Railway Square; tel: 051 381572. Open Jun–Aug.*

**ⓗ Splashworld €€**
*Tel: 051 390176; www.splashworld.ie. Open daily 1000–2200 in summer; phone for winter timetable.*

The ancient Celts must have recognised the town's tourism potential when they named it *Tra Mor* ('the Great Beach'). Tramore has been a seaside getaway since Georgian times, and is now Ireland's biggest coastal resort. Its fine sandy beach, 3 miles (5km) long, attracts more Irish families than foreign tourists. A huge fun park sprawls along the promenade, with amusements such as Celtworld, a miniature railway and a boating lake. **Splashworld**, an indoor water park, is also a hit with children. At the west end of the beach a coastal path leads to the steep Doneraile Cliffs.

# WATERFORD

**ⓘ Waterford Tourist Information Office**
*The Granary, Merchants Quay; tel: 051 875823; fax: 051 876720. Open year-round.*

**ⓗ Waterford Museum of Treasures €€**
*The Granary; tel: 051 304500. Open Jun–Aug Mon–Sat 0900–1800, Sun 1100–1800; Sept–May Mon–Sat 1000–1700, Sun 1100–1700.*

**Waterford Crystal Visitor Centre**
*Tel: 051 31700; www. waterfordvisitorcentre.com. Open Jun–Sept Mon–Sat 0900–1800, Sun 1030–1800, factory tours Mon–Sat 0900–1615, Sun 1030–1615; phone for winter hours.*

**ⓠ** Entertaining walking tours (€€) of Waterford leave from the Waterford Museum of Treasures. Details from the Tourist Office.

Set alongside the River Suir (pronounced 'Sure'), Waterford is a busy, vibrant city with traces of its great heritage woven around its waterfront and modern central shopping district. The attractive quays with their central Victorian clock tower run for nearly a mile (1.6km) along the river. A wide range of rare and beautiful artefacts is brilliantly displayed at the **Waterford Museum of Treasures**. At the east end of the quays is the bulky **Reginald's Tower**, with walls 10ft (3m) thick (*tel: 051 304220, open daily*); it was used as a residence by Anglo-Norman kings. Their leader Strongbow had captured the city in 1170 and succeeded to the throne.

Some of the city's finest Georgian architecture can be seen along The Mall, including town houses, the City Hall and the adjacent Bishop's Palace. The neoclassical **Christ Church Cathedral**, with its Corinthian colonnade, was built in the 1770s by the local architect John Roberts. Inside, a gruesome effigy of a rotting corpse marks the tomb of James Rice. Roberts also designed **Holy Trinity**, the city's Catholic cathedral, with a more subdued façade but highly ornate interior. It's worth seeking out the remnants of Waterford's **city walls**, some of the best preserved in Ireland. The finest section can be found near the watchtower on Castle Street.

The first Waterford glasshouse began producing its exquisite patterned glassware in 1783. In the town centre, the **Waterford Crystal** factory, the largest of its kind in the world with an extensive visitor centre, is a popular attraction. Guided tours take visitors through the production area to watch the craftsmen at work.

# YOUGHAL

This charming heritage town grew up at the wide mouth of the River Blackwater. Its name, pronounced 'Yawl', comes from the Yew

🅷 **Youghal Tourist**
**Office** *Market Square;*
*tel: 024 92447. Heritage*
*Centre (€) open May–Sept*
*daily Oct–Apr weekdays.*
*Historical walking tours at*
*1100 daily Jul–Aug, other*
*times by appointment.*

**Right**
The Clock Gate, Youghal

woodlands that once covered the area. Occupied from Viking times, under the English it became a 'closed borough' (*see page 100*), with the Irish population living outside the town walls. The Clock Gate straddles the main street of the brightly painted old town. The Watergate connects the town to the picturesque quayside. Among the sights of interest are **Myrtle Grove**, a Tudor manor house once lived in by Sir Walter Raleigh; **St Mary's Collegiate Church**, which dates from the 11th century; the Dutch-style **Red House**; medieval almshouses, priory ruins and remnants of the old town walls. With its long, sandy Blue Flag beach and funfair, Youghal is a popular seaside resort.

## Suggested tour

**Total distance:** The main route is 137 miles (221km). The detour to Ardmore is 12 miles (19km). The detour to Mitchelstown is 28 miles (45km).

**A whale of a time**

Youghal's Market Square may look vaguely familiar to film buffs. It was the location for the director John Huston's production of *Moby Dick*. The film crew's watering hole was Moby Dick's Pub, where you can still enjoy a brew. Gregory Peck, never out of character in his role as Captain Ahab, signed the guestbook 'Death to Moby Dick'.

**Time:** You will need a full day's driving time to complete the main route, as the narrow scenic roads along the coast and through the Blackwater Valley require slower speeds. If you want to explore several of the towns and sights, two days are recommended. The detour to Ardmore will add only a few minutes' driving time to your journey; the detour to Mitchelstown about half an hour – plus exploring time. Those with little time should visit Waterford City, Youghal and Lismore.

**Links:** This route adjoins the tours of County Wexford (*see page 112*), Kilkenny (*see page 98*) and the Midlands (*see page 88*).

Leave **WATERFORD ❶** on the R683, which leads to **Passage East** on the Waterford Harbour, where there is a car ferry crossing to Ballyhack in County Wexford (*see page 113*). After about 2½ miles (4km) turn right

The car ferry (€€) from Passage East to Ballyhack operates year-round; *closed 25 and 26 Dec.* First sailings are *0700 Mon–Sat, 0930 Sun.* Last sailings are *2200 Apr–Sept, 2000 Oct–Mar.* There is continuous service and the crossing time is 10 minutes. Buy tickets on board. *Tel: 051 382480 or 382488; www.passageferry.ie*

South East Tourism publishes guides to Walking & Cycling, Equestrian Activity, Angling and Golfing in Waterford, Wexford, Kilkenny, Carlow and Tipperary.

**The Metal Man**

The *Metal Man* sculpture, near the Doneraile Cliffs at Tramore, stands atop a tower at Great Newtown Head. Though it is intended as a landmark for sailors, it was erected on the site of an ancient stone used in fertility rites. It is said that if a woman hops around the pillar three times on one foot, she will be married within the year. The custom is still jokingly observed.

on to the R684 for **DUNMORE EAST ❷**, 7½ miles (12km) further on. Along the way you'll pass a turn-off for **Woodstown Strand**, a beautiful sandy beach along the harbour. From Dunmore East, the R684/R685 heads inland to the busy resort of **TRAMORE ❸**, 10 miles (16km) away.

Leave Tramore on the R675, following signs for 'Newtown' and the 'Dungarvan Coast Road'. It wends through some pretty pastoral scenery before reaching the coast at **Annestown**, 7 miles (11km) west. This smaller resort is backed by cliffs and the ruins of Dunhill Castle. It also has a good sandy beach, as does **Bunmahon**, 5 miles (8km) beyond. The latter is a fishing village set above the sea on impressive cliffs. Further on are more splendid beaches at **Stradbally** and **Clonea**, just outside **DUNGARVAN ❹**. Then take the Cork Road, N25, southwest to Youghal, just over the Cork county boundary.

**Detour:** About 7 miles (11km) from the edge of Dungarvan, turn left on to the R673 to **ARDMORE ❺**. The road continues on to rejoin the N25 outside Youghal.

As you enter **YOUGHAL ❻**, you cross a large bridge over the wide mouth of the River Blackwater. Just past the bridge, note the turn-off to the right for the **Blackwater Valley Drive**. After exploring the town, return and take this turning. This is a scenic drive along a narrow road, winding first past the tall wooded banks of the broad river, then opening out on to views across the fertile valley to the distant mountains before disappearing again into thick forests. It leads to **CAPPOQUIN ❼**, 20 miles (32km) away. **LISMORE ❽** is 3½ miles (6km) to the west on the N72.

From Lismore, the R668 towards Clogheen leads up over the lovely Knockmealdown Mountains. The landscape changes from woodland to pasture to windy moorland until, at the scenic viewpoint known as 'The Vee', an impressive vista of the bright green plains of Tipperary below is revealed. **Clogheen** is 4 miles (7km) on, at the foot of the mountains.

**Detour:** West of Clogheen on the R665 is the town of **Ballyporeen**, where Ronald Reagan's great-grandfather was baptised in the village church. You can have a drink in the pub named after the former president. The **MITCHELSTOWN CAVES ❾**, 4 miles (6km) from here, lie off the R639 and are well signposted. Take the R639 northeast to rejoin the main route at Cahir.

As you leave Clogheen, keep your eyes peeled for the small road (with its small signpost) veering off to the left for **CAHIR ❿**, 7½ miles (12km) away. This is still the R668, but it is easy to miss as the main road appears to go straight on. From Cahir, the N24, a good primary road, has pretty views of the round-topped Knockmealdown Mountains as it heads east for 8 miles (13km) to **CLONMEL ⓫**. It carries on for 12 miles (20km) through the valley of the River Suir to **CARRICK-ON-SUIR ⓬**, and from there back to Waterford.

## Also worth exploring

The R671 and R672, north of the N72 from Dungarvan, run through the **Nier Valley**, a scenic landscape of woodlands and tumbling streams between the Comeragh and Knockmealdown mountains. Another beautiful drive through the mountains is on the R676 via the village of **Lemybrien**. Northwest of Cahir, the **Glen of Aherlow** is a verdant river valley backed by the Galtee Mountains. **Glengarra Wood**, southwest of Cahir off the R639, is a short but charming nature trail lined with exotic plants and trees. From Carrick-on-Suir, the R697 leads north to some outstanding carved high crosses at **Ahenny** and **Kilkieran**. At Portlaw, northwest of Waterford, is **Curraghmore House and Gardens**.

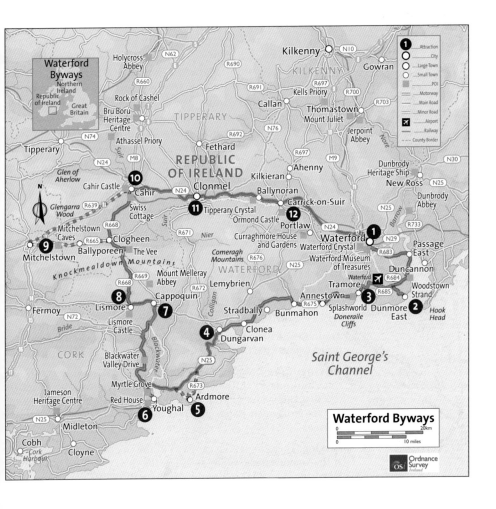

# Cork City

203-216-7094

## Ratings

| | |
|---|---|
| Art | ●●●●● |
| Cathedrals/churches | ●●●●● |
| Walking | ●●●●● |
| Architecture | ●●●●○ |
| History | ●●●●○ |
| Art and craft | ●●●○○ |
| Food and drink | ●●●○○ |
| Shopping | ●●●○○ |

Cork is the Republic of Ireland's second-largest city. Its Irish name, *Corcaigh*, means 'marshy place', a reference to the estuary of the River Lee, where it grew up on islands in the 6th century. Its heart lies on an island still, formed by two channels of the river, and the many bridges give it a continental character. The city prospered from the butter trade in the 17th and 18th centuries, when many of the attractive Georgian buildings with their bowfront windows were built. Until around 1800, when the river was dammed, Patrick Street, the Grand Parade and other main streets were still under water. Cork's independent-minded citizenry gave only nominal obedience to the English crown. A hotbed of the nationalist Fenian movement, 'Rebel Cork' was burned in the War of Independence, 1919–21, but significant restoration has created a bright and attractive city with a lively nightlife and an acclaimed arts scene.

## Getting there and getting around

**ℹ Cork Tourist Information Office**
*Grand Parade;*
*tel: 021 425 5100;*
*fax: 021 425 5199; email:*
*corkkerryinfo@failteireland.*
*ie; www.discoverireland.ie/*
*cork. Open year-round.*

**Airport:** Cork International Airport, *tel: 021 431 3131, www.corkairport.com*, is 4 miles (6km) south of the city.

**Train:** Kent Rail Station, *tel: 021 455 7277*, is on the north side of the river, opposite the Custom House.

**Driving:** Cork's one-way traffic system crosses and recrosses the river and quays, and can be confusing when you drive here for the first time, so arm yourself with a good map before you arrive. Try to avoid rush hours, when you're likely to experience traffic jams.

**Parking:** There are several car parks in the city centre, including those at the Grand Parade, South Mall, Lavitt's Quay near the Opera House, Merchant's Quay and across the river at St Patrick's Quay.

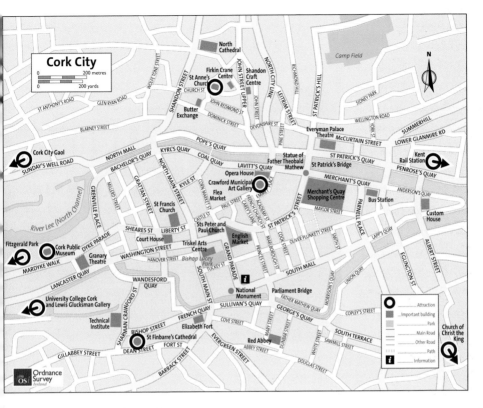

## Sights

**Crawford Municipal Art Gallery** *Emmet Place; tel: 021 490 7855; www.crawfordartgallery.ie. Open Mon–Sat 1000–1700 (Thur till 2000). Closed Sun.*

### Crawford Municipal Art Gallery

The building itself is one of Cork's finest. Its handsome façade of red brick dressed with limestone was built in 1724, and it served as the Custom House until 1832, when Emmet Place was still the King's Dock. It then became a drawing academy and was converted into a gallery for Ireland's finest public art collection outside Dublin. Jack B Yeats, James Barry and Nathaniel Grogan are among the important Irish painters represented. There is also a room dedicated to contemporary Irish artists. The stained-glass rooms on the second floor contain pieces by Harry Clarke, regarded as the country's finest stained-glass craftsman of his time. Special exhibitions are also held here. The gallery café, run by the acclaimed Ballymaloe cookery school, is superb.

### Fitzgerald Park

Fitzgerald Park is bordered to the north by the River Lee and to the south by the Mardyke, a riverside walk. Housed in a Georgian

**ⓘ Cork Public
Museum** Tel: 021
427 0679; email:
museum@corkcity.ie.
Open Mon–Fri 1100–1300,
1415–1700, Sat 1100–
1300, 1415–1600; also
Apr–Sept Sun 1500–1700.

**St Anne's Church €€**
Church Street; www.
shandonbells.org. Open Jun–
Sept Sat 1000–1700, Sun
1130–1630; Mar–May &
Oct Mon–Sat 1000–1600,
Sun 1130–1530; Nov–Feb
Mon–Sat 1000–1500.

**St Finbarre's Cathedral**
€ Bishop Street; tel: 021
496 3387; http://stfinbarres.
wordpress.com. Open Apr–
Nov Mon–Sat 0930–1730,
Sun 1230–1700; Nov–Apr
Mon–Sat 1000–1245, Sun
1400–1700.

mansion in the centre of the park is the **Cork Public Museum**, which
traces the social and political history of the town, including the
conflicts of the 20th century. There are some good archaeological
exhibits dating back to 3000 BC, and an important collection of
18th-century silver.

### St Anne's Church
Visitors climb up the steep north bank to St Anne's (1722) to see the
**Bells of Shandon**, made famous in a popular 19th-century tune. The
eight bells were cast in Gloucester in 1750. You can climb the 120ft
(36m) tower and ring them, playing a tune with the help of 'music'
cards. The weathervane on top of the steeple is shaped like a salmon,
the Celtic symbol of knowledge. The clock face is known to locals as
'the four-faced liar' because each face showed slightly different times
until it was repaired in 1986.

### St Finbarre's Cathedral
This triple-spired French Gothic cathedral, rich in sculptural
decoration, was designed by William Burges and completed in 1878. It
was built on the site where St Finbarre, Cork's founder and patron
saint, established a monastery in the 7th century. Among its
highlights are the west front, mosaic pavements, Bishop's Throne and
the beautiful rose window. There is also a 3,000-pipe organ.

**Above**
River Lee

**University College Cork €** *Western Road; tel: 021 490 3000. Honan Chapel open Mon–Fri 0800–2000, Sat 1000–1800. The chapel may be closed during college holiday periods and for weddings; check with the tourist office.*

The **Lewis Glucksman Gallery** *University College Cork, main entrance; tel: 021 490 1844; www.glucksman.org. Open Tue–Sat 1000–1700, Sun 1400–1700. This cultural and education centre promotes the visual arts through a variety of exhibitions, workshops, films and lectures. It has won many architectural awards, including Best Public Building in Ireland in 2005.*

## University College Cork

Founded in 1845 as Queen's College, the university was designed by Sir Thomas Deane in the style of a typical Oxford college and has an attractive riverside quadrangle. The **Honan Chapel**, built in 1915, was modelled on Cormac's Chapel at the Rock of Cashel. It contains some exquisite stained-glass windows, many by Harry Clarke, as well as fine mosaic, enamelwork and other elaborate decoration. The college also has a significant collection of ogham stones (*see page 146*) on display.

## Suggested walk

**Time:** You can easily cover the main route in 2 hours, though an extra hour for lingering will not go amiss. The walk to Fitzgerald Park takes about 15 minutes each way. The walk to the Custom House will add an extra 20 minutes to the journey.

**Links:** The Cork environs hold many attractions for pleasant day trips (*see page 134*).

Start at the tourist information office and walk up the Grand Parade. Over the road is **Bishop Lucey Park ❶**, a peaceful place with sculptures by Cork artists. Remnants of the old city walls were found during its excavation. Just beyond is the **Triskel Arts Centre ❷**, a venue for theatre, film, and art and crafts exhibitions. The **English Market ❸**, situated between the Grand Parade and St Patrick Street, is a covered food market dating from the early 17th century. Look for the ornate cast-iron fountain as you wander through. Turn left at Washington Street to the **Court House ❹**, built in 1835 with a Corinthian portico.

**Detour:** Continue west along Washington Street, which becomes Lancaster Quay. Ahead on the left is **UNIVERSITY COLLEGE CORK ❺**. Cross over the road and continue along Lancaster Quay, before turning north into **FITZGERALD PARK ❻**. Return to the Court House to continue the main tour.

Behind the Court House on Liberty Street, **St Francis Church ❼** is worth a visit to see its beautiful interior, with a sparkling mosaic reredos, domed ceiling, ornate archways and marble pillars. At the end of the street, continue straight on along Castle and Paul streets. Off to the left is the open-air **flea market** on Corn Market Street. **Paul Street** is the heart of the old French Quarter, where Huguenots sought refuge from religious persecution. The piazza is a lively spot for buskers and street theatre, while the little side lanes, notably Carey's Lane and French Church Street, have interesting shops, bookshops and cafés. Another leads to **Sts Peter and Paul Church ❽**, a dark Gothic Revival edifice of 1866, replete with woodcarving. Paul Street leads into Emmet Place, where some beautiful old buildings have been spruced up with characterful pubs and shopfronts. Here, too, is the CRAWFORD MUNICIPAL ART GALLERY ❾. Opposite is the **Opera House ❿**; the ornate original was destroyed by fire but it has recently been given a new façade.

Cross over the bridge and continue straight ahead up the hill along John Street, turning left on John Redmond Street to reach the famous Shandon bells at **ST ANNE'S CHURCH ⓫**. Nearby are the **Firkin Crane Centre ⓬**, a small venue for the performing arts, and the **Shandon Craft Centre ⓭**, where you can watch artists at work. Both are part of the former Butter Exchange, where butter was graded and exported from 1770 to 1924. Return to the quay and turn left, following the river east to **St Patrick's Bridge ⓮**. Cross back to the city centre, where you'll see one of Cork's best-known landmarks, the **Statue of Father Theobald Mathew ⓯** (1790–1856), the 'Apostle of Temperance'. His drive against the demon drink became a national cause, but his success in keeping thousands sober hit a standstill in the misery of the famine years.

**Detour:** Continue east along Merchant's Quay, where tall ships used to load their cargoes of butter before heading downstream to the harbour. It leads past the bus station to the **Custom House ⓰** at the tip of the island where the river channels join. Its classical façade was designed by William Hargrave in 1818 and displays the Cork coat of arms. Return along Lapp's Quay to rejoin the main tour in the South Mall.

From the statue, walk into the heart of the city along **St Patrick's Street ⓱**, which curves gracefully down to the Grand Parade. Cork's main thoroughfare was the scene of heavy fighting during the War of Independence, but the Georgian buildings have been beautifully restored, their stately bowed windows overlooking the bustle of high-street shoppers. Off to the left, several side streets with charming shopfronts beckon to be explored. The little statue of the Echo Boy stands at the entrance to the pedestrianised **Cook Street ⓲**. Follow this down to the **South Mall ⓳**. Along the South Mall are large street-level gateways with steps above them leading to the main door. These are former boathouses, where merchants entered their warehouse by water. Turn left and, when you reach Parliament Bridge, cross over to the south side of the river. Turn right and continue west along Sullivan's Quay and French Quay, passing the ivy-laden **Elizabeth Fort ⓴**, built in the 16th century and later a prison. Just beyond is **ST FINBARRE'S CATHEDRAL ㉑**. From here, follow Sharman Crawford Street and Wandesford Quay to cross back over the river to the Court House.

## Also worth exploring

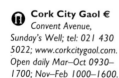

**Cork City Gaol €**
Convent Avenue, Sunday's Well; tel: 021 430 5022; www.corkcitygaol.com. Open daily Mar–Oct 0930–1700; Nov–Feb 1000–1600.

The restored **Cork City Gaol**, west of the town centre, re-creates prison life in the 19th and 20th centuries. There is also a museum of radio memorabilia. Cork has many beautiful churches, including **St Mary's Cathedral**, north of Shandon, and **St Mary's Dominican**

Church with its Ionic columns and miraculous statue. The **Church of Christ the King** in Turners Cross, to the south of the city centre, was designed by Barry Byrne, a Chicago architect and student of Frank Lloyd Wright. The **Red Abbey**, a remnant of an Augustinian abbey, is Cork's oldest building.

## Shopping

The major high-street chains can be found along **St Patrick's Street**. Debenham's is the largest store in town, while Brown Thomas, next door, carries more upmarket fashions. At the top of the street, near the bridge, is a huge shopping complex at **Merchant's Quay**. The **English Market**, off Princes Street and the Grand Parade, sells a wonderful variety of foodstuffs, from Irish farm cheeses, smoked salmon, fruit and veg to more acquired-taste specialities such as tripe and black pudding. The shops in the old **French Quarter** around Paul Street are noted for modern Irish crafts and design, and you'll also find

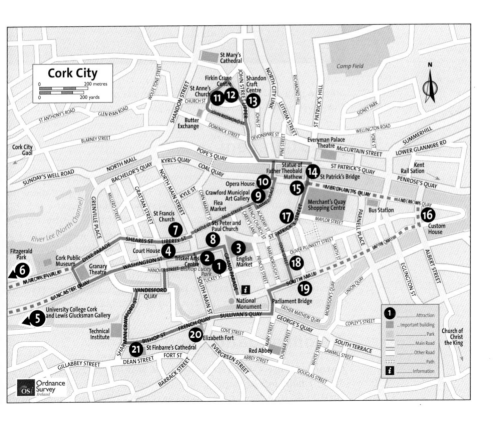

antique shops in Paul's Lane. Bargain hunters may enjoy the open-air **flea market** on Corn Market Street, also called Coal Quay.

## Entertainment

Cork has a reputation for a creative and nonconformist approach to the arts. Cork **Opera House** (*tel: 021 427 0022*) is the major venue for touring performers and shows. The **Everyman Palace Theatre** (*tel: 021 450 1673*) with its Victorian interior, the **Firkin Crane Centre** and the **Cork Arts Theatre** are smaller venues with a range of productions. The **Cork International Choral Festival**, held in City Hall in April/May, welcomes choirs and dance teams from around the world. The **Cork Folk Festival** takes place in September to October. In October, the great faces of jazz appear at the **Cork Jazz Festival**. The **Cork Film Festival**, Ireland's oldest cinematic event, is held in November.

## Accommodation and food

**Garnish House** €–€€ *Western Road; tel: 021 427 5111; fax: 021 427 3872; email: info@garnish.ie; www.garnish.ie.* This lovely Victorian guesthouse is located across from University College, a 5-minute walk from the town centre. Mrs Lucey's splendid hospitality begins with tea and a tray of scrumptious home-made cakes and scones on arrival. Rooms are comfortable and nicely decorated, with all amenities and thoughtful touches such as fresh fruit; some have whirlpools. Enjoy the flowers in the public areas. Tip: have a light dinner, the better to enjoy the fabulous breakfast that awaits you in the morning. For starters, try the house speciality of porridge oats topped with Bailey's Irish Cream. Pancakes, French toast, eggs *en cocotte* and vegetarian rissoles are a few of the alternatives to a full Irish breakfast. The warm welcome and great location make this a wonderful base for touring the area. Off-street parking available.

**Right**
St Finbarre's Cathedral

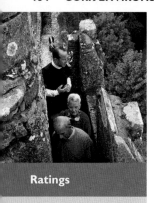

# Cork environs

## Ratings

| | |
|---|---|
| Castles | ●●●●● |
| Coastal towns/villages | ●●●●● |
| Restaurants | ●●●●● |
| Scenery | ●●●●● |
| Cathedrals/churches | ●●●●○ |
| History | ●●●●○ |
| National parks | ●●●●○ |
| Beaches | ●●●○○ |

While the sights of Cork can easily be seen in a day, its environs hold many options for pleasant day trips. You can be at Blarney Castle, where millions come to kiss the Blarney Stone, within a quarter of an hour. To the west, the River Lee runs through quintessential Irish countryside – lush woodland and green pastures with dairy cows grazing on the riverbank. The river's source at Gougane Barra is surrounded by the beautiful backdrop of the country's first forest park.

The south Cork coast is delightful, with its brightly painted waterside villages, stone circles and cliff-cornered headlands to explore. Kinsale, only 16 miles (26km) from Cork but a world apart, is one of Ireland's loveliest towns and a yachting and gourmet capital. To the east, at Cork Harbour, the historic port of Cobh, where millions of emigrants departed for new lands, is guarded by its striking cathedral.

## BLARNEY CASTLE

**Blarney Castle €€**
Tel: 021 438 5252;
www.blarneycastle.ie. Open
Mon–Sat: May & Sept
Mon–Sat 0900–1830;
Jun–Aug 0900–1900;
Oct–Apr 0900–sunset; Sun
0900–1730 summer,
0900–sunset winter.

Whether or not you want to kiss the Blarney Stone and risk catching the gift of the gab, don't miss Blarney Castle. It rises up amid wooded parkland, a glorious setting that doesn't fail to delight, in spite of the number of tourists who flock to one of Ireland's most popular castles. Built by Cormac MacCarthy in the 15th century, the fortress is a well-preserved ruin; you can let your imagination loose as you climb the spiral stone stairs through the rooms, picturing for yourself what the Young Ladies' Bedroom, the Great Hall and so forth must have looked like in their time. At the top, there are wonderful panoramic views from the ramparts as you queue up to kiss the famous Stone (*see page 139*). Here you must lie on your back and lean your head backwards into a crevasse to achieve this feat, helped by a guard and watched by the castle photographer who will capture this graceless moment for posterity. Take care when descending from the

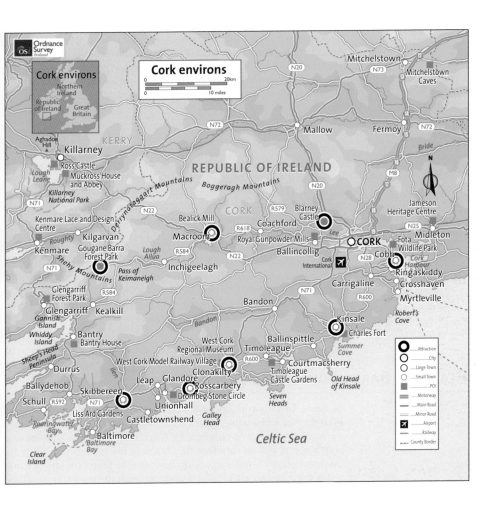

top of the castle, as the winding steps are very narrow and slippery. Afterwards, explore the pretty path that leads to the Rock Close, Druid circle and fairy glen – a truly enchanting spot.

# CLONAKILTY

**Clonakilty Tourist Information Office**
25 Ashe Street; tel: 023 88 33226. Open year-round.

Clonakilty was founded in 1588 by the Great Earl of Cork, Richard Boyle. The **West Cork Regional Museum** €€ (*Western Road. Open May–Oct Mon–Sat*) in the old schoolhouse traces the town's industrial past, while many buildings from that era along the quayside have been restored. The town is known for its traditional shopfronts with hand-painted signs, some of which sell the town's speciality, black pudding. The **West Cork Model Railway Village** €€ (*Inchydoney Road; tel: 023 88 33224. Open daily 1100–1700*) portrays the town in the 1940s. The nearby Inchydoney beach is very popular. Also in the vicinity is the reconstructed Lisnagun Ring Fort.

# COBH

Cobh can be reached by train from Cork City.

One-hour cruises on Cork Harbour (€€) are operated by **Marine Transport** from Cobh's Kennedy Pier; tel: 021 420 2900 May–Sept daily.

**The Queenstown Story** €€ Cobh Heritage Centre; tel: 021 481 3591; www.cobhheritage.com. Open May–Oct daily 0930–1800; Nov–Apr daily 0930–1700.

Cobh (pronounced 'cove') is situated on an island in Cork Harbour and joined to the mainland by a causeway. It was a quiet fishing village until the Napoleonic wars of the early 1800s, when the harbour flourished as a refuelling station for both naval and commercial ships. It later became an embarkation point for passenger vessels and the country's busiest port of emigration. In 1912 the *Titanic* made her last stop here before her fateful voyage. The history of the town – and its temporary name change – is told in **The Queenstown Story**, a multimedia exhibition housed in the Victorian railway station. **St Coleman's Cathedral**, a Gothic Revival edifice designed by Pugin in 1868, soars above the Victorian terraces lining the waterfront. Its carillon of 47 bells is the largest in Ireland.

# GOUGANE BARRA FOREST PARK

Gougane Barra, set around a lake at the source of the River Lee, was Ireland's first forest park. Against a spectacular backdrop of rugged crags – a broad brown face streaming with waterfalls after it rains – St Finbarre built a hermit cell on the lake's tiny island in the 6th century, where he lived and prayed before journeying downriver to found the city of Cork. A tiny Romanesque chapel on the spot preserves its timeless tranquillity. There is an annual pilgrimage on the Sunday nearest his feast day, 25 September. You can drive or walk around the 2-mile (3km) thickly forested nature trail, which circles the streams running beneath towering trees. Picnic tables and hiking trails invite you to linger.

# KINSALE

Kinsale Tourist Information Office Pier Road; tel: 021 477 2234; fax: 021 477 4438. Open year-round.

Kinsale is one of Ireland's most picturesque coastal towns. Set around a large harbour on the estuary of the River Bandon, it is filled with yachts and fishing boats and hosts international sailing events. Narrow streets lined with colourful, upmarket shops, restaurants and pubs run back from the waterfront and up into the hills. Kinsale has become known as a gourmet capital, due to the quality of both the local seafood and the international chefs the town attracts.

A turning point in Irish history occurred at the Battle of Kinsale in 1601, when English forces defeated the rebels and their Spanish allies. The subsequent 'Flight of the Earls', in which the Irish royalty abandoned their lands and left for the Continent, opened the way for the English Plantation (*see page 35*). As you wander through town, look out for the Old Courthouse, now a regional museum; St Multose Church, dating from Norman times; and the ruins of Desmond Castle. Nearby at Summer Cove is **Charles Fort**, a star-shaped bastion built around 1677 and in use until 1922. It has splendid views of Kinsale Harbour.

The Spaniard Bar, a long yellow building perched on a hillside opposite the town centre, is an atmospheric pub with log walls, low ceilings, an open fire and sawdust-covered floors. A favourite haunt of local fishermen, it often has traditional music. There is also a restaurant.

## Accommodation and food in Kinsale

**The White House €–€€€** *Pearse Street; tel: 021 477 2125; fax: 021 477 2045; email: info@whitehouse-kinsale.ie; www.whitehouse-kinsale.ie.* This excellent bar, restaurant and guesthouse in Pearce Street has newly refurbished bedrooms and cheerful places to eat. The informal bar and bistro serves a fantastic seafood chowder accompanied by home-baked brown bread, as well as steaks, salads and pasta dishes. Their more formal restaurant, Le Restaurant d'Antibes, is a member of the Kinsale Good Food Circle.

**Right**
Charles Fort

**Charles Fort** €€
*Tel: 021 477 2263.
Open mid-Mar–Oct daily
1000–1800; Nov–mid-Mar
daily 1000–1700.*

**Max's Wine Bar** €€ *48 Main Street; tel: 021 477 2443.* Classic, Irish-French dishes in a relaxed, intimate setting.

**Old Bank House** €€–€€€ *11 Pearse Street; tel: 021 477 4075; fax: 021 477 4296; email: info@oldbankhousekinsale.com; www.oldbankhousekinsale.com.* This luxury Georgian guesthouse has consistently been voted one of the top 100 places to stay in Ireland. The spacious bedrooms and suites are individually designed and decorated to the highest standard, and feature exquisite period pieces and original art. Its great location – in the town centre – is matched by excellent service. An award-winning restaurant, **blu**, is located in its sister hotel, the Blue Haven, featuring modern Irish cuisine with international accents and an excellent wine list.

# MACROOM

Set along the river in a lush landscape backed by mountains, Macroom is the market town for the Gaeltacht region (*see page 201*) to the west. Its pubs are great places to hear traditional music. Off the square, the ruins of **Macroom Castle** date from the 13th century and were a stronghold of the MacCarthys of Muskerry, who also built Blarney Castle. It was later granted to Admiral Sir William Penn, whose son William, founder of the colony of Pennsylvania in the United States, spent his early childhood here.

# ROSSCARBERY

This pretty little village traces its roots to a monastery founded by St Fachtna in the 6th century. A Benedictine abbey was later built on the site, which is now occupied by an attractive 17th-century Church of Ireland church. The **Drombeg Stone Circle** lies 2 miles (3km) outside town via the R597 Glandore road. There are many stone circles in County Cork and this one, dating back to the 2nd century BC, is among the best preserved, with 17 standing stones forming a circle 30ft (9m) in diameter. Nearby is a Stone Age cooking pit. There are also some sandy beaches and the ruins of Benduff Castle in the area.

# SKIBBEREEN

**Skibbereen Tourist
Information Office**
*Town Hall, North Street;
tel: 028 21766.*

Skibbereen is a lively market town, with weekly cattle and country markets on Wednesdays and Fridays. It sits at the head of Baltimore Bay alongside the River Ilen and is a good spot for salmon fishing. The

**Liss Ard Gardens**
€€ *On the Castletownshend road; tel: 028 40000. Open Mon–Fri 1000–1630.*

**Romancing the stone**

The legend that the Blarney Stone imparts the gift of eloquence is a relatively recent one, thought to date from the late 18th century. However, it was Queen Elizabeth I who made the name Blarney synonymous with 'nonsense'. Her attempts to persuade Lord Blarney to will his estate to the Crown were repeatedly met with elaborate excuses and fawning flattery. In exasperation she allegedly exclaimed, 'This is all Blarney! What he says he rarely means.'

town was particularly hard-hit by the famine in the 1840s, and there are mass famine graves among the ruins at Abbeystrewery Abbey, a mile (1.6km) west of town. The **Liss Ard Gardens** comprise a series of lakeside gardens covering 40 acres (16 hectares), designed to showcase the natural environment in an artistic manner. They will reach maturity in 30–50 years. The Sky Garden by American artist James Turrell is particularly interesting.

## Suggested tour

**Total distance:** The main route is 136 miles (218km). The detour back to Cork through Kinsale adds about 5 miles (8km) to the distance.

**Time:** Allow up to 4 hours' driving time for the main route. Although the route through Kinsale is only slightly longer in distance, it could take you an extra half-hour or longer because of the slower roads. Those with little time should concentrate on visiting Blarney Castle and Kinsale.

**Links:** Attractions on this tour can be visited on day trips from Cork City (*see page 126*). It overlaps with the tour of Southwest Cork (*see page 146*) at Bantry. Gougane Barra Forest Park can be easily reached from here. Youghal, a heritage town on the east Cork coast, is well worth a visit (*see page 122*).

**Above**
Kissing the Blarney Stone

BLARNEY CASTLE ❶, 5 miles (8km) from the west end of Cork, is well signposted from the city. As you leave Blarney, follow signs for Killarney, turning right at the junction on to the R579. Just beyond, make a quick left-hand turn on to the R622, still signposted Killarney. At the T-junction, turn right on to the R618, heading west towards Macroom. This is a lovely road along the River Lee, with a viewpoint outside Coachford where you can stop to admire the quintessential Irish countryside. Just north of **MACROOM** ❷, **Bealick Mill** has been restored and is open to the public.

Take the N22 back towards Cork. Just outside Macroom, take the turn-off to the right on to the R584 for **GOUGANE BARRA FOREST PARK** ❸, which is 20 miles (33km) away. At Inchigeelagh, the River Lee broadens into **Lough Allua**; you can drive or walk around it. Gougane Barra is 10 miles (16km) beyond. Near the entrance to the park is a large Crucifixion monument, a common feature around Ireland. On your way back out, turn right on to the R584 and head up through heavily forested slopes to the **Pass of Keimaneigh**, the 'pass of the deer's step'. At the top there is a large stone memorial to local 'White Boys' who died in a battle with Crown forces here in 1822. Views across the green pastures of the valley are gorgeous as you descend to **Kealkill**, a pretty town with a narrow bridge guarded by a ruined tower. Carry on for 5 miles (8km) to **Bantry** (*see page 142*).

Stay on the N71 Cork road; to the right the land stretches out into the Sheep's Head and Mizen Head peninsulas (*see page 145*). After 20 miles (32km) you reach **SKIBBEREEN** ❹. About 5 miles (8km) further on is the sweet village of **Leap**, where the River Leap empties into the Glandore Harbour. Its Irish name translates as 'O'Donovan's Leap', which recalls the story of a local chieftain who jumped across the ravine to escape his enemies. Roads either side of the harbour run to **Glandore** and **Unionhall**, pretty fishing and resort villages. Continue on through **ROSSCARBERY** ❺ and **CLONAKILTY** ❻. From here it is 33 miles (53km) back to Cork via Bandon.

**Detour:** To explore the coastal villages of the south Cork coast, take the R600 from Clonakilty to **Timoleague**, with the waterside ruins of an early 14th-century Franciscan abbey. There are occasional open days at **Timoleague Castle Gardens**, on the grounds of a 13th-century castle, little of which remains. The road south along the waterfront leads to the picturesque town of **Courtmacsherry** with its row of brightly painted cottages and sandy beaches. Beyond lies the **Seven Heads** Peninsula, with scenic back roads to explore. Continue on the R600 through Ballinspittle to **KINSALE** ❼. The **Old Head of Kinsale**, 7 miles (11km) south of town off the R600, is now a scenic golf course with its magnificent cliffs topped by a castle. The *Lusitania* was sunk offshore by a U-boat in 1915. From Kinsale, it is 16 miles (26km) back to Cork.

**Adam and Eve**

There are two islands in Glandore Harbour, one named Adam and the other, smaller one named Eve. Boats entering the harbour were given the sailing direction 'Avoid Adam and hug Eve'.

## Also worth exploring

The **Royal Gunpowder Mills** at Ballincollig are just west of Cork on the main road to Macroom. Among the attractions situated around Cork Harbour are the **Fota Wildlife Park** and the **Jameson Heritage Centre** at Midleton, where you can take a guided tour of the old whiskey distillery.

Cloyne, 18 miles (29km) to the east of Cork, has an enormous 13th-century cathedral and round tower. Near Crosshaven, home of the **Royal Cork Yacht Club**, the world's oldest, there are good beaches at **Myrtleville and Robert's Cove**. The picturesque villages of **Castletownshend** and **Baltimore** lie on the peninsula south of Skibbereen; the latter has some interesting offshore islands.

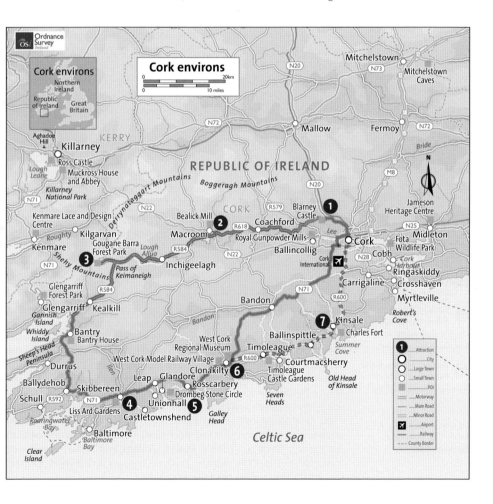

# Southwest Cork

## Ratings

| | |
|---|---|
| Coastal towns/villages | ●●●●● |
| Scenery | ●●●●● |
| Walking | ●●●●● |
| Manor houses/stately homes | ●●●●○ |
| Mountains | ●●●●○ |
| Beaches | ●●●○○ |
| Gardens | ●●●○○ |
| Prehistoric sites | ●●●●○ |

Southwest Cork is a region of rocky peninsulas stretching like long bony fingers into the Atlantic. The Beara Peninsula, some 30 miles (48km) long, lies between the Kenmare River and Bantry Bay. The Caha Mountains run along its spine, and form the dividing line between counties Cork and Kerry. Many people find the drive around the Ring of Beara more impressive and enjoyable than the more famous, and far busier, Ring of Kerry to the north. Pleasant harbour towns and brightly painted villages form a delightful contrast to the rocky landscape, and everywhere there are beautiful views of the sea. The region is also littered with stone circles and the mysterious ogham stones (*see page 146*). Bantry House and its gardens are splendidly situated along the waterfront. The town makes an excellent base for exploring the Beara and the smaller peninsulas of Sheep's Head and Mizen Head, with fine beaches, to the south.

## BANTRY

 **Bantry Tourist Information Office**
*The Old Courthouse; tel: 027 50229. Seasonal opening.*

**Bantry House €€€**
*Tel: 027 50047. www.bantryhouse.ie. Open mid-Mar–Oct daily 1000–1800. Joint or separate ticket for the 1796 Bantry French Armada Exhibition Centre.*

This pleasant town with its broad square sits at the head of Bantry Bay. **Bantry House** enjoys a glorious setting, perched above the town with sweeping vistas over the bay. Built in 1720, it was the seat of the earls of Bantry, whose descendants live here today. Richard White, the first earl, was awarded the peerage for his efforts in repelling the French Armada in 1796. The furnishings are as impressive as the drawing-room views: Gobelin and Aubusson tapestries, some made for Marie Antoinette's wedding to the Dauphin; huge Italian alabaster urns, early Waterford crystal chandeliers, and a peacock-blue dining room with an ornately carved sideboard. Concerts are often held in the library. There are formal Italian gardens and terraces. In a side courtyard is the **1796 Bantry French Armada Exhibition Centre**, which tells the story of the failed invasion.

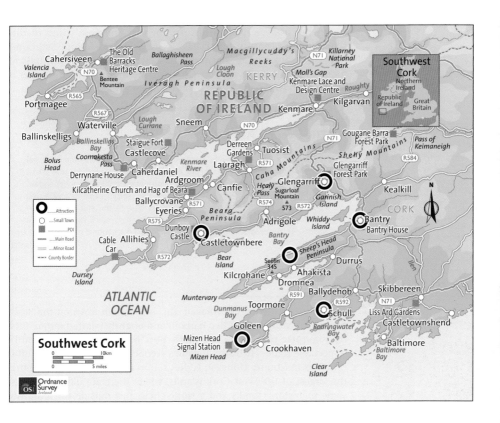

Bantry is the site of the **Bantry Mussel Fair**, held in early May, a long weekend of music, dancing, street entertainment, cooking competitions and, of course, plenty of mussels from Bantry Bay.

## Accommodation and food in Bantry

**Westlodge Hotel €€** *Tel: 027 50360; fax: 027 50438; email: reservations @westlodgehotel.ie; www.westlodgehotel.ie.* Set in 30 acres (12 hectares) of landscaped grounds about a mile (1.5km) outside of town, this large modern hotel has beautiful views of Bantry Bay and the surrounding mountains. Rooms are spacious and comfortable with all amenities. Guests can use the adjoining health and leisure centre. The restaurant serves a set menu and à la carte meals, and a bar menu is also available.

**O'Connor's Seafood Restaurant €€–€€€** *Main Street; tel: 027 50221.* Mussels are the speciality at this cute and cosy restaurant on Bantry's main street, which also features daily seafood specials, live lobsters, steaks, and oysters from a sea-water tank. Lighter meals are served in the back bar.

**Bantry House €€€** *Tel: 027 50047; fax: 027 50795; email: info@bantryhouse.com; www.bantryhouse.com.* For those who want to experience a piece of Irish history, the east and west wings of this splendid 18th-century house have guest accommodation. Bedrooms have en-suite facilities, and residents can use a sitting room, billiard room and balcony TV room overlooking the Italian Garden. Dinner is available on weekdays, May–October (advance notice required).

## The French Armada

In the winter of 1796, Wolfe Tone, leader of the United Irishmen, set sail from Brest with an armada of 50 French warships bound for the Cork coast. Their aim was to drive out the British and establish an independent Irish Republic. Richard White, who became the 1st Earl of Bantry, gathered volunteers to defend the territory at Bantry Bay. In the end, the invasion was thwarted by heavy storms, in which ten ships were lost. One, the *Surveillante*, was rediscovered in 1982 and declared a national monument.

# CASTLETOWNBERE

Also called Castletown Bearhaven, this is the main town on the Beara peninsula, with an attractive harbour and brightly painted restaurants. Its romantic past as a smuggler's port has given way to a more respectable trade – it boasts Ireland's second-largest fishing fleet, after Killybegs in County Donegal. Ferries run to **Bear Island**, just offshore, the largest of the West Cork islands, where there are old naval forts, some prehistoric tombs and a stone circle. Just outside town are the shattered remains of **Dunboy Castle**, the last bastion of resistance in the uprising of 1601–02. The ruined mansion nearby was once home to the Puxley family, who owned the copper mines at Allihies; the novel *Hungry Hill* by Daphne du Maurier was based on their lives.

# GLENGARRIFF

**Glengarriff Tourist Information Office**
Tel: 027 63084. Seasonal opening.

**Garinish Island €€**
Tel: 021 425 5100.
Open Apr–Jun & Sept Mon–Sat 1000–1830, Sun 1200–1830; Jul–Aug Mon–Sat 0930–1830, Sun 1100–1830; Oct Mon–Sat 1000–1600, Sun 1300–1700.

Sheltered beneath the Caha Mountains at the top of Bantry Bay, this village enjoys one of Ireland's finest settings. Its mild climate enables many Mediterranean plant species to flourish here, creating a lush landscape of flowers and foliage. It also contains one of the few remaining patches of the original oak forest which once covered the entire country. There are some beautiful woodland walks in **Glengarriff Forest Park**. Boat trips run throughout the day to **Garinish Island**, also called Ilnacullin, which is covered with luxuriant gardens. Created in 1910, its centrepiece is a formal Italianate garden, and the 37 acres (15 hectares) contain rock gardens, follies, pools and a host of exotic plants and shrubs. Watch for seals in the harbour on your way to and from the island.

# MIZEN HEAD

**Mizen Head Signal Station** €€ *Tel: 028 35115; www.mizenhead.ie. Open mid-Mar–May, Sept & Oct daily 1030–1700; Jun–Aug daily 1000–1800; Nov–mid-Mar weekends only 1100–1600.*

**O'Sullivan's Pub,** opposite the pier at Crookhaven, is a popular gathering place and serves chowder, soups, sandwiches and desserts.

Mizen Head is Ireland's most southwesterly point and its name gave rise to the saying: 'from Fair Head to Mizen Head', meaning, the length and breadth of Ireland (Fair Head is in County Antrim). The road from Schull (*see below*) runs along a dramatic rocky coastline, sliced by small coves and pounded by breaking waves, for 17 miles (27km) to these spectacular sandstone cliffs, which rise to over 755ft (230m). The views are fabulous, but the drops are sheer, so take care! The lighthouse here, built in 1910, was automated in 1993. Some of the buildings have been reopened as a visitor attraction, such as **Mizen Head Signal Station,** which has exhibits about local lore. The road out to the point runs through the villages of Toormore and Goleen. **Crookhaven** is a delightful fishing and holiday village, with a sailing centre. **Barleycove** is another popular small resort with a wonderful sandy beach.

# SCHULL

With its broad sheltered harbour, Schull (pronounced 'Skull') has become a popular resort and yachting centre. It looks out across Roaringwater Bay, dotted with many little islands; in summer, ferries run to Clear Island. The planetarium at Schull Community College puts on Star Shows for visitors. Mount Gabriel, rising 945ft (288m) above the town, still has traces of its Bronze Age copper mines. There are splendid views from the top. The town also has good restaurants and a number of craft shops.

# SHEEP'S HEAD PENINSULA

This long, narrow peninsula runs between Bantry Bay and Dunmanus Bay for 15 miles (24km) to its tip at Muntervary, or Sheep's Head. With a rugged, rocky landscape, it is the least visited of Cork's southwestern peninsulas. It is surprisingly well populated, with many attractive homes rising into the hills as far as Kilcrohane, after which the landscape suddenly becomes empty. An unclassified road from Durrus runs along the shore, with beautiful views of the rocky outcrops and tiny islands. At **Ahakista**, 6 miles (10km) along, there are good sandy beaches and a memorial to those who died when an Air India plane crashed offshore in 1985. The road climbs high above the sea, passing steep stone-walled pastures and the hamlet of **Dromnea** where the O'Dalys had a famous bardic school in medieval times. At the main village of **Kilcrohane** there is another good beach. Intrepid explorers can continue straight on across a rather desolate stretch to a car park, where a footpath leads to land's end at the **Sheep's Head**. Most follow the scenic **Goat's Path**

Road, signposted at Kilcrohane, which crosses the peninsula, climbing up into the mountains along Seefin, the highest peak. At the summit is a religious shrine. You can walk up to the top of the mountain for fantastic views over the peninsula, and there are gorgeous views over Bantry Bay and the Caha Mountains as you descend the other side.

## Suggested tour

**Total distance:** From Bantry the main route around the Beara Peninsula is 120 miles (192km). The detour around the Mizen Head and Sheep's Head peninsulas is 79 miles (128km).

**Time:** Allow 4 hours' driving time for the main route around the Beara Peninsula, though you could easily spend a leisurely day here exploring the side roads and enjoying the views. Those with little time should take the short cut over Healy Pass, which cuts off a good 2 hours. The detour to Mizen Head and Sheep's Head combined will take about 3½ hours.

**Links:** Although, given an early start and fine weather, you could conceivably cover all three peninsulas in one day, you will enjoy them more if you visit them separately, perhaps combining Mizen Head and/or Sheep's Head with a journey along the south Cork coast (*see page 140*) or inland to Gougane Barra Forest Park (*see page 136*). North of the Beara Peninsula is the Iveragh Peninsula and the famous Ring of Kerry (*see page 150*).

From **BANTRY ❶** take the N71 north along the wide curve of Bantry Bay; this is a beautiful stretch, crossing several rivers that empty into the bay as the road rises from the water's edge high above the shore. At **GLENGARRIFF ❷**, 7½ miles (12km) on, turn left on to the R572, signposted Ring of Beara and Castletownbere. There are gorgeous vistas over the bay and its islands along this coastal ribbon, with the Caha Mountains and Sugarloaf Mountain, 1,880ft (573m), rising up to your right. Watch for the viewpoint near the sign for Seal Harbour. The town of **Adrigole** straggles out from the bridge near the head of the little harbour. There is a good beach here, signposted 'the Strand'.

**Detour:** At Adrigole bridge, the R574 runs over **Healy Pass** to Lauragh, 8 miles (13km) away. Begun in the famine years, the road was only completed in 1931 and named for Tim Healy, the first governor-general of the Irish Free State. The road climbs through the rugged mountain landscape, opening out into a high, wide valley. There is a Crucifixion shrine at the top, near a viewing point that, on a clear day, affords splendid views. As you cross the Cork–Kerry border and snake down the northern slope past Glanmore Lake, you can see across the Kenmare River to Macgillycuddy's Reeks. This road is a good short cut if you don't have time to drive the entire Ring of Beara. At

## Ogham stones

Ogham is an ancient system of writing comprising 20 characters formed by combinations of lines and notches. Its origins are unknown, but it is thought to have derived from the Latin alphabet. The purpose of the stones appears to have been commemorative, recording the names of individuals and their tribal affiliations. They may also have marked territorial boundaries. Some 300 ogham stones have been found in Ireland, more than 80 of them in County Kerry alone. Once considered a pagan form of writing, recent studies date the majority of these stones to the 5th and 6th centuries, Ireland's early Christian era.

**Right**
Summer colour

Lauragh, turn right for Kenmare, and right again on to the N71 for the magnificent road back to Glengarriff.

From Adrigole, **CASTLETOWNBERE** ❸ is 10 miles (16km) to the west. You can take a short cut across the mountains to Eyeries, but the main road carries on around the peninsula for 12 miles (19km) to Allihies. About 3 miles (5km) past the signpost for Dunboy Castle, you will see a signpost off to the right for Allihies. Ignore this short cut and keep to

The roads running around the southwestern peninsulas are generally good but very narrow, so expect to drive slowly and exercise caution around the bends. The Sheep's Head Peninsula has some rough spots.

**Derreen Gardens** €€ Lauragh; tel: 064 83103. Open Apr–Oct daily 1000–1800 (but closed Mon–Thur in Aug).

**Adrigole Arts,** located in Adrigole village, tel: 027 60234, sells handmade paper, picture frames, jewellery, woollens, pottery and a range of gifts by local artisans. It is the home and studio of the Irish painter John McConnell.

the left on the coast road, which narrows as it winds through lovely hillside pastures. As you round the tip, there are dramatic views of the sea and the waves crashing against the rocky shore, seen through breaks in the hedgerows and grass-covered drystone walls. At a junction, the side road to the left leads to **Dursey Island**, about 5 miles (8km) away, a mountainous island whose high cliffs are home to a gannetry. It is connected to the mainland by Ireland's only cable car; check times of operation locally if you decide to visit. The main road (now the R575) carries on towards Allihies.

Despite a scattering of farms and houses, this rocky, sea-pounded end of the Beara feels very remote. The tall, bright blue, yellow, peach and purple-coloured houses of **Allihies** announce a momentary return to civilisation. This is a charming village, with two small pubs and old stone buildings on the edges of town. Set in a stark, rocky landscape, it makes a striking contrast to its surroundings, even on a rainy day. The hills are littered with ruins and mine shafts from the abandoned copper mines. Take the next 4½ miles (7km) slowly – not only for safety but to better enjoy the nature of this narrow, roller-coaster road which winds around the dark boulders and sharp curves, climbing up for awesome vistas over field and sea and dropping down again. Suddenly, the road straightens and you're sailing along to **Eyeries**, 10 miles (16km) on. Be sure to enter the village itself, another brightly painted gem with a peach-coloured Mediterranean-style church in the middle of the square. Follow signs for the Ardgroom Coast Road leading out of town, and at the end of the narrow lane turn left for **Ballycrovane Harbour**, where there is an **ogham stone** measuring over 17ft (5m) high, the tallest in Europe. Nearby are the ruins of **Kilcatherine Church** and the strangely shaped rock known as the **Hag of Beara**; local lore claims it is the petrified remains of a Celtic harvest goddess. Follow the road signposted to **Ardgroom**, 4 miles (6km) ahead. At the petrol station, the main road (R571) curves around to the right, signposted to Kenmare, 22 miles (35km) away. There is a fine **stone circle** at Canfie, signposted from the main road just beyond town. This is another scenic stretch with alternating views of the coast, mountains and forest.

About 6 miles (10km) along, at the hamlet of **Lauragh**, a right turn marks the start of the Healy Pass road to Adrigole, described on pages 146–7. To the left, the minor road signposted Kenmare Coast Road adds only a couple of miles to the journey but is much slower. It squiggles through thick woodland past the entrance to **Derreen Gardens**, filled with tree ferns, bamboos and other exotic plants, before opening out into peaceful views of Kilmakilloge Harbour, with its backdrop of mountains. There are boat trips from the pier, sea and shore angling, and walking trails. The fine scenery alternates between frothing surf, inland pastures and sweeping views across the mint-green waters to the Iveragh Peninsula. At **Tuosist**, another hamlet with an information kiosk, turn left to rejoin the main R571 into Kenmare (*see page 152*),

Garden lovers should ask for the 'West Cork Garden Trail' leaflet, available at tourist offices, which lists a number of private and public gardens open during the summer season.

Cork Kerry Tourism publishes a guide to long distance walking routes, including the Beara Way, Sheep's Head Way, the Kerry Way and Dingle Way. It is available from tourist information offices.

which also makes a good base for the Beara, and for a trip around the Ring of Kerry. To return to Bantry, turn right on to the N71. The 18-mile (29km) stretch between Kenmare and Glengarriff must rate as one of the most spectacular scenic roads in Ireland. It is known as the 'Tunnel Road', as it traverses the mountains through two tunnels – one very long and dark – hewn out of the solid rock. In between it hugs the rocky slopes, affording grand sweeping views across the valleys, glorious skies, streaming waterfalls and a stunning vista as you approach Bantry Bay.

**Detour:** Take the N71 Cork road south from Bantry for 10 miles (16km) to **Ballydehob**, where many craft workshops are set around the pretty harbour. Take the R592 for 5 miles (8km) to **SCHULL ❹**. Continue on this main road, signposted to Goleen, to explore the **MIZEN HEAD PENINSULA ❺**. The R591 leads back along Dunmanus Bay to the village of Durrus. From here you can return to Bantry, or follow signs for Ahakista and Kilcrohane to explore the **SHEEP'S HEAD PENINSULA ❻**.

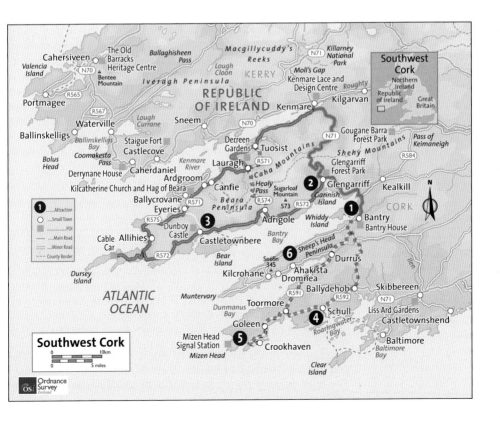

# The Ring of Kerry

## Ratings

Coastal towns/
villages   ●●●●●

Mountains   ●●●●●

National parks
            ●●●●●

Scenery   ●●●●●

Walking   ●●●●●

Prehistoric sites
            ●●●●○

Manor houses/stately
homes   ●●●○○

Outdoor activities
            ●●●○○

The Ring of Kerry circles the Iveragh Peninsula and is famous for its vistas of mountains and sea. This drive is the biggest draw in the west of Ireland, so don't expect to enjoy it in blissful solitude. Along with other drivers and cyclists, this is tour coach heaven. The views are magnificent, though arguably no more so than other western peninsulas. On a clear sunny day, it is magic; on a foggy, rainy day the grand views are obscured. If this is what you came to see, plan to spend a few days in the area so you can wait out any bad weather. A good plan is to start from Kenmare and drive clockwise around the Ring, breaking the journey at Killarney. This will give you plenty of time to savour the views, explore the side roads and Killarney National Park, and enjoy both of these delightful towns.

## CAHERSIVEEN

ℹ **Cahersiveen
Tourist Office** *The
Barracks; tel: 066 947
2589. Seasonal.*

🏛 **The Old Barracks
Heritage Centre** €
*Tel: 066 947 2777. Open
daily.*

At the foot of Bentee Mountain, Cahersiveen is the primary market town for the region. Look for the traditional hand-painted shop signs along its long main street. The **O'Connell Memorial Church**, a neo-Gothic church built of granite and black limestone in 1888, honours Daniel O'Connell (1775–1847), 'The Liberator'. By championing the cause of Catholic emancipation, he helped secure voting rights for Catholics in 1829. Uniquely, this is the only church in Ireland dedicated to a layman, rather than a saint. The house where he was born in 1775 lies in ruins about a mile (1.6km) outside of town. **The Old Barracks Heritage Centre** has interesting displays on local history. The ruins of many stone ring forts can be found in the area and are signposted from town.

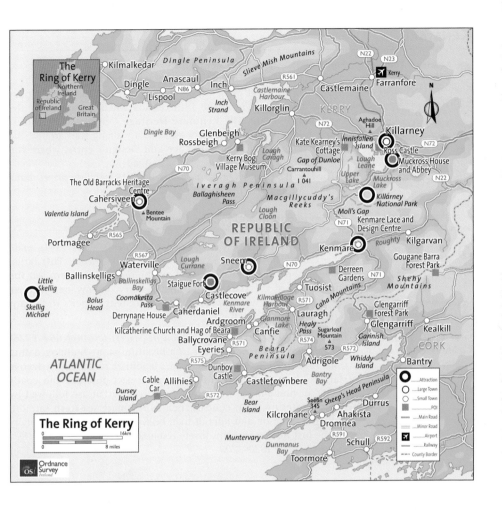

## Up against a wall

The parade of tour coaches, with which you'll share the road, drive the Ring of Kerry anticlockwise from Killarney. If you don't want to view the Ring round the back end of a bus, you can either leave at the crack of dawn and endeavour to stay ahead of them, or drive it clockwise. In that case, you'll be battling these behemoths head on round hairpin curves and on narrow roads that just aren't big enough for the both of you. If you spot an enormous red road hog bearing down upon you, brace yourself – some drivers have no compunction about taking your share of the tarmac.

# KENMARE

**ℹ Kenmare Tourist Office and Kenmare Heritage Centre** *The Square; tel: 064 664 1233. Open Easter–May, Sept & Oct Mon–Fri 0915–1700; Jun Mon–Fri 1015–1800; Jul–Aug daily 0915–1900.*

**P** Street parking is free in Kenmare, but there is a 2-hour limit from June to the end of September.

**ℹ Kenmare Lace and Design Centre** € *The Square; tel: 064 664 2636.*

**✆** Seafari cruises (€€€) on the Kenmare River to see seals and other wildlife operate from Kenmare Pier *(Apr–Oct).* Cruises last 2 hours. *Call 064 664 2059 for times and reservations; www.seafariireland.com*

Kenmare is a delightful heritage town with bright buildings, good shops and restaurants and traditional hand-painted signs. Its buildings and X-shaped street plan, which converges in a pleasant triangular square, date largely from the 18th century when it was part of the Landsdowne estate. The **Kenmare Heritage Centre**, at the tourist office, traces the town's history and has a walking trail around the town. Upstairs is the **Kenmare Lace and Design Centre**, where you can see how the town's distinctive lace is made.

The **Druid's Circle** is an impressive ring of 15 standing stones and a dolmen, located near the river off Market Street.

## Accommodation and food in Kenmare

**Kenmare Bay Hotel** €€ *Tel: 064 664 1300; fax: 064 664 1541; email: info@kenmarebayhotel.com; www.kenmarebayhotel.com.* This large, modern hotel has a great location on the outskirts of town, on the Sneem road at the start of the Ring of Kerry. Rooms are spacious, comfortable and well appointed. The excellent Jasper's restaurant serves good steaks and fresh seafood.

**Lime Tree Restaurant** €€ *Shelbourne Street; tel: 064 664 1225; www.limetreerestaurant.com.* Set in a beautiful stone building dating from 1832, the Lime Tree is Kenmare's landmark restaurant. Seductive starters like poppy seed tart with roast sweet potatoes and goat's cheese or home-made free-range duck liver parfait are followed by mouth-watering main courses such as Kenmare sea-fresh salmon, butterfish, venison and fillet of Irish beef. A contemporary art gallery on the first floor makes this lovely restaurant even more special. *Open Easter–Oct daily 1830–2200.*

# KILLARNEY

**ℹ Killarney Tourist Information Office** *Town centre car park, Beech Road; tel: 064 663 1633; fax: 064 663 4506. Open year-round.*

**✆** Killarney is notorious for its traffic jams, as crowds throng its narrow streets. Use the ring road to avoid the town centre if you're just passing through.

As the main tourist centre for the Ring of Kerry, Killarney is a busy town and often crowded, but once you're out of the car and on foot you can begin to appreciate its charms. A host of colourful little lanes, some still cobbled, run off the main streets. **St Mary's Cathedral**, designed by Pugin in the 1840s, is a splendid neo-Gothic Revival building with beautiful stained-glass windows. The Franciscan Friary and St Mary's Church of Ireland are also worth a visit. Killarney is known for its lively nightlife. The town is particularly busy during the Killarney Rally in May, the Killarney Races in July and during the Gathering Folk Festival in February and March.

# KILLARNEY NATIONAL PARK

**ⓘ Killarney National Park** *Tel: 064 663 1440; www. killarneynationalpark.ie*

Killarney National Park covers 25,000 acres (10,000 hectares), encompassing the three lakes of Killarney and the surrounding mountains. It contains Ireland's largest area of natural oak woodlands, and the only remaining herd of native red deer. Among the many places of interest are **Ross Castle** on the shores of Lough Leane, **Innisfallen Island** with its ruined abbey, **Torc Waterfall**, and **Ladies' View**, with its superb vistas over the valley. A spectacular view of the lakes of Killarney can be had from **Aghadoe Hill**, north of the park on the Killarney–Tralee road. There are ruins of a round tower, castle and church. To the west of the park are the impressive peaks of **Macgillycuddy's Reeks**, which contain Ireland's highest mountain, **Carrantouhill**, rising 3,406ft (1,041m). The **Gap of Dunloe**, a glacier-carved pass, is a popular walking and horse-riding route, with dramatic views of deep gorges and lakes. It runs from **Kate Kearney's Cottage**, where 19th-century travellers stopped off for *poteen* (illegal liquor), to **Moll's Gap**.

## Accommodation and food in Killarney

**Muckross Park Hotel & Cloisters Spa €€–€€€** *Muckross Village; tel: 064 662 3400; fax: 064 663 1965; email: info@muckrosspark.com; www. muckrosspark.com.* Beautifully situated in Killarney National Park, opposite the grounds of Muckross Abbey, Killarney's oldest hotel dates from 1795. This former coaching inn, visited by Queen Victoria and Prince Albert in 1861, is now a luxurious retreat. Bedrooms are large and splendidly appointed, with king-size beds. The drawing room is elegant and relaxing; service is superb. The Bluepool Restaurant, overlooking landscaped gardens leading down to the river and forest walk, has innovative cuisine and fine wines. Adjoining the hotel is Molly Darcy's, a large, lively pub and restaurant.

**Below**
Local business

## MUCKROSS HOUSE AND ABBEY

ℹ️ **Muckross House (€€)** and **Muckross Traditional Farms (€€)**
Tel: 064 667 0144;
www.muckross-house.ie.
House open Jul & Aug daily 0900–1900, Sept–Jun daily 0900–1730, last admission 1 hour before closing; farm open Apr, Sept & Oct, Sat–Sun 1300–1800, May daily 1300–1800, Jun–Aug daily 1000–1800. Joint ticket available.

🅿️ As you approach Muckross from Killarney, you will pass two parking areas for Muckross House, but these are at the opposite end of the grounds and are useful only if you want to approach by jaunting cart. Continue past the Muckross Park Hotel and the main entrance and car park are signposted to the right. If you only want to visit the abbey, park by the hotel and the entrance is just opposite.

There's a well-loved, homely feel to this elegant, 19th-century Elizabethan-style mansion. You can imagine its residents relaxing around the exquisite inlaid games tables in the sitting room, which has fabulous views over Muckross Lake. In the basement of the house there are exhibits on stonework, bookbinding and traditional crafts. The gardens have beautiful displays of rhododendrons and azaleas, a water garden and a superb limestone rock garden. Also in the grounds are **Muckross Traditional Farms**, working farms that demonstrate the lifestyle and farming practices of Kerry countrymen in the 1930s, before the use of electricity.

**Right**
Muckross Abbey

## THE SKELLIGS

🔘 Cruises to the Skelligs **(€€€)** operate from The Skellig Experience on Valencia Island; tel: 066 947 6306, Apr–Sept (call for cruise times). Landing is not allowed without a special permit. Local fishermen sometimes run unofficial trips from Ballinskelligs or Portmagee.

The Skelligs are a group of three conical rock islands lying about 9 miles (14km) off the Iveragh Peninsula. The largest is **Skellig Michael**, or Great Skellig, which rises more than 700ft (213m) out of the sea. Early Christian monks built a settlement of beehive huts, oratories and two churches atop the rock, living here from the 6th to 12th centuries. It is amazingly well preserved and is reached by a precipitous stairway carved out of the rock. **Little Skellig**, like its bigger brother, has steep cliffs that are home to breeding colonies of gannets, puffins, stormy petrels and other seabirds.

# SNEEM

This charming village, at the head of an estuary pouring into the Kenmare River, is set round a picturesque bridge and village green. Salmon fishing is plentiful here, and the weathervane of the 18th-century Protestant church is shaped like the fish. The sculpture park beside the parish church contains 'the pyramids' – traditional tall stone structures with stained-glass insets by James Scanlon, a Kerry artist. Sneem means 'the knot' in Irish.

# STAIGUE FORT

Dating from around 1000 BC, this is one of Ireland's best-preserved Iron Age sites. Built of stone, the circular fort measures 75ft (23m) in diameter, with walls 13ft (4m) wide and standing 18ft (5.5m) high. The sole entrance is on the south side; within the fort, stairways lead to lookout platforms. You have to cross private land to reach the fort, and the owner may request a small fee for access.

# Suggested tour

**The Kerry Way**
The Kerry Way long-distance walking trail covers 134 miles (215km), beginning in Killarney National Park and continuing around the Iveragh Peninsula. A booklet describing the route and a map guide are available from Cork Kerry Tourism. There are also several walks on Valencia Island. Kenmare holds walking festivals at Easter and Whitsuntide.

**Total distance:** It is 110 miles (176km) around the Ring of Kerry. Distances for short detours off the main road are listed below.

**Time:** Allow a full day to drive this route. Two days are recommended, especially if you want to visit the Skelligs or explore the trails in Killarney National Park.

**Links:** This route links with the tours of the other Southwest Cork peninsulas (*see page 146*) and the Dingle Peninsula (*see page 163*).

Leave **KENMARE ❶** on the N70 for **SNEEM ❷**, 15½ miles (25km) away. The road runs along the Kenmare River, and there are fine views of the Caha Mountains, across the water on the Beara Peninsula. As you continue to **Caherdaniel**, 13 miles (21km) from Sneem, the road turns inland through a valley bordered by conifer-covered slopes and rugged mountains, then returns to the rocky coast with islands dotting the mint-coloured sea. At Castlecove, 3 miles (5km) before town, turn right at the signpost for **STAIGUE FORT ❸**, 2½ miles (4km) inland. Just beyond Caherdaniel is the turning for **Derrynane House**, the former home of Daniel O'Connell, 'The Liberator'. Now a museum commemorating his life and political career, it is surrounded by a national park.

There are stunning views over the ocean as the road climbs up the Coomakesta Pass. These are best enjoyed from the fine viewpoint beside the Scarriff Inn. You then descend to **Waterville**, set low on the

**Derrynane House**
€ *Tel: 066 947 5113.
Open Apr, Oct & Nov
Wed–Sun 1030–1700;
May–Sept daily 1030–1800.*

**The Skellig Experience**
€€ *Tel: 066 947 6306;
www.skelligexperience.com.
Open May–Jun & Sept daily
1000–1800; Jul–Aug daily
1000–1900; Mar, Apr, Oct
& Nov 1000–1700 (ring for
opening days).*

**Kerry Bog Village
Museum** €€ *Tel: 066 976
9184; www.kerrybogvillage.ie.
Open daily 0830–1800.*

**Jaunting carts**
Jaunting carts are a
popular attraction around
Killarney. These horse-
and-traps can be hired for
a spin around the grounds
of Muckross House, or for
day-long sightseeing
excursions through the
valley, during which the
jarveys (drivers) will fill
your ears with local lore.
Negotiate the price before
you start the ride.

shores of Ballinskelligs Bay. Its excellent golf course and game fishing, in the bay and behind the town at Lough Currane, make it a popular resort. The main road now cuts inland across the peninsula to **CAHERSIVEEN** ❹, 10 miles (16km) beyond.

**Detour:** Just beyond Waterville, the left turning onto the R567 leads to **Ballinskelligs**, a Gaeltacht village 5 miles (8km) away. There are ruins of an ancient castle and abbey, and a magnificent sandy beach stretching for 4 miles (6km). Also off the N70, the R565 runs to Portmagee and the land bridge to **Valentia Island**, about 6 miles (10km). This lush, scenic island is a departure point for boat trips to the **SKELLIGS** ❺, which can be seen offshore. The **Skellig Experience**, located near the causeway, tells the story of the early Christian monastery there, the lighthouse and the wildlife. Valencia Island can also be reached by ferry from Cahersiveen.

The N70 north from Cahersiveen is one of the finest stretches of the Ring, with superb views across Dingle Bay to the peaks of the Slieve Mish Mountains (weather permitting). The road hugs the coast, then climbs into the rugged mountains before dropping down again into **Glenbeigh**, 17 miles (27km) away. This small village, a good base for hiking and fishing, is built on a seaside bog. The **Kerry Bog Village Museum**, beside the Red Fox Inn, re-creates life here in the early 1800s. Nearby at **Rossbeigh** there is a beautiful strand backed by high dunes. **Killorglin**, 6 miles (10km) on, is a pleasant town, famous for its Puck Fair in August, when a large goat is crowned King of the Fair. From here it is 13 miles (21km) to **KILLARNEY** ❻ on the N72. Follow the N71 along Lough Leane to Muckross, about 4 miles (7km) away,

## The Puck Fair

Killorglin's Puck Fair, three boisterous days of non-stop merrymaking in mid-August, begins when a large male goat is crowned and installed on a pedestal as King of the Fair. It dates from the early 17th century, but is thought to have its origins in a more ancient ritual honouring the Celtic god Lug. The Gaelic word for August is Lughnasa, which means 'festival of Lug'.

**Above**
Pick up some lunch at a bakery

where you can tour lovely **MUCKROSS HOUSE** ❼ and the ruins of **MUCKROSS ABBEY**, a Franciscan friary dating from 1448. These lie within the boundaries of **KILLARNEY NATIONAL PARK** ❽. The N71 continues on through Moll's Gap back to Kenmare.

## Also worth exploring

The interior of the Iveragh Peninsula usually takes second billing to the Ring of Kerry drive, but has many places of interest to explore. A scenic unclassified road between Waterville and Killorglin runs over the **Ballaghisheen Pass**, and past the lake areas of loughs Cloon, Glencar and Caragh. The latter is encircled by another scenic road along its shores. East of Kenmare, **Kilgarvan** in the Roughty Valley is a pleasant village with good fishing rivers and several prehistoric sites.

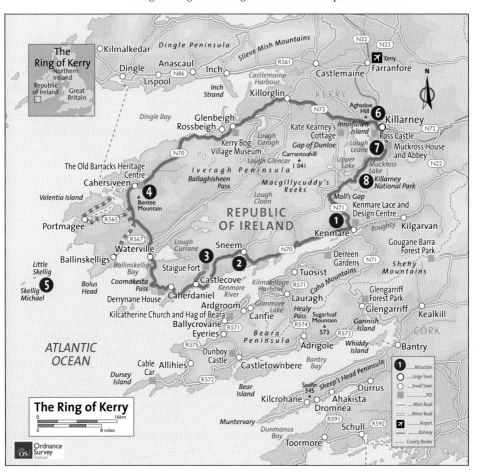

# The Dingle Peninsula

## Ratings

| | |
|---|---|
| Beaches | ●●●●● |
| Coastal towns/ villages | ●●●●● |
| Mountains | ●●●●● |
| Prehistoric sites | ●●●●● |
| Scenery | ●●●●● |
| Traditional music | ●●●●● |
| Walking | ●●●●● |
| Art and craft | ●●●●○ |

There's a touch of magic to the Dingle Peninsula. It stretches just 35 miles (56km) as the crow flies from Kerry's county town of Tralee to Slea Head, which looks out over the Blasket Islands, Ireland's 'last parish before America'. But within its bounds are rugged mountains, dramatic seascapes, idyllic beaches and steep slopes of the brightest green, peppered with stone cottages, fences and curious beehive huts. It's no wonder the region is rich in Celtic legends. It also holds a wealth of tangible ancient sites, from the promontory fort at Dunbeg to the remarkable Gallarus Oratory. The western half of the peninsula is a Gaeltacht area, a stalwart of traditional culture where Irish is the first language (*see page 201*). Villages such as Dingle, with its music pubs and famous dolphin, and Dunquin and Ventry, with their pottery workshops, provide a delightful complement to the stunning scenery.

## BALLYFERRITER

**Ballyferriter Heritage Centre**
€€ *Tel: 066 915 6333.
Open Easter–Sept daily
1000–1700; rest of the year
by request.*

With many fine walks in the area, this village is a popular holiday spot. The **Ballyferriter Heritage Centre**, housed in the old schoolhouse, traces the history of the Dingle Peninsula with artefacts and old photographs. On Main Street, the West Kerry Co-op, which has sponsored important projects in farming, tourism and language studies to revive the Dingle economy, publishes a good illustrated guide to the region's antiquities. About 2 miles (3km) north of town, near the fine beach at Smerwick Strand, are the ruins of the 16th-century fortress of **Dún an Óir** (the 'golden fort'). It was built by a Spanish invasion force, come to aid their Irish Catholic allies against the English. The fort was bombarded and its 600 survivors brutally slaughtered. To the east of town are the remains of a 7th-century monastic settlement at **An Riasc**.

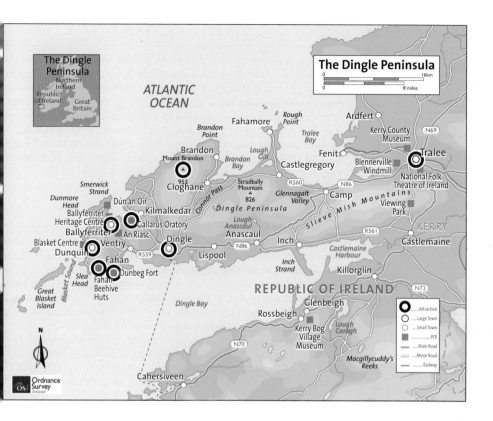

The Dingle Peninsula

The Dingle Peninsula

Northern Ireland

Republic of Ireland

Great Britain

ATLANTIC OCEAN

0 _____ 16km

0 _____ 8 miles

Rough Point

Fahamore

Ardfert

Brandon Point

Tralee Bay

Kerry County Museum

N69

Brandon Mount Brandon

Lough Gill

Fenit

Brandon Bay

Castlegregory

Blennerville Windmill

Tralee

953

Cloghane

Stradbally Mountain

826

R560

N86

National Folk Theatre of Ireland

Smerwick Strand

Glennagalt Valley

Camp

Viewing Park

Dunmore Head

Dún an Óir

Kilmalkedar

Dingle Peninsula

Slieve Mish Mountains

KERRY

Ballyferriter Heritage Centre

Gallarus Oratory

Lough Anascaul

R561

Ballyferriter

An Riasc

Anascaul

Castlemaine

Blasket Centre

Ventry

Dingle

Inch

Castlemaine Harbour

Dunquin

R559

Lispool

N86

Slea Head

Fahan

Inch Strand

Killorglin

Great Blasket Island

Fahan Beehive Huts

Dunbeg Fort

REPUBLIC OF IRELAND

N72

Dingle Bay

Glenbeigh

Rossbeigh

Kerry Bog Village Museum

Lough Caragh

Attraction

Large Town

N70

Small Town

POI

Main Road

Minor Road

Railway

Macgillycuddy's Reeks

N

Cahersiveen

Ordnance Survey Ireland

# DINGLE

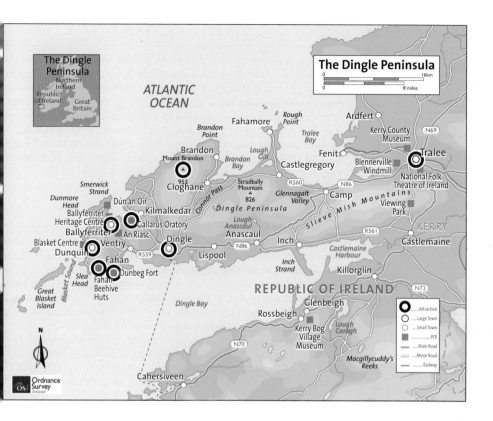

**Dingle Tourist Office** *The Quay; tel: 066 915 1188. Open year-round.*

In a town known for its traditional music, one name that always pops up is **O'Flaherty's** (UaFlaibeartaig), on Bridge Street, near the town entrance. Its simple, rustic interior is the scene of impromptu music sessions on most summer nights.

The peninsula's main town is a lively place whose population doubles during the summer season. The small streets winding up from the fishing harbour are lined with bright shops, good seafood restaurants and pubs renowned for their traditional music. The Old Presbytery contains historical photos and memorabilia. On the west edge of town, a selection of local crafts is sold at the Ceardlann Craft Village, including leather and handwoven goods and *uilleann* pipes.

In recent years, Dingle has become a hideaway haunt of Hollywood actors, who discovered its charms while filming in the area. The biggest star, however, is Fungie the bottlenose dolphin, who came to Dingle Bay in 1983 and made the harbour his home. Local boatmen at the quayside will take you out to see him (€€), or you can don a wetsuit and join him for a swim.

# DUNBEG FORT

**Dunbeg Fort €€**
Tel: 066 915 9755.
Easily accessible.

Very few promontory forts remain in Ireland, and Dunbeg, clinging dramatically to the sheer black cliffs high above Dingle Bay, is one of the best preserved. It dates from the Iron Age (500 BC–AD 500). With its inner stone rampart measuring over 20ft (6.35m) thick and some 10ft (3m) high, it was a defensive structure, rather than a homestead. The fort possibly served as a refuge for residents of the *clochans*, or beehive huts (*see below*), that stood on the hillsides of Mount Eagle, behind the fort. Its raised earthen banks, souterrain and central causeway can still be seen, and in the interior is a single *clochan*.

# DUNQUIN

**Blasket Centre €**
Dunquin; tel: 066 915 6444 or 915 6371. Open Apr–Oct daily 1000–1800.

If the scenery around Dunquin looks vaguely familiar, it may be that you've seen the film *Ryan's Daughter*, which was filmed here in 1969. The **Blasket Centre** recounts the way of life of the Blasket Islanders, whose small population eked out a harsh living from fishing until 1953, when they were moved to the mainland. They were grand storytellers, and their language and heritage were faithfully recorded in some beautifully written biographies. Boat trips to the islands can be arranged with local boatmen in the summer months; enquire at Dunquin Pier. Here you'll see upturned *curraghs* (traditional Irish fishing boats covered in canvas and painted with black tar) and the surrounding cliffs of colourful Silurian rock, over 400 million years old and rich in fossils.

# FAHAN BEEHIVE HUTS

The tip of the Dingle Peninsula is littered with *clochans* – small stone beehive huts that were lived in by prehistoric people in the early Christian era. Around 414 have been counted from around Slea Head to Dunquin. Some of the finest can be seen at Fahan, about a mile (1.6km) beyond Dunbeg Fort. You can enter these amazing little dwellings, which are held together without mortar and yet remain watertight. The sweeping vistas over the sea from the green and rock-strewn slopes of Mount Eagle are equally impressive. The Fahan Beehive Huts are on private land, and the farmer asks a small fee to enter.

# GALLARUS ORATORY

One of Ireland's finest early Christian sites is this small church, built in the 7th or 8th century. Its unusual shape, resembling an upturned boat, represents the height of an architectural technique known as corbelling, which was first developed by the builders of

**Above**
Gallarus Oratory

Neolithic tombs. Unmortared stones, projecting inward and placed at an angle so that they were slightly lower on the outside, enabling rainwater to run off, were built up from both sides until they met at the top.

## MOUNT BRANDON

Rising to 3,127ft (953m), Mount Brandon has been a holy mountain since ancient times. The mountaintop was the site of the harvest festival of Lughnasa, dedicated to the Celtic god Lug. Like most other pagan sites, it was appropriated by an early Christian saint – Brendan, in this case – who built a hermitage where he had the vision of Hy-Brasil, a promised land, which launched his great sea voyage to the New World (*see page 162*). Pilgrims still climb up here to pray on the last Saturday in June, but you'll be blessed with a great vision of Dingle on any clear day by taking the 'Saint's Road' footpath from Kilmalkedar Church, or the path from the village of Cloghane.

## TRALEE

**① Tralee Tourist Information Office**
*Ashe Memorial Hall, Denny Street; tel: 066 712 1288; fax: 066 712 1700. Open year-round.*

The capital of County Kerry was made famous years ago by the old Irish ballad 'The Rose of Tralee'. Each August the town holds a festival of the same name, in which women from Irish communities around the world compete for the title; music, dancing, parades and a horse race also mark the event. The **National Folk Theatre of Ireland** (*tel:*

**i** **South West Walks Ireland** 28 The Anchorage, Tralee, Co Kerry; tel: 066 712 8733; email: swwi@iol.ie; www. southwestwalksireland.com. Mail order for Ordnance Survey maps, books, walking information, waymarked trails, routes and accommodation for the whole of Ireland.

**m** **Kerry County Museum €€€** Ashe Memorial Hall, Denny Street; tel: 066 712 7777; www.kerrymuseum.ie. Open Jan–Apr & Sept–Dec Tue–Sat 0930–1700; May–Aug daily 0930–1730.

**Blennerville Windmill €€** Tel: 066 712 1064. Open Apr–Oct daily 1000–1800.

The **Aqua Dome €€** Dingle Road; tel: 066 712 8899 or 066 712 9150; www.aquadome.ie. Open Jul–mid-Aug Mon–Fri 1000–2200, Sat & Sun 1000–2100; mid-Aug–Jun Mon–Fri 1000–2200, Sat & Sun 1100–2000.

**The Dingle Way** circles the peninsula on a 111-mile (179km) walking route. Details are available from tourist information and Cork Kerry Tourism.

066 712 3055; www.siamsatire.com), Siamsa Tíre, is based here and there are performances of traditional music and dance throughout the summer. **Kerry County Museum** tells the county's history from prehistoric times using modern interpretive media alongside the artefacts and displays. The Medieval Experience is a time-travel stroll through the sights, sounds and smells of medieval Tralee. Other exhibits focus on Kerry's colourful characters and give an overview of the region's sights and scenery.

The **Tralee and Dingle Steam Railway** is under restoration; it runs for 3 miles (5km) to the **Blennerville Windmill**, which has been turned into a visitor centre with craft workshops, an audiovisual theatre and a birdwatching area. There is also an emigration museum, whose star attraction is the *Jeanie Johnston* commemorative quilt. Made by local women, it remembers the 19th-century vessel that transported thousands of emigrants to North America on 16 voyages and never lost a single passenger or crew member to accident or disease. The **Aqua Dome** is Ireland's largest water park with water slides, rapids and a wave pool.

## Accommodation and food in Tralee

**Brook Manor Lodge €–€€** Fenit Road; tel: 066 712 0406; fax: 066 712 7552; email: brookmanor@eircom.net; www.brookmanorlodge.com. This luxury four-star country guesthouse is 2 miles (3km) from Tralee town centre, set in 3½ acres (1.5 hectares) of private grounds against the backdrop of the Slieve Mish Mountains. Sandra and Jerome Lordan are genial and attentive hosts, and their eight bedrooms are beautifully furnished, with all amenities. There's a cosy guest lounge with an open fire, and a delicious breakfast is served in the conservatory, a bright spot even on a rainy day.

## The Voyage of St Brendan

A group of Irish monks led by St Brendan the Navigator may have reached the New World in the 6th century, long before the Vikings or Columbus. Brendan was born in the village of Fenit, near Tralee, and founded several monasteries, including Clonfert. According to a medieval manuscript, the *Navigato Brendan*, Brendan and his band set sail in hide-covered *curraghs* across the Atlantic in search of a promised land he had seen in a vision. During their seven-year odyssey they encountered fire-hurtling demons, a floating crystal column and a sea creature as large as an island. Could these have been a volcanic eruption on Iceland, an iceberg, a whale? If the Utopian world that Brendan duly reached was indeed North America, no archaeological proof has been found, yet many latter-day explorers believed it, and place names from the saga appear on some medieval maps and charts. Timothy Severin, an English explorer, built a replica of St Brendan's boat and in 1976 successfully retraced the epic voyage, proving it was possible that the Irish could have been the first Europeans to reach the New World. The boat can be seen at Craggaunowen (see page 168).

## Suggested tour

**Total distance:** The main route covers 97 miles (156km). The detour inland to Camp is 13 miles (21km).

**Time:** Allow at least half a day for the main route, though a full day is best to enable you to explore the towns and savour the sights at leisure. The detour will add about half an hour.

**Links:** This route connects with the Ring of Kerry tour (*see page 155*) and the Shannonside tour (*see page 172*).

Leave **TRALEE** ➊ on the N70 heading south for Castlemaine, 10 miles (16km) away, with the beautiful **Slieve Mish Mountains** on your right.

**Detour:** About a mile (1.6km) before you enter Castlemaine, look for the small sign (opposite the Mountain View B&B) for the 'Viewing Park'; turn right and follow this minor road up into the hills for 2½ miles (4km). At the top there are wonderful views of Castlemaine Harbour and across the valley to the mountains around Killarney.

From Castlemaine, take the R561 west along the mountains; the road soon drops down along Castlemaine Harbour, affording spectacular views across the water to the Iveragh Peninsula. At Inch, 12 miles (19km) along, stop off at **Inch Strand**. This is a stunning 4-mile (6km) sandy beach, backed by dunes, stretching along a spit into the harbour. Take a stroll along the gentle surf, or just sit and admire the peaceful view. The village of **Anascaul** (Abhainn an Scáil), a short distance beyond, is a popular stop with two well-known pubs: the brightly painted **Dan**

**Above**
Slea Head shrine

Dunquin boasts the most westerly pub in Europe. **Kruger's** (*tel: 066 915 6127*), which offers sessions and set dancing, is named for the late, local hero Kruger Kavanagh, who was a soldier, impresario, storyteller, political activist and bodyguard to Eamonn de Valera.

Foley's, and the **South Pole Inn**, so named because its former owner, Tom Crean, was part of the Scott expedition to the Antarctic.

**Detour:** To explore the interior of the peninsula, about 7 miles (12km) west of Castlemaine take the minor road signposted to the right which cuts across the mountains to Camp, 5 miles (8km) away. Then take the N86 towards Anascaul, back into the mountains. About 2 miles (3km) along is a viewpoint with wonderful views over the north coast. The road continues through the broad, green **Glennagalt Valley**. The Irish name means 'valley of the mad', so called because water from a well in the valley was said to cure insanity. Rejoin the main route at Anascaul. Nearby Lough Anascaul is a beauty spot also worth a detour.

The N86 (R561) continues west through huge, rounded bright-green hills and the village of Lispool (Lios Poil) to **DINGLE ❷** (An Daingean), 10 miles (16km) away. You are now entering the Gaeltacht proper, and most road signs will be in Irish only. From Dingle, continue west on the R559, which is signposted 'Slea Head Drive'. **Ventry** (Ceann Trá), set along its turquoise harbour, has a lovely beach of white sand where you can see *curraghs*. The beach was the scene of a mythological battle between the hero Fionn MacCumhaill and the King of the World. About 4 miles (6km) further on, **DUNBEG FORT ❸** (An Dún Beag) clings to the dramatic black cliffs. One mile (1.6km) beyond are the **FAHAN BEEHIVE HUTS ❹**.

After fording a small rocky stream running down the slopes and across the road, you round the promontory to **Slea Head** (Ceann Sléibhe), marked by a Crucifixion shrine known as 'The Cross' (An Cros). The view over Blasket Sound is magnificent, with Great Blasket Island rising like an enchanted castle offshore. Inhabited until 1953, the **Blasket Islands** were often called 'the last parish before America'. Their history is told at the **Blasket Centre**, 2 miles (3km) further on at **DUNQUIN ❺** (Dún Chaoin). Off to the left, **Dunmore Head** (Ceann an Dúin Mhoir) is the most westerly point on the mainland. This stretch of coast has a treacherous beauty, and is not safe for swimming. Many ships have been wrecked in Blasket Sound, including two from the Spanish Armada (one has been excavated by divers).

The Slea Head Drive continues around the tip of the peninsula past Clogher Strand to **BALLYFERRITER ❻** (Baile an Fheirtéaraigh). Shortly beyond the town, follow signs for 'Dingle via Gallarus', making a left and then a right turn for **GALLARUS ORATORY ❼** (Séipéilín Ghallrois). When you leave Gallarus, turn left out of the drive, which brings you to a T-junction. Turn left again, which brings you to another T-junction at the top of the hill. Turn right for Dingle, about 3 miles (5km) away. To the left is **Kilmalkedar** (Cill Maolchéadair), where the ruins of a Romanesque church stand on an ancient pagan site; the graveyard contains early crosses, a sundial and ogham stones (*see page 146*).

At Dingle, the road across the rugged mountains over **Connor Pass** is signposted from the roundabout, before the town centre. It is 4 miles (6.5km) to the summit, at 1,509ft (460m), where there are sweeping views back to Dingle and ahead to Brandon and Tralee bays. To the left is **MOUNT BRANDON ⑧**, Dingle's highest peak. The steep descent brings you down to **Brandon Bay**, said to be the site where St Brendan the Navigator set sail on his voyage to the New World. Continue east to **Castlegregory** (Caisleán Ghriaire). **Lough Gill**, near Castlegregory, is a bird sanctuary favoured by many unusual migrating species. Turn right on the R560 towards Camp. There are fine beaches along this shore beside Tralee Bay. From Camp it is 10 miles (16km) back to Tralee.

## Also worth exploring

**Ardfert**, north of Tralee, has interesting ruins of a cathedral and churches dating from the 12th century, as well as remnants of a Franciscan friary. The nearby village of **Fenit** on Tralee Bay is said to be the birthplace of St Brendan the Navigator. Inland from Tralee there are scenic minor roads through the Stacks Mountains.

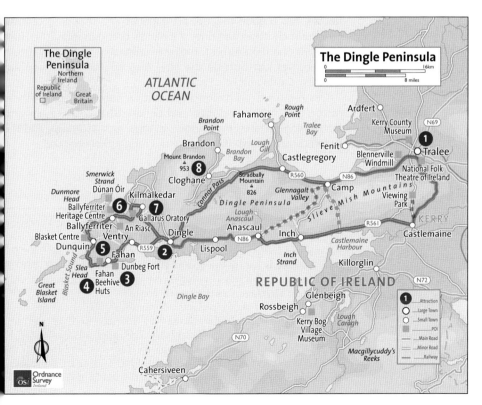

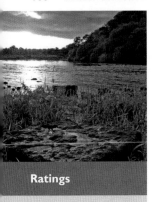

# Shannonside

## Ratings

| | |
|---|---|
| Castles | ●●●●● |
| Family attractions | ●●●●● |
| History | ●●●●● |
| Museums | ●●●●○ |
| Prehistoric sites | ●●●●○ |
| Cathedrals/ churches | ●●●○○ |
| Scenery | ●●●○○ |
| Beaches | ●●○○○ |

The Shannon is the longest river in Ireland, running for 170 miles (274km) from its source in County Cavan to its meandering mouth, which divides counties Limerick and Clare. Gentle rolling hills follow the south banks of the estuary until it meets the sea at the fine beaches of Ballybunion, home to one of Ireland's top golf courses.

The historic city of Limerick, with its handsome Georgian houses, has a good theatre, art galleries and shopping centres, numerous churches and one of Ireland's best museums, the Hunt Museum. Shannon Airport, the international gateway to western Ireland, lies just outside the city. Also nearby is the popular Bunratty Castle and Folk Park.

This region is brimming with castles, some in ruins, others restored as hotels and medieval banquet halls. There are also archaeological sites, picturesque villages such as Adare, and the fine reconstructions of Celtic life at Craggaunowen.

## ADARE

**ⓘ Adare Tourist Information Office**
*Adare Heritage Centre; tel: 061 396255. Seasonal.* There are guided walking tours of the town's historical highlights.

**ⓟ** There is a large, free car park behind the Adare Heritage Centre which visitors are encouraged to use. Parking restrictions apply elsewhere.

People come to Adare to see the row of charming thatched cottages, several of which now house restaurants and craft shops, along its busy main street. With upmarket modern homes spreading out from the centre, Adare is hardly the quaint village you would expect, but the stone buildings and ruins are highly attractive and well worth a visit. The **Adare Heritage Centre**, which contains the tourist office and knitwear and craft shops, presents a historical exhibition on the town. Next door is the **Trinitarian Monastery**, founded in 1230, and now incorporated into the Catholic church. The order was established in France to rescue hostages taken during the Crusades, and this was the only known branch in Ireland. Across the River Maigue are the ruins of **Desmond Castle**. Nearby, a short walk across the golf course, are the ruins of the **Franciscan Friary**.

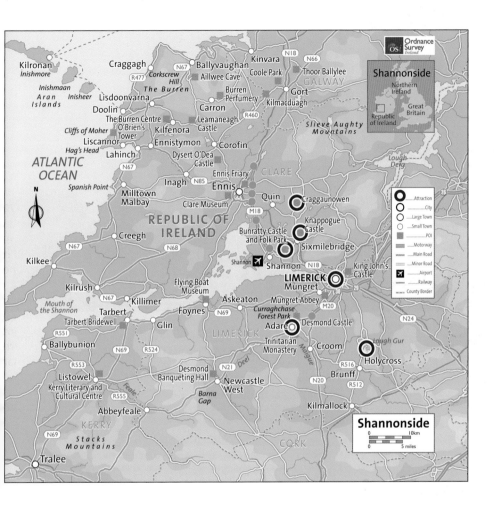

Shannonside

0    10km
0    5 miles

# Bunratty Castle and Folk Park

 **Bunratty Castle and Folk Park €€€**
Tel: 061 360788;
www.shannonheritage.com.
Open Jun–Aug Mon–Fri
0900–1730, Sat & Sun
0900–1800; Sept–May daily
0900–1730; last admission
45 minutes before closing.

One of Ireland's most popular castles, **Bunratty Castle** was built in 1425, though its origins date back to Viking times. It has been restored to its medieval glory and filled with a superb collection of medieval furniture that greatly enhances its atmosphere. Highlights include the great hall with its timbered roof and tapestries, the 'murder holes' through which enemies were drenched in boiling oil, and the banqueting hall, where the popular medieval banquets take place. Surrounding the castle is the delightful **Folk Park**, where there are re-creations of a village street, fisherman's cottage, farmhouses, a forge and other period buildings that illustrate all walks of life in days gone by. The costumed staff work hard to explain traditional crafts and the way

**Above**
Bunratty Castle

of life. While it may be a bit too touristy for some tastes, children love it so it's a good day out for families and the food is reasonable.

## Medieval banquets

If quaffing mead and feasting on roast beast in a genuine medieval dining hall strikes your fancy, you've come to the right region. Bunratty Castle, Knappogue Castle and Dunguaire Castle at Kinvara (*see page 184*) hold medieval banquets twice nightly in season (year-round at Bunratty). These royal repasts are accompanied by music, entertainment and merrymaking. Bunratty also holds traditional Irish Nights in the Great Barn. For information contact Shannon Castle Banquets, *tel: 061 360788*, or the tourist offices' website *www.shannonheritage.com*

# CRAGGAUNOWEN

**Craggaunowen €€**
Tel: 061 361511.
Open May–Sept daily 1000–1700 (last admission 1600).

Craggaunowen is more than a tourist attraction. The project was the brainchild of the late John Hunt, known in his day as one of the best medievalists in Europe. After restoring the 16th-century castle, he set about reconstructing dwellings that portray the lifestyle of the ancient Celts. A fine *crannog*, or lake dwelling, a ring fort and a hunter's cooking site are set along a woodland trail. The Iron Age field and the *togher* – a relic of an ancient wooden roadway built across a bog –

provide insight on how they survived. A fascinating piece of recent history is *The Brendan*, the leather-hulled boat in which Tim Severin crossed the Atlantic in 1976 in an effort to authenticate the voyage of St Brendan the Navigator (*see page 162*). Rare breeds such as Kerry cattle and Soay sheep, which have died out in the rest of Ireland, are fostered here. Craggaunowen also serves as a climatological station for Ireland and daily readings are taken year-round.

# KNAPPOGUE CASTLE

**Knappogue Castle**
€€ Tel: 061 360788.
Open May–Sept daily
0930–1700 (last admission
1615). Banquets Apr–Oct
daily at 1830.

Knappogue Castle, one of 42 belonging to the powerful MacNamara clan, was built in 1467. It is a typical example of the type of fortified tower house favoured by the Irish and Anglo-Irish ruling class. The tower consists of four storeys connected by a spiral staircase. The upper floors were used as living and sleeping quarters, with the lord of the castle residing at the top. The ground floor was primarily used for storage and is now made up of the banquet hall and the reconstructed rooms of a 19th-century extension. The bawn wall, which encloses the castle and its outbuildings, protected residents of nearby farmsteads and livestock in times of danger. The 19th-century walled garden has been restored.

# LIMERICK

**Limerick Tourist
Information Office**
Arthur's Quay; tel: 061
317522; fax: 061 317939;
www.limerick.ie

**The Angela's Ashes
Walking Tour**
€€€ Tel: 061 317522.
Tour departs from the tourist
information office at Arthur's
Quay.

**Hunt Museum €€**
Custom House, Rutland
Street; tel: 061 312833;
www.huntmuseum.com.
Open Mon–Sat 1000–1700,
Sun 1400–1700.

The Republic's fourth-largest city shot to fame in 1996 as the setting for Frank McCourt's novel *Angela's Ashes*. While some natives take issue with his portrayal of their city, it has nonetheless sparked visitor interest. The slums of McCourt's childhood have long gone, and Limerick's beautifully renovated Georgian buildings – best seen along the Crescent and O'Connell Street – and its prosperous city centre create a fine impression of the city today.

With its strategic location on the Shannon, Limerick dates back to Celtic times. In its long and often turbulent history it has been settled by the Vikings, walled and segregated by the English, and defended by Irish patriots against Cromwell and during the Jacobite wars. A self-guided walking route, 'Limerick – the Past Revisited' (€€), highlights the many places of interest. It has walking trails through English Town and New Town and is available from the tourist information office or the Limerick Civic Trust opposite King John's Castle. Alternatively, you can see the sights on two open-top bus tours, one covering medieval and Georgian Limerick, the other visiting the settings in McCourt's novel.

Limerick's attractions include the **Hunt Museum**, with a superb collection of art and antiquities amassed by John and Gertrude Hunt, specialists in medieval art. They advised many of the great

**Limerick City Museum €** *Nicholas Street; tel: 061 417826. Open Tue–Sat 1000–1300, 1415–1700.*

**St Mary's Cathedral €** *Bridge Street; tel: 061 310293. Open Mon–Sat year-round.*

**King John's Castle €€** *Tel: 061 360788. Open daily 1000–1700 (last admission 1600).*

international collectors of the 1930s and 40s such as William Randolph Hearst. The museum displays Celtic and medieval treasures as well as Irish and European paintings, including works by Picasso, Renoir and Yeats. It also hosts visiting exhibitions in a purpose-built gallery. **Limerick City Museum** also has a fine collection of artefacts, including a brass-topped stone pillar known as 'the Nail'; this once stood in the Exchange (now gone), where business transactions were finalised with cash 'on the Nail'. The museum is housed in two of the attractive Georgian buildings at St John's Square. In the old medieval city, **St Mary's Cathedral**, which dates from the 12th century, has interesting tombs, and **King John's Castle**, a Norman fortress, houses good historical exhibitions. The castle stands alongside the River Shannon, and there are wonderful views over the city from the battlement walks. Alongside the castle is **Castle Lane**, an authentic 18th- to 19th-century streetscape. Across Thomond Bridge is the **Treaty Stone**, where the treaty that ended the siege of the Williamites was signed.

Limerick has many beautiful churches that are worth a look. Whether or not you're a McCourt fan, pay a visit to **Mungret Abbey**, where Angela's ashes were finally scattered in the churchyard. These atmospheric ruins lie on the southwest outskirts of town and date back to the 6th century.

## Accommodation and food in Limerick

**Alexandra Guest House €** *5–6 O'Connell Avenue; tel: 061 318472; fax: 061 400433; email: info@alexandra.iol.ie.* This pleasant Victorian house is only a 5-minute walk from the heart of the city centre. For literature fans, it's also located on the popular Angela's Ashes trail. Eleven en-suite guestrooms.

**Woodfield House Hotel €€** *Ennis Road; tel: 061 453022; fax: 061 326755; email: woodfieldhotel@eircom.net; www.woodfieldhousehotel.com.* Convenient location within walking distance of the city centre, quays and main attractions. Twenty-seven rooms, a bar and good food served in the Bistro.

## The washerwomen of Mungret

It is said that a long-standing rivalry existed between the monks of Mungret Abbey and Clonmacnoise as to who were the greatest scholars. They decided to settle the matter once and for all with an early Christian version of *University Challenge*. On the day their guests were due to arrive, the monks of Mungret dressed as washerwomen and went down to the *shrahan*, a little trench used for laundering clothes. When the monks of Clonmacnoise passed by and asked directions to the abbey, they answered them in Greek and Latin. At that, the visitors decided that if the washerwomen of Mungret were this well-educated, there was no point in challenging the monks, and they returned to Clonmacnoise.

# LOUGH GUR

**Lough Gur Visitor Centre** €€ *Tel: 061 360788. Open May–Sept daily 1030–1700 (last admission 1630). Walking tours of the archaeological sites are also conducted at regular intervals.*

The remains of one of Ireland's earliest settlements are scattered around Lough Gur, an idyllic lake in the Limerick countryside. By 3000 BC, Neolithic farmers had cleared the forests and built the first homesteads. Gold and bronze spearheads, shields and other objects found in the water indicate the lake was a sacred site well into Christian times. The earls of Desmond built two castles here, whose ruins still stand. An interpretive centre modelled after the Neolithic dwellings traces the history of this important site in detail. There are fine walks and a small swimming area. The Lough Gur wedge tomb can be seen along the road that leads to the visitor centre. This communal grave, dated to around 2500 BC, was a ritual site and early Bronze Age beakerware pottery was found here. A stone circle on the west side of the lake can be reached off the Limerick road.

**Above**
Lough Gur

# Suggested tour

**Total distance:** The main route is 85 miles (136km). The detour to Ballybunion covers 42 miles (67km). The detour to Lough Gur is an additional 22 miles (35km).

**Time:** It will take about 2 hours to drive the main route. Plan to take an extra hour for the detour to Ballybunion, and slightly more for the detour to Lough Gur, due to the small roads.

**Links:** This route adjoins the tour of western County Clare (*see page 182*) and is a short distance from the Dingle Peninsula (*see page 158*) and the Midlands (*see page 80*).

Leave **LIMERICK ①** on the N69 through Mungret to Askeaton, 17 miles (27km) away. On the way you'll pass the turn for the **Celtic Theme Park and Gardens**, a re-created prehistoric settlement, and **Curraghchase Forest Park**, a 618-acre (250-hectare) plantation with forest walks, a lake and arboretum. **Askeaton** was the medieval stronghold of the Desmonds, whose ruined castle with its enormous great banqueting hall sits on an island in the River Deel in the centre of town. Also on the riverbanks are the well-preserved cloisters of a 15th-century Franciscan friary. The most scenic portion of this drive begins at the small port of **Foynes**, 7 miles (11km) further on. The **Flying Boat**

**⊞ Curraghchase Forest Park €€**
Kilcornan; tel: 061 337322.
Open daily 0700–2200
(winter 0800–1830).

**Flying Boat Museum**
€€ Foynes; tel: 069 65416;
www.flyingboatmuseum.com.
Open Apr–Oct daily 1000–
1800.

**Tarbert Bridewell €€**
Tel: 068 36500. Open
Apr–Sept daily 1000–1800;
Oct–Mar Mon–Fri 1000–
1800.

**Kerry Literary and Cultural Centre €€**
24 The Square, Listowel;
tel: 068 22212; www.
kerrywritersmuseum.com.
Open Jun–Sept daily 0930–
1730 (last tour 1630); Oct–
May Mon–Fri 1000–1600
(last tour 1500).

**Left**
Lough Gur wedge tomb

**The limerick**

The true origin of the 5-line bawdy rhymes known as limericks is a matter of some debate, but some claim that they were first written by a group of 18th-century poets who lived near Croom as light-hearted jibes and drinking songs. They were translated into English in the 1840s and became very popular when Edward Lear published them in his Book of Nonsense.

**Museum** documents the transatlantic seaplane service that operated here in the 1930s and 40s. The road continues through pastoral riverside landscape to **Glin**. This small Shannonside town has been the seat of the Fitzgeralds, Knights of Glin, since the 14th century, and the ruins of an early castle overlook the river. The present Glin Castle (*not open to the public*) dates from 1785, though battlements and Gothic details were added in the 19th century to reflect the family's long history here. Turn left on the R524 for 15 miles (24km) to **Abbeyfeale**, a market town at the foot of the mountains beside the River Feale; the only remains of the 12th-century abbey after which it is named have been incorporated into the Catholic church.

**Detour:** From Glin, continue west on the N69 to **Tarbert**, where there is a handy car ferry that crosses the Shannon Estuary to Killimer in County Clare. The **Tarbert Bridewell** courthouse and gaol re-creates the fate of a prisoner in the 1830s. The R551 continues west to **Ballybunion**, a premier seaside resort with a championship golf course. Its lovely beach is backed by striking ruins and stunning cliff walks. Take the R553 to **Listowel**, which is famous for writing and racing. The town's literary heritage is examined in the **Kerry Literary and Cultural Centre**, and a racing festival takes place in September. Continue southeast on the R555 to rejoin the main tour at Abbeyfeale.

Now take the N21 northeast to **Newcastle West**. Next to the town square are the impressive ruins of a 12th-century castle built by the Knights Templar. Its banqueting hall is so well preserved that concerts and exhibitions are held here. Continue on the N21 to **ADARE ❷**. From here it is 10 miles (16km) back to Limerick.

**Detour:** Leave Adare on the N21 towards Limerick. Pass the castle and the golf course, and turn right at the old gatehouse, which the locals call the Lantern Inn, on to the minor road signposted to Croom. From here, follow signs for the R516 to Bruff, 8 miles (13km) away. At the junction with the R512, turn left and follow signs for Lough Gur. About a mile (1.6km) outside of town, turn right at the Reardon Inn to reach **LOUGH GUR ❸**. The wedge tomb is on your right about half a mile (0.8km) down this road. The interpretive centre is 2 miles (3km) further on (signposted). Return to Reardon's pub and turn right on the R512. The stone circle is signposted to the right about half a mile (0.8km) along. Follow the R512 back to Limerick, 13 miles (21km) on.

To visit the attractions north of the Shannon in County Clare, leave Limerick on the N18, signposted Shannon Airport. **BUNRATTY CASTLE AND FOLK PARK ❹** is well signposted and is about 10 miles (16km) west of the city centre. **KNAPPOGUE CASTLE ❺** and **CRAGGAUNOWEN ❻** can also be reached off the N18 via Sixmilebridge; or follow signposts from the car park at Bunratty Castle. The village of **Quin**, 4½ miles (7km) from Craggaunowen, has beautiful abbey ruins with a castle tower and Franciscan church and cloister, founded in 1402.

Shannon Development publishes guides to fishing, golfing, horse riding and other outdoor activities in the region. Enquire at the tourist information office, or *tel: 061 361555; www.discoverireland.ie/ shannonregion*

## Also worth exploring

**Killaloe**, birthplace of Brian Ború, Ireland's great high king, has a heritage centre and cathedral with magnificent carving. It lies at the tip of Lough Derg, which is encircled by a signposted scenic drive. **Castleconnell**, a Georgian spa town, is northeast of Limerick on the banks of the Shannon. **Kilmallock**, south of Lough Gur, has an attractive abbey and castle ruins. The N21 south from Newcastle West offers panoramic views from the viewing platforms at **Barna Gap**.

**Opposite**
King John's Castle, Limerick

# Irish castles

Some 2,500 castles and tower houses still stand throughout Ireland. The majority are found in the west and southwest of the country. Around 400 can be seen in County Clare alone. They were so numerous in this region that it is believed the inhabitants of any given castle could always see and signal to a neighbouring one. The motte and bailey ruins of eastern Ireland are all that remain of the early wooden fortifications built by the first wave of Norman invaders. The large-scale construction of stone castles began towards the end of the 12th century, and the fortified tower houses proliferated from around 1420 through to the 16th century.

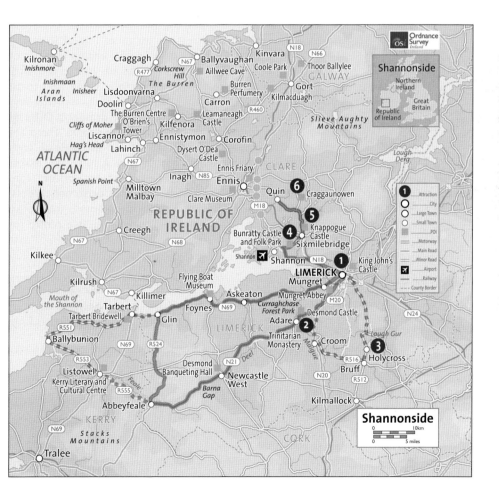

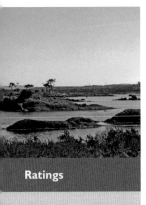

# County Clare

**Ratings**

| | |
|---|---|
| Geology | ●●●●● |
| Prehistoric sites | ●●●●● |
| Scenery | ●●●●● |
| Traditional music | ●●●●● |
| Coastal towns/ villages | ●●●●○ |
| Nature | ●●●●○ |
| Castles | ●●●○○ |
| Monastic sites | ●●●○○ |

Western County Clare contains one of Ireland's most fascinating landscapes, the sweeping limestone plateau known as the Burren. It stretches for miles inland from the Atlantic, with rare and delicate wild flowers adding splashes of colour to its grey canvas. The rocky hillsides are littered with sites of archaeological interest, from prehistoric stone ring forts, dolmens and cairns to the ruins of 12th-century churches and medieval castles. Along the coast are the dramatic Cliffs of Moher, another of the country's geological wonders. There are magnificent seascapes driving north around Black Head, with vistas across to the Aran Islands and beyond. A sunny day makes all the difference here. The region is full of surprises, from seaside resorts and a spa town to a remote perfumery. Yeats' tower home is nearby. Ennis, the county town, makes an excellent base and, like several smaller villages, is a centre for traditional Irish music.

## BALLYVAUGHAN

**Monk's Bar and Seafood Restaurant**
€ Tel: 065 707 7059.
Seafood is the speciality at this popular bar, located on the main road near the pier. The chowder is great, and so is the atmosphere.

**Aillwee Cave €€€**
Tel: 065 707 7036;
www.aillweecave.ie. Open year-round daily from 1000; Dec by appointment only.

This attractive fishing village is a popular spot for holidaymakers renting its whitewashed thatched cottages, as well as for day-trippers from around the region. On a sunny weekend you may encounter a small traffic jam as everyone vies for a parking spot near the popular **Monk's Bar**. There are boat trips from the harbour to the Aran Islands, and a number of good craft shops. Just outside town is the **Aillwee Cave**, a vast cavern formed more than two million years ago by an underground river, full of fantastic formations and a waterfall. You can see the cave on a 30-minute guided tour. There is a warren of caves throughout the Burren, but this is the only one accessible to the public.

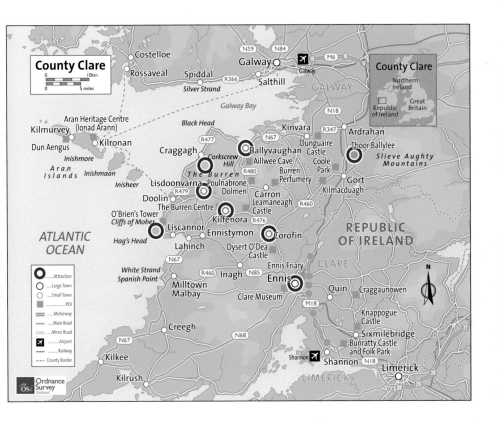

# THE BURREN

🛈 Please don't pick the flowers from this delicate habitat; many are rare and they will not flourish elsewhere.

The Burren, a sweeping area of rocky hills and plateaux, covers 62 square miles (160sq km) in northwest County Clare and is unique in Ireland. It has no bogs and few trees or pastures. The land is covered by huge pavements of limestone, called 'clints', which are broken by vertical fissures called 'grikes'. These have allowed the rainwater to drain through and carve out an extensive system of underground caves. At first glance these vast fields of grey seem a lonely and desolate place. On closer inspection, splashes of colour appear between the crevices. The Burren is a botanist's paradise, for the microclimate here nurtures an amazing number of rare plant species, including alpine and Mediterranean varieties seldom found in Ireland. Among the blue gentians, rock roses and mountain avens are 22 varieties of orchid. The flowers in turn attract some 28 species of butterfly. May to August is the best time to see this floral display (the plants are tiny, so you will have to get out of the car and explore on foot). In winter, shallow lakes called turloughs, which dry out in summer, fill up again and attract wildfowl.

**Left**
Whitewashed cottage, Ballyvaughan

# CLIFFS OF MOHER

**Cliffs of Moher**
**O'Brien's Tower** €
*Tel: 065 708 6141; www.*
*cliffsofmoher.ie. Open daily:*
*Nov–Feb 0915–1700; Mar*
*& Oct 0900–1800; Apr*
*0900–1830; May & Sept*
*0900–1900 (later on Sat,*
*Sun & bank holidays); Jun*
*0900–1930; Jul & Aug*
*0900–2130.*

**Above**
The Cliffs of Moher

These sheer striated cliffs, rising over 700ft (215m) out of the Atlantic, are one of the west coast's most impressive natural sights. Stretching for nearly 5 miles (8km) along the coast, they form a massive housing estate for nesting gulls, kittiwakes, puffins and other seabirds. **O'Brien's Tower**, built in the 19th century as a viewpoint for Victorian tourists, sits atop the highest cliff; on a clear day you can see the mountains of Connemara. Regrettably, the site is spoiled by its own popularity. Many will find it hard to appreciate the awesome beauty of the cliffs amid hordes of tourists marching up the hill to the tower, which, naturally, contains a shop. Travellers with outstretched yoghurt cartons approach you for money in the car park, while assorted buskers and CD vendors lend it all the atmosphere of a carnival pier. The best way to experience the cliffs is to set off on the path to Hag's Head, about an hour south; a walking guide can be purchased in the visitor centre.

# COROFIN

**Clare Genealogical Centre €€**
Tel: 065 683 7955;
www.clareroots.com. Open Mon–Fri 0900–1730.

**Dysert O'Dea Castle €€**
Tel: 065 683 7401;
www.dysertcastle.com. Open May–Sept daily 1000–1800.

Corofin is home to the **Clare Genealogical Centre**, which provides a professional service to people wishing to trace their Clare ancestry. The adjacent **Heritage Centre** is located in the former St Catherine's Church, built in 1718. Exhibits portray the traumatic period of Irish history between 1800 and 1860 under such themes as the Famine, emigration, language and music. **Dysert O'Dea Castle**, on the edge of town, houses an archaeology centre that displays numerous artefacts from the Burren. Within a short radius of the castle are 25 monuments, including holy wells, Celtic forts, a high cross and two Romanesque churches, which can be seen on a walking trail.

# ENNIS

**Ennis Tourist Information Office**
Arthur's Row (off O'Connell Street); tel: 065 682 8366. Open year-round. There is a walking trail to sights of interest in the town.

**Ennis Friary €**
Abbey Street. Currently closed for conservation work; call for reopening times.

**Clare Museum €€**
Arthur's Row; tel: 065 682 3382. Open Tue–Sat 0930–1300, 1400–1730 (last admissions 1230 and 1630).

**Custy's Traditional Music Shop**, Cookes Lane; tel: 065 682 1727; www.custysmusic.com, is a charming little shop with a good selection of traditional music and instruments including bodhráns, fiddles and flutes.

Clare's county town dates from 1240 when the O'Briens, kings of Thomond, invited the Franciscans to establish a settlement on an island, or 'Inis', formed by two streams of the River Fergus. The **friary** still stands and is famous for its richly carved monuments, particularly the 15th-century McMahon tomb. The town is a lively and characterful place, with narrow winding streets and bright shopfronts in the town centre. In O'Connell Square, a statue atop a high pedestal commemorates Daniel O'Connell, 'The Liberator' (*see page 36*), who was MP for County Clare between 1828 and 1831. Numerous mementos from Irish political history can be seen in the **Clare Museum**. Above all, Ennis is famous for traditional music and hosts the annual Fleadh Nua music festival at the end of May.

## Accommodation and food in Ennis

**Cruise's Pub and Restaurant €** *Tel: 065 684 1800*. Next to the friary in Abbey Street is one of the best known of many pubs in Ennis where you can hear traditional music and enjoy some authentic Irish food.

**Glenomra House €** *Limerick Road; tel: 065 682 0531; email: glenomra@hotmail.com; www.glenomrahouse.com*. There's a warm welcome at this large, friendly B&B, a 5-minute walk from the centre of town. The comfortable rooms are all en-suite with TV and tea- and coffee-making facilities. It's well located across from St Flannan's College, on the Limerick road at the east end of town. Off-street parking is available.

**Town Hall Cafe €–€€** *O'Connell Street; tel: 065 689 2333*. Set in one of Ennis's most historic buildings adjacent to the Old Ground Hotel, the high ceilings and large artworks give this busy restaurant an airy, contemporary feel. Locals drop in for freshly baked scones and the bistro-style lunch menu served throughout the day. The food is a mixture of Irish and continental cuisine with such dishes as grilled goat's cheese, braised lamb shank or beer-battered monkfish, perfectly cooked. *Open daily 1000–1630, 1800–2145 (2130 Sun).*

# KILFENORA

**The Burren Centre** €€ *Tel: 065 708 8030; www.theburrencentre.ie. Open Mar–May, Sept & Oct daily 1000–1700; Jun–Aug daily 0930–1730.*

Comprising only 13 parishes, Kilfenora is the smallest Catholic diocese in Ireland, yet by some hierarchical twist its bishop is none other than the Pope! The village is known as the 'City of the Crosses' because of the fine high crosses which adorned the grounds of its cathedral; the Doorty Cross near the door and the West Cross or 'Cross in the Field' are among the finest to survive. The cathedral is actually a small 12th-century church, now roofless but with fine sculpted capitals, tombs and other medieval details. **The Burren Centre** contains excellent models and exhibits that explain the geology, flora and fauna of this unique landscape.

# LISDOONVARNA

**Spa Wells Health Centre** €€ *Tel: 065 707 4023. Open Jun–Sept daily 1000–1800. Book in advance for the baths and treatments.*

Lisdoonvarna grew up as a spa town in Victorian times, and its sulphurous waters are still the main attraction today. You can have a sulphur bath, massage and other treatments at the **Spa Wells Health Centre**. The complex is set in parkland on the edge of town, and is Ireland's only working spa. The town's other claim to fame is its Matchmaking Festival, held in late September. Lisdoonvarna was a traditional gathering spot for bachelor farmers in search of a wife.

# THOOR BALLYLEE

This 'tower set by a stream's edge' was the summer home of William Butler Yeats for 12 years. He bought the abandoned 14th-century

## Ring forts

Ring forts were circular enclosures made of earthen walls or banks and topped by a wooden fence. In the rocky landscape of western Ireland or when a stronger structure was needed, they were built of stone. People lived in ring forts from the Iron Age, around 600 BC, through the Middle Ages, though they are generally associated with the early Christian period. They were built as isolated homesteads, rather than defensive structures, and are seldom found in groups. Dwellings, workshops and outbuildings were located inside the walls. Ring forts often had underground passages, called souterrains, which were used primarily for storing food but could also serve as a place of refuge or avenue of escape in times of attack. Around 40,000 ring forts exist throughout the countryside; most are little more than eroded banks or ditches, but in County Clare the remains of 2,300 stone forts, also called *cahers* or *cashels*, still survive.

**Thoor Ballylee €€**
*Tel: 091 631436 or
091 537700 out of season.
Open late May–Sept
Mon–Sat 0930–1700.*

**Coole Park €** *Tel: 091
631804. Park open daily
1000–dusk; visitor centre €,
open May–Aug daily
1000–1700; Sept–Apr
Wed–Sun 1000–1700.*

**Below**
O'Brien's Tower and the Cliffs
of Moher

fortified tower for £35 in 1916, shortly after his marriage, and converted it into a home. He wrote much poetry here, including 'The Winding Stair' and 'The Tower'. It has been restored to look as it did when the Yeats family lived here, and the self-guided tour is enhanced by recorded readings of Yeats' works. An audiovisual programme also gives an introduction to the man and the influences on his work. There is a magnificent view of the surrounding countryside from the top of the tower and a pretty walk beside the stream to a restored mill race. **Coole Park**, the home of Yeats' patron Lady Gregory, is 4 miles (6km) away. The house is gone and the grounds are now a national park; you can still see the Autograph Tree where many famous literary figures carved their initials.

**Above**
The Burren coastline

## Suggested tour

**Total distance:** The main route is 122 miles (196km). The detour to Milltown Malbay is 19 miles (30km). The detour through Carron cuts about 21 miles (33km) off the main route.

**Time:** Allow a full day for the main route, including the detours.

**Links:** This route is a natural extension of the tour of Shannonside (*see page 172*) and is also close to Galway City (*see page 186*).

Leave **ENNIS** ❶ on the N85, heading northwest. This is a scenic drive right from the start, with rolling hills covered in furze and pastures, broken by rocky ridges. In the centre of Ennistymon, 6 miles (10km) beyond Inagh, take the left turn signposted to Cliffs of Moher. **Lahinch** is just over a mile (2km) away. The splendid beach has made this small village, which is known for traditional music, into a popular resort. A long promenade looks out to sea over the boulder-strewn foreshore; break your journey here for a stroll, or watch the surfers and kayaks from the pub terrace. At the end of the pavement, a path carries on around the bay past the championship golf course set in the dunes.

**Detour:** At Inagh, turn left on to the R460 to **Milltown Malbay**, 10½ miles (17km) away. This is another Clare town famous for its traditional music. There are workshops, concerts and recitals during the summer school held here in July. On the coast is **Spanish Point**, where many of the ships from the Spanish Armada were wrecked in 1588; the unfortunate sailors who made it to shore were slaughtered. Nearby is a good swimming beach at **White Strand**. Follow the coast north to rejoin the main tour at Lahinch.

Leave Lahinch on the road running around the bay through Liscannor to the **CLIFFS OF MOHER ❷**, 6 miles (10km) away. Long, low walls of flat limestone rocks run like grey veins through the vast fields inland. Continue north along the coast, turning left after about 3 miles (5km) on the R479 for **Doolin**. The small village, quite spread out along the coast, is famous for traditional music; O'Connor's pub is a focal point. You can also catch a boat from the pier to Inisheer in the Aran Islands (*see page 194*). From here, follow the coast road (R477) – keep to your left at the fork and head towards the sea – which runs north for 18 miles (29km) to **BALLYVAUGHAN ❸**. This is a fabulous scenic drive around the tip of the coastline at Black Head, with surf splashing high against the rocks and distant castles glimpsed across the limestone plateau. On a clear day you can see the Aran Islands and Connemara across Galway Bay.

**Right**
Poulnabrone Dolmen

**Burren Perfumery**
*Carron; tel: 065 708 9102; www. burrenperfumery.com. Open May, Jun & Sept daily 1000–1800; Jul & Aug daily 0900–1900; Oct–Apr daily 1000–1700.* Fragrances, aromatherapy bath oils and shower gels, and scented soaps are for sale.

**The Burren Way** walking route runs for 28 miles (45km) and passes many ruined churches and archaeological sites.

## The Druid's Altar

The term 'dolmen' is derived from two Breton words meaning 'stone table'. Traditionally, a dolmen was called a 'Druid's Altar'. In Irish folklore they were said to be night-time refuges for the lovers Diarmuid and Gráinne on their flight from a wrathful king.

Leave Ballyvaughan on the N67, signposted Lisdoonvarna, and just outside town turn left on to the R480 towards Aillwee Cave. You are now entering the heart of **THE BURREN** ❹. About 4½ miles (7km) down this road, keep an eye out for the **Poulnabrone Dolmen** on your left. In spite of its size, it blends into the wide, rocky landscape and the only sign is a tiny descriptive plaque along the roadside. The farmer asks a small donation to cross his field, which is littered with hundreds of mini-dolmens built by playful locals. This impressive portal tomb, which was once covered by a mound, is dated to 2500–2000 BC.

There are several other prehistoric sites in the vicinity, including the Gleninsheen wedge tomb and the stone forts at Cahermore and Caherconnell. Continue south to the junction with the R476; alongside are the ruins of **Leamaneagh Castle**. From here you can turn left to return to Ennis via Corofin. To continue the tour through the Burren, turn right for **KILFENORA** ❺. The spa town of **LISDOONVARNA** ❻ lies 5 miles (8km) beyond.

**Detour:** Just after the Poulnabrone Dolmen, take the minor road on the left signposted to Carron, 3 miles (5km) away. From here, follow the signs to the **Burren Perfumery**. Hidden away down quiet lanes, Ireland's oldest working perfumery is a delightful spot, lined with dark bottles reminiscent of an apothecary's shop. Wonderful fragrances such as the fragrant orchid-based Ilaun or the woody Man of Aran are produced from wild flowers gathered in the Burren. The short audio-visual is a good introduction to the region's flora. As you leave the perfumery, turn right on to an unclassified road which leads through some of the Burren's most magnificent scenery; if you're lucky you may spot wild goats along here. After about 5 miles (8km), turn left at the T-junction. At the next crossroads, about a mile (1.6km) beyond, continue straight ahead and this will bring you into Kinvara.

On the main route, from Lisdoonvarna, take the N67 north, which brings you back to Ballyvaughan, 10 miles (16km) further on, via the scenic and challenging **Corkscrew Hill**, with splendid views over the town to Galway Bay. Continue east along the N67 to **Kinvara**, a pleasant town with the picturesque **Dunguaire Castle** set on a promontory jutting into the bay. This 17th-century tower house holds medieval banquets. Turn right opposite the castle on the R347 signposted to Ardrahan, 5 miles (8km) away. At the junction, turn right on to the N18 heading south. About 2 miles (3km) on you will see a large sign for **THOOR BALLYLEE** ➐. The actual turn, to the left, is about half a mile (0.8km) beyond the sign on to a small country road; from there it is signposted for just over a mile (2km) to the car park.

Return to the N18 and turn left for Gort, about 3 miles (5km) away. The R460 leads back through the Burren, passing the monastic settlement of **Kilmacduagh**, with its tilting round tower, for 13 miles (21km) to **COROFIN** ➑. From here, it is 8 miles (13km) back to Ennis. Or you can also stay on the N18 for a faster return journey.

### Also worth exploring

The towns of **Kilrush**, at the mouth of the Shannon, and **Kilkee**, on the Atlantic, are popular resort areas with fine scenery and many activities and family attractions.

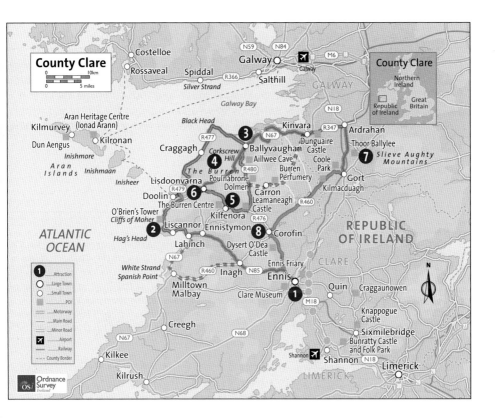

# Galway City

**Ratings**

Architecture ●●●○

The arts ●●●●

Entertainment ●●●●

History ●●●●

Beaches ●●●○○

Family attractions ●●●○○

Shopping ●●●○○

Parks ●●○○○

Set along Galway Bay at the mouth of the River Corrib, Galway City is one of the fastest-growing cities in the country. It is also one of the most pleasant, with a compact and colourful centre that still bears traces of its medieval past. Founded in the 13th century, the city became an Anglo-Norman bastion amid the fiercely Irish lands of Connacht. Maritime trade with France and Spain brought great prosperity, especially to its 14 ruling families, known as the 'tribes of Galway'. Today, as the centre for the Gaeltacht (*see page 201*), it's the Irish traditions that hold sway, from the hand-painted wooden shop signs along its cobbled streets to the traditional music and Irish-language theatre. It is also a lively university town and a magnet for artists and writers. The resort of Salthill, with beaches and a splendid promenade, lies just beyond the city centre.

## Getting around

**ⓘ Galway Tourist Information Office**
*Aras Failte, Forster Street;*
*tel: 091 537700;*
*fax: 091 537733;*
*www.discoverireland.ie/west.*
*Open year-round.*

### Parking
Both Pay and Display and a parking permit system operate on the streets of Galway. You can buy the permits online at *www. galwaycity.ie*. There are several car parks in the city centre. Two of the most convenient for this tour are those at the Eyre Square Shopping Centre and the Forster Street Car Park, across from St Patrick's Church. Much of the city centre is a pedestrian zone from 1100 to 1930 each day. This includes William, Shop, High, Quay, Main Guard and Castle streets, and parts of Abbeygate Street.

### River cruises
Scenic cruises aboard the *Corrib Princess* sail up the river into Lough Corrib. *Tel: 091 592447. Daily sailings May–Sept from Woodquay.*

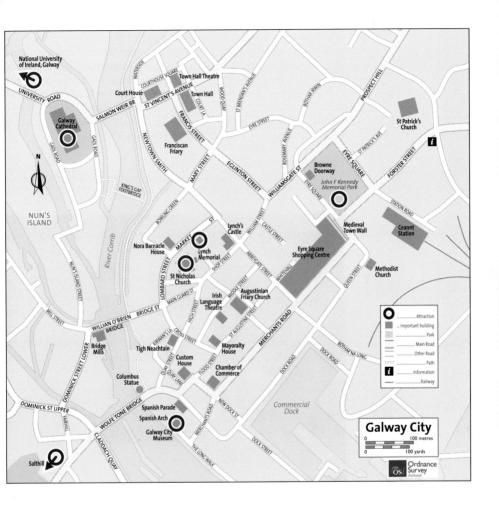

Galway City

0    100 metres
0    100 yards

OS Ordnance
Survey
Ireland

## Sights

### Eyre Square (John F Kennedy Memorial Park)

With its grassy lawns and monuments, Eyre Square is a gathering point for Galwegians. The park is also known as John F Kennedy Memorial Park, in honour of the US president who visited here in 1963. The focal point of Eyre Square is the **fountain**, erected in 1984 for the city's quincentenary. Its striking sculpture represents the rust-coloured sails of a Galway 'hooker', the region's traditional sailing boat, emphasising the importance of maritime trade to the growth of the city. The park's entrance is through the **Browne Doorway**, which was moved here from an old mansion; it bears the arms of the Browne and Lynch families and is dated 1627. The square underwent a complete remodelling in 2004, which saw an increase in green space and the planting of 95 new trees. The iron cannons at the top of the square were moved to City Hall, while the statue of Pádraic O'Conaire (1882–1928), an important literary figure who wrote his short stories in the Irish language, was moved to the civic museum. A replica now stands in the square's new sculpture garden. Other additions include a pedestrianised mall and a children's play area.

### Galway Cathedral

The Cathedral of Our Lady Assumed into Heaven and Saint Nicholas – the full name of Galway's cathedral – commands the skyline from

**Right**
Galway Cathedral by night

**St Nicholas Church**
*Lombard Street;*
*tel: 091 521 914.*
*Open year-round. Donation.*

**Leisureland €€** *Tel: 091*
*52145; www.leisureland.ie.*
*Open daily year-round;*
*summer 0800–2200.*

**Galway City Museum**
**€€** *Spanish Arch;*
*tel: 091 532460;*
*www.galwaycitymuseum.ie.*
*Open Mon 1400–1700,*
*Tue–Sat 1000–1700.*

Nun's Island, formed by channels of the River Corrib. It was one of the last cruciform churches to be built in Ireland, and was dedicated in 1965 by Boston's Cardinal Cushing. The exterior, of plain cut limestone, is a conglomeration of styles: Renaissance dome, Romanesque windows, Spanish Baroque cupolas. The surrounding pavement and car park detract from its appearance, but go inside, and the immense space, massive pillars and statues, and Connemara marble flooring are indeed impressive.

## Lynch Memorial
This black marble stone set above a Gothic doorway recalls the harsh justice of James Lynch Fitzstephen, Mayor of Galway in 1493, who condemned his own son to death for the murder of a Spanish sailor who had flirted with the lad's girlfriend. No one in town was willing to carry out the execution, so the mayor, determined to see the law upheld, hanged the boy himself, then became a recluse. Some say this tragic event was the origin of the term 'to lynch'.

## St Nicholas Church
The Collegiate Church of St Nicholas was built by the Normans in 1320 on the site of an older chapel. Tradition claims that Christopher Columbus prayed here before his voyage to the New World. Extensions in the 15th and 16th centuries created its unusual shape, and it is the largest medieval parish church in the country still in constant use. Cromwell's forces commandeered it as a headquarters and destroyed many of its features, but it contains fine sculptural work and gargoyles, as well as the tomb of that sorry soul Mayor Lynch (*see above*).

## Salthill
Salthill is Galway City's seaside resort, just 2 miles (3km) west of the town centre, and a holiday destination in its own right. Many of the city's large hotels are located here. It has good beaches, nightlife and family attractions, such as **Leisureland**, with a variety of pools as well as amusement park rides. Salthill's best feature is its 2½-mile (4km)-long promenade, the longest in Ireland. This is associated with a strange tradition: local strollers kick the wall when they reach the end of the prom. No one knows how the custom originated, but it goes back generations.

## Spanish Arch
One of Galway's most famous landmarks, the Spanish Arch was built in the 16th century to protect the quays where Spanish ships unloaded their cargoes. It actually comprises two arches. At the front of the arch, adjoining the **Spanish Parade**, is the old fishmarket area, where Claddagh women sold the catches of the village fishermen. On the other side is The Long Walk, a promenade for the gentry in times past. Next to the arch is the **Galway City Museum**.

# Suggested walk

**Time:** Allow about 2 hours for the main walk, slightly longer if you add the detours.

**Links:** Galway City is a good base for a tour of Connemara (*see page 202*). There are good connections to County Clare and Limerick via the N18, to the Midlands via the N6 and to County Mayo via the N84.

Begin at the tourist information office. Walk down Forster Street to the Eyre Square Shopping Centre. Here you can see a section of Galway's **medieval town wall ❶**, built by the Normans in the 13th century. Cross over the road to **EYRE SQUARE ❷**. From the top of the square, walk down Williamsgate Street, which leads into the heart of old Galway. The central shopping district begins here along William Street, which becomes Shop Street after it crosses Abbeygate Street. On the right-hand corner is **Lynch's Castle ❸**, a fine example of a fortified house dating to around 1320. Notice the Spanish-style decoration around the stone lintels. The castle now houses a branch of the Allied Irish Banks. Shortly beyond, a pedestrian walkway to the right leads to the **LYNCH MEMORIAL ❹**, next to **ST NICHOLAS CHURCH ❺**. Continue across Market and Lombard streets to the **Nora Barnacle House ❻** at No 8 Bowling Green, the former home of James Joyce's wife; it is now a small museum.

Continue south along Lombard Street, which curves left on to Cross Street. At the corner with Quay Street is the **Tigh Neachtain ❼** pub (Naughton's in English, pronounced 'knock-tons'). It was once the town house of Richard Martin of Ballynahinch, in Connemara, known as 'Humanity Dick' (*see page 203*). Turn right on to Quay Street. This is

**Below**
County Galway crafts centre

## The Claddagh ring

The Claddagh ring – two hands holding a heart with a crown on top – represents love, loyalty and friendship. This Galway tradition originated in the fishing village of Claddagh, which was located on the west bank of the river just outside the medieval walled city (now a suburb). It is said to have been made in the 1730s by Richard Joyce, who was captured by Moorish pirates and trained as a goldsmith. When King William ordered his release, he made the ring to express his gratitude. It became popular as a wedding ring and to symbolise friendship or betrothal. If the ring is worn with the heart pointing inward, it signifies the wearer's heart is taken. If the heart points outward, the wearer's heart is open.

the nucleus of activity in the city, with all the best bars, restaurants, gift shops and art galleries packed into the colourful little streets and alleyways. As you wander down towards the river, look for **Kirwan's Lane** ❽ on the right, one of Galway's last medieval lanes.

**Detour:** If Quay Street gets claustrophobic, other nearby streets are worth a wander. From Tigh Neachtain, continue straight on along Cross Street, and turn left on Middle Street. About halfway along, past the **Irish Language Theatre**, the Augustinian Friary Church has a beautiful stained-glass artwork depicting the Crucifixion behind the altar. At the top of the road, turn right on Abbeygate Street and right again on St Augustine Street, which takes you back down past the **Mayoralty House** into Flood Street and on to the waterfront, where you can rejoin the main walk at the Spanish Arch.

Quay Street continues on down to the river, where the **Columbus Statue** ❾, erected on the 500th anniversary of his discovery of America, stands near the Wolfe Tone Bridge. To the left is the **Spanish Parade** and the **SPANISH ARCH** ❿. The banks of the wide, rushing river are a favourite spot for students and workers to relax on a sunny day. From the Columbus memorial, a signposted riverside walk takes you north along the River Corrib to the **Salmon Weir Bridge** ⓫. The views from the bridge are particularly wonderful from mid-April to early July, when shoals of salmon gather in the water to begin leaping their way upriver to their spawning grounds in Lough Corrib. Cross the bridge to **GALWAY CATHEDRAL** ⓬. Cross back over the bridge and veer to the left along Waterside, passing the courthouse, for wide views across the river. Turn right at the end of the street, right again into St Vincent's Avenue, and left at the traffic lights in front of the town hall into Francis Street. This runs past the Franciscan friary and into Eglinton Street. At Williamsgate Street, turn left to return to Eyre Square.

**Detour:** For a longer walk, from the cathedral, cross the bridge along University Road, which leads to the **National University of Ireland,**

Galway **⓭**. It was built during the Great Famine (1845–9), and was then called Queens University. Today it is known as a centre for Irish language and Celtic studies. The Victorian Quadrangle is its finest architectural feature. Return to the corner of Canal Road, turn right and follow it along the water, continuing south on Henry and Dominick streets which bring you back to Wolfe Tone Bridge. Cross the bridge to return to the town centre.

# Shopping

On Saturday mornings, a lively **street market** sets up shop in the pedestrian street beside St Nicholas Church (*0800–dusk*). The **Eyre Square Shopping Centre** has a range of offerings, from the antique market and fashions to the heraldry gifts in the Shoemakers Tower. **Claddagh Jewellers** is one of many merchants in the area selling the traditional Claddagh rings (*see page 191*). The **Cornstore** in Middle Street is a complex of stylish shops; **Mulligan**, in the same street, has a good selection of traditional music.

# Entertainment

Galway is a city of the arts, with several theatre groups, dance groups, a film industry and numerous arts events. One home troupe, the Druid Theatre Company, made it to Broadway with its highly acclaimed production of 'The Beauty Queen of Leenane'. The **Town Hall Theatre**, Courthouse Square, is Galway's main venue for plays, concerts, films and events; *tel: 091 569777 for information and bookings*. Galway also has a vibrant music scene, where you can hear traditional Irish music or check out some excellent nightclubs with a variety of dance music.

Galway's biggest party is the **Galway Arts Festival** in July, with a variety of concerts, theatre productions, comedy, film and visual arts. Another time to catch the city in full swing is during the **Galway International Oyster Festival**, held in the latter part of September.

# Accommodation and food

**McDonagh's Seafood House €–€€** *22 Quay Street; tel: 091 565001; www.mcdonaghs.net.* This Galway landmark caters for all budgets and appetites. You can relax over a restaurant meal of fresh mussels, Galway oysters or the catch of the day, or have a cheap and cheerful – but equally delicious – snack from the fish and chips bar.

**Tigh Neachtain €–€€** *17 Cross Street; tel: 091 568820.* This popular bar and bistro is housed in a historic pub in Galway's medieval quarter. The downstairs pub is famous for traditional music; the bistro upstairs serves seafood and steaks.

**The House Hotel €€** *Spanish Parade; tel: 091 538900; fax: 091 568262; email: info@thehousehotel.ie; www.thehousehotel.ie.* This luxury boutique hotel in the heart of the city combines cosy comfort with chic style. Rooms are individually designed with thoughtful amenities such as a laptop safe. The Parlour Bar and Grill serves modern international cuisine.

**Hotel Meyrick €€€** *Eyre Square; tel: 091 564041; fax: 091 566704; email: reshm@monogramhotels.ie; www.hotelmeyrick.ie.* De-luxe accommodation at a desirable address. The hotel was built in the mid-19th century for the arrival of the railway. Rooms in the original building are the most elegant; the fifth-floor bedrooms are now all suites with great views of Galway Bay. All are beautifully appointed with every amenity. There is an indoor pool and sauna, two bars and a restaurant.

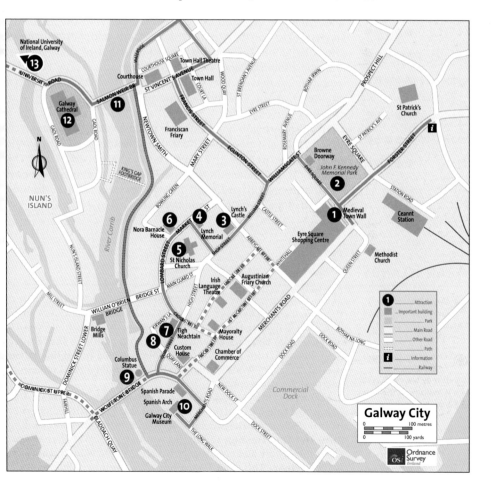

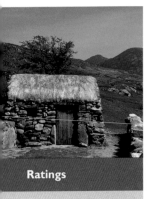

**Ratings**

| | |
|---|---|
| Art and craft | ●●●●● |
| Coastal towns/ villages | ●●●●● |
| Lakes | ●●●●● |
| Mountains | ●●●●● |
| National parks | ●●●●● |
| Scenery | ●●●●● |
| Walking | ●●●●● |
| Prehistoric sites | ●●●○○ |

# Connemara

Connemara is one of the wildest and most beautiful areas in all Ireland. This westward expanse of County Galway would be a peninsula were it not for the mountain barrier that thwarts the joining of the fjord-like Killary Harbour with the Republic's largest lake, Corrib. Around the southern and western coasts, the Atlantic has taken great jagged bites out of the shoreline; tranquil fishing villages lie scattered along the rocky bays and across the causeways that bridge the islet stepping stones. This is the heart of the Gaeltacht, home to thousands of native Irish speakers (*see page 201*).

Inland the region is a kaleidoscope of beauty, with sapphire-blue lakes, vast bogs and heathlands, and stunning sculpted mountains such as the Twelve Pins, centred round the wilderness of Connemara National Park. Spend at least two days here, especially if you want to visit the remote Aran Islands. Every road is a scenic one, and there is much to explore.

## ARAN ISLANDS

🛈 **Aran Tourist Information Office**
*Kilronan; tel: 099 61263. Open year-round.*

 One of the best ways to get around the islands is by bicycle. Bicycle hire is available at the quay in Kilronan.

The three Aran Islands, formed of a limestone base similar to that of the Burren region (*see page 177*), lie off the south coast of Connemara in Galway Bay. Many age-old Irish traditions are still part of everyday life here, from language and dress to methods of fishing and farming. Aran knitwear, with its distinctive motifs, is highly prized throughout Ireland (*see page 196*). The islands also contain important prehistoric and early Christian remains.

At 8 miles (13km) long and 2 miles (3km) wide, **Inishmore** (Inis Mór) is the largest of the three. Ferries arrive at **Kilronan** (Cill Rónáin), its main village, where passengers are met by minibuses and jaunting carts. The **Aran Heritage Centre (Ionad Áran)** is a good place to learn about the history and culture of the islanders. The island's main sight is **Dun Aengus**. This stone fort, dating from the Iron or Bronze Age, is

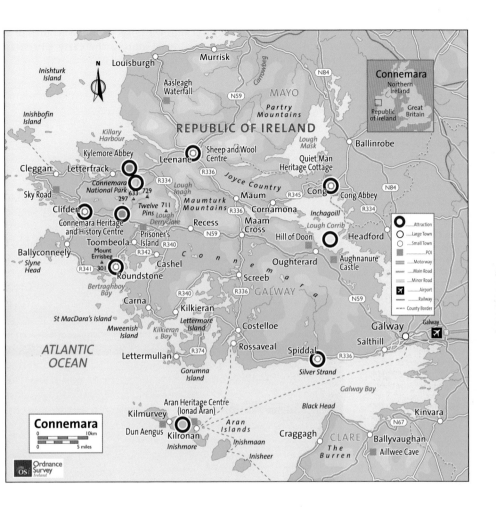

**Ionad Áran – Aran Heritage Centre**
€€ Tel: 099 61355;
fax: 099 61454;
www.visitaranislands.com.
Open Jun–Aug daily 1000–1900; Apr–May & Sept–Oct daily 1100–1700.

one of Europe's most important prehistoric sites. It covers 11 acres (4.5 hectares) and is protected by three concentric stone battlements and sharp-pointed rock stakes designed to injure unsuspecting enemies. The views from the inner rampart are spectacular. There are other stone forts on Inishmore, but the island is also known for its early Christian ruins. St Enda established a monastery here in the 5th century and for centuries it was the island of saints and hermits. Enda's church and those of St Ciarán and others can be seen. Many sights are near **Kilmurvey** (Cill Mhuirbhigh), which also has a good beach.

**Inishmaan** (Inis Meáin), the middle island, with a population of around 300, also has an abundance of ancient monuments, including the fort of Dun Conor (Dun Chonchubhair).

Cars cannot be taken to the Aran Islands. Passenger ferries leave daily from Rossaveal for Inishmore, with extra sailings in summer. For details of these sailings and for inter-island schedules, contact **Inismór Ferries**, the islanders' own ferry, *tel: 091 56653*; or **Island Ferries**, *tel: 091 568903 or 572273 (after 1900); email: islandferries@eircom.net; www.aranislandferries.com*

**Aran Doolin Ferries** provides ferry services to the islands from Doolin; *tel: 065 707 4455; email: info@doolinferries.com; www.doolinferries.com*

**Aer Arann Islands** operates daily flights to the Aran Islands year-round from Connemara Regional Airport at Inverin, near Spiddal; *tel: 091 593034; www.aerarann.islands.ie*

Take a sweater or jacket on the ferry to the Aran Islands, as the return trip can be cold and wet. Sunscreen is also recommended. If you want to stay on the islands, accommodation is limited and difficult to find in high season, so book before you leave the mainland.

The smallest island, **Inisheer** (Inis Oírr), has the ruined church of St Gobnait, the only woman allowed among the early Christian brethren, and the 15th-century O'Brien's Castle.

## Aran sweaters

The traditional oiled wool Aran sweaters protected fishermen against the elements. Each family had their own pattern of stitches, so that the wearer could be identified in case of an accident at sea. The stitches were also symbols: for example, the cable was the fisherman's rope, for safety and good luck; the trellis stood for the stone-walled fields; the diamond signified success and wealth.

# CLIFDEN

ⓘ **Clifden Tourist Information Office** Galway Road; tel: 095 21163. Seasonal.

**Clifden Chamber of Commerce**, The Square; tel: 095 30776; email: info@clifdenchamber.ie; www.clifden.ie, has local maps and information. Open year-round Mon–Fri 0930–1300, 1400–1730.

ⓦ **Michael Gibbons' Walking Ireland**, Market Street, tel: 095 21492 or 21379; email: walkwest@indigo.ie, has guided walks and mountain treks graded for beginners to advanced, and study tours by an Irish archaeologist.

🅐 A Clifden highlight is the **Connemara Pony Show**, held in August, with festivities celebrating this sturdy breed that evolved on the rocky slopes of the region.

Opposite
Connemara landscape

Set in forested hills between the mountains and the sea, on the western edge of County Galway, Connemara's largest town is a great base for exploring the region. It's a pretty place whose distinguishing landmarks are the two pointed church spires; the Protestant church has a copy of the Cross of Cong (*see page 198*). There are several good restaurants and pubs. Along the beach road are the ruins of Clifden Castle, built in 1815 by the town's founder, John D'Arcy, a Galway sheriff who dreamed of establishing law and order in the Connemara wilderness.

The **Sky Road** is a scenic 7-mile (11km) circular drive west of Clifden, single-track for much of the way, with spectacular views from the 'low' road above the sea or the 'high' road which climbs to over 500ft (152m).

## Accommodation and food in Clifden

**Mitchell's Restaurant** €€ *Market Street; tel: 095 21867.* Seafood is superb at this popular restaurant, housed in a turn-of-the-20th-century building with a pleasant décor of wood and stone. The gigantic mound of mussels is a favourite choice, though it competes with monkfish with red pepper sauce, fresh salmon, oysters, and a variety of other fresh fish, based on the catch of the day.

**The Quay House** €€ *Beach Road; tel: 095 21369; fax: 095 21608; email: res@thequayhouse.com; www.thequayhouse.com.* Built for the harbour master around 1820, the Quay House is Clifden's oldest building and has been a Franciscan monastery and convent in its long history. Now it's an award-winning four-star guesthouse, beautifully furnished with antiques and family portraits. The 14 bedrooms have large bathrooms and period furniture, some have working fireplaces and balconies, and most overlook the harbour. Breakfast is served in the conservatory and features home-baked breads, locally smoked salmon and other delights.

# CONG

ⓘ **Cong Tourist Information Centre** Tel: 094 954 6542. Open Mar–Oct Mon–Sat.

ⓦ **Quiet Man Heritage Cottage** €€ Circular Road; tel: 094 954 6089. Open Mar–Nov daily 1000–1700.

**Cong Abbey** € Always accessible.

Cong (the name means 'the narrow neck of land') sits on an isthmus between loughs Corrib and Mask. Film buffs have been making a beeline for this picturesque village in County Mayo since 1952, when it was the setting for John Ford's *The Quiet Man* starring John Wayne. The **Quiet Man Heritage Cottage**, opposite a bend in the river, is a replica of the one used in the film. At the top of the street is the tourist information office, housed in the old court-house, and the entrance to **Cong Abbey**. The ruins of this Augustinian abbey date from the 13th century, and the sculpture around its doorways and windows is some of the finest stone carving in Ireland.

**Corrib Cruises** sail from Cong to Inchagoill Island in Lough Corrib. *Tel: 091 557798; www. corribcruises.com. Sailings at 1100 and 1445 daily, Apr–Oct.*

The Cross of Cong, believed to contain a relic of the True Cross and now in the National Museum in Dublin, came from here. The abbey stands alongside the river and beautiful woodlands. Ashford Castle is now a luxury hotel, but its grounds are open to the public.

## CONNEMARA HERITAGE AND HISTORY CENTRE

**Connemara Heritage and History Centre** *Dan O'Hara's Homestead €€ On the N59, 4 miles (6km) from Clifden; tel: 095 21808; www.connemaraheritage.com. Open Apr–Oct daily 1000–1800.*

This visitor attraction strikes the right note between informing and entertaining. It centres around the homestead of Dan O'Hara, a Connemara farmer whose life was shattered when he was evicted for non-payment of a windows tax. Forced to emigrate, his wife and three of their seven children died on the passage, and Dan ended his days selling matches on the streets of New York. After learning how the family lived in happier times, a little train takes you up the steep hill to the restored cottage. Some Neolithic burial sites have been excavated nearby. Back at the heritage centre, there is a replica of a *crannog* (lake dwelling), ring fort and stone oratory.

## CONNEMARA NATIONAL PARK

**Connemara National Park** € *Tel: 095 41054; www. connemaranationalpark.ie. Visitor centre open mid-Mar–mid-Oct daily 0900–1730; park open all year. The walking trails near the visitor centre are wide and there are well-groomed gravel paths, suitable for pushchairs and wheelchairs.*

Covering 7,307 acres (2,957 hectares), Connemara National Park contains expanses of bog and heath, grasslands and four peaks of the majestic Twelve Pins (also known as the Twelve Bens). The entrance to the park at Letterfrack leads to an excellent visitor centre, where there are exhibits on the bogs and the park's flora and fauna. Walking trails start from the visitor centre, one leading past a paddock where there are Connemara ponies. There is a good tearoom and picnic area, and in the summer guided walks, talks and activities.

**Right**
Pony in Connemara National Park

## Will o' the Wisp

Strange glowing lights can sometimes be seen on the bog at night. Some say it is Jack O'Lantern, a shoemaker who was condemned to wander the bog for murdering a child. Such lights can cause a person to stray from the path and fall into a bog hole. To ward off this evil, people are advised to turn their coats inside out immediately on sighting the Will o' the Wisp.

# KYLEMORE ABBEY

**Kylemore Abbey and Garden €€€**
Tel: 095 41146; www.kylemoreabbey.com. Open daily: Mar–Jun 0900–1800; Jul & Aug 0900–1900; Sept & Oct 0930–1800; Nov–Feb 1000–1630.

Built in 1868 as a private home, Kylemore Abbey is one of Ireland's great neo-Gothic castles. In 1920, it was purchased by Benedictine nuns fleeing war-torn Belgium; they converted it into an abbey and girls' school. Two reception rooms and the main hall are open to visitors, as is the beautiful 6-acre (2.5-hectare) Victorian walled **garden**, the country's finest in its day. Also on the grounds is a Gothic church with beautiful stained-glass windows, marble columns and intricate stone carvings. Visitors can enjoy the lake and woodland walks or watch the abbey's distinctive pottery being made in the studio.

# LEENANE

**Sheep and Wool Centre €€**
Tel: 095 42323; www.sheepandwoolcentre.com. Open Apr–Oct daily 0930–1800.

This tiny village is surrounded by a giant of a landscape, set on the edge of Killary Harbour between the billowing curves of the Maumturk Mountains and the peak known as Devilsmother. The mountain walls shelter this long, narrow fjord, which maintains a constant depth, making it one of the safest anchorages in the world. In the 1990s, Leenane was the setting for the filming of John B Keane's play, *The Field*. The **Sheep and Wool Centre** focuses on the area's sheep and wool industry, with demonstrations of spinning, weaving and dyeing. Nearby, on the road to Louisburgh, is the impressive **Aasleagh Waterfall**.

# LOUGH CORRIB

**Oughterard Tourist Information Office**
Tel: 091 552808; fax: 091 552811. Open year-round.

Lough Corrib is the largest lake in the Irish Republic, covering 42,000 acres (17,000 hectares). It is also among the most scenic, dotted with numerous islands. One of these, **Inchagoill**, contains early Christian monastery ruins, another a 13th-century castle. **Oughterard**, the largest town on its western shore, is a centre for brown trout and salmon fishing. Whether or not you want to take the boat trip out on the lake to Inchagoill, take the minor road, signposted from town,

**Aughnanure Castle**
€ Tel: 091 552214.
Open Apr–Oct daily
0930–1800.

down to the pier; it's a beautiful spot to sit in the cool breeze and admire the islands. Another fine lakeside drive is the Glann road, also signposted from the centre, which runs along the lake shore for 7 miles (11km) to the **Hill of Doon**. The ruins of **Aughnanure Castle**, built around 1500, are just east of town on the shores of the lake.

# ROUNDSTONE

**O'Dowd's**, tel: 095 35809; www.odowdsbar. com, is a popular bar and restaurant serving delicious seafood. Specialities include their mouthwatering chowder with lobster bits.

This picturesque village, whose Irish name means 'rock of the seals', rises up the hill from its small harbour. It attracts visitors seeking quiet holidays, as well as many craftspeople and artists. In the IDA Crafts Centre on the edge of town, you can watch *bodhráns* (pronounced 'bow-rawn'), the traditional Irish goat-skin drums, being made (just don't try to take any photos). For wonderful views, ascend the slopes of Mount Errisbeg, 987ft (301m).

# SPIDDAL

**Spiddal Craft Village**
Tel: 091 553376; email: info@ceardlann.com; www.ceardlann.com. Open year-round Mon–Sat 0900–1800, Sun 1400–1800.

**Standún**, on the outskirts of Spiddal, tel: 091 553108; www. standun.com, is a family-owned shop established in 1946 with a large range of high-quality clothing and other goods.

Spiddal is a delightful village at the start of the Gaeltacht, and makes a good base for day trips to the Aran Islands. Its name is an anglicisation of the Irish word for 'hospital'; the original hospital is now a convent, next to the church. There is a fine Blue Flag beach, the Silver Strand, which was formerly the bathing place for the gentry; in those days, there were separate beaches for men and women. You can also fish or, in summer, watch the *curragh* races along the shore. At the edge of town, **Spiddal Craft Village** (Ceardlann An Spideil) is an attractive complex of cottages housing workshops where you can watch weavers, potters, candlemakers, woodturners and other artisans at work.

## Accommodation and food in Spiddal

**Tuar Beag B&B** € *Tel: 091 553422; fax: 091 553010; www. bandbgalway.com.* This splendid B&B has a great location and an interesting history. Set on a hillside overlooking Galway Bay on the west edge of the village, it is a modern home incorporating the original stone walls and fireplace of the 19th-century cottage built by Eamonn Feeney's great-grandfather. Several generations back, the family was related to Sean Feeney, the real-life *Quiet Man* upon whom the film was based; the ruined homestead still stands nearby. The six rooms have a view of the sea and the Aran Islands, and are beautifully furnished with all amenities. Siobhan serves a fabulous breakfast menu. Three-star self-catering apartments are also available.

**Above**
Drying turf

## The Gaeltacht

A Gaeltacht is a region where traditional Irish language (Irish Gaelic) and culture still hold sway. Irish is spoken as the first language, although almost everybody is bilingual; signs, however, are generally in Irish only. Gaeltachts are primarily found in western Ireland, in counties Kerry, Cork, Galway, Mayo and Donegal, and also in Waterford. The southern Connemara Gaeltacht is the most populous in Ireland. People throughout the country send their children to stay with families in these regions during summer holidays to learn Irish firsthand. The Gaeltachts often lie in remote areas that are on the margins economically, and creative initiatives have been in operation since 1956 to support these areas and encourage people to stay. For visitors, Gaeltachts are a place to hear an ancient tongue in everyday use and to enjoy some of Ireland's best traditional music.

There are walks of varying lengths and difficulties in the region, including the Aran Islands; details and maps are available from tourist information offices. There are magnificent views from Benlevy Mountain, 1,375ft (418m), on the isthmus between Lough Corrib and Lough Mask.

# Suggested tour

**Total distance:** The main route is 118 miles (189km). The coastal detour through Carna and Roundstone adds an extra 25 miles (40km). The R344 from Kylemore Abbey to Recess is 10 miles (16km). The detour to Cong from Maum is 28 miles (64km) return.

**Time:** Whether you follow the main route or the coastal detour, you will want to devote at least a full day to this tour, as there is much to explore. The coastal detour can be rather slow going, due to the narrow, winding roads and the likelihood of getting lost in the Gaeltacht, so figure half a day for this part of the route. Allow an hour and a half for the detour to Cong, as the roads here can also cause delays.

**Links:** This tour is a natural extension of a visit to Galway City (*see page 186*). The N59 continues on a scenic drive to Westport in County Mayo (*see page 210*).

Leave Galway on the R366 through Salthill (*see page 189*). **SPIDDAL** ❶ (An Spidéal) is 11 miles (18km) beyond. You are now entering southern Connemara's Gaeltacht area, and road signs are generally in Irish only. **Rossaveal** (Rós a Mhíl) is the ferry port for the **ARAN ISLANDS** ❷. There's no reason to drive down to this port area unless you are catching a boat; if you are, watch out for the tricky turn-off, about 10 miles (16km) beyond Spiddal. The R336 curves sharply to the right, while the minor road to Rossaveal goes straight on. For the main route, continue north on the R336 through Costelloe (Casla) and Screeb (Scriob); **Maam Cross** (An Maam) is 5 miles (8km) beyond. Turn left on to the N59 for **Clifden** (An Clochán), 21 miles (34km) to the west. This is a stunning road, running alongside idyllic lakes and backed by the magnificent mountains known as the Twelve Pins (Benna Beola). It is also fast, wide and well paved – a joy to drive, especially after a spell on the back roads. About 15 miles (24km) along, look out on your left for the tower on **Prisoner's Island** in Ballynahinch Lake. In the early 19th century, Richard Martin, known as Humanity Dick, used to imprison his tenants there if they mistreated the animals on his estate. Martin went on to found the Royal Society for the Prevention of Cruelty to Animals. About 4 miles (6km) before Clifden, the turn for the **CONNEMARA HERITAGE AND HISTORY CENTRE** ❸ is on your right.

**Detour:** To explore Connemara's rocky sea coast, turn left at **Screeb** (Scriob) on to the R340 signposted to Gortmore (An Gort More). The narrow road winds around Kilkieran Bay to the lobster-fishing villages of **Kilkieran** (Cill Chiaráin) and **Carna**. From the latter, you can follow a side road across a bridge to **Mweenish Island**, where there are sandy beaches, or you can take a boat trip to **St MacDara's Island**. At the junction beyond the village, the main road turns to the right, signposted Clifden; the left-hand 'coast road' only leads out on to another headland. There are fine views of the Twelve Pins in the

**Above**
Lough Inagh

distance as you head north through the landscape of bog grasses. Just outside Cashel, you can continue north for 3 miles (5km) to rejoin the main tour. To continue the detour, turn left on to the R342 towards the village of **Cashel** (An Caiseal). This winding road has beautiful views over Bertraghboy Bay and of the mountains inland, and there are plenty of shaggy Connemara ponies grazing in the fields. At Toombeola, turn left on the R341 to **ROUNDSTONE** ❺ (Cloch na Rón), 4 miles (6km) to the south. Continue around the headland, past the fine beaches at Gorteen Bay and Dog's Bay, through **Ballyconneely** (Baile Conaola), a large village strung out along the bay. About 1½ miles (2.5km) beyond, a memorial marks the site where Alcock and Brown landed after the first non-stop transatlantic flight in 1919. Rejoin the main tour at **CLIFDEN** ❹ (An Clochán), 6 miles (9km) further on.

From Clifden, take the N59 north towards Westport. This road has magnificent panoramic views of the Twelve Pins on its way to **CONNEMARA NATIONAL PARK** ❻; the entrance to the visitor centre is just beyond Letterfrack (Leitir Fraic), about 9 miles (14km) away. **KYLEMORE ABBEY** ❼ is 3 miles (5km) further on. From there it is 9 miles (14km) to **LEENANE** ❽ (An Lionán). Turn right on the R336 for a scenic drive through the Maam Valley, known as 'Joyce Country', bordered by the Maumturk Mountains. At Maum, turn right on the R336 for a 5-mile (8km) drive back to Maam Cross.

**Detour:** Just beyond Kylemore Abbey, a right turn off the N59 on to the R334 signposted to **Recess**, 10 miles (16km) away, takes you south along one of the most scenic roads in Connemara. It runs through a broad valley with sweeping tracts of bogland either side, encircled by the Maumturk Mountains and the Twelve Pins. The ground is marked with dark ridges where peat has been dug, and you will see piles of cut turf stacked and drying in the sun. It makes a wonderful follow-up to the exhibits in the abbey visitor centre. Further along, the bog gives way to forest along **Lough Inagh**, its deep blue waters filling a crescent at the base of the range, with its equally photogenic neighbour, **Lough Derryclare**. At the junction with the N59, you can turn right to return to Clifden, carry on south on the R340 to connect with the Roundstone detour (*above*), or turn left to rejoin the main tour at Maam Cross.

**Detour:** Another scenic detour can be made from Maum along the north shore of Lough Corrib. Continue straight ahead on the R345 towards **Cornamona** (Corr na Móna). After 2 miles (3km) look out for the **Hen's Castle**, roosting on Castlekirk Island in the lake. This 12th-century tower is said to have been built in a single night by a witch and her hen. Continue through the village and along the road to **CONG** ❾, with lovely lake views, steep-sided hills, pasture and woodlands. The turns in the main road are fairly well signposted bar one: when you reach the unmarked 'Y' junction just outside town, take the right-hand fork which will bring you into the town centre. To rejoin the main tour, retrace the 14 miles (23km) back to Maum.

On the main route, turn left at Maam Cross on to the N59, which continues through more lovely lakeland for 9 miles (15km) to **Oughterard** on the shores of **LOUGH CORRIB ⑩**. Galway is 17 miles (27km) further on.

## Also worth exploring

From Costelloe, the R374 leads out across the islands of **Lettermore** (Leitir Móir) and **Gorumna** to **Lettermullan** (Leitir Mealláin), along a narrow road that crosses bridges and causeways connecting this stony landscape. Views are lovely but driving is slow. **Cleggan**, northwest of Clifden, is a centre for outdoor activities such as pony trekking and fishing. There are also regular sailings from here to **Inishbofin Island**, 6 miles (10km) offshore, with historical sites, beaches and wildlife.

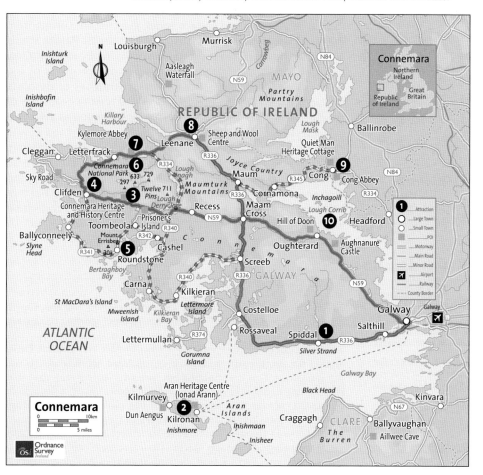

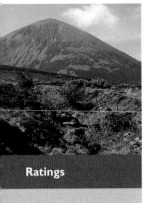

# County Mayo

## Ratings

| | |
|---|---|
| Prehistoric sites | ●●●●● |
| Religious sites | ●●●●● |
| Beaches | ●●●●○ |
| Outdoor activities | ●●●●○ |
| Coastal towns/ villages | ●●●○○ |
| Scenery | ●●●○○ |
| Family attractions | ●●○○○ |
| Mountains | ●●○○○ |

County Mayo has two very different faces. Most people live on its southern and eastern edges, in a crescent curving from Westport up to Killala Bay. Its highlights are St Patrick's holy mountain, the miraculous shrine of Knock, the beaches of Clew Bay and the holiday island of Achill. To the northwest of the Nephin Beg Mountains, there are vast stretches of desolate bogland that end in the dramatic cliffs and remote headlands of the Gaeltacht. This lonely landscape may strike you as awesome or oppressive, depending on the weather and your mood as well as your point of view. But however it moves you, it *is* amazing, particularly when you think that it was once completely covered in trees. This is an environment largely caused by man, and evidence of the thriving settlement that existed here in prehistoric times can be seen at Céide Fields. Here, civilisation was turned into wilderness, rather than the other way round.

## ACHILL ISLAND

ℹ️ **Achill Tourist Information Office**
*The Sound; tel: 098 45384; www.discoverireland.ie/west. Open Mon–Sat in summer.*

**Achill Tourism** *Cashel, tel: 098 47353 or 098 47392; www.achilltourism. com. Open Jun–Sept daily 0900–1700; Oct–May Mon–Fri 0900–1700.*

At 15 miles (24km) long and 12 miles (19km) wide, Achill is Ireland's largest island. It has splendid cliff scenery, picturesque villages, superb game fishing and fine sandy beaches, five of them sporting the quality Blue Flag. A trip to Achill Island is best undertaken on a sunny day when you can enjoy the views. If it's misty or dark, the **Atlantic Drive** around the south coast, signposted as you leave Achill Sound, is not recommended. This is a stunning but somewhat hair-raising road that winds along high, sheer cliffs. It passes Kildownet Castle, a stronghold of Grace O'Malley (*see page 210*), and the ruins of a 12th-century church. It rejoins the main road at **Keel** (An Caol), the island's main resort. Between **Dooagh** (Dumha Eige) and Keel are the Minaun Cliffs and the strange Cathedral Rocks; these are best explored from a sightseeing boat. Further west, basking sharks – a harmless variety –

County Mayo

0 _____ 16km
0 _____ 8 miles

Portacloy
Belderrig
Céide Cliffs
Céide Fields
Broadhaven
Belmullet
R314
Glenamoy
Belmullet Peninsula
Bunnahowen
R313
Bangor Erris
Blacksod
N59
Slievemore Mountain
Doogort
N59
Dooagh 671
Keel
Keem
Minaun Cliffs
Achill Island
Corraun Peninsula
R319
Claggan Mountain
380
Mulrany
Rockfleet Castle
Newport
Clare Island
Clew Bay
National Famine Monument
Murrisk
Westport House and Country Park
N5
Westport
N84
Louisburgh
R335
Croagh Patrick 765
Inishturk Island
Aasleagh Waterfall
N59
Inishbofin Island
Killary Harbour
Kylemore Abbey
Letterfrack
Leenane
Sheep and Wool Centre
R336
Cleggan
Connemara National Park 633 729
297
Twelve 711 Pins
R334
Joyce Country
Maumturk Mountains
Maum
R345
Cong
Clifden
Cornamona
Inchagoill
Recess
Maam Cross
Lough Corrib
Ballyconneely
Toombeola
R340
N59
Hill of Doon
R341
Mount Errisbeg
R342
301
Connemara
Cashel
Roundstone
Bertraghboy Bay
R340
Carna
Kilkieran
St MacDara's Island
Mweenish Island
Kilkieran Island Bay
Lettermore Island
Costelloe
ATLANTIC OCEAN
Lettermullan
R374
Rossaveal
Spiddal
R366
Gorumna Island
Silver Strand
Galway Bay

Donegal Bay

Dún Briste
Céide Cliffs
Downpatrick Head
Ballycastle
R314
Killala Bay
Killala
Moyne Abbey
Rosserk Friary
N59
Ballina
Moy
MAYO
Nephin Beg Range
Feeagh Lough
Furnace Lough
Lough Conn
Foxford
N26
N58
Swinford
N5
Burrishoole Abbey
Museum of Country Life
Kiltimagh
Castlebar
R320
Knock-Ireland West
R323
N83
Knock
N60
N17
Ballyhaunis
Ballintober Abbey
Claremorris
REPUBLIC OF IRELAND
R331
Lough Mask
Ballinrobe
N17
N83
Quiet Man Heritage Cottage
Cong Abbey
Tuam
Headford
N84
N17
Aughnanure Castle
Oughterard
GALWAY
N63
Screeb
R366
N59
Galway
M6
Salthill
N18

Skreen
Ox Mountains
SLIGO

County Mayo

Northern Ireland
Republic of Ireland
Great Britain

○ Attraction
○ Large Town
○ Small Town
■ POI
Motorway
Main Road
Minor Road
✈ Airport
Railway
County Border

Ordnance Survey Ireland

can be seen in **Keem Bay**. On the north coast at **Doogort** (Dumha Goirt), a fishing village at the base of Slievemore Mountain, you can hire boats to visit Seal Caves.

# CÉIDE FIELDS

**Céide Fields €**
*Located on the R314, 5 miles (8km) from Belderrig and 5 miles (8km) from Ballycastle; look for the silver pyramid roof rising out of the bogland; tel: 096 43325; www.ceidefields.com. Open Apr–May & Oct daily 1000–1700; Jun–Sept daily 1000–1800; last admission 1 hour before closing; rest of the year pre-booked groups only.*

Lying beneath the blanket bog on the slopes of the north Mayo coast, Céide (pronounced 'Cay-ja') Fields is the most extensive Stone Age monument in the world. Excavations have revealed a highly organised layout of dwellings, tombs, walls and fields covering over 3,700 acres (1,500 hectares). It represents the earliest known land enclosure, dating back some 5,500 years. Why the site was abandoned remains a mystery, but it is thought that with the growth of the bog the land could no longer support the population.

Céide, which means 'flat-topped hill', was discovered in the 1930s by Patrick Caulfield, who recognised a pattern in the stones he found when digging peat in the fields. His theories were ignored, but his son Seamus became an archaeologist and returned to study the site, uncovering some of the most valuable data known about this environment. Excellent displays in the visitor centre provide background on the settlement, and a guide takes you into the fields to interpret the site. Little of the actual ruins can be seen, but it is impressive all the same to picture what this must have looked like in prehistoric times. The panoramic views over the coastline, from the Stacks of Broadhaven to Downpatrick Head and beyond, are spectacular. Across the road from the car park, a viewing platform affords dramatic views down over the Céide Cliffs.

# CROAGH PATRICK

**P** Beware of thieves in the large car park at the base of Croagh Patrick. Put any valuables out of sight *before* you get there, as they have even been known to break into the boots of cars while visitors are on the mountain.

**Croagh Patrick Visitor Centre**
*Tel: 098 64114; www.croagh-patrick.com. Open Apr–Oct daily.*

Croagh Patrick, rising 2,510ft (765m), is the holy mountain where St Patrick is said to have driven the snakes from Ireland. (In fact, Ireland never had any snakes to begin with, as the reptiles failed to make it across the land bridge that briefly connected it to the mainland after the last Ice Age.) However, the holy man did spend 40 days praying and fasting atop the mountain in his mission to convert the country to Christianity, and every year on Reek Sunday, the last Sunday in July, thousands of pilgrims make the ascent – many in bare feet – performing ritual prayers at three stations. It takes about two hours to reach the top, which is flat – not conical as it appears from below – and crowned by a chapel. The views over Clew Bay and its islands are fantastic. You can see them just as well from the statue of the saint at the start of the trail, only a 10-minute climb from the car park.

Opposite the car park in the village of Murrisk is the **National Famine Monument**, erected in 1997. John Behan's moving sculpture depicts skeletal bodies on a coffin ship, a tribute to those who fled the country and died. County Mayo was one of the regions hardest hit by the famine, with over 100,000 victims. The little road near the entrance runs down to the ruins of Murrisk Abbey.

## The Famine Walk

In 1847, the Choctaw Indians of the southern United States learned of the Great Famine from Irish refugees and sent money to a relief fund in Ireland. Six years earlier, the Choctaws had been driven from their homelands in Mississippi and forced to walk the 'Trail of Tears' to reservations in Oklahoma. Each year in May, a memorial Famine Walk takes place from Doolough to Louisburgh, often accompanied by a representative from the Choctaw Nation.

# KNOCK

**Knock Tourist Information Office**
Tel: 094 938 8193. Open May–Sept.

**Knock Shrine €**
Tel: 094 938 8100; programme of ceremonies and devotions, late Apr–mid-Oct; call for information; email: info@knock-shrine.ie; www.knock-shrine.ie

In 1879, 15 people witnessed an apparition of the Blessed Virgin in this small impoverished town. It has since become an international Marian Shrine, visited by 1.5 million pilgrims seeking cures or forgiveness every year. The basilica built to accommodate them has 32 pillars, one donated from each of the counties in Ireland; the four medieval windows represent the four provinces. It is surrounded by several chapels and peaceful, landscaped grounds. Pope John Paul II commemorated the centenary of the apparition during a visit here in 1979. To the south of the church, the **Knock Museum €** (*tel: 094 937 5034. Open May–Oct daily 1000–1800, Nov–Apr daily 1200–1600*) portrays life in rural Ireland in the 19th century, and documents the story of the apparition.

# NEWPORT

Newport is an attractive little town nestled between the mountains and Clew Bay. The seven-arch viaduct you cross upon entering the town was built in 1892 to carry the old railway line. The most striking landmark is **St Patrick's Catholic Church**, built of stone in 1914 in the Irish Romanesque style. Inside is a beautiful marble communion rail and a stained-glass window depicting the Last Judgement by Harry Clarke. Just outside town are the ruins of 15th-century **Burrishoole Abbey**. Nearby are **Rockfleet Castle** (also called Carrigahowley Castle), a stronghold of Grace O'Malley, and the ancestral home of the late Princess Grace of Monaco.

## The pirate queen

Grace O'Malley, or Granuaile, Ireland's famous pirate queen, was born in 1530 to a clan who ruled Mayo's islands. When her first husband was murdered by a rival clan, she established a string of forts around Clew Bay, and attacked cargo vessels from her base on Clare Island. As the English stepped up their conquest of the Irish chieftains, Grace sailed to London to make peace with Queen Elizabeth I, who offered her a title. Grace refused, saying that she was a queen in her own right! She died peacefully in 1603, and bridged the gap between the old Gaelic ways and the new order as her son became the first Viscount Mayo. Her story is told in the Granuaile Centre in Louisburgh.

# WESTPORT

**ℹ Westport Tourist Information Centre**
*James Street; tel: 098 25711; email: westport@failteireland. ie. Open year-round.*

**🏠 Westport House and Country Park**
*€€€ Tel: 098 27766; email: info@westporthouse.ie; www.westporthouse.ie. Open Mar–Oct; call or see website for details.*

Westport, one of the few planned towns in the country, was designed by James Wyatt in the 18th century. The graceful tree-lined Mall which straddles the Carrowbeg River, the lovely Georgian houses and the bright shopfronts on Bridge Street make this heritage town a popular base for visitors. **Westport House and Country Park**, near the quay, is the home of Lord Sligo, a descendant of the pirate queen Grace O'Malley. The house was built in 1730 and has many outstanding features, including ceilings by Richard Castle, a dining room by James Wyatt and exquisite period furnishings. On the grounds are a children's zoo, a log flume ride, a miniature railway and various other family attractions.

## Accommodation and food in Westport

**Brooklodge B&B €** *Deerpark East, Newport Road; tel: 098 26654; email: brooklodgebandb@eircom.net; www.brooklodgebandb.com.* A warm welcome and a friendly chat over tea and scones await at this pleasant B&B, 5 minutes from the town centre. Two of the four large, comfortable rooms are en-suite; there is also a TV lounge and private car park. *Open all year except Christmas week.*

A farmers' market is held on Thursday mornings at **The Octagon**, in the town's central square.

**Matt Molloy's**, owned by a member of The Chieftains, is one of the most popular venues for traditional music in Westport. This busy pub is on Bridge Street, and the music is in a room at the back.

**Torrinos €–€€** *10 Market Lane, Middle Bridge Street; tel: 098 28338; www.torrinos.ie.* Located down a little passageway off Bridge Street, this charming Italian restaurant has a wide selection of meat, poultry and seafood dishes, pasta and gourmet pizzas. Good wine list and friendly, attentive service. Very popular, so book ahead in high season. *Open daily 1730–2200, and also for lunch Thur–Sat from 1230.*

## Suggested tour

**Total distance:** The main tour is 132 miles (212km). The detour to Achill Island is 28 miles (45km) each way from Mulrany to Keel. The detour to Knock is 57 miles (91km).

**Time:** The main tour will take you one long day. Allow half a day for the detour to Achill Island, and 2 hours for the detour to Knock. If you want to cover the entire main route and detours, you will need to spend at least 2 days in the area.

**Links:** The N59 connects County Mayo with Connemara (*see page 194*) in the south and Sligo (*see page 220*) to the east. Sections of this tour work well as a linking route to other regions.

**Below**
Clew Bay from Croagh Patrick

Leave **WESTPORT ❶** on the R335 Louisburgh road. After 6 miles (10km) you enter the village of **Murrisk**, at the foot of **CROAGH PATRICK ❷**. Return to Westport and take the N59 north for 7 miles (11km) to **NEWPORT ❸**, crossing an area of drumlins (small hills) that are rich in archaeological remains. The Dyra hoard of bronze and gold treasures, now in the National Museum in Dublin, was found here, and there are many ring forts, holy wells and *crannogs* (lake dwellings). Just beyond Newport, on the N59, a minor road to the right, signposted to Furnace, leads up into the Nephin Beg Mountains and the scenic countryside around Furnace and Feeagh loughs. The N59 continues around Clew Bay, past fringes of sandy beach and a lush landscape of wild fuchsias. At **Mulrany** there are gorgeous views across to Croagh Patrick on the opposite shore. A footpath leads down to the wide sandy beach.

**Detour:** Just beyond Mulrany, turn left on the R319 for **ACHILL ISLAND ❹**. This should be treated as a separate excursion, as it is unlikely you would be able to drive around the island and make the circuit around the north coast in the same day.

**❶ Ballina Tourist Information Office**
*Cathedral Road; tel: 096 70848. Open May–Sept.*

**Castlebar Tourist Information Office**
*Linenhall Street; tel: 094 902 1207. Open Apr–Sept.*

**Above**
St Patrick's Church, Newport

Beyond Mulrany, the N59 winds around the base of Claggan Mountain, then suddenly drops into a flat, open area of peatland where piles of turf cut by local people are stacked along the road to dry. The rapidly deteriorating road surface signals your entry into the hinterland. At Bangor Erris, a small dusty town 19 miles (31km) away, turn left on to the R313 towards Belmullet. About a mile (1.6km) outside of town, an unclassified road to your right is signposted to Glenamoy and Céide Fields, 8 miles (13km), but if you prefer to stick to the main roads, continue on the R313 to Bunnahowen (Bun na hAbhna), 9 miles (14km) ahead, and turn right on to the R314, signposted to Ballina. The hamlet of Glenamoy is the only speck of civilisation in this lonely expanse of sweeping bogland. After 17 miles (27km) you near the coast at **Belderrig**. The next few miles are some of the most dramatic coastline in Ireland. The road suddenly plunges into a series of dangerous bends that carry you down a deep ravine, with glimpses of the jagged stratified cliffs. You'll be looking seaward

**Foxford Woollen Mills Visitor Centre**
€€ St Joseph's Place; tel: 094 925 6104. Open Mon–Sat 1000–1800, Sun 1200 or 1400–1800.

Three long-distance walking trails traverse County Mayo. The **Newport–Bangor Trail**, 28 miles (48km), takes you through the Nephin Beg Mountain Range. The **Foxford Way**, 54 miles (86km), winds through the Ox Mountains and past many archaeological sites; in summer, there are guided walks along sections of the trail. It is linked to the **Western Way**, a 106-mile (170km) long-distance route across the wild boglands to Killary Harbour. Contact the tourist information offices for details.

**Granuaile Centre €**
Louisburgh; tel: 098 66341, tells the story of the pirate queen Grace O'Malley. Open Jun–mid-Sept 1100–1700.

**Family trees**
If you're tracing your ancestors in County Mayo, there are two genealogical research centres that may be of help: the **Mayo North Family Heritage Centre** in Ballina, tel: 096 31809, and the **South Mayo Family Research Centre** in Ballinrobe, tel: 094 954 1214; www.mayo.irishroots.net

as you climb up the other side, but also keep an eye out for the entrance to **CÉIDE FIELDS ❺**, about 5 miles (8km) along on your right, which is not signposted and easy to miss if you're distracted by the coastal views. Look for the silver pyramid roof of the visitor centre peeking out above the brown peatlands.

The R314 continues east along the coast, with more fine views of **Downpatrick Head** and its amputated tip, Dún Briste; on a clear day you can see the coast of Donegal across the bay. Around Ballycastle, the landscape changes to pasture. Continue straight on the R314 for 9 miles (14km) to **Killala**, an attractive town with old stone buildings set along the harbour and a fine round tower. A couple of miles east of town on Killala Bay are the ruins of **Moyne Abbey**. Nearby are the better-preserved remains of **Rosserk Friary**. Both date from the 15th century and were Franciscan communities. **Ballina** (pronounced 'Bal-in-náh'), Mayo's largest town, is about 3 miles (5km) further south. Set on the River Moy, it is a centre for salmon and trout fishing. The Victorian Cathedral of St Muredach and ruins of a 14th-century friary can be found here. Take the N26 south to **Foxford**, where you can tour the **Foxford Woollen Mills**, and continue south on the N58, which joins the N5, where you turn right for **Castlebar**, Mayo's county town. It is home to the **Museum of Country Life** with its fascinating portrayal of the traditions of rural life in Ireland from 1850 to 1950 (*Turlough Park; tel: 094 903 1773; www.museum.ie. Open Tue–Sat 1000–1700, Sun 1400–1700*). From here it is 11 miles (18km) back to Westport.

**Detour:** From Foxford, continue on the N26 to Swinford, then take the R320 south to Kiltimagh. Turn left on the R323 for 5 miles (8km) to **KNOCK ❻**. Take the N17 south to Claremorris, then follow the R331 southwest to **Ballinrobe**, surrounded by mountains, lakes and woodland. The village of **Cong** (*see page 197*) is just 7 miles (11km) to the south. Then take the N84 north past **Ballintober Abbey**, where Mass has been celebrated continuously since its construction in 1216, to rejoin the main tour at Castlebar.

## Also worth exploring

**Belmullet Peninsula**, in the far northwest of the county, is a Gaeltacht region with remote beaches and fine views. The small beaches around **Portacloy** are backed by cliffs with views of the Stacks of Broadhaven offshore. County Mayo has 13 Blue Flag beaches, and many of them can be found around Clew Bay. These include Louisburgh, Murrisk and Mulrany, as well as those at Achill Island and **Clare Island**. The latter was the stronghold of the pirate queen Grace O'Malley (*see page 210*), whose castle can be visited; ferries run from Roonah Quay near Louisburgh. The narrow coast road around the south side of the Corraun Peninsula that connects the mainland with Achill Sound is very scenic with fine views out to Clare Island.

## Ireland's boglands

Ireland's boglands are some of the largest in Europe. They cover about 17 per cent of the country. Bogs were formed thousands of years ago, due to a combination of factors. Prehistoric settlers burned large tracts of the primeval forests that once covered the land to make pastures for their animals and fields for cereal crops. This produced charcoal, which impeded soil drainage. With Ireland's heavy rainfall and cool climate, the soil became waterlogged, creating conditions for the development of humus and peat. Dead trees and vegetation sank into the marshy pools but could not fully decompose in the watery conditions. Over the centuries, the bog built up and spread outwards. Only certain mosses, grasses and heathers could thrive in this acidic environment. There are two types of bogland: blanket bog, which covers mineral soil and is found mainly in the west; and raised bogs, which can be up to 98ft (30m) deep.

Because of a lack of oxygen, peat acts as a preservative; everything from pollen and huge trees (bog oak) to human bodies have been found in the bogs. For centuries the Irish have cut turf by hand for use as fuel, but large-scale commercial harvesting and increased energy needs are rapidly depleting this unique and irreplaceable habitat. Some 4,000 years ago, Ireland had 2,890,000 acres (1,178,000 hectares) of peatlands, most of which were still undisturbed in 1645. By 1990, only 373,000 acres (151,000 hectares) remained – a loss of 87 per cent in less than 400 years.

**Below**
View from Mulrany

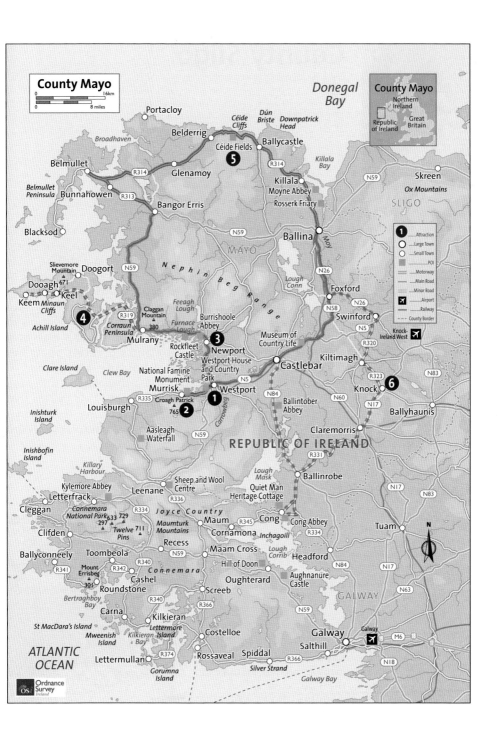

County Mayo

0 ........... 16km
0 ........... 8 miles

Donegal Bay

County Mayo
Northern Ireland

Republic of Ireland | Great Britain

Portacloy
Céide Cliffs
Dún Briste
Downpatrick Head
Belderrig
Broadhaven
Céide Fields
Ballycastle
Belmullet
R314
Glenamoy
R314
Killala Bay
Belmullet Peninsula
Bunnahowen
R313
Bangor Erris
Killala
Moyne Abbey
Rosserk Friary
N59
Skreen
Ox Mountains
SLIGO
Blacksod
N59
Ballina
Moy
MAYO

1 ........... Attraction
O ........... Large Town
O ........... Small Town
........... POI
........... Motorway
........... Main Road
........... Minor Road
✈ ........... Airport
........... Railway
........... County Border

Slievemore Mountain
Doogort
N59
Nephin Beg Range
Lough Conn
N26
Foxford
Dooagh 671
Keel
Keem Minaun Cliffs
Feeagh Lough
Claggan Mountain
R319
Corraun Peninsula
Furnace Lough
380
Mulrany
Burrishoole Abbey
N58
Swinford
N26
N5
Achill Island
Clare Island
Clew Bay
Rockfleet Castle
Newport
Westport House and Country Park
National Famine Monument
Murrisk
Croagh Patrick
765
Westport
Louisburgh
R335
Inishturk Island
Museum of Country Life
Castlebar
Kiltimagh
Knock-Ireland West ✈
R320
R323
N83
Knock
N84
Ballintober Abbey
N60
N17
Ballyhaunis
Aasleagh Waterfall
N59
Carrowbeg
Claremorris
REPUBLIC OF IRELAND
R331
Inishbofin Island
Killary Harbour
Sheep and Wool Centre
Lough Mask
Ballinrobe
N17
N83
Kylemore Abbey
Letterfrack
Leenane
R336
Quiet Man Heritage Cottage
Cleggan
Connemara National Park 633 729
R334
Joyce Country
Maumturk Mountains
Maum
R345
Cong
Cong Abbey
R334
Tuam
N17
Clifden
297
Twelve Pins 711
Cornamona
Inchagoill
Recess
Maam Cross
Lough Corrib
Headford
N84
Ballyconneely
Toombeola
R340
N59
Hill of Doon
Aughnanure Castle
N63
Mount Errisbeg
R341
R342
Connemara
Cashel
301
Roundstone
Oughterard
Screeb
GALWAY
Bertraghboy Bay
R340
R366
N59
Carna
Kilkieran
St MacDara's Island
Mweenish Island
Kilkieran Island Bay
Lettermore
Costelloe
Galway
Galway ✈
M6
ATLANTIC OCEAN
Lettermullan
R374
Rossaveal
Spiddal
Salthill
R366
N18
Gorumna Island
Silver Strand
Galway Bay

N

Ordnance Survey Ireland

# County Sligo

## Ratings

| | |
|---|---|
| Literary connections | ●●●●● |
| Mountains | ●●●●● |
| Prehistoric sites | ●●●●● |
| Scenery | ●●●●● |
| Traditional music | ●●●●● |
| Walking | ●●●●○ |
| Art | ●●●○○ |
| Beaches | ●●●○○ |

Sligo is Yeats country, and you can see why the poet and the painter were inspired by this stunning landscape of placid lakes, enchanting glens, glorious seascapes and striking table mountains. This often-overlooked corner of Ireland may come as a surprise to visitors who aren't expecting such a visual feast. At its heart is lovely Lough Gill, whose Irish name means 'lake beauty'. Everywhere you turn there are sculpted mountains of great character: atop Knocknarea is the grave of a legendary warrior queen, while one of Ireland's greatest poets lies beneath 'bare Benbulben'. The landscape is a museum of prehistoric remains. More than 5,000 archaeological sites have been recorded, and it is said that there is not a field in Sligo that doesn't contain a ring fort, cairn or standing stone. The region is also famous for its traditional fiddle music, which can be heard in the booming capital, Sligo Town.

## CARROWMORE MEGALITHIC TOMBS

**ⓘ Carrowmore Megalithic Tombs**
€ Tel: 071 916 1534.
Open Apr–mid-Oct daily 1000–1800 (last admission 1700).

Carrowmore is Ireland's largest Stone Age cemetery. The megalithic graves here predate those at Newgrange (see page 60) by 700 years and are among the oldest and most important in Europe. More than 60 passage tombs (see page 68) and dolmens have been excavated in the fields surrounding the visitor centre; many more were destroyed in the 19th century. Ring forts, standing stones and other

**Right**
Tomb at Carrowmore

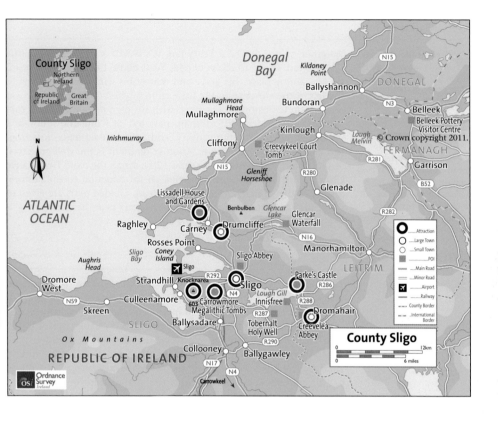

prehistoric remains indicate that a significant hunter-gatherer settlement existed here for thousands of years. There are beautiful views of the countryside as you walk around the sites.

# DROMAHAIR

This pretty village set along the River Bonet has a pivotal place in Irish history. In the 12th century, Dervorgilla, wife of Tiernan O'Rourke, eloped from the now-ruined Breffni Castle with Dermot MacMurrough, King of Leinster, setting in motion events that led to the Anglo-Norman conquest of Ireland (*see page 35*). On the opposite bank of the river is **Creevelea Abbey**, the last Franciscan friary to be built before the suppression of the monasteries in the mid-16th century. Its lovely peaceful ruins are worth a visit; there's a footpath signposted from the town. To drive in, take the minor road between two round stone walls, to the left off the R287 just before the junction for the town centre; it's not signposted so you may need to ask for directions.

# DRUMCLIFFE

**Drumcliffe Church and Visitor Centre**
€ Tel: 071 914 4956. Open Mon–Sat 0900–1800; Sun 1200–1800. Refreshments and gift shop.

**Yeats Tavern Restaurant** € On the N15 at Drumcliffe; tel: 071 916 3117. This busy family-run establishment is a cheery place with pub and adjoining restaurant serving above-average fare.

Whether or not you're a Yeats fan, it's worth a stop at Drumcliffe Churchyard. Poetic to the very end, Yeats chose this peaceful spot for his last resting place. His grave and that of his wife Georgie lie just to the left of the entrance to the little church where his grandfather was rector. The tombstone is inscribed with his own epitaph: 'Cast a cold eye/On life, on death,/Horseman, pass by!' St Colmcille founded a monastery here in the 6th century, and a fine carved high cross from this earlier church still stands. Another remnant is the well-preserved round tower, built between 900 and 1200, across the road. **Drumcliffe Church and Visitor Centre** provide an introduction to the cultural history of the church, Drumcliffe and Yeats. Guided tours are given of the church and site. There is a pretty river walk near the cemetery.

# KNOCKNAREA

The distinctive cairn-topped mountain Knocknarea (pronounced 'Knock-na-ray') dominates the Sligo coastline for miles around. The cairn is said to be the grave of Queen Maeve, the warrior queen of Connacht, whose feats of battle are glorified in the ancient Celtic tale *Taín Bó Cuilgne*. Maeve is believed to have lived in the 1st century AD, although the grave is much older, dating to around 2500 BC. The huge cairn, whose circumference measures 590ft (180m), has never been excavated. A scenic drive along the lower slopes of the mountain is signposted from the R292, about a mile and a half (2.5km) outside Strandhill. You can climb to the summit, 1,978ft (603m) high, but, if you do, local tradition advises that you add a stone to the cairn as a protection against fairies.

# LISSADELL HOUSE AND GARDENS

**Lissadell House and Gardens** €€
Tel: 071 916 3150; www.lissadellhouse.com. Visitor reception centre open Aug–Oct; access to house and gardens by permission only.

An atmosphere of faded grandeur exists behind the imposing façade of 'that old Georgian mansion', as described by W B Yeats. Built in 1834, it is still a family home and houses exhibitions on Yeats and Constance Markievicz. Yeats was a frequent visitor here, calling on the two sisters, Eva and Constance, immortalised in one of his poems. Constance was a revolutionary who participated in the Easter Rising; she became the first woman elected to the British House of Commons, but took her seat in the Dáil instead (*see page 37*). Murals of the sisters and other members of the family were painted on the dining-room wall by Constance's husband, Count Casimir Markievicz. The house is surrounded by beautiful woodlands stretching down to the lake which are now a wildlife and forestry reserve.

**Above**
Lissadell House

## Accommodation and food near Lissadell

**Ardtarmon House €–€€** *11 miles (17km) from Sligo Town on the Drumcliffe–Raghley road; tel/fax: 071 916 3156; email: enquiries@ardtarmon.com; www.ardtarmon.com.* Experience the gracious ambience and tranquil setting of Yeats' day at this large, handsome house, just down the road from Lissadell. A family home since 1852, it is filled with original furniture, in both the spacious bedrooms and public areas. The genial hosts have decorated the four guest bedrooms, all en-suite, in lovely light colours that complement the period furnishings. The house is surrounded by extensive grounds with a tennis court, orchards, woodlands and lovely views of Knocknarea and the Mayo Mountains. A private beach is just a 3-minute walk through the fields. Dinner is available with advance notice. There are also self-catering cottages in the gatehouse and converted stable block.

# PARKE'S CASTLE

**Parke's Castle €**
*Tel: 071 916 4149.*
*Open Apr–Sept 1000–1800.*

The finest thing about Parke's Castle is its setting, right at the water's edge of Lough Gill. Built in 1609, this fortified manor house set within a walled enclosure is typical of Irish plantation settlements. It was erected on the site of an earlier O'Rourke stronghold, whose clan chief was executed for having extended his hospitality to a shipwrecked officer of the Spanish Armada. His confiscated lands were then granted to Captain Robert Parke. The castle has been restored using Irish oak and traditional craftsmanship. The stone mullioned windows, diamond-shaped chimneys and parapet walls are some of its outstanding features. The interior contains an exhibition on the castle's restoration and the topography and archaeology of the surrounding countryside.

# SLIGO TOWN

**ℹ Sligo Tourist Information Office** Temple Street; tel: 071 916 1201; fax: 071 916 0360; email: northwestinfo@ failteireland.ie. Open year-round.

**Ⓨ Yeats Memorial Building** Hyde Bridge; tel: 071 914 2693; www. yeats-sligo.com. Open year-round Mon–Fri 1000–1700 (closed for lunch 1300–1400).

**The Model Arts and Niland Gallery** The Mall; tel: 071 914 1405; www.modelart.ie. Open Tue–Sat 1100–1730 (Thur till 2000), Sun 1200–1700.

**Sligo Abbey** €€ Abbey Street; tel: 071 914 6406. Open mid-Apr–mid-Oct daily 1000–1800; mid–end Oct Fri–Sun 0930–1630.

**The Sligo County Museum** Stephen Street; tel: 071 914 1623. Open: Jun–Sept Tue–Sat 1000–1200, 1400–1650; Oct–May Tue–Sat 1400–1650. The museum displays memorabilia connected with both Yeats and Countess Markievicz, as well as local artefacts.

The northwest's largest town spans the River Garavogue and covers the neck of land between Lough Gill and Sligo Bay. It's a lively place, with a college and a compact town centre of traditional façades. The town is also known as a centre for the arts and for Irish music. Its greatest appeal for many visitors is its associations with W B Yeats. At Hyde Bridge, a striking bronze statue of the poet by Rohan Gillespie stands across from the **Yeats Memorial Building**, where the Yeats Summer School of poetry readings, lectures and other events is held in August. The W B Yeats Exhibition here contains a film, photographic displays and heritage objects associated with the poet. **The Model Arts and Niland Gallery** is home to the Niland Collection of paintings by Jack B Yeats, the poet's brother, and their father John B Yeats. The gallery also hosts temporary exhibitions of Irish and international contemporary art. **Sligo Abbey**, founded in 1253, is the only medieval building remaining in the town, and most of the ruins date from the 15th century. The cloisters and altar have beautifully carved stonework. Other notable buildings include the courthouse, Dominican friary and several churches.

## The brothers Yeats

The poet William Butler Yeats (1865–1939) and his artist brother Jack (1871–1957) were members of a prominent Sligo family. Although they spent their childhood in London, where their father John struggled to earn a living as a portrait painter, during summer holidays they visited their maternal grandparents, the Pollexfens, who were merchant shippers in Sligo. This idyllic landscape inspired them throughout their lives. Jack, one of Ireland's foremost 20th-century painters, declared 'Sligo was my school, and the sky above it.' William credited Sligo as the inspiration for the poems that earned him the Nobel Prize for Literature in 1923.

# Suggested tour

**Total distance:** The main route is 50 miles (80km). The detour to Innisfree is about 5 miles (8km) return. The detour to Bundoran is 54 miles (87km).

**Time:** The main route can be driven in a couple of hours, not counting sightseeing stops. The detour to Bundoran will add another hour and a half.

**Links:** From Manorhamilton, it is only 25 miles (40km) to the Fermanagh Lakeland (*see page 224*). The N15 continues north through the attractive town of Ballyshannon to Donegal (*see page 235*). There are several roads to County Mayo (*see page 206*) from Sligo Town.

Leave **SLIGO TOWN ❶** on the R292 to **Strandhill**. This seaside village with its smart white houses sloping down to the strand has a modern, almost Californian feel. The beach here is fabulous, with sweeping vistas and a promenade for watching the Atlantic surf breaking against the shore. There is a more sheltered beach nearby at **Culleenamore**. Continue on the R292 around the headland, which circles **KNOCKNAREA ❷**, following signs for **CARROWMORE MEGALITHIC TOMBS ❸**, about 4 miles (7km) away.

To avoid going back through Sligo and to continue the scenic route around Lough Gill, turn right out of the car park at Carrowmore and take the first minor road on your right. Take the next left-hand turn down a pretty country lane, and then the next right (at the road's end), which brings you to a roundabout. Take the second exit off the roundabout (signposted Dromahair) and then an immediate left again towards Dromahair; you will then see a sign for Lough Gill, indicating you are on the right road (R287). About a mile (1.6km) beyond, a short detour signposted to the left leads to the **Tobernalt Holy Well**, a peaceful shady spot surrounded by a cliffside grotto. Mass was celebrated here in secret during the years of the Penal Laws. Continue on the R287, with the shores of Lough Gill coming into view. On the left is the **Dooney Rock** nature trail, a 3/4-mile (1.2km) loop that takes you past the inspiration for Yeats' poem, 'The Fiddler of Dooney'. The road carries on through beautiful woodland, with tantalising glimpses of the island-dotted lake. At the junction, take the left fork signposted to **DROMAHAIR ❹**, 4 miles (6km) ahead.

**Detour:** Yeats fans may want to make a pilgrimage to see the Lake Isle of **Innisfree**, celebrated in his famous poem. After the junction, look for the brown 'Yeats Country' sign on your left. The minor road through the farmlands is well signposted, ending at the car park just above the lake (2½ miles/4km). Walk down to the shore to see the tiny tree-covered island; boat trips may be available from the house beside the pier. There are also views across the lake to Parke's Castle and the mountain called the Sleeping Warrior. Rejoin the main tour at Dromahair.

**PARKE'S CASTLE ❺** is 4 miles (7km) from Dromahair on the R288/R286. Continue west along the north shore of Lough Gill for 6 miles (10km) back to Sligo Town. Leave town on the N15 north for **DRUMCLIFFE ❻**. Turn left at the Yeats Tavern and after about a mile

**Walking** Sligo is great walking country. The Glencar Valley, with its lake and waterfall, and other glens northeast of Lough Gill have splendid scenery. It's a good idea to ask permission when crossing private land; some farmers can take offence. There are also good walks through the Kinlough Forest from the picnic site by the village. Knocknarea is the easiest mountain to climb, and the view from here is as rewarding as any.

If you're headed to the Fermanagh Lakeland from here, fill up with petrol before you cross the border, as it costs more in Northern Ireland.

North West Tourism produces guides to Hiking and Biking, Golfing and Equestrian activities in the region, available from the tourist office.

**VOYA Seaweed Baths** €€€ *Strandhill;* tel: 071 916 8686; *www.voyaseaweedbaths.com.* Open Mon–Tue 1200– 2000, Wed–Fri 1100–2000, Sat & Sun 1000–2000.

**The Organic Centre** € *Rossinver; tel: 071 985 4338; www.theorganiccentre.ie.* Open mid-Mar–Nov daily 1100–1600 (till 1500 Fri). Specialises in organic food production. Display gardens include a children's garden, a taste garden, a heritage garden, an unusual vegetable and salad garden, and an edible flower garden.

## The Lake Isle of Innisfree

*I will arise and go now, and go to Innisfree,*

*And a small cabin build there, of clay and wattles made:*

*Nine bean-rows will I have there, a hive for the honey-bee,*

*And live alone in the bee-loud glade.*

*And I shall have some peace there, for peace comes dropping slow,*

*Dropping from the veils of the morning to where the cricket sings;*

*There midnight's all a glimmer, and noon a purple glow,*

*And evening full of the linnet's wings.*

*I will arise and go now, for always night and day*

*I hear lake water lapping with low sounds by the shore;*

*While I stand on the roadway, or on the pavements grey,*

*I hear it in the deep heart's core.*

William Butler Yeats, 1890

(1.6km), turn left in the village of Carney on the road to Raghley (pronounced 'Rock-ly'); the entrance to **LISSADELL HOUSE AND GARDENS 7** is about 3 miles (5km) along this road. After your visit, you could continue on to Raghley, a picturesque fishing harbour about 5 miles (8km) away. To return to Sligo, follow the 'exit' sign from Lissadell and continue straight through the forest grounds to the lake shore, where the road curves to the left and leads back to the main road. Turn right, which brings you back through Carney to the N15.

**Detour:** For a longer tour that explores the glens of Leitrim and the northern coastline, take the N16 north from Sligo Town towards Manorhamilton. The spectacular views of Benbulben make it difficult to keep your eyes on the sharp curves in the road. About 4½ miles (7km) along, a signposted side road off to your left leads to **Glencar Lake** down in the valley below. At its eastern end is the lovely **Glencar Waterfall**. On the N16, just beyond the turn for the lake, is a lay-by where you can stop and admire the view of these sculpted mountains, dressed in a patchwork cloak of fields and timber beneath a rocky crown. There's another, very sharp left turn for the waterfall about 2½ miles (4km) further on. At Manorhamilton, you can take the R280 north through another lovely glen, **Glenade**, or turn left on the

R282 and left again on the R281 along the shores of Lough Melvin to **Kinlough**. There are ruins of an abbey and castle here. Continue on the R280 to the busy seaside resort of **Bundoran**, with a good beach and cliff walks. The N15 takes you back down the coast towards Sligo Town. There is much to explore along the way, including the **Creevykeel Court Tomb**, 8 miles (12km) south of Bundoran, the picturesque fishing village of **Mullaghmore** and the **Gleniff Horseshoe**, a signposted scenic loop around the mountains inland from Cliffony. Rejoin the main tour at Drumcliffe.

## Also worth exploring

The R291 from Sligo Town leads to a magnificent stretch of sandy beach at **Rosses Point**. More Bronze Age passage tombs can be seen at **Carrowkeel**, south of Castlebaldwin on the N4. West of Sligo Town, there is a pretty coastal stretch along Sligo Bay from Ballysadare to Skreen; from here there are roads into the scenic Ox Mountains.

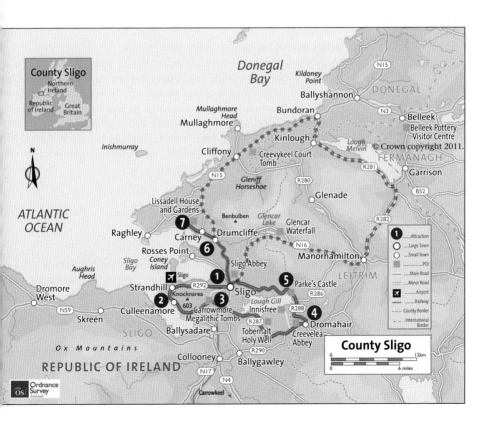

# Fermanagh Lakeland

## Ratings

| | |
|---|---|
| Lakes | ●●●●● |
| Outdoor activities | ●●●●● |
| Nature | ●●●●○ |
| Parks | ●●●●○ |
| Prehistoric sites | ●●●●○ |
| Stately homes | ●●●●○ |
| Monastic sites | ●●●○○ |
| Scenery | ●●●○○ |

The gentle, manicured landscape of Fermanagh is a sudden contrast to the wilder mountain lands to the west. This is Ireland's lakeland, and much of the county lies under water. Lower Lough Erne, sprinkled with nearly a hundred tiny islands, forms a broad arc from Belleek to the county town of Enniskillen, where it is joined to Upper Lough Erne by a narrow channel. It provides an important habitat for wildlife and a fine playground for visitors. The fishing is superb, and several country parks and forests dotted around the shore offer peaceful woodland walks, hidden castle ruins and outdoor activities. Boatmen ferry visitors out to the islands to see early Christian monastic ruins, and there are mysterious pagan relics in this region as well. The remarkable Marble Arch Caves, the great houses of Castle Coole and Florence Court, and the famous Belleek Pottery are further attractions in this pretty pocket of Ulster.

## BELLEEK

**Belleek Pottery Visitor Centre ££**
Tel: 028 6865 9300;
www.belleek.ie. Tours
Mon–Fri 0930–1215,
1345–1600 (last tour
1500 on Fri). Visitor centre
open Mar–Oct daily;
Nov–Dec Mon–Sat; Jan–Feb
Mon–Fri.

Belleek is a pleasant village, the most westerly in Northern Ireland. It is famous for the **Belleek Pottery**, which produces fine Parian china and porcelain. Ireland's oldest pottery, it was established in 1857 after John Caldwell Bloomfield inherited the Castle Caldwell estate and sought to provide employment for his tenants in the aftermath of the potato famine. At the visitor centre, you can take a guided tour of the pottery to see how craftspeople design, shape and decorate the delicate basketware, vases and figurines. The museum contains some of the outstanding pieces created here, which are crafted by extruding thin strands of clay which are then laid over and under each other to create a complex and delicate lattice pattern.

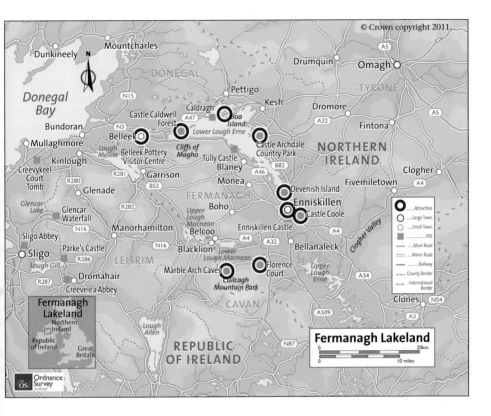

© Crown copyright 2011

# BOA ISLAND

Boa (pronounced 'Bo'), the largest island in Lower Lough Erne, is connected to the mainland by a bridge at either end. Its name comes from Badhbha, war goddess of the Ulster Celts, and a Druidic cult survived here well into Christian times. A curious remnant of this can be seen in the old cemetery at **Caldragh**, signposted down a track at the island's western end. The stone idol with a face on either side, called a Janus figure, is thought to have been used in rituals. The smaller figure alongside it was moved here from Lusty Beg Island. The little graveyard is itself a magical spot, overgrown and, in spring, full of bluebells and edged with ancient, blossoming trees.

# CASTLE ARCHDALE COUNTRY PARK

This popular park on the shores of Lower Lough Erne was created from the demesne of the 18th-century Archdale manor house; only the courtyard buildings remain, which house a visitors' centre and several

White Island Ferry
££ Castle Archdale
Marina; tel: 028 6862 1156.
Ferries leave every hour on
the hour; Apr–Jun & Sept Sat
& Sun 1100–1700; Jul &
Aug daily 1100–1700.

small museums. The ruins of an earlier castle, destroyed in 1689, can be seen in Castle Archdale Forest. The marina, developed as an RAF airbase during World War II, is now a mecca for pleasure boats, and fishing trips with a ghillie, or guide, can be arranged. A ferry runs to **White Island**, where you can see the remains of a 12th-century church; carved into one wall are eight enigmatic figures, pagan in style but thought to belong to an earlier Christian monastery. With a huge caravan park, youth hostel and activities such as pony trekking, this is a busy place in season, but you can still find peace on the woodland trails where you may see red deer.

# CASTLE CALDWELL FOREST

Castle Caldwell
Forest 7km (4 miles)
east of Belleek on the A47;
tel: 028 6634 3165;
www.forestserviceni.co.uk.
Free access dawn–dusk.

Castle Caldwell Forest covers an area of promontories and small islands on the western shores of Lower Lough Erne. It is one of the oldest state forests in the British Isles, and an important nature reserve for elusive animals such as otters and pine martens; you can observe a variety of birds from hides along the shore. A short trail from the car park leads through a canopy of beech trees to the derelict castle, built in 1612 and now enveloped by vines, mosses and trees – a wonderfully atmospheric and peaceful spot. Longer trails continue through the forest. As you drive into the grounds, notice the **Fiddler's Stone** beside the entrance arch, a memorial to Denis McCabe, a fiddler who fell from the Caldwells' barge and drowned in 1770. The epitaph concludes: 'On firm land only exercise your skill/There you may play and drink your fill'.

**Below**
Castle Caldwell Forest

# CASTLE COOLE

**Castle Coole ££**
2 miles (3km) from
Enniskillen on the A4; tel:
028 6632 2690. House
open mid-Mar–May & Sept
weekends 1100–1700; Jun
Fri–Wed 1100–1700;
Jul–Aug daily 1100–1700;
Oct weekends 1300–1700.
Grounds open Nov–Feb
1000–1600; Mar–Oct
1000–1900.

Set in a landscaped park amid oak woodlands southeast of Enniskillen, this splendid neoclassical mansion is considered to be one of Ireland's finest houses. It was designed in the 1790s for the 1st Earl of Belmore, and is largely the work of the English architect James Wyatt. Portland stone for the grand façade was shipped from Dorset to Donegal and transported overland. The colonnaded pavilions that frame the central block and portico create a graceful symmetry. Its glory, however, is the lavish interior, adorned with richly ornamented plasterwork and containing nearly all of the original furniture and portraiture. The finest room is the oval saloon, or ballroom, with gilded Regency furniture and a sweeping oak floor. The present earl resides in one wing of the house.

# DEVENISH ISLAND

**Devenish Island**
ferry £ Trory Point,
2 miles (3km) north of
Enniskillen; tel: 028 6862
1588. Scheduled sailings
1000, 1300, 1500, 1700 in
summer; reduced service in
spring and autumn.

The monastery founded on this tiny island by St Molaise in the 6th century was one of the most important in Ulster and, despite Viking attacks, it remained so into the early 17th century. Its finest structure is the 12th-century round tower, with five storeys rising 82ft (25m) high. Look for the human faces carved above the four windows at the top – a unique feature. Other surviving buildings include the Teampall Mor church near the jetty and the 15th-century St Mary's Priory, with a carved stone cross nearby. A small museum houses a collection of antiquities and stone carvings found on the island.

# ENNISKILLEN

**Fermanagh Tourist
Information
Centre** Wellington Road;
tel: 028 6632 3110; fax:
028 6632 5511. Open year-
round.

**Buttermarket £**
Tel: 028 6632 4499.
Open Mon–Sat 1000–1700.

**Enniskillen Castle £**
Tel: 028 6632 5000;
www.enniskillencastle.co.uk.
Open year-round Mon
1400–1700, Tue–Fri
1000–1700; also May–Sept
Sat 1400–1700; Jul & Aug
Sun 1400–1700.

Fermanagh's capital is an attractive town built on an island between Upper and Lower Lough Erne. Traditional pubs and red-brick Georgian buildings line Townhall and High streets, its main thoroughfares. **Enniskillen Castle**, built by the Maguire chieftains in the 16th century, has a striking watergate with corbelled towers and turrets. It houses a heritage centre, county museum and the Royal Inniskilling Fusiliers Museum. In the old **Buttermarket**, you can watch craftspeople at work in the Enniskillen Craft and Design Centre. Oscar Wilde and Samuel Beckett attended the **Portora Royal School**, established in 1608; it lies across the West Bridge. Atop a hill on the east side of town, the **Cole Monument**, a tall Doric column, has fine views over the town.

## Accommodation and food in Enniskillen

**Rossahilly House ££** *Trory Bay; tel: 028 6632 0976; www. rossahillyhouse.com.* The views over Lough Erne are fabulous from this lakeside home; the conservatory could well be the best spot on the lake to view the sunset. The en-suite bedrooms, each named after an island, are beautifully decorated with quality furniture, fluffy duvets and power showers. The hosts extend a friendly welcome and superb hospitality. There's a tennis court on-site. Light meals or a five-course dinner are available, with advance notice. To reach the house, you must cross the local airport runway, but don't let that throw you – flights are few and this is a most tranquil place to unwind and enjoy the scenery.

## FLORENCE COURT

**Florence Court ££**
Tel: 028 6634 8249.
House open Jun & Sept
Wed–Mon 1100–1700;
Jul–Aug daily 1100–1700;
also Mar–Apr & Oct
weekends; grounds open
year-round.

This neoclassical mansion was built in the mid-18th century by John Cole and named after his English wife. Their son, who became the 1st Earl of Enniskillen, added the arcades and pavilions flanking the central house in the 1770s. The staterooms were decorated with flamboyant rococo plasterwork by John West, painstakingly restored after a fire in 1955. The house is surrounded by hills and beautiful grounds; there are several walks and nature trails, one of which leads to the Florence Court yew tree, progenitor of all Irish yews.

## MARBLE ARCH CAVES

**Marble Arch Caves**
**££** Marlbank Scenic
Loop; tel: 028 6634 8855
(advance booking
recommended); www.
marblearchcaves.net. Open
Mar–Sept daily, weather
permitting, 1000–1630 (last
tour); Jul–Aug last tour 1700.
Tours last for 75 minutes.

These spectacular caves were carved by streams running down from Cuilcagh Mountain. You begin with an underground boat trip past stalactites and stalagmites and continue on foot past limestone formations, rivers and waterfalls. Outside, the River Cladagh emerges from underground into the glen, where the 30ft (9m) Marble Arch stands. From here there are fine walks further into the glen, filled with wild flowers in season. Wear comfortable shoes and a warm sweater.

## Suggested tour

**Total distance:** The main route is 78 miles (126km). The forest drive detour is 7 miles (11km).

**Time:** Allow 2–3 hours for the main tour and detour, plus extra for sightseeing.

**Links:** From Belleek, County Sligo (see page 216) via the N16, and County Donegal (see page 232) via the B52; are each under 30 minutes' drive. From Enniskillen, the A32 runs north to Omagh (see page 244).

**Right**
Castle Caldwell

Leave **ENNISKILLEN ❶** on the A32 north towards Omagh. After 2 miles (3km) look for the signpost to **DEVENISH ISLAND ❷**.

🅟 **Cruises** Guided cruises on Lower Lough Erne on the **MV Kestrel** leave from Round O'Quay in Enniskillen *Easter–Sept; tel: 028 6632 2882; 1 hour 45 minutes; booking not necessary.*

The *Inishcruiser* has 90-minute pleasure cruises on Upper Lough Erne from the Share Holiday Village, *3 miles (5km) south of Lisnaskea on the B127.* Sailings *Sun & bank holidays, Easter–Aug; tel: 028 6772 2122; www.sharevillage.org.* Viking Longship tours available to private parties on request.

🅗 **Manor House Hotel ££** *Killadeas; tel: 023 6862 2200; www.manor-house-hotel.com.* The restaurant of this resort hotel and leisure complex has beautiful views over Lough Erne. The extensive menu features fresh local produce and a good wine list. Snacks are available all day in the hotel's two bars.

Continue along Lower Lough Erne, keeping to the left-hand fork on the B82. **CASTLE ARCHDALE ❸** is on the left, 7 miles (11km) on. Turn left as you leave the park and continue on the B82 for 2 miles (3km), then turn left on to the road signposted 'Kesh Scenic Route', a pretty country lane that passes the Castle Archdale Forest. After a mile (1.6km) you reach a viewpoint that looks out across the lake and its islands. At Kesh, turn left at the junction, following signs for Belleek Potteries, and forking left again on to the A47. A couple of miles beyond, you cross the bridge to **BOA ISLAND ❹**. (Watch for the small sign to Caldragh, about 3 miles/5km from the east bridge.) When you cross back to the mainland, look out for the entrance to **CASTLE CALDWELL FOREST ❺**, about 3 miles (5km) on your left. Continue on into **BELLEEK ❻**. Leave Belleek on the A46 towards Enniskillen.

**Detour:** Leave Belleek on the B52 south towards Garrison and follow signposts to the **Lough Navar Forest Drive**. This is a scenic 7-mile (11km) loop through pine forest that leads to a panoramic viewpoint overlooking Lough Erne from atop the Cliffs of Magho, which are more than 1,000ft (305m) high. The road rejoins the A46 at Blaney.

About 12½ miles (20km) from Belleek, the ruins of **Tully Castle** on the lake shore are fringed with a pretty herb garden. Just beyond, turn right off the A46, following signs to **Monea** (pronounced 'Mon-ay'). This well-preserved Plantation castle ruin is surrounded by marsh. It was built in 1618 by settlers from Scotland, and the two circular towers and

**Above**
Belleek

corbelling are reminiscent of the Scottish style. Turn left as you leave Monea, and left again towards Enniskillen. Take a right turn, following signs for Boho (5 miles/8km), where you turn right again for **Belcoo**, situated between Upper and Lower Lough Macnean. Continue into the adjoining town of **Blacklion**, which lies in the Republic, to catch the road along the south shore of Lower Lough Macnean. Turn right on the Marlbank Scenic Loop to reach the **MARBLE ARCH CAVES** ❼, 3 miles (5km) away. South of the caves is **Cuilcagh Mountain Park** and its extensive peatlands. As you leave the caves, turn left and then right for **FLORENCE COURT** ❽, 4 miles (6km) away. From here, turn right, and then left on to the A32 to return to Enniskillen.

## Also worth exploring

The A4 runs east from Enniskillen past **Castle Coole** and on through the charming **Clogher Valley**; its villages were once stations on the old railway through the valley. Upper Lough Erne is a maze of waterways winding around dozens of tiny islands; the marina at **Bellanaleck** gives you a taste of this scenery.

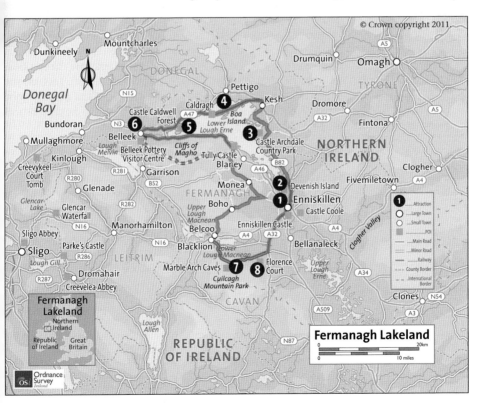

© Crown copyright 2011

# County Donegal

## Ratings

| | |
|---|---|
| Gardens | ●●●●● |
| National parks | ●●●●● |
| Scenery | ●●●●● |
| Art | ●●●●○ |
| Beaches | ●●●●○ |
| Shopping | ●●●●○ |
| Traditional music | ●●●●○ |
| Villages | ●●●●○ |

Donegal is Ireland's third-largest county, sparsely populated and a stalwart region of the Gaeltacht. Here, in this remote northwestern corner, the landscape has top billing. The Atlantic has carved a spectacular coastline of rocky inlets and secluded beaches. There are grand peninsular drives and a heart-pounding track to the top of Europe's highest sea cliffs. Inland are the majestic Derryveagh Mountains. The magnificent gardens at Glenveagh National Park are not to be missed. In spite of the rocky landscape, there's a feeling of softness to northern Donegal, with its rounded mountains, its green valleys brushed by dark forests and limpid lakes, its low, grey skies. Villages here are muted, too – more pebbledash, less bright paint. But when the sunbeams break through, the play of light is magic, igniting the blood-red cliffs and purple heathers, and draping the boglands in a cloak of tawny gold.

## ARDARA

**Ⓗ Ardara Heritage Centre €** *On the main street; tel: 074 954 1704. Open Feb–Dec 0900–2000.*

**Ⓢ** There are several factory outlet shops selling hand-loomed sweaters and knitwear, tweed jackets and other goods. These include **John Molloy**, on the outskirts of town, **Bonners**, **Kennedy's** and **Triona Design**.

Although the woollen mills and shops make Ardara (pronounced 'Ardrah' by the locals) popular with visitors, its L-shaped main street retains a local rather than a touristy character and is all the more attractive for it. The village chipper (fish-and-chip shop) is the real thing, housed in a square caravan whose flattened tyres make it a permanent fixture on the main street, right across from a row of pubs with traditional music.

The centre of town is known as the Diamond; this was the old marketplace where a monthly fair was held from 1760. Dealers came from as far away as London to purchase the region's famous tweed. The **Ardara Heritage Centre** tells the story of Donegal tweed production, from sheep shearing to woven cloth, and you can watch a weaver at work. Nearby, the church of the Holy Family has good modern stained glass by the artist Evie Hone. Ardara is a good base for walking holidays; the **Caves of Maghera** and **Assaranca Falls** are also nearby.

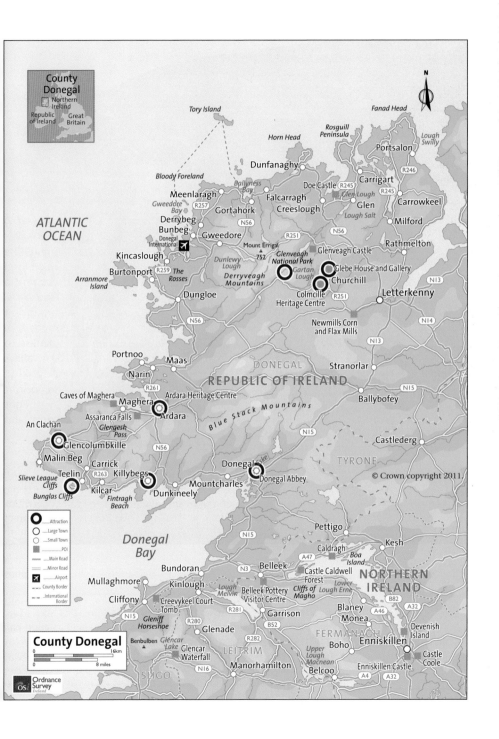

N

County
Donegal

Northern
Ireland

Republic     Great
of Ireland   Britain

Tory Island

Fanad Head

Rosguill
Peninsula

Horn Head

Lough
Swilly

Portsalon

Bloody Foreland

Dunfanaghy

R246

Ballyness
Bay

Doe Castle

R245

Carrigart

R245

Meenlaragh

Falcarragh

Glen Lough

Gweedore
Bay

R257

Gortahork

Creeslough

Glen

Carrowkeel

ATLANTIC
OCEAN

Derrybeg

N56

Lough Salt

Milford

Bunbeg

Donegal
International

Gweedore

R251

N56

Rathmelton

Kincaslough

Mount Errigal

752

Glenveagh
National Park

Glenveagh Castle

Burtonport

R259

Dunlewy
Lough

Derryveagh
Mountains

Gartan
Lough

Glebe House and Gallery

Arranmore
Island

The
Rosses

Churchill

N13

Dungloe

Colmcille
Heritage Centre

R251

Letterkenny

N56

Newmills Corn
and Flax Mills

N14

N13

Portnoo

Maas

Stranorlar

Narin

R261

REPUBLIC OF IRELAND

N15

Caves of Maghera

R263

Ardara Heritage Centre

Ballybofey

Maghera

DONEGAL

Assaranca Falls

Ardara

Blue Stack Mountains

An Clachan

Glengesh
Pass

N15

Glencolumbkille

N56

Castlederg

Malin Beg

Carrick

Donegal

TYRONE

Slieve League
Cliffs

Teelin

R263

Killybegs

© Crown copyright 2011

Bunglas Cliffs

Kilcar

Fintragh
Beach

Dunkineely

Mountcharles

Donegal Abbey

Attraction

Large Town

Small Town

Pettigo

POI

N15

Main Road

Caldragh

Kesh

Minor Road

Donegal
Bay

Boa
Island

Airport

Bundoran

N3

Belleek

A47

Castle Caldwell
Forest

County Border

Mullaghmore

Kinlough

Lough
Melvin

Belleek Pottery
Visitor Centre

Cliffs of
Magho

Lower
Lough Erne

NORTHERN
IRELAND

International
Border

Cliffony

Creevykeel Court
Tomb

R281

Garrison

Blaney

B82

A32

N15

Gleniff
Horseshoe

R280

Glenade

B52

Monea

Devenish
Island

County Donegal

Benbulben

Glencar
Lake

R282

Boho

Enniskillen

FERMANAGH

0

16km

Glencar
Waterfall

LEITRIM

Upper
Lough
Macnean

Castle
Coole

0

8 miles

N16

Manorhamilton

Belcoo

Enniskillen Castle

A4

A32

SLIGO

Ordnance
Survey
Ireland

**Above**
Bunglas Cliffs

## Accommodation in Ardara

**Bay View Country House €** *Portnoo Road; tel/fax: 074 954 1145; email: chbennett@eircom.net.* This pleasant B&B has a quiet location half a mile (1km) from town on the coast road. There is a fine view of the bay from the spacious guest lounge. The six comfortable guest rooms are all en-suite; one is a family room with separate bedrooms and two baths. Tasty scones are baked fresh for breakfast every day, and there is creamy porridge on the menu as well.

COUNTY DONEGAL   235

# BUNGLAS CLIFFS

The 2½-mile (4km) track up to the viewpoint atop Bunglas Cliffs is one of the most exciting drives in Ireland. It's not for the faint-hearted, as the narrow road runs right along the edge of these rugged cliffs, but it is well worth the terror. Bunglas is the lower side of the Slieve League Cliffs, which, at 1,972ft (601m), are the highest sea cliffs in Europe. There is an ample car park at the top where you can enjoy a gull's-eye view. A short path leads to an overlook down to the Giant's Desk and Chair, a rock formation in the water far below. Vertigo sufferers may want to skip the 15-minute walk to One Man's Pass, with a sheer drop on both sides. To the left of the car park, 'Tir Eire' or 'Country Ireland' is written in stone on the heather-covered banks. This was to inform aircraft in the 1940s that Ireland was a neutral country.

# COLMCILLE HERITAGE CENTRE

**Colmcille Heritage Centre €€** *Gartan, Churchill; tel: 074 913 7306. Open Easter & first Sun in May to last Sun in Sept, Mon–Fri 1030–1830, Sun 1300–1800.*

St Colmcille (pronounced 'Colm-*keel*'), or Columba, is one of Ireland's three patron saints. Born a prince of Tyrconnell, he chose the life of a monk. He founded 37 monasteries in Ireland – Derry, Durrow and Kells among them – and was one of the foremost scholars of his day. It is said that his copying of a book of psalms led to a battle in which many died, and in repentance he chose the life of an exile; at the age of 42 he set sail and landed on the island of Iona off the west coast of Scotland, where he founded a monastery and brought Christianity to the Picts.

The Colmcille Heritage Centre traces the life of the saint through artistic reproductions of early monastic life and art such as manuscripts and stained glass, and looks at the rise of Christianity in Ireland. It is thought that St Colmcille was born in 521 amid the stunning landscape of Gartan Lough. A large cross marks the start of a footpath into Glenveagh National Park, and there are other relics, such as the Natal Stone, nearby.

# DONEGAL TOWN

Donegal Town is a gateway into the wilder parts of the northwest. Its Irish name, Dun na nGall, means 'fort of the foreigners', a name which referred to the Vikings who set up a base here in the 9th century, but seems equally fitting today, judging by the number of visitors to this small town. It is set on a crossroads where the River Eske flows into Donegal Bay, and centred around the attractive central market square, known as the Diamond, which was built during the Plantation period in the early 17th century. The obelisk rising 20ft

**ℹ Donegal Tourist Information Office**
*The Quay; tel: 074 972 1148; fax: 074 972 2762; www.irelandnorthwest.ie. Open year-round.*

**🏠 Donegal Castle €€**
*Tel: 074 972 2405. Open mid-Mar–Oct daily 1000–1800; Thur–Mon 0930–1630 rest of the year.*

**🚤 The Donegal Bay Water Bus Tour**
*€€€ takes you on a scenic 90-minute cruise of Donegal Bay and its islands. Tickets from the booking office at Donegal Pier; tel: 074 972 3666; www. donegalbaywaterbus. com*

**🛍 Magee of Donegal,** established in 1866, is famous for its hand-woven tweed jackets, which are reasonably priced, at its shop on the Diamond. Outside town on the Ballyshannon road, **Donegal Craft Village** is a group of workshops making batik, pottery, jewellery and *uillean* pipes, among other goods.

(6m) here is dedicated to the Four Masters. These four Franciscan friars set out to preserve as much of Celtic culture as possible and compiled one of the earliest historic texts, the *Annals of the Four Masters*, between 1632 and 1636; it is now in the National Library. The ruins of **Donegal Abbey**, the friary where they laboured, lie a few minutes' walk south of town. Beside the Diamond, **Donegal Castle**, built by an O'Donnell chieftain in the 15th century, had a manor house added in the 17th century. The town is also a centre for the tweed industry.

## Food in Donegal Town

**Dom Breslin's Bar & Restaurant €–€€** *Pier 1, Quay Street, Donegal Town; tel: 074 972 2719; www.domspier1.ie.* Set in the Pier 1 building on the old harbour, this restaurant complex offers a range of dining options, from the popular Carvery to a relaxed steak or seafood meal with fine wines in peaceful surroundings overlooking Donegal Bay. Bar food is served all day in the six nautical-themed bars, which are spread over different levels. There is live music entertainment nightly in summer and on weekends throughout the year.

### St Columba's valley

According to legend, when St Patrick was converting Ireland to Christianity in the 5th century, a group of demons sought refuge in what is now Glencolumbkille, raising a fog and turning the river into a fiery stream so that no Christian could enter. A hundred years later, Colmcille was preaching nearby when a demon threw a rod of holly out of the glen, killing one of his assistants. The furious saint hurled the stick back and when it hit the ground it began to grow. The demons were terrified and fled, but Colmcille chased them, throwing stones, and driving them into the sea. He then founded several churches in the valley. On a cliff top north of the village is a small stone oratory said to have been used by the saint himself. Each year on 9 June, St Colmcille's feast day, a *turas*, or station, is performed, which involves a 3-mile (5km) walk with prayers around 15 cairns and carved stones associated with the saint.

# GLEBE HOUSE AND GALLERY

**🏠 Glebe House and Gallery €** *Churchill, Letterkenny; tel: 074 913 7071. Open Easter daily 1000–1830; Jun & Sept Sat–Thur 1100–1830; Jul & Aug daily 1100–1830. Access by guided tour only.*

This Regency manor, set in woodland beside Gartan Lough, was the home of the landscape and portrait painter Derek Hill, who gave the house and its contents to the state in 1981. The house is richly furnished with William Morris wallpapers and textiles, Japanese and Islamic artworks, and unusual *objets d'art*. The gallery holds Hill's collection of 300 works by leading 20th-century artists, including ceramics and etchings by Picasso and lithographs by Kokoschka. Irish art is well represented, with paintings by Jack B Yeats and art from the Tory Islands. The 25 acres (10 hectares) of gardens are beautifully landscaped down to the lake's edge.

# GLENCOLUMBKILLE

**An Clachan €**
Tel: 074 973 0017;
www.glenfolkvillage.com.
Open Easter–Sept Mon–Sat
1000–1800, Sun
1200–1800; or by
appointment.

This remote village, threaded through 'the valley of Colmcille' at the western tip of Donegal, is a symbol of hope and success to Gaeltacht villages throughout Ireland. In the 1950s, Glencolumbkille's (pronounced 'glen-colm-*keel*') economic prospects were grim, but with the help and determination of Father James McDyer and a cooperative aimed at preserving the traditional culture of the area, they turned a dying village into a thriving community. Its centrepiece is **An Clachan** (Father McDyer's Folk Village Museum), which is a re-created traditional village with houses of 1750, 1850 and 1900, a schoolhouse and craft shop. The shebeen sells unique home-made produce, including wines made from fuchsias and carageen (seaweed) and whiskey marmalade; the tea house is renowned for its Guinness cakes. An Clachan opened in 1967, before tourism was even heard of in this part of Donegal, and since that time many other folk museums have modelled themselves after this one.

Glencolumbkille is rich in traditional music and folklore. The landscape is indeed fit for a saint, with glorious mountains and a heavenly coast that can be admired on the Seaview Drive. There is a sandy beach behind the folk museum. Walks lead into the hills where there are many archaeological sites, including some fine portal dolmens.

**Below**
An Clachan, Glencolumbkille

# GLENVEAGH NATIONAL PARK

**Glenveagh National Park €€**
Tel: 074 913 7090; www.
glenveaghnationalpark.ie.
Open Mar–Oct daily
1000–1800; Nov–Feb daily
0900–1700 (last admission
1 hour before closing).

Some people choose to
walk the 2½ miles (4km)
between the visitor centre
and the castle. There's a
lovely lakeside view, but be
warned that it's an open
road with little shade so
take sunscreen, a hat and
some water on a hot
sunny day.

Set among the Derryveagh Mountains, whose name means 'forest of
oak and birch', Glenveagh National Park covers 40,870 acres (16,540
hectares) of woodland, lakes, bogs and mountains. It encompasses
Donegal's highest peaks, Mount Errigal, rising to 2,467ft (752m),
and Slieve Snacht, and is home to one of Ireland's two large red deer
herds. The estate was created between 1857 and 1859 by John George
Adair, who built **Glenveagh Castle** in 1870–73. The lakeside setting of
this castellated mansion is magnificent, but the grounds and castle as
they stand today are the work of a wealthy American businessman,
Henry McIlhenny of Philadelphia, who owned the estate from 1937 to
1981, when he gave it to the Irish nation.

**Left**
Glenveagh Castle Gardens

**Below**
Killybegs Harbour

The visitor centre at the entrance to the grounds has an audiovisual show and displays about the park and its natural history; there is also a nature trail and picnic area here. You cannot drive within the grounds; a shuttle bus takes you up to the castle, which you can visit on a guided tour. It remains as it was in McIlhenny's day, when he entertained film stars and aristocracy. The real glory of the park, however, is the 27 acres (11 hectares) of gardens, each with a different theme, largely informal. Highlights include the pleasure gardens with exotic plants, the view garden with vistas over the landscape, and the Swiss garden, a tranquil woodland path where you can hear the cuckoo and other birdsong. It's hard to tear yourself away from such beauty, so allow at least a couple of hours for the gardens, especially on a sunny day.

# KILLYBEGS

**Melly's € Killybegs; tel: 074 973 1093.** For fish so fresh it melts in your mouth, try this bright and cheerful chipper which looks out over the harbour. Also quiche, chicken, desserts and weekday café lunches. *Open till 2230. Takeaway meals available till late.*

You will smell this town before you see it. Killybegs is the northwest's largest fishing port, and the scent of its processing industry wafts on the sea breeze. The town's main street overlooks its broad harbour, which is filled with enormous fishing vessels. It's an amazing sight to watch the daily 'silver harvest' being unloaded on the pier, or simply to marvel at the array of nets, ropes and giant cables that fill the boats docked here. Needless to say, seafood is at its freshest here, so stop off at one of the pubs or chippers set around the pleasant town centre.

## Suggested tour

**Total distance:** The main tour is 161 miles (259km). The detour to the top of Bunglas Cliffs is 8 miles (13km) return. The detour around the Rosses is 14 miles (23km). The detour along the north coast from Gortahork to Letterkenny is 100 miles (160km), including the drives around the three peninsulas.

**Time:** Two days are recommended for this tour, especially if you want to follow any of the detours. Allow up to an hour for the detour to Bunglas Cliffs, including viewing time. The detour around the Rosses will take about half an hour. The north coast detour will take you 4½ hours. Those short on time should take in the gardens at Glenveagh National Park, or concentrate on southern Donegal from Donegal Town to Glencolumbkille.

**Links:** From Letterkenny the N13 connects with Derry and the Central Ulster tour (*see page 249*). Donegal Town connects with the Sligo (*see page 220*) and Fermanagh (*see page 228*) tours via Ballyshannon, to the south on the N15.

Leave **DONEGAL TOWN** ❶ on the N56, heading west between the Blue Stack Mountains and the rocky shores of Donegal Bay. After passing through the hillside village of **Mountcharles** (Moin Séarlas) and the fishing village of Dunkineely (Dún Clonnaola), you reach **KILLYBEGS** ❷, 17 miles (28km) away. Continue west along the coast on the R263, a narrower road which climbs higher above the bay, with fine views ahead to the mountains and across the bay. Below is the impressive stretch of sand at **Fintragh Beach**. A scenic route to Kilcar is signposted off to the left, but it is very narrow and there are plenty of fine views on the main road. **Kilcar** (Cill Charthaigh) is a pleasant Gaeltacht village known for its woollens, crafts and traditional music, as is **Carrick** (An Charraig), 3 miles (5km) further on. From here, it is 6 miles (9km) on through bogland; before you make the steep descent

**Above**
Glenveagh National Park

into **GLENCOLUMBKILLE ❸** (Gleann Cholm Cille), look for the viewpoint signposted to the left for a stupendous vista over the valley.

**Detour:** Turn left at Carrick on a minor road signposted to **Teelin** (Tieleann). After an idyllic 2-mile (3km) stretch along the river, turn right on the road to the **BUNGLAS CLIFFS ❹**. Return to Carrick and continue on the main route to Glencolumbkille.

From Glencolumbkille, take the scenic road over the **Glengesh Pass** for 15 miles (24km) to **ARDARA ❺** (Ard an Ratha). You may need to ask directions locally to find the start of this road, which is signposted from the outskirts of town. It climbs into the mountains and crosses high bogland, incredibly beautiful at sunset, to a magnificent viewpoint, before making the ear-popping descent. From Ardara, take the R261 towards **Narin** and **Portnoo** (Port Nua), twin resorts with a magnificent beach 2½ miles (4km) long. At Maas, continue north on the N56 to Dungloe (An Clochán Liath) and on to Gweedore (Gaoth Dobhair).

**Detour:** At Dungloe, the R259 leads out along the coast towards **Burtonport** (Ailt an Chórrain) on the peninsula known as **The Rosses**, a strong Gaeltacht area. The rocky landscape, sprinkled with lakes and channels, has some nice views over the water; there are a surprising number of houses here in this rather bleak terrain. At the Y-junction, the left fork leads to the harbour for trips to Arranmore Island. Follow the right fork, signposted to the airport, around through Kincaslough (Cionn Caslach) and Annagry (Anagaire). Turn left on to the main N56 to rejoin the main tour at Gweedore.

Turn left on to the R257, a quick turn as you enter Gweedore and signposted only in Irish for **Bunbeg** (An Bun Beag), which runs through a continuous string of houses to Derrybeg (Doiri Beage). About 5 miles (8km) after the turn, you come to an unmarked intersection; take the left-hand fork which runs along **Gweedore Bay**. There are some magnificent views over the sea coast and islands. After 3½ miles (6km), you reach the headland known as the **Bloody Foreland** (Cnoc Fola), a gentle spot in spite of its name, which comes from the red colour of the rocks at sunset. The road carries on through a splendid landscape of sandy cliffs, dunes and bogland sweeping down to the sea, passing **Meenlaragh** (Min Larach), the port for trips to Tory Island (Toraigh). It winds down along the shores of Ballyness Bay; just before Gortahork (Gort an Choirce), turn right on to the N56 and head south to the junction with the R251. Turn left towards Letterkenny (Leitir Ceanainn), passing the foot of **Mount Errigal** (An Earagail), the distinctive peak that you see from all directions in this region. On the right is **Dunlewy Lough**. A track from the abandoned church leads to the **Poisoned Glen**; local lore says that God dropped poison there and henceforth no bird has been heard, but it probably gets its name from a toxic plant that used to grow there. The road carries on along the beautiful Derryveagh Mountains to the entrance to **GLENVEAGH NATIONAL PARK ❻**. Turning right out of the park, continue on the R251; near Gartan Lough, take the right turn signposted to **GLEBE HOUSE AND GALLERY ❼**. Return to the R251 and just beyond the turn, turn right again on to the R254 in Churchill for the **COLMCILLE HERITAGE CENTRE ❽**. Return to the R251 – the **Newmills Corn and Flax Mills** powered by a large waterwheel are also signposted off this road – and continue on to **Letterkenny**, with its long main street. It is the largest town in Donegal and one of the fastest growing in all of Ireland. From here take the N13 and N15 south to Donegal Town.

**Detour:** To further explore the coastline, continue on the N56 from Gortahork through **Falcarragh** (An Fál Carrach) to **Dunfanaghy** (Dún Fionnachaidh). This attractive village has a splendid wide sandy beach backed by a golf course. **Horn Head Drive**, a scenic 7-mile (11km) circuit signposted from town, is arguably the finest of the north peninsular drives, with dramatic views of the cliffs and wonderful vistas over the beach. Continue on the N56 to Creeslough (An Craoslach). About a mile (1.6km) beyond town is the turn, to your left, on to the R245 to Carrigart, which leads past **Doe Castle** on the shores of the inlet. The signposting for this road is particularly bad – look for a clutter of mangled and vandalised brown signs pointing to what appears to be a forest road on the left and that's your turn. If you miss it don't despair. A few miles beyond, a minor road which *is* signposted leads past pretty **Glen Lough** and through the village of Glen to Carrigart (Carraig Airt). From here, you can follow the signposted **Atlantic Drive**. This 9-mile (15km) drive circles the rocky **Rosguill Peninsula**, with scenic views of the cliffs, beaches and dunes along the coast. When you return to Carrigart, take the R245 to Milford. (By now signs are bilingual again.) From here you can explore yet another peninsula, **Fanad Head**, by taking the R246 to Carrowkeel (Kerrykeel) and Portsalon; the minor roads for Fanad Head and Fanad Drive are signposted off this road. The views are pretty in spots but it is generally less spectacular than the other headlands. Return to Milford and take the R245 through **Rathmelton** (also called Ramelton) to Letterkenny to return to Donegal Town on the N13 and N15.

## Also worth exploring

A signposted drive known as the 'Inishowen 100' (which refers to its length of 100 miles) starts from Bridgend and circles the **Inishowen Peninsula** (*see page 245*), taking in Ireland's most northerly tip at Malin Head. Apart from the small coastal resorts, it is a largely unspoilt landscape of mountains, cliffs and green pastures bordered by Lough Swilly, Lough Foyle and the Atlantic.

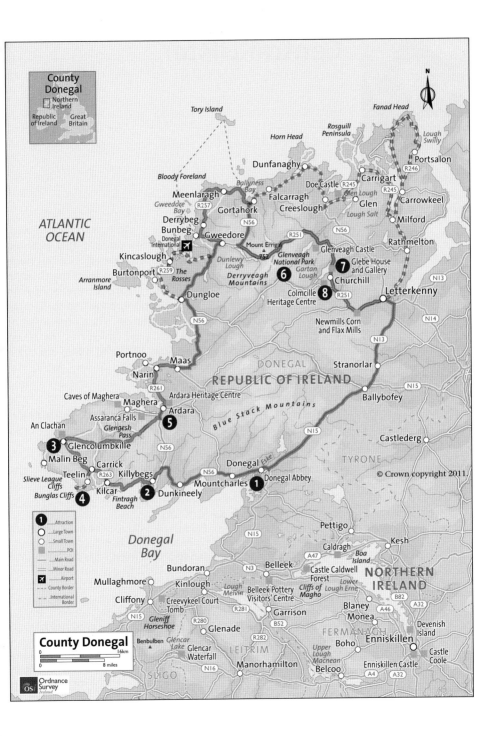

County
Donegal

- Northern
  Ireland

Republic    Great
of Ireland   Britain

N

Tory Island

Fanad Head

Rosguill
Peninsula

Lough
Swilly

Horn Head

Dunfanaghy

Portsalon

R246

Bloody Foreland

Ballyness
Bay

Doe Castle  R245

Carrigart

R245

Meenlaragh

Falcarragh

Glen Lough

Glen

Carrowkeel

Gweedore
Bay

R257

Gortahork

Creeslough

Lough Salt

Milford

ATLANTIC
OCEAN

Derrybeg

Bunbeg

Donegal
International

N56

N56

Gweedore

R251

Rathmelton

Mount Errigal

Glenveagh Castle

Kincaslough

752

Glenveagh
National Park

Glebe House
and Gallery

7

Burtonport  R259  The

Dunlewy
Lough

Gartan
Lough

Churchill

N13

Arranmore
Island

Rosses

Derryveagh
Mountains

6

Letterkenny

Dungloe

Colmcille

8

R251

N56

Heritage Centre

Newmills Corn
and Flax Mills

N14

N13

Portnoo

Maas

Stranorlar

N15

Narin

R261

DONEGAL

REPUBLIC OF IRELAND

Caves of Maghera

Ardara Heritage Centre

Ballybofey

Maghera

Ardara

Blue Stack Mountains

Assaranca Falls

An Clachan

Glengesh
Pass

5

N15

Castlederg

N56

TYRONE

3

Glencolumbkille

Malin Beg

Donegal

Eske

© Crown copyright 2011

Teelin

Carrick

R263

Killybegs

N56

Donegal Abbey

Slieve League
Cliffs

Kilcar

2

Dunkineely

Mountcharles

1

Bunglas Cliffs

4

Fintragh
Beach

1 ........Attraction
O ........Large Town
O ........Small Town
■ ........POI
──── ........Main Road
──── ........Minor Road
✈ ........Airport
─ ─ ........County Border
▪ ▪ ........International
        Border

Donegal
Bay

Pettigo

N15

Kesh

Caldragh

Boa
Island

A47

Bundoran

N3

Belleek

Castle Caldwell
Forest

NORTHERN
IRELAND

Mullaghmore

Kinlough

Lough
Melvin

Belleek Pottery
Visitors' Centre

Cliffs of
Magho

Lower
Lough Erne

B82

Cliffony

Creevykeel Court
Tomb

R281

Garrison

Blaney

A46

A32

B52

Monea

County Donegal

0           16km

NI5

Gleniff
Horseshoe

R280

Glenade

R282

FERMANAGH

Devenish
Island

Benbulben

Glencar
Lake

Glencar
Waterfall

LEITRIM

Upper
Lough
Macnean

Boho

Enniskillen

Castle
Coole

0           8 miles

SLIGO

NI6

Manorhamilton

Belcoo

Enniskillen Castle

A4

A32

Ordnance
Survey
Ireland

# Central Ulster

## Ratings

| | |
|---|---|
| History | ●●●●● |
| Museums | ●●●●● |
| Prehistoric sites | ●●●●● |
| Mountains | ●●●●○ |
| Nature | ●●●●○ |
| Parks | ●●●●○ |
| Cathedrals/ churches | ●●●○○ |
| Scenery | ●●●○○ |

While the name Ulster today is often synonymous with Northern Ireland only, in olden times it also included three northern Republican counties. The chieftains of this huge province were the fiercest in the land, ruling from the Grianán of Aileach, a great stone ring fort just over the border in Donegal. But in 1607, the beaten Ulster nobility fled to Europe, opening the way for the English Plantation. The Corporation of London built the historic city of Derry, which has the finest medieval walls in Ireland. Between 1700 and 1900, over two million people from all religions and social classes left the province for North America. Their story is told in the fascinating Ulster American Folk Park, near Omagh. At the heart of the region are the beautiful Sperrin Mountains, while to the east is Lough Neagh, the largest lake in the British Isles.

## DERRY

 **Derry Tourist Information**
**Office** *44 Foyle Street;*
*tel: 028 7126 7284;*
*fax: 028 7137 7992;*
*email: info@derryvisitor.com;*
*www.derryvisitor.com.*
*Open year-round.*

In the 6th century, St Columba founded a monastery in an oak grove, or 'daire', beside the River Foyle. Nearly a thousand years later, in the Plantation era (*see page 35*), English merchants built the magnificent town walls that give Derry so much character today; it is the only completely walled city in Ireland. The town's Plantation name, 'Londonderry', is still used today, mainly by those who favour continued union with Britain. Derry is also famous as the place where Amelia Earhart landed in 1932 on her first solo flight across the Atlantic.

The highlights of this historic city are best seen on a walk around the top of the **town walls**, a circuit of about a mile (1.5km). Completed in 1618, they stand 20ft (6m) high and were never breached, despite three sieges, one of which – the 105-day Siege of Derry which began in December 1688 – was the longest in British history. Panels set into the wall near the eight bastions and four original gates explain the historical background of the nearby

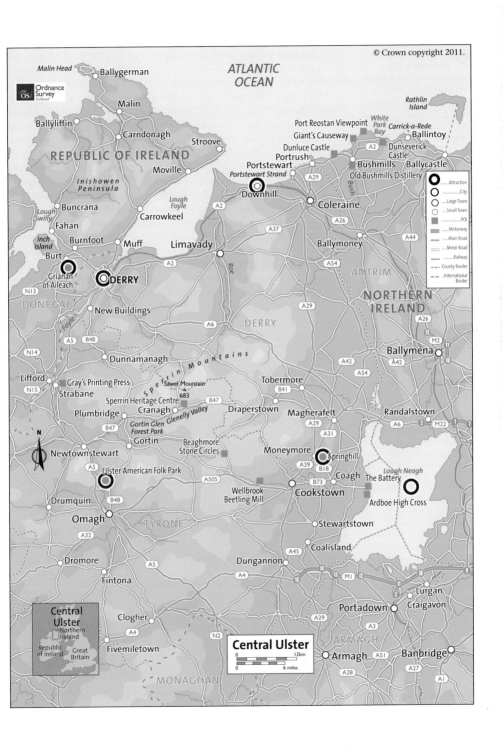

© Crown copyright 2011.

Malin Head
Ballygerman

ATLANTIC
OCEAN

Ordnance
OSi Survey
Ireland

Malin

Rathlin
Island

Ballyliffin

Port Reostan Viewpoint
Giant's Causeway
White
Park Carrick-a-Rede
Bay

Carndonagh
Stroove

Ballintoy

REPUBLIC OF IRELAND

Dunluce Castle
Portrush
Portstewart

A2
Dunseverick
Castle

Moville

Bushmills Ballycastle
Old Bushmills Distillery

Inishowen
Peninsula

Portstewart Strand
A29

Attraction

City

Large Town

Small Town

POI

Motorway

Main Road

Minor Road

Railway

County Border

International
Border

Lough
Foyle

Downhill

Coleraine

Lough
Swilly
Buncrana

Carrowkeel

A2

A26

Fahan

A37

Inch
Island
Burnfoot
Muff
Limavady

Ballymoney

A44

Burt

A2

Roe

A54

Grianán
of Aileach
DERRY

ANTRIM

N13

A29

NORTHERN
IRELAND

DONEGAL

New Buildings

A6

DERRY

A26

Foyle

A5
B48

12

M2

N14

Dunnamanagh

Ballymena

A42

A42

Lifford
Gray's Printing Press
Sperrin Mountains
Sawel Mountain

Tobermore

A54

NI5
Strabane

683

B41

Sperrin Heritage Centre
B47

Plumbridge
Cranagh
Draperstown
Magherafelt

Randalstown

B47
Gortin Glen
Forest Park
Glenelly Valley

A29

A6

M22

N
Gortin

A31

Newtownstewart

Beaghmore
Stone Circles

Moneymore

Springhill

A5
Ulster American Folk Park

A29
B18

Coagh
Lough Neagh
The Battery

A505

B73

Drumquin
B48

Wellbrook
Beetling Mill
Cookstown

Ardboe High Cross

Omagh

TYRONE

Stewartstown

A32

Coalisland

Dromore

A5

Dungannon

A45

A4

MI

Fintona

Lurgan

Central
Ulster
Northern
Ireland

Clogher

A29
Portadown
Craigavon

A3

Republic
of Ireland
Great
Britain

A4

Fivemiletown

N2

Central Ulster

ARMAGH

0        12km

0        6 miles

Armagh
A51
Banbridge

MONAGHAN

A28

A27

A1

**ℹ Tracing your ancestors** The genealogy centre for Derry is located in the Harbour Museum; *Harbour Square; tel: 028 7137 7331; http://derry.rootsireland.ie. Open Mon–Fri 0900–1700.*

**🏛 Guildhall £** *Tel: 028 7137 7335. Open Mon–Fri 0900–1700. Free guided tours during Jul, Aug and other times on request.*

**Tower Museum ££** *Union Hall Place; tel: 028 7137 2411. Open Tue–Sat & bank holidays 1000–1700; Jul–Aug Mon–Sat 1000–1700.*

**Harbour Museum** *Guildhall Street and Harbour Square; tel: 028 7137 7331. Open Mon–Fri 1000–1300, 1400–1630.*

**St Columb's Cathedral and Chapter House Museum £** *London Street; tel: 028 7126 7313; www.stcolumbscathedral.org. Open Apr–Sept Mon–Sat 0900–1700; Oct–Mar Mon–Sat 0900–1300, 1400–1600.*

**🚶 Walking tours (££)** of the historic city lasting 1½ hours are organised from the Derry Tourist Office at 44 Foyle Street; tel: 028 7126 7284. Tours Jul–Aug Mon–Fri 1115 and 1515; 1430 rest of the year.

buildings and features such as the great cannon, Roaring Meg. From the ramparts there are sweeping views across the great swathe of housing estates that comprises much of modern-day Derry.

The centre of the walled city is **The Diamond**, with a memorial to those who died in the two World Wars. The **Guildhall**, at the entrance to Shipquay Gate, was built in 1890 and is the city's town hall; it has splendid stained-glass windows. The **Tower Museum**, housed in the 17th-century O'Doherty's Tower, tells the 'Story of Derry' from ancient to modern times from the Plantation to the Siege of Derry and the Troubles of recent years. There is also an exhibition on the Armada shipwreck. The **Harbour Museum** is a museum and picture gallery that focuses on the region's maritime history.

**St Columb's Cathedral**, built in 1633, is one of the earliest Protestant cathedrals and contains the country's oldest and largest bells. It has many relics from the Siege of Derry, including an enormous mortar ball fired over the wall, and other treasures in the **Chapter House Museum**. Other buildings of interest include the charming **St Augustine's Church** (thought to stand on the site where

**Right**
Roaring Meg Cannon, Derry town walls

## A walled garden

In the 1800s when life was peaceful and prosperous, Derry's city walls no longer served a defensive purpose. People built homes against the outside of the walls and also on top of them. They even planted gardens in the bastions, one of which still existed up until 1990.

**The Craft Village,** off Shipquay Street, tel: 028 7126 0329, is a warren of craft shops and apartments where you can watch demonstrations. **Austin's,** Ireland's oldest department store, adjoins the Diamond and has a selection of quality gifts.

Derry has a thriving arts scene. The **Gordon Gallery,** Pump Street, and the **Context Gallery,** 5–7 Artillery Street, hold contemporary art exhibitions. Several theatre companies perform at the **Foyle Arts Centre** (tel: 028 7126 6657), **The Playhouse** (tel: 028 7126 8027) and **Millennium Forum** (tel: 028 7126 4455).

Columba founded his early church), the **1st Derry Presbyterian Church,** the **Apprentice Boys Memorial Hall** and, outside the walls, the neo-Renaissance **St Columba's 'Long Tower' Church.**

### Accommodation and food in Derry

**Mange2** ££ 110–115 Strand Road; tel: 028 7136 1222; www. mange2derry.com. A friendly, family-owned restaurant with a riverside location. The sophisticated menu combines fresh local beef, lamb, salmon and seafood with French and global influences. The excellent wine list features old and new world wines, including hand-picked vintages from small producers. Lunch is served Tue–Fri 1230–1430, Sun 1200–1530, dinner daily 1700–late.

**Beech Hill Country House Hotel** ££–£££ 32 Ardmore Road; tel: 028 7134 9279; fax: 028 7134 5366; www.beech-hill.com. Just 2 miles (3km) from Derry city centre, this luxurious country-house hotel is set in extensive landscaped grounds with fine old beech trees, beautiful gardens, streams and a pond. The house, with its distinctive porch and bow windows, was built in 1729 by Captain Thomas Skipton, head of a prominent Plantation family. Bedrooms are elegantly furnished, some with antiques, and have all amenities. Beech Hill is a favoured hideaway for prominent politicians, not least because of the superb Ardmore Restaurant, with a sophisticated menu prepared by a top chef.

# DOWNHILL

**Downhill** £ Tel: 028 2073 1582. Hezlett House open Apr–Sept daily 1000–1700; grounds open year-round daily dawn–dusk.

Downhill is a landscaped estate laid out in the late 18th century by Frederick Hervey, Earl of Bristol and Bishop of Derry. A well-travelled and extravagant character, he built the palatial house, now in ruins, for entertaining and to house a grand art collection, which he purchased with the episcopal revenues. He adorned the grounds with artificial ponds, cascades, family memorials and the classical Mussenden Temple, perched on the cliff top. The grounds contain beautiful gardens, woodland and cliff-top walks.

# GRIANÁN OF AILEACH

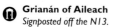

**Grianán of Aileach**
*Signposted off the N13.*

Just over the border in Donegal, near the village of Burt, this formidable Iron Age ring fort commands a hilltop overlooking the coast. No one knows exactly when it was built, but it is thought to be the royal residence recorded by the geographer Ptolemy around AD 140. From the 5th century, Grianán Fort (pronounced 'grann-an'), as it is known locally, was occupied by Ulster's royal dynasty, the O'Neills, and it was the political centre of Ulster until it was destroyed in the 12th century. It was restored in the 1870s. Surrounding the high stone walls are two earthen defences covering 5½ acres (2 hectares). The fort itself has a diameter of about 76ft (23m). You can enter the enclosure and walk around the tiered ramparts, which give spectacular views of Lough Swilly, Inch Island, the coastline and surrounding countryside. Some controversial work has taken place in recent years to repair a collapsed wall. The site remains open to visitors.

# LOUGH NEAGH

Lough Neagh is the largest lake in the British Isles, covering 153 square miles (400sq km). Its remarkable similarity in shape and size to the Isle of Man gave rise to the story that the legendary giant Finn MacCool scooped out a huge chunk of earth and threw it into the Irish Sea. The lump of earth formed the Isle of Man, while the hole filled with water and became Lough Neagh. Its 75-mile (120km) shoreline is fringed with small harbours, beaches and woodland, but the roads seldom parallel the water's edge, giving only fleeting glimpses of this huge inland sea, which measures 20 miles (32km) long and 10 miles (16km) across.

# SPRINGHILL

**Springhill ££** *1 mile (1.6km) from Moneymore on the B18; tel: 028 8674 8210. Grounds open May–Sept daily 1000–1700; Oct–Apr daily 1000–1600. House open Mar–Jun & Sept Sat & Sun 1300–1800; Easter, Jul & Aug daily 1300–1800.*

This whitewashed Plantation manor house was built in the 17th century, and has mid-18th- and early 19th-century additions. It contains family furniture, paintings and curios. The outbuildings are also of interest; one houses an important costume collection. There is a fortified barn dating from the 17th century, and two barns in the Dutch style. The grounds also contain a secluded walled garden and woodland walks.

# ULSTER AMERICAN FOLK PARK

**Ulster American Folk Park ££** *Mellon Road (A5), 5 miles (8km) north of Omagh; tel: 028 8224 3292; www.folkpark. com. Open Mar–Sept Tue–Sun 1000–1700; Oct–Feb Tue–Fri 1000–1600, Sat & Sun 1100–1600; last admission 1½ hours before closing.*

**Right**
Traditional crafts at the Ulster American Folk Park

Plan to spend some time at this fascinating folk park that traces the history of Ulster emigrants from their pre-famine homesteads to life in the New World. An impressive array of dwellings representing different walks of life has been superbly reconstructed, with costumed interpreters who demonstrate spinning, cooking over a turf fire and other facets of everyday life. The trail leads down an Ulster high street to the most moving exhibit in the park: an enormous coffin ship that re-creates the appalling conditions suffered by the emigrants on their Atlantic voyage. You emerge into a 19th-century streetscape of an American port town, and head on to a log cabin in the wilderness. The indoor Emigrants exhibition, which looks at the historical background to this mass exodus and the contributions of emigrants in the New World, tells an inspirational story of the resilience of the human spirit, and is a tribute to the experience of emigrants the world over. Also in the grounds is the Centre for Migration Studies.

## Tracing your ancestors

The Centre for Migration Studies at the Ulster American Folk Park has a reference library and emigration database for genealogical research. For information, *tel: 028 8225 6315; fax: 028 8224 2241; email: centremigstudies@ni-libraries.net; www.qub.ac.uk/cms and www.folkpark.com. Open Mon–Fri 1030–1700.*

# Suggested tour

**Omagh Tourist Information Office** *Strule Arts Centre, Townhall Square; tel: 028 8224 7831. Open year-round.*

**Cookstown Tourist Information Office** *Burn Road; tel: 028 8676 9949. Open year-round.*

**Total distance:** The main route is 127 miles (204km). The detour to Cookstown and Ardboe is 56 miles (90km).

**Time:** Allow a full day for the main route, including visits to some of the attractions. The alternative route to Plumbridge on the B48 adds 10–15 minutes, depending on traffic. The detour to Cookstown and Ardboe can take up to 1½ hours.

**Links:** From Derry, the N13 leads west to Donegal (*see page 235*). The A2 connects with the tour of the Antrim coast (*see page 259*).

**Gray's Printing Press and Printers' Museum £** *49 Main Street, Strabane; tel: 028 7188 0055. Admission is by guided tour only. Please telephone for times and dates.*

**Gortin Glen Forest Park £** *Tel: 028 8167 0666. Open daily 1000–dusk.*

Leave **DERRY** ❶ on the A5, which runs along the River Foyle to **Strabane**. Its main attraction is **Gray's Printing Press**, an 18th-century print shop with original machinery and exhibits. John Dunlap, who printed the American Declaration of Independence, learnt his trade here. Another native son of Strabane is the writer Flann O'Brien. Nearby is the ancestral homestead of American president Woodrow Wilson. Continue south through Newtownstewart. The entrance to the **ULSTER AMERICAN FOLK PARK** ❷ is off the A5, 5 miles (8km) before Omagh.

**Detour:** For an alternative route south, take the B48, signposted left off the A5 at New Buildings, about 5 miles (8km) outside of Derry. This is a pretty country road that runs along the edge of the Sperrins. At Plumbridge, take the B47 southwest to rejoin the main tour at Newtownstewart.

From **Omagh**, Tyrone's county town, take the B48 north towards Gortin. Continue north through **Gortin Glen Forest Park**, which has walking trails and a forest drive through coniferous woodland. At the village of Plumbridge, turn right on to the B47, which runs through the

**Sperrin Heritage
Centre £** Cranagh;
tel: 028 8164 8142. Open
Easter–Oct Mon–Fri 1130–
1730, Sat 1130–1800,
Sun 1400–1800.

**Left**
Campbell House, Ulster
American Folk Park

**Above**
Pennsylvania Log Farmhouse,
Ulster American Folk Park

Glenelly Valley at the base of the Sperrin Mountains. About 8 miles (13km) along, just past the village of Cranagh, is the **Sperrin Heritage Centre**. From ancient times people have panned for gold in these quiet hills. From the centre you can make the ascent to the top of Sawel, the highest peak in the Sperrins, which rises to 2,240ft (683m).

Continue to Draperstown, about 12 miles (19km) away at the valley's eastern end. Travel on the B41 for 3 miles (5km) to Tobermore, where you join the A29 north (signposted Coleraine). At the roundabout outside Coleraine, take the A2 northwest to the coast at **DOWNHILL** ❸. Continue on to **Limavady**, situated in the beautiful Roe Valley and framed by mountains. The A2 continues west along Lough Foyle back to Derry.

**Detour:** From Omagh, head east on the A505 to Cookstown. The road itself is not particularly scenic, running through an area of heath and

**① Limavady Tourist Information Office**
*7 Connell Street; tel: 028 7776 0307. Open year-round.*

**① Beaghmore Stone Circles** *Between Cookstown and Gortin, 10 miles (16km) west of Cookstown, signposted off the A505. Free access at all times.*

**Wellbrook Beetling Mill £** *4 miles (6km) west of Cookstown on Wellbrook Road; tel: 028 8675 1735. Open mid-Mar–Jun & Sept weekends 1400–1800; Jul–Aug Sat–Thur 1400–1800. National Trust.*

bogland, but there are several attractions along the way. After 17 miles (27km), a road to the left leads to the **Beaghmore Stone Circles**, one of Ulster's primary archaeological sites; it comprises seven stone circles, stone rows and burial mounds. They date from around 1600 BC, but they lay buried in thick layers of peat for centuries until they were uncovered during peat cutting in the 1940s. Beaghmore, which means 'moor of the birches', is one of dozens of such ancient stone rings scattered around the Sperrin Mountains. Flint tools and other deposits suggest that the site was in use much earlier in Neolithic times. Three miles (5km) further on is the turn for the **Wellbrook Beetling Mill**, a water-powered linen mill with its original 18th-century machinery.

At Cookstown you can make a detour to see the **Ardboe High Cross**, which stands on the site of a 6th-century monastery on the shores of **LOUGH NEAGH ④**. Turn on to Molesworth Street and continue past the tourist information office on the B73 to Coagh (pronounced 'coke'). The signposting to Ardboe can seem a bit like a wild goose chase, but keep on the B73 towards the Battery, veering right to the abbey and high cross as you near the shores of the lake. Dating from the 10th century, it is one of the best crosses in the region, standing over 165ft (50m) high with 22 sculpted panels depicting biblical scenes. Return to Coagh and take the B18 north to Moneymore. Nearby is the manor house of **SPRINGHILL ⑤**. Continue north on the A29 to rejoin the main tour at Tobermore.

## Accommodation and food in Omagh

**Silverbirch Hotel ££** *5 Gortin Road, Omagh; tel: 028 8224 2520; fax: 028 8224 9061; email: info@silverbirchhotel.com; www.silverbirchhotel.com.* This pleasant, comfortable hotel on the B48 on the outskirts of Omagh is well situated for visiting the Ulster American Folk Park, which is just down the road. Also nearby are the woodlands of Gortin Glen and the Sperrin Mountains. The Barreta Bar and Grill serves good food.

## A Londonderry Air

In 1851, Jane Ross was sitting in her home on Limavady's main street when she heard a haunting tune played by a travelling fiddler, blind Denis O'Hempsey. She wrote it down and called it 'Londonderry Air'. The tune is believed to have been composed in the 16th century. Better known now as 'Danny Boy', it became one of Ireland's best-known songs.

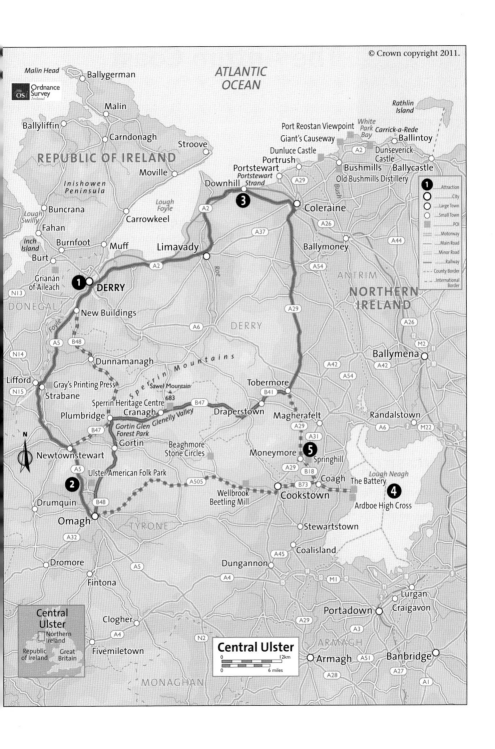

© Crown copyright 2011.

Malin Head
Ballygerman
ATLANTIC OCEAN

Ordnance Survey Ireland

Malin
Rathlin Island

Ballyliffin
Carndonagh
Stroove

Port Reostan Viewpoint
White Park Bay
Carrick-a-Rede
Ballintoy

Giant's Causeway
Dunluce Castle
Dunseverick Castle
A2

REPUBLIC OF IRELAND
Moville
Portrush
Portstewart
Bushmills
Ballycastle

Portstewart Strand
Downhill
Old Bushmills Distillery

Inishowen Peninsula
Lough Foyle
❸
A29
Bush

Buncrana
Carrowkeel
A2
Coleraine

Lough Swilly
Fahan
A37
A26

Inch Island
Burnfoot
Muff
Limavady
Ballymoney
A44

Burt
A2
Roe
A54

Grianán of Aileach
❶
DERRY
ANTRIM
NORTHERN IRELAND

N13
New Buildings
A29

DONEGAL
Foyle
A6
DERRY
A26

A5
B48
M2

N14
Dunnamanagh
Sperrin Mountains
A42
Ballymena

Lifford
Gray's Printing Press
Sawel Mountain
Tobermore
A54
A42

N15
Strabane
683
B41

Sperrin Heritage Centre
B47

Plumbridge
Cranagh
Draperstown
Magherafelt
Randalstown

B47
Gortin Glen Forest Park
Glenelly Valley
A29
A6
M22

Gortin
Beaghmore Stone Circles
Moneymore
❺
A31

N
Newtownstewart
Springhill

A5
Ulster American Folk Park
A29
B18
Coagh
The Battery
❹

❷
A505
Lough Neagh

Drumquin
B48
Wellbrook Beetling Mill
Cookstown
B73
Ardboe High Cross

Omagh
TYRONE
Stewartstown

A32
Coalisland

Dromore
A5
Dungannon
A45

Fintona
A4
M1

Lurgan
Craigavon

Central Ulster
Clogher
Portadown
A29
A3

Northern Ireland
A4
N2

Republic of Ireland
Great Britain
Fivemiletown
ARMAGH

Central Ulster
0          12km
0      6 miles
Armagh
A51
Banbridge

MONAGHAN
A28
A27
A1

Attraction
City
Large Town
Small Town
POI
Motorway
Main Road
Minor Road
Railway
County Border
International Border

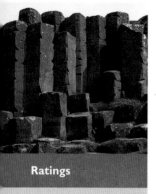

# The Antrim Coast

## Ratings

| | |
|---|---|
| Beaches | ●●●●● |
| Children | ●●●●● |
| Geology | ●●●●● |
| Scenery | ●●●●● |
| Walking | ●●●●● |
| Whiskey | ●●●●● |
| Mountains | ●●●●○ |
| Coastal towns/ villages | ●●●○○ |

The Giant's Causeway, which Thackeray called 'a remnant of chaos' left over from the creation of the world, is the most visited sight in Northern Ireland. The 18-mile (30km) stretch of the Causeway Coast between Portrush and Ballycastle is a designated Area of Outstanding Natural Beauty, with dramatic cliffs, headlands, dunes and volcanic rocks rising high above the sea. And it doesn't stop there. The entire Antrim coast is a scenic feast. The A2, known as the Antrim Coast Road, continues south to Larne, a magnificent drive on a ribbon of road between the steep mountain walls of the Antrim Glens and the sea. Along the way you can visit Bushmills, the world's oldest distillery; cross the spine-tingling Carrick-a-Rede rope bridge; hike to the waterfalls in Glenariff Forest Park; explore charming coastal villages; lounge on fine sandy beaches; or tee off at one of Ireland's top golf courses.

## BALLYCASTLE

**ⓘ Ballycastle Tourist Information Office**
7 Mary Street; tel: 028 2076 2024; fax: 028 2076 2515. Open year-round.

**Ⓐ** The Oul' Lammas Fair has been held in Ballycastle since 1606, making it possibly the oldest fair in Ireland. It takes place over the August bank holiday, with traditional games, market, music and horse trading.

**Above right**
Ballycastle Harbour

Ballycastle is a pleasant town at the northern end of the Antrim Glens. There are lovely old shops and pubs in the town centre, where many buildings date from Georgian times. These can be explored on the Ballycastle Heritage Trail, a self-guided walking trail available from the tourist office. From the main square, the Diamond, Quay Road leads down to the harbour, where there is a fine beach and promenade. The Marconi Memorial celebrates the transmission of the world's first wireless message across the sea from Ballycastle to Rathlin Island by Gugliemo Marconi in 1891. You can take the ferry to Rathlin for hiking and birdwatching.

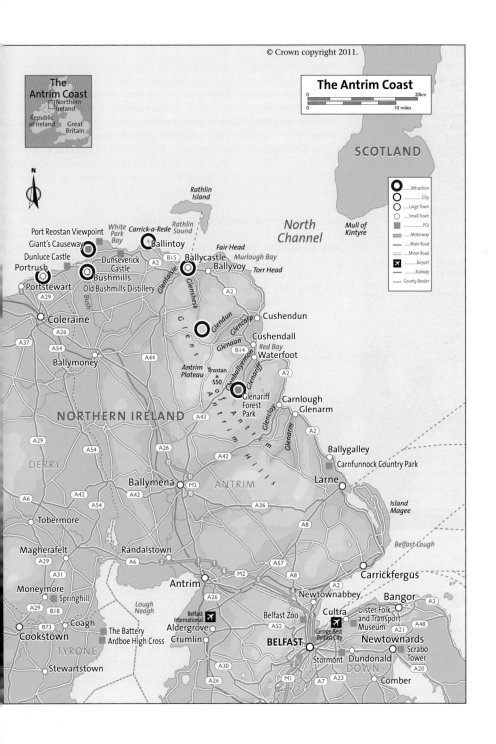

© Crown copyright 2011.

**The Antrim Coast**

The Antrim Coast
- Northern Ireland
- Republic of Ireland
- Great Britain

0 ___ 20km
0 ___ 10 miles

SCOTLAND

Rathlin Island

○ Attraction
○ City
○ Large Town
○ Small Town
■ POI
Motorway
Main Road
Minor Road
✈ Airport
Railway
County Border

Port Reostan Viewpoint
Giant's Causeway
Dunluce Castle
Portrush
Portstewart

White Park Bay
Carrick-a-Rede
Dunseverick Castle
Bushmills
Old Bushmills Distillery

Rathlin Sound
Ballintoy
Ballycastle
Ballyvoy

North Channel

Mull of Kintyre

Fair Head
Murlough Bay
Torr Head

A2
B15
A2
A29
Bush

Coleraine
A26
A37
A54
Ballymoney
A44

Cushendun
Cushendall
Red Bay
Waterfoot

Glendun
Glencorp
Glenaan
B14
A2

Antrim Plateau
Trostan ▲ 550

Glenariff Forest Park
Carnlough
Glenarm

NORTHERN IRELAND
A43

Ballygalley
Carnfunnock Country Park

A29
A54
A26
A42
Ballymena M2
DERRY
A6
A42
A54
A42
A36

Larne

Island Magee

A8

Belfast Lough

Tobermore

Magherafelt
A29
A31
Randalstown
A6

A57

Carrickfergus

Moneymore
Springhill
A29 B18
Coagh
B73
Cookstown
TYRONE
The Battery
Ardboe High Cross

Antrim
A26

Lough Neagh
Belfast International ✈
Aldergrove
Crumlin

Newtownabbey
Belfast Zoo
A52

BELFAST
George Best Belfast City ✈

A2
Cultra
Bangor
Ulster Folk and Transport Museum

A21
A48

Newtownards
Scrabo Tower

Stewartstown
A30
A26

Stormont
A7 A23
M1

Dundonald
DOWN

Comber
A20

# BUSHMILLS

 **Old Bushmills Distillery ££**
Tel: 028 2073 3272; www.bushmills.com. Open Mar–Oct Mon–Sat 0915–1700, Sun 1200–1700, opens 1100 on Sun Jul–Sept, last tour 1600 each day; Nov–Mar open daily, phone for tour times. Closed Good Friday, 4 & 12 July.

Bushmills the town grew up around Bushmills the distillery. The former is an attractive village set on the River Bush, which teems with salmon and trout. The latter is the world's oldest legal whiskey distillery, granted a licence by King James I in 1608, but the famous 'water of life' (*see page 260*) is known to have been made here as early as the 13th century. You can take a guided tour of the **Old Bushmills Distillery** to see how this leading malt whiskey is made, and learn about the processes of mashing, fermentation, distillation, maturation and bottling. There's a whiskey tasting at the end.

## Accommodation and food in Bushmills

**Below**
Old Bushmills Distillery

**Opposite**
Giant's Causeway

**The Bushmills Inn** *££–£££ 25 Main Street, Bushmills; tel: 028 2073 3000; fax: 028 2073 2048; email: mail@Bushmillsinn.com; www.bushmillsinn.com.* This atmospheric hotel, set in a historic coaching inn, is an Ulster favourite. The main hotel was built in the 1830s, and the character of this era is evoked by the gaslights in the Victorian bar, the flagstoned kitchen with an open turf fire, now a cosy lounge, the grand staircase, oil lamps, and the circular library with its secret room. Bedrooms in the coaching inn are furnished in comfortable cottage style. The oak-beamed loft leads to the Mill House, where the spacious modern bedrooms, all with a sitting-room area and small dressing room, overlook the River Bush. The restaurant, with whitewashed walls and intimate snugs, looks out on to the courtyard garden. The excellent Taste of Ulster menu is prepared from fresh local produce.

# CARRICK-A-REDE

**Carrick-a-Rede** Tel: 028 2076 9839. Open daily, weather permitting; Feb–May, Sept & Oct 1000–1800; Jun–Aug 1000–1900; Nov–Dec 1030–1530.

Carrick-a-Rede, which means 'the rock in the road', is a rocky island off the shore near Ballintoy. Every spring, salmon fishermen put up a swinging rope bridge to connect it to the mainland so they can reach their favoured fishing spot. Crossing the bridge across the chasm has become a popular challenge for visitors with a head for heights. The bridge is reached across the limestone headland of Larrybane, a former quarry that is a haven for birdlife. The bridge is normally taken down in mid-September.

### Giant's Causeway

It is said that the Giant's Causeway was built by the legendary giant Finn MacCool in order to lure his rival Benandonner to Ireland for a battle. When the Scottish giant arrived, he was bigger than expected, so Finn's wife Oonagh swaddled her frightened husband in a blanket, covered his head with a large bonnet and rocked him in an enormous cradle. Benandonner was so terrified by the size of this 'baby' that he had no desire to meet its father. He fled back to Scotland, ripping up the causeway as he went to avoid pursuit.

# GIANT'S CAUSEWAY

ℹ **Giant's Causeway Tourist Information Office**
44 Causeway Road, Bushmills; tel: 028 2073 1855. Open year-round.

🏛 **Giant's Causeway**
Tel: 028 2073 1582. Open for walking all year; visitor centre open year-round daily dawn–dusk. Charge for parking.

🍴 There is a restaurant at the Giant's Causeway visitor centre, but on a fine day you'd be better off bringing a picnic to enjoy on the benches overlooking the coast.

This incredible geological phenomenon is the most visited sight in Northern Ireland. The 40,000 basalt columns that make up the Giant's Causeway were formed by the cooling and cracking of lava from a volcanic explosion some 60 million years ago. They form a series of stepping stones reaching far into the sea, following the underwater fissure and resurfacing at the Scottish island of Staffa. When you see the causeway for the first time, you may be surprised to find that it is not as big as you were led to expect from all those well-composed guidebook photographs. What is most impressive are the shapes of this army of columns and its dramatic backdrop of cliffs, which rise as high as 328ft (100m). There are two approaches. It's an easy half-mile (1km) walk on the road leading down from the visitor centre (take the shuttle bus if you prefer). Alternatively, a longer path takes you along the top of the cliffs and down the Shepherd's Steps – all 162 of them – where you'll have splendid views of the cliff-face columns known as the Organ. It's worth walking the extra 550 yards (500m) to the **Port Reostan Viewpoint** for a spectacular vista back across the causeway. Near here, at Port na Spaniagh, is the wreck of the Spanish Armada galleon, the *Girona*, whose treasure hoard can be seen in the Ulster Museum in Belfast. The visitor centre has interpretive displays and an audiovisual theatre.

# GLENARIFF FOREST PARK

**Glenariff Forest Park** *Tel: 028 2955 6000. Open daily 1000– dusk. Small charge for parking.*

Glenariff, the 'queen of the glens', is arguably the most beautiful of the nine Antrim Glens. It covers 2,928 acres (1,185 hectares), more than three-quarters of which have been planted with trees. The main species is Sitka spruce, a North American conifer, which flourishes on the poor soil, but areas of old broad-leaved woodland also exist in the park. There are small lakes and recreation areas, rocky gorges and spectacular waterfalls created by two rivers, the Inver and the Glenariff. The glen has been designated a national nature reserve. Trails from half a mile to 5 miles long (1–9km) start from the car park. There is also a visitor centre.

# GLENS OF ANTRIM

**The Ulster Way** The Ulster Way is a waymarked trail that runs through the Antrim Glens.

Stretching from Ballycastle in the north to Larne in the south, the nine Glens of Antrim were carved out of the high green hills by glaciers at the end of the last Ice Age. In the 1830s, the building of the Antrim Coast Road linked these remote glens to the rest of Ulster. It is a magnificent drive on a narrow, winding ribbon of road between the steep hillsides and the sea. Narrower side roads wind up into the glens, where numerous trails are a paradise for hikers, to the escarpment of the Antrim Plateau. The glens are steeped in myth and legend. A chambered 'horned' cairn in Glenaan is said to be the grave of Ossian, the legendary Ulster hero who journeyed to Tir-na-nOg, the land of eternal youth.

**Below**
Dunluce Castle, near Portrush

# PORTRUSH

Set on a promontory jutting into the Atlantic, Portrush is Northern Ireland's largest seaside resort town, which flourished during Victorian times with the coming of the railway. There are many family attractions here, including amusement parks and a Waterworld. From the harbour, there are boat trips along the Causeway Coast and to the Skerries, the little rocky islands offshore. Just to the east of town are the romantic ruins of **Dunluce Castle**, dating from the 13th century. It is so precariously perched on the cliffs that in 1639 its kitchens – with the cooks in them – were swept into the sea during a storm. The nearby Royal Portrush championship golf course is one of the top four in Ireland. To the west is the twin resort of **Portstewart**, with a beautiful 2-mile (3km) stretch of beach, the **Portstewart Strand**, managed by the National Trust.

## Suggested tour

**Total distance:** The main route along the Antrim coast is 74 miles (119km). The detour to Fair Head and Murlough Bay is 16 miles (26km). To return to Portrush from Larne is 52 miles (84km).

**Time:** You can drive the main route in 2–3 hours, but allow plenty of time to linger and walk the paths at the Giant's Causeway. Allow up to an hour for the Fair Head detour.

**Links:** Belfast (*see page 262*) is 20 miles (32km) from Larne. This route also adjoins the tour of Central Ulster (*see page 249*).

From **PORTRUSH ❶**, take the A2 east along gorgeous coastal scenery of dunes and headlands for 5 miles (8km) to **BUSHMILLS ❷**. The famous **GIANT'S CAUSEWAY ❸** is just 2 miles (3km) from the centre of town. Turn left out of the car park, following signs to Ballycastle, and drive across the headland past the remains of **Dunseverick Castle**. At the junction, turn left on to the A2, which runs past White Park Bay and its sandy beach. Just beyond, the A2 curves right, but continue straight ahead on the B15 to **Ballintoy**. Just before the village, turn left on the side road for Ballintoy Harbour, which winds past the pretty village church and down to the shore. This picturesque spot with its rocky islets and sea caves is a gem on the Causeway Coast shoreline, while **Rourke's Kitchen**, a café in an old stone fisherman's cottage, will tempt you to stay awhile. Continue through the village and on the outskirts follow signs for **CARRICK-A-REDE ❹**. Turn left on to the B15 and continue on to **BALLYCASTLE ❺**, which marks the start of the **GLENS OF ANTRIM ❻**. Continue on the A2 for 11 miles (17km) to **Cushendun**. Set around a wide sandy bay, the striking black-and-white buildings of the town square were designed by Clough Williams-Ellis, the architect for Portmeirion in Wales.

**ⓘ Ballintoy Harbour Café** £ *Tel: 028 2076 3632.* This charming café is called **Rourke's Kitchen**, after the former owner of the old stone fisherman's cottage. It serves home-cooked shepherd's pie, lasagne, burgers, sandwiches, salads and Ulster fry. If you're not hungry, you will be when you see the scrumptious home-baked cakes, scones, fruit pies and pastries, accompanied by a nice pot of tea. You can also get ice cream, drinks and snacks. *Open 1100–1900.*

### The Water of Life

*Uisce Beatha*, which means the 'water of life' in Gaelic, has been produced for over a thousand years. The raw materials for making it are barley and pure water, and it is these two ingredients that give individual products their unique character. For example, the water from St Columb's Rill, a tributary of the River Bush, is said to give Bushmills its special flavour. Apart from the 'e' in the spelling, Irish malt whiskey differs from its Scottish counterpart in two main ways. The barley is dried in closed kilns without the use of a peat fire, so the characteristic smoky taste of many Scotch whiskies is absent. Irish whiskies are generally distilled three times, as opposed to twice for most Scottish brands.

**Detour:** Just past the village of Ballyvoy, when the A2 curves right, continue straight ahead on the signposted **Torr Head–Cushendun Scenic Route**. This road, which leads out through the rural headland, becomes extremely narrow and winding, with steep grades and very sharp bends, and is not recommended if you're uncomfortable with this sort of driving. Signs lead to the car park above Murlough Bay, and there are several walking routes, including one to the rugged Fair Head. A steep, rough track snakes down to an idyllic wooded spot on the rocky shore. Continue around the headland, where the promontory of Torr Head can also be explored. There are fantastic views out to sea, and down over the sandy beach as you approach Cushendun, where you rejoin the main tour.

Take the A2 south for 5 miles (8km) to **Cushendall**, a pretty village set along the sandy Red Bay, at the foot of three of the Antrim glens – Glenaan, Glenballyemon and Glenariff. From here the mountain scenery becomes higher and more dramatic. Continue along the waterfront, passing beneath an archway cut through the overhanging rock, topped by castle ruins, for 1 mile (1.5km) to Waterfoot. Here you turn right on the A43 for the beautiful 6-mile (10km) drive up the green, steep-sided Glenariff to **GLENARIFF FOREST PARK ❼**. Turn left out of the park, and continue for 1 mile (1.5km) on the A43, then take the right turn on to the B14, signposted Cushendall/Cushendun. This leads back down to the coast through the more barren Glenballyemon, passing beneath the slopes of Trostan, at 1,805ft (550m) the highest point in the glens. There are sweeping views of the ocean ahead, in the 'V' where the two glens meet. At Cushendall, turn right and continue south on the A2.

For the next 21 miles (34km) the road hugs the coast all the way to Larne, often with only a little rock wall between you and the sea. It passes the villages of **Carnlough**, set along a broad bay with a sandy beach, and **Glenarm**, with its neo-Tudor castle. Just beyond Ballygalley is the **Carnfunnock Country Park**, with its walled garden, time garden and amazing maze in the shape of Northern Ireland. **Larne**, 4 miles (6km) further on, is an important port for the north coast. From here you can continue on to Belfast, or return to Portrush via Ballymena on the A8/A36/A26.

## Also worth exploring

**Carrickfergus**, situated on Belfast Lough south of Larne, has an attractive harbour and several visitor attractions.

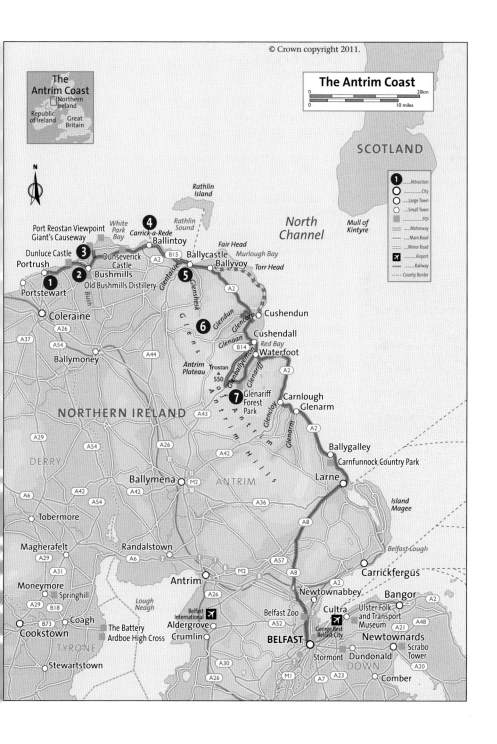

# Belfast

## Ratings

| | |
|---|---|
| Architecture | ●●●●● |
| Entertainment | ●●●●● |
| Shopping | ●●●●● |
| Cathedrals/churches | ●●●●○ |
| Food and drink | ●●●●○ |
| Gardens | ●●●●○ |
| Museums | ●●●●○ |
| Parks | ●●●●○ |

Overshadowed by the political affairs of Northern Ireland, Belfast is often avoided as a holiday destination. This is a pity, for what emerges from the smokescreen of the past Troubles is a vibrant city with much to offer. Belfast enjoys a lovely setting on the shores of a sea lough, backed by green hills. It is young as Irish cities go, dating largely from the 19th century when it flourished as a port and commercial centre, the linen mills and shipyards forming the backbone of its wealth. Grand buildings were erected, such as City Hall and the great warehouses and commercial buildings around Donegall Square. It was a cultured city, with a Grand Opera House and splendid Botanic Gardens, and so it remains. Belfast has a fine university, a top arts festival and a lively nightlife, with smart, sophisticated bars and restaurants standing alongside the characterful Victorian saloons.

## Getting there and getting around

ℹ **Belfast Welcome Centre** 47 Donegall Place; tel: 028 9024 6609; fax: 028 9031 2424; email: info@belfastvisitor.com; www.gotobelfast.com. Open year-round.

**Belfast International Airport** at Aldergrove is 19 miles (30km) from the city centre, a 30-minute drive on the M2. There is a shuttle service between the airport and city centre. *Tel: 028 9448 4848.*

**George Best Belfast City Airport** is 3 miles (5km) from the city centre and can be reached by train from Great Victoria Street station (*tel: 028 9093 9093*). There is a regular rail service to Dublin and other cities in Northern Ireland and the Republic. Northern Ireland Railways enquiries: *tel: 028 9093 9093.*

### Public transport
**Bus:** Citybus provides a regular service to all parts of the Belfast area. Tickets can be bought from the driver, or multi-journey tickets are available in local shops or at the Citybus kiosk in Donegall Square West. Enquiries: *tel: 028 9066 6630.*

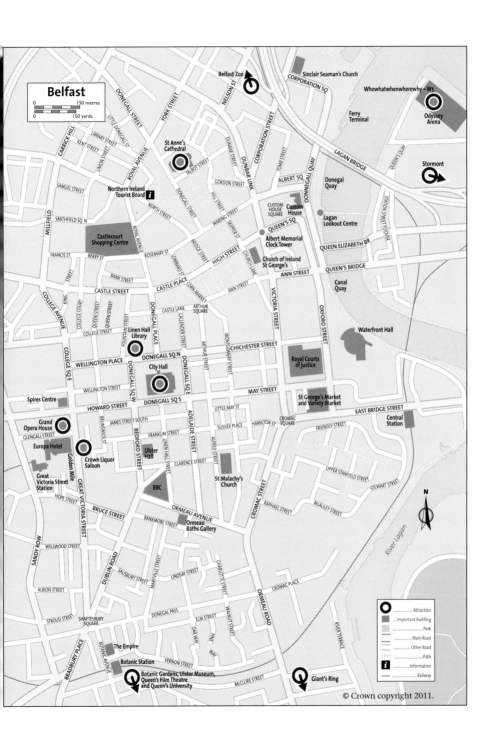

# Belfast

0       150 metres
0       150 yards

Belfast Zoo

Sinclair Seaman's Church

CORPORATION SQ

Whowhatwhenwherewhy – W5

Ferry Terminal

Odyssey Arena

St Anne's Cathedral

Stormont

Northern Ireland Tourist Board

Donegal Quay

Lagan Lookout Centre

Castlecourt Shopping Centre

CUSTOM HOUSE SQUARE   Custom House

QUEEN'S SQ

Albert Memorial Clock Tower

QUEEN ELIZABETH BR

Church of Ireland St George's

QUEEN'S BRIDGE

Canal Quay

CASTLE STREET   CASTLE PLACE

Linen Hall Library

Waterfront Hall

DONEGALL SQ N

City Hall

Royal Courts of Justice

WELLINGTON PLACE

Spires Centre

DONEGALL SQ S

St George's Market and Variety Market

EAST BRIDGE STREET

Central Station

Grand Opera House

Europa Hotel

Crown Liquor Saloon

Ulster Hall

St Malachy's Church

Great Victoria Street Station

BBC

Ormeau Baths Gallery

The Empire

Botanic Station

Botanic Gardens, Ulster Museum, Queen's Film Theatre and Queen's University

Giant's Ring

River Lagan

N

| | Attraction |
| --- | --- |
| | Important building |
| | Park |
| | Main Road |
| | Other Road |
| | Path |
| *i* | Information |
| | Railway |

© Crown copyright 2011.

BELFAST

**Taxis:** Taxi ranks for metered cabs are located at Central Station, both bus stations and at City Hall. They look like London black cabs and have a yellow disc on the windscreen. If other taxis do not have meters, be sure to ask the fare before setting off.

**Tours:** There are several walking tours of Belfast. They include **Belfast, the Old Town of 1660–1685** (*tel: 028 9024 6609*), and **Belfast Pub Tours** (*tel: 028 9268 3665; www.belfastpubtours.com*). Contact the tourist office for a full list.

**Parking**

On-street metered parking is limited to an area around St Anne's Cathedral on the north side of the city, and behind City Hall on the south side. There is free street parking in the streets around Queen's University and the Ulster Museum, but always check the parking regulations locally as you may be required to park on alternate sides of the street at certain times of day. There are many car parks around the city centre, but they are expensive, as in most big cities.

**Right**
Titanic Memorial, Belfast City Hall

ⓝ **Botanic Gardens**
*Tel: 028 9032 4902.*
*Gardens open 0730–dusk;*
*Palm House and*
*Tropical Ravine open*
*Apr–Sept weekdays*
*1000–1700, weekends*
*1300–1700; closed for*
*lunch; closed from 1600*
*Mon–Fri in winter.*

**City Hall** *Donegall Square;*
*tel: 028 9027 0456. Open*
*Mon–Thur 0830–1700, Fri*
*0830–1630.*

**Crown Liquor Saloon**
*Great Victoria Street;*
*tel: 028 9027 9901;*
*www.crownbar.com. Open*
*Mon–Sat 1130–midnight,*
*Sun 1230–2200.*

**Grand Opera House**
*Great Victoria Street;*
*tel: 028 9024 1919*
*(tickets); www.goh.co.uk*

# Sights

## Botanic Gardens

Belfast's Botanic Gardens were laid out in 1827 between Queen's University and the River Lagan. Here, paths lined with wrought-iron benches wind past shady trees, flowerbeds and a rose garden. The **Palm House**, designed by Charles Lanyon in 1839, is one of the earliest curvilinear glass and cast-iron glasshouses. A variety of temperate species billow into the 49ft (15m)-high dome, added in 1852. By contrast, you'll gaze down into the **Tropical Ravine** from a steamy walkway lush with hanging vines and exotic flowers. Band concerts, showjumping and other events are held in these gardens.

## City Hall

This grand Renaissance-style building with its façade of Portland stone was built in 1906. Its finest features are the main entrance, the main dome and the grand staircase, designed in three types of Italian marble. Even if you're not taking in one of the free guided tours, step inside for a look at the stained-glass windows, decorative plasterwork and ornate central dome, rising 173ft (53m) high from the foyer. To the right of the entrance is a small exhibition about the city. You can pick up a guide to the statues and monuments that adorn the spacious grounds. These include the statue of Queen Victoria in front of the main entrance and the Titanic Memorial on the building's east side. The grounds are surrounded by barley-twist steel railings. Look for the city's coat of arms on the front entrance gates. On either side are ornate lamps decorated with cherubs and sea horses, symbolising the city's industrial and manufacturing heritage.

## Crown Liquor Saloon

You'll be ready for a pint after a look at this dazzling Victorian bar, opposite the opera house. Now owned by the National Trust, it is the most perfectly preserved bar of its era in the province. A visit here is like entering a kaleidoscope of bright stained glass, gleaming brasswork, geometric Italian tilework, embossed ceilings and bevelled mirrors. It has scalloped gaslights and a long bar inlaid with coloured glass. If you're lucky, you'll be able to claim a seat in one of the ten wood-panelled snugs (booths with closing doors for privacy); notice the brass match-strikers.

## Grand Opera House

It's worth seeing a show just for the privilege of sitting in this opulent opera house, designed in 1894 by Frank Matcham. Lavish gilt mouldings, ornamental plasterwork, and a magnificent frescoed ceiling by Irish artist Cherith McKinstry are all part of its Victorian glory. The elephants supporting the boxes and the imitation Sanskrit add an oriental touch. Pavarotti made his British debut here in 1963 as

**Linen Hall Library**
17 Donegall Square;
tel: 028 9032 1707;
www.linenhall.com. Open
Mon–Fri 0930–1730, Sat
0930–1600.

**St Anne's Cathedral**
Donegall Street;
tel: 028 9032 8332;
www.belfastcathedral.org.
Open Mon–Sat 1000–1600,
Sun before and after
services.

**Whowhatwherewhen
why – W5@Odyssey** 2
Queen's Quay; tel: 028 9046
7700; www.w5online.co.uk.
Open Mon–Thur 1000–
1700, Fri–Sat 1000–1800,
Sun 1200–1800 (last
admission 1 hour before
closing).

Lieutenant Pinkerton in *Madame Butterfly*. The opera house was restored after bomb damage in the early 1990s.

### Linen Hall Library
Housed in a charming building on Donegall Square, Belfast's oldest library has been lending books since 1788. It houses local history and literature collections as well as an extensive archive of documents relating to the Troubles. A visit here is a must for anyone who cherishes the atmosphere of old-fashioned reading rooms, which are rapidly becoming an endangered species around the world. The library is for members' use only, but you can go in for a look around, a browse through the day's newspapers and a cup of coffee in the little café.

### St Anne's Cathedral
The construction of this Romanesque Revival-style cathedral, begun in 1899, was directed by eight architects over 80 years, and is still not entirely finished. Basilican in plan, its sombre character is somewhat relieved by an ornately carved west front, a decorative baptistery and some fine stained glass and 1920s mosaics. A crossing tower was part of the original design but has never been added. The Unionist leader Lord Carson, who was instrumental in keeping the six counties of Northern Ireland within the United Kingdom, is buried in the cathedral.

### Whowhatwherewhenwhy – W5
One of Belfast's major attractions, the W5 interactive discovery science centre is a great place for the whole family to visit. Based at the Odyssey Complex in central Belfast, the museum has five main exhibition areas comprising 160 interactive exhibits: START, SEE, GO, DO and WOW. Each area offers different and creative interactive activities. W5 also presents live science shows and serves as a venue for corporate events and even birthday parties. It is a not-for-profit charitable organisation.

## Green Belfast

Despite – or perhaps because of – its industrial origins, Belfast has a wealth of parks in or near the city centre. In addition to the Botanic Gardens, there is Sir Thomas and Lady Dixon Park, fragrant with over 20,000 roses; Ormeau Park, the city's oldest and one of its largest parks; Grovelands Park, with heather and alpine gardens; Lagan Meadows, a wildlife haven with woodland, marsh and meadows; and Barnett Demesne, a landscaped estate. To the north of the city, Belfast Castle is set within Cave Hill Country Park, with nature reserves and archaeological sites among the heath, moors and woodland.

**Above**
Belfast Botanic Gardens

## Suggested walk

**Time:** You can walk the main route in 1–2 hours. The detour to the Botanic Gardens will add an extra half-hour, not counting sightseeing time in the gardens.

**Links:** The Belfast environs tour (*see page 277*) and the Antrim Coast tour (*see page 259*) are both easily approached from the city.

Begin in the heart of Belfast at **Donegall Square ❶**. The grounds of the magnificent **CITY HALL ❷** fill the square and make a pleasant place to sit. Surrounding the square are some of Belfast's grandest buildings. At No 1, on the north side, Marks & Spencer occupies one of the great linen warehouses of the 19th century. The **LINEN HALL LIBRARY ❸** is at No 17. On the west side is the Baroque Scottish Provident Institution, built in 1899; to the east is the Gothic Pearl Assurance building of the same date; and on the south side Jaffe Brothers is housed in another linen warehouse decorated with busts of Isaac Newton and Christopher Columbus, among others. Walk north along Donegall Place, a pedestrianised shopping street, and turn right on Castle Place. As you reach Cornmarket, you may hear a band playing in the afternoon. Carry straight on into High Street, and explore the little 'entries', or narrow lanes, running through to Ann Street. Here you'll find small shops and some of Belfast's most characterful pubs, such as the Morning Star, along Pottinger's Entry, and White's Tavern, the city's oldest pub, along Winecellar Entry. At the end of High Street is the **Albert Memorial Clock Tower ❹**, called 'the Albert Clock' by

**i** **Queen's University**
   **Visitor Centre £**
*Tel: 028 9097 5252. Open
May–Sept Mon–Sat
0930–1630, Sun
1000–1300; Oct–Apr
Mon–Fri only.*

locals, a tribute to Queen Victoria's consort. This well-loved landmark leans slightly, due to its foundation on wooden piles driven into the muddy reclaimed land. Behind it is the **Custom House** ❺, designed by Sir Charles Lanyon in 1854. You can also see Samson and Goliath, two enormous yellow cranes in Harland & Wolff's shipyards on Queen's Island. The ill-fated ocean liner *Titanic* was built there.

Turn left at the clock tower, then left again on Waring Street, then right on Donegall Street, which leads to **ST ANNE'S CATHEDRAL** ❻. The **Northern Ireland Tourist Board** ❼ is just opposite in St Anne's Court, reached via North Street. Carry on along Donegall Street and turn left on to Royal Avenue, and soon you'll see the Castlecourt Shopping Centre on the right. Next, turn right on Castle Street, passing the tourist information office for the Irish Republic. Turn left on Queen Street and continue south to Howard Street, by the Spires Mall. Turn right, and then left into Great Victoria Street. On your right is the **GRAND OPERA HOUSE** ❽. Next door is the **Europa Hotel** ❾, a Belfast landmark. Over the road is the **CROWN LIQUOR SALOON** ❿. This trio sits at the top end of the **Golden Mile** ⓫, where much of Belfast's nightlife takes place. To peruse the district, continue south on Great Victoria Street to its tip at Shaftesbury Square, then head north up Dublin Road and Bedford Street to return to Donegall Square.

**Detour:** From Shaftesbury Square, head south along Botanic Avenue. This is one of Belfast's nicest streets, lined with attractive restaurants, bars and shops that cater for a university clientele. The street leads into **Queen's University** ⓬, with handsome Tudor-revival buildings designed by Charles Lanyon and built in 1849. Its highlights are the red-brick and sandstone main building, and University Square, an impressive terrace. There are exhibitions in the visitor centre. At the end of the street is the entrance to the **BOTANIC GARDENS** ⓭. Leave the gardens via Stranmillis Road; turn right and continue up University Road, past Queen's University, back to Shaftesbury Square.

## Also worth exploring

**Belfast Zoo** is a fun day out for the children. The **Giant's Ring** is a Neolithic circular earthwork with a dolmen in the centre, just 4 miles (6km) outside the city centre. **Stormont**, Northern Ireland's Parliament House, can only be visited by advance arrangement, but you can view its impressive façade of Portland stone from the Newtownards Road (A20). Belfast has many churches. Among the most interesting are Church of Ireland St George's (High Street); St Malachy's (Alfred Street); Sinclair Seaman's Church (Corporation Square off Donegall Quay) and Knockbreda Parish Church, the city's oldest, on Church Road in south Belfast.

# Shopping

Belfast's grand old buildings and pedestrianised streets are a shopper's delight. **Donegall Place** has many of the familiar chain stores as well as family-owned establishments. Try **Chinacraft** for crystal, china and other Irish quality gifts. To the left of Donegall Place, through the **Queen's Arcade**, is the **Fountain Area**, where there is a multitude of speciality shops. Donegall Place becomes **Royal Avenue**, where you'll find the **Castlecourt Shopping Centre**, an indoor mall. **High Street** is another main shopping thoroughfare, with narrow 'entries', or lanes, running off it. The **Spires Centre**, housed in a former Presbyterian church building, is filled with upmarket designer shops. **St George's Market**, on May Street, is a Friday-morning food market, with the **Variety Market** next door. **Donegal Pass**, off Shaftesbury Square, has a row of antique shops and a Saturday-morning flea market.

# Entertainment

You can hear all kinds of music in Belfast's pubs, from traditional Irish to country and rock, to jazz and blues. Some of the most atmospheric can be found around the Crown Liquor Saloon. Nightclubs are also plentiful, with many located in the Golden Mile and university area. These stay open later, until 0100–0300. **King's Hall** (*tel: 028 9066 5225*) is a major venue for rock and pop concerts. The **Empire** (*tel: 028 9032 8110*), in a former church on Botanic Avenue, has stand-up comedy as well as music. Film buffs should check out the **Queen's Film Theatre** (*tel: 028 9097 1097*), an art cinema showing foreign and independent films (*closed between terms*). To find out what's on where, look for the free listings papers called '*the big list*' and *That's Entertainment*. The *Belfast Telegraph* also has a good 'What's On' section. Or log on to *www.culturenorthernireland.org*

Belfast is a vibrant centre for the performing arts, attracting many international artists from a variety of fields. The **Belfast Festival at Queen's** is Ireland's biggest arts festival, which runs for three weeks every autumn and hosts world-class stars in theatre, dance, comedy, opera, jazz, folk and classical music. **Waterfront Hall** (*tel: 028 9033 4455*) is the city's state-of-the-art concert and conference venue. The **Grand Opera House** (*tel: 028 9024 1919*) presents drama, ballet, musicals and pantomime, as well as opera, and has hosted many of the world's top stars. **Ulster Hall** (*tel: 028 9032 3900*) is home to the Ulster Orchestra. Classical and contemporary Irish drama is featured at the **Lyric Theatre** (*tel: 028 9038 1081*). A new **Metropolitan Arts Centre**, the **MAC**, is due to open in late 2011. Permanent and temporary art exhibitions can be seen at the **Ormeau Baths Gallery** (*tel: 028 9032 1402*). The **Odyssey Arena** (*tel: 028 9073 9074*) hosts live music concerts.

# Accommodation and food

**Madison's** *££ 59–63 Botanic Avenue, Belfast BT7 1JL; tel: 028 9050 9800; fax: 028 9050 9808; email: info@madisonshotel.com; www.madisonshotel.com.* Everything about Madison's says 'style', from the Art Nouveau-style doors to the amusing sculpture of a man peering out of a top-floor window. It's brilliantly located, 5 minutes' walk from the university, 10 minutes' walk from the city centre, and surrounded by good restaurants, bars and nightclubs. Service is friendly and top-notch. Rooms are comfortable with pleasant décor and all amenities, including satellite TV. The spacious bar and restaurant are a feast for the eye as well as the palate, with a fantastical twisting iron staircase and ultra-modern décor. The food is excellent bistro fare – seafood, steak, poultry, pasta and vegetarian dishes with Eastern spices. Great selection of wines by the glass or bottle from 'The Collection' of their hand-picked wines.

**Nick's Warehouse** *££ 35 Hill Street; tel: 028 9043 9690; www.nickswarehouse.co.uk.* Built as a warehouse for Bushmills Whiskey in 1832, this popular restaurant in the cathedral quarter serves a delectable menu of dishes made from local produce ranging from wild boar to local seafood, accompanied by interesting wines at affordable prices. *Open Tue–Fri 1200–1500 & 1700–2200, Sat 1200–1500 & 1800–2200. Reservations advised.*

**Deanes** *£££ 36–40 Howard Street; tel: 028 9033 1134; www.michaeldeane.co.uk.* Irish and British cuisine tops the menu at Belfast's only Michelin-starred restaurant. Beneath the elegant upstairs restaurant for serious dining there's a bustling brasserie serving modern Irish cooking (*open Mon–Sat 1000–1500, 1800–2200*).

**Malmaison Belfast** *£££ 34–38 Victoria Street, Belfast BT1 3GH; tel: 028 9022 0200; fax: 028 9022 0220; www.malmaison.com.* Four-star luxury in a classical Italianate building designed in the 1850s from two former warehouses. The spacious, elegant rooms have every amenity. Fine restaurant and café bar. Located near the river and clock tower, just a few minutes' stroll from the city centre.

## Tracing your ancestors

If you're tracing ancestors in Northern Ireland, the **Public Record Office** on Balmoral Avenue has some 33 miles (53km) of records dating back to the early 17th century. The PRO is open again from May 2011 after its move to the Titanic Quarter. *Tel: 028 9025 5905; www.proni.gov.uk.* Another source is the **Ulster Historical Foundation**, *49 Malone Road, Belfast BT9 6RY, tel: 028 9066 1988; fax: 028 9066 1977; email: enquiry@uhf.org.uk; www.ancestryireland.com. Open Mon–Fri 1000–1230, 1430–1630.*

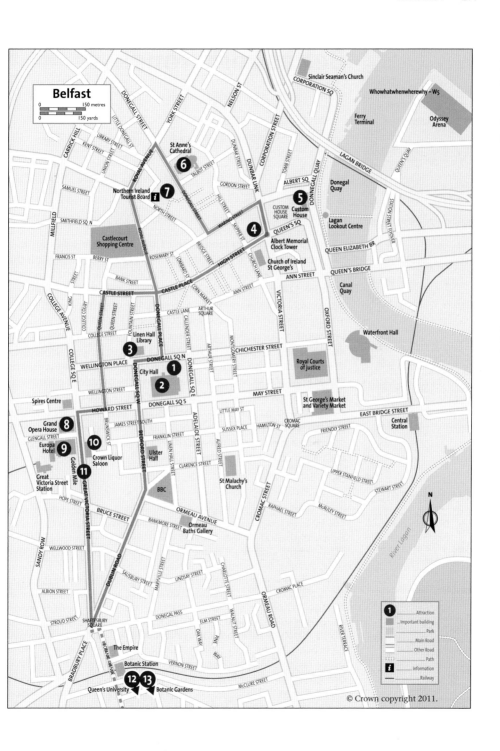

Belfast

0 — 150 metres
0 — 150 yards

Sinclair Seaman's Church
CORPORATION SQ
Whowhatwhenwherewhy – W5
Ferry Terminal
Odyssey Arena
St Anne's Cathedral
⑥
Northern Ireland Tourist Board ⑦
Castlecourt Shopping Centre
Albert SQ
Donegal Quay
⑤
Custom House
Lagan Lookout Centre
④
Albert Memorial Clock Tower
QUEEN ELIZABETH BR
Church of Ireland St George's
QUEEN'S BRIDGE
Canal Quay
Linen Hall Library
③
Waterfront Hall
City Hall ①
②
Royal Courts of Justice
Spires Centre
St George's Market and Variety Market
EAST BRIDGE STREET
Central Station
Grand Opera House ⑧
⑩
Europa Hotel ⑨
Crown Liquor Saloon
Ulster Hall
⑪
Great Victoria Street Station
BBC
St Malachy's Church
The Empire
Botanic Station
⑫ ⑬ Botanic Gardens
Queen's University
Ormeau Baths Gallery

① Attraction
Important building
Park
Main Road
Other Road
Path
i Information
Railway

© Crown copyright 2011.

# Belfast environs

## Ratings

| | |
|---|---|
| Mountains | ●●●●● |
| Religious sites | ●●●●● |
| Wildlife | ●●●●● |
| Beaches | ●●●●○ |
| Family attractions | ●●●●○ |
| Gardens | ●●●●○ |
| Manor houses/stately homes | ●●●●○ |
| Museums | ●●●●○ |

The pretty, rolling landscape of the Ards Peninsula runs in a scenic crescent from Belfast to Portaferry. Together with the north shores of County Down, it encircles Strangford Lough, a 15-mile (24km) lake that empties into the sea through the Narrows. These waters are a haven for grey seals and other marine life – in summer some 20 per cent of Ireland's seals can be found basking along its shores – as well as flocks of wildfowl and wading birds. Six national nature reserves have been designated in the area. One of Ireland's finest museums, the Ulster Folk and Transport Museum, and the fabulous gardens of Mount Stewart, are also found here. South Down is characterised by the Mourne Mountains, considered by many to be the loveliest in the country. You can relax on the splendid sandy beaches around Newcastle, or follow in the footsteps of Ireland's patron saint at Downpatrick.

## DOWNPATRICK

**Down Cathedral £**
English Street; tel: 028 4461 4922. Open Mon–Sat 0930–1630, Sun 1400–1630.

**Down County Museum**
The Mall, English Street; tel: 028 4461 5218; www. downcountymuseum.com. Open Mon–Fri 1000–1700, Sat & Sun 1300–1700.

The modern town sprawls below the Hill of Down, which is topped by **Down Cathedral**. It was founded as a Benedictine monastery in the 12th century, and rebuilt in the 18th and 19th centuries in the Gothic style. Among its features are a medieval baptismal font, a unique pulpitum on which the Telford organ is built, return chapter stalls and Georgian box pews. The **churchyard** is the reputed burial place of Ireland's three patron saints: Patrick, Brigid and Colmcille. An enormous stone (placed here in 1900) with the inscription 'Patric' marks the site where the Norman knight John de Courcy reinterred their bones in the 12th century, fulfilling a prophecy that the three would be buried in the same place. On the road below the cathedral is the **Down County Museum**. It is housed in the old county gaol, which was built between 1789 and 1796, and is the most complete example of its era in Ireland. A tableau of prison life has been

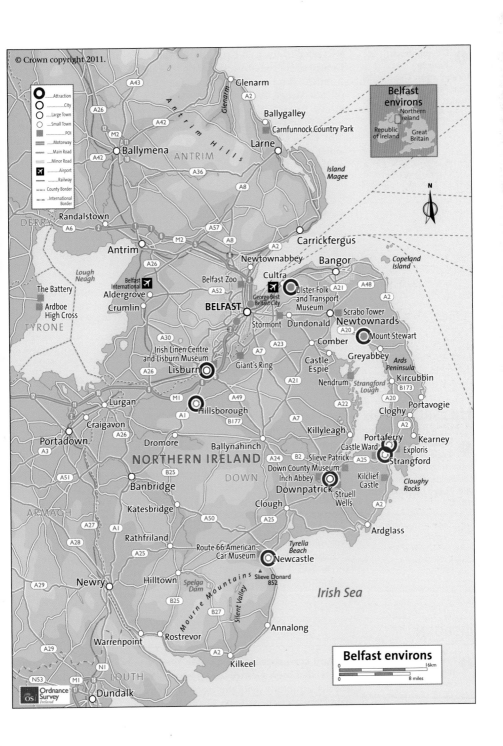

© Crown copyright 2011.

**Belfast environs**

Northern Ireland
Republic of Ireland
Great Britain

Attraction
City
Large Town
Small Town
POI
Motorway
Main Road
Minor Road
Airport
Railway
County Border
International Border

N

Glenarm
A43
A2
A26
Ballygalley
A42
Carnfunnock Country Park
M2
Larne
Ballymena
ANTRIM
A42
A36
Island Magee
A8

DERRY
Randalstown
A6
A57
A8
A2
Carrickfergus
Antrim
M2
A26
Newtownabbey
Bangor
Copeland Island
Lough Neagh
Belfast International
Belfast Zoo
Cultra
The Battery
Aldergrove
A52
George Best Belfast City
Ulster Folk and Transport Museum
A21
A48
A2
Ardboe High Cross
Crumlin
BELFAST
Scrabo Tower
TYRONE
Stormont
Dundonald
Newtownards
A30
A23
Comber
A20
Mount Stewart
Irish Linen Centre and Lisburn Museum
A7
Greyabbey
Ards Peninsula
A26
Lisburn
Giant's Ring
Castle Espie
Nendrum
Strangford Lough
Kircubbin
A21
B173
A49
A22
A20
Lurgan
M1
Hillsborough
A7
Cloghy
Portavogie
A1
B177
Craigavon
A26
Killyleagh
A2
Portadown
Dromore
Ballynahinch
Portaferry
Kearney
A3
A24
B2
Slieve Patrick
Castle Ward
Exploris
NORTHERN IRELAND
B25
Down County Museum
A25
Strangford
A51
DOWN
Inch Abbey
Kilclief Castle
Cloughy Rocks
Banbridge
Downpatrick
Struell Wells
A2
Katesbridge
Clough
A50
A25
Rathfriland
Ardglass
A27
A1
A28
A25
Route 66 American Car Museum
Tyrella Beach
Newry
Hilltown
Spelga Dam
Slieve Donard 852
Newcastle
A29
Mourne Mountains
Silent Valley
Irish Sea
B25
B27
Warrenpoint
Rostrevor
Annalong
A29
A2
Kilkeel
NI
LOUTH

**Belfast environs**
0                    16km
0          8 miles

N53
M1
Ordnance Survey Ireland
Dundalk

**ⓘ Downpatrick Tourist Information Centre** *The Saint Patrick Centre, 53A Market Street; tel: 028 4461 2233. Open year-round.*

re-created in the Cell Block. In the gatehouse, the **St Patrick Heritage Centre** traces the life of the saint. The alleged site of his first church is 2 miles (3km) away at the village of Saul. Other sites in the area include **Struell Wells**, a pagan holy well blessed by Patrick; the hill of **Slieve Patrick**, a pilgrimage site with a statue of the saint at the summit; and the ruins of **Inch Abbey**, in a pretty marshland setting.

**St Patrick's Way** is a walking route from 1 to 7 miles (1.5–11km) along paths and quiet roads that pass many of the sites associated with St Patrick.

## St Patrick

St Patrick was a Roman Briton, born into a wealthy Christian family near Hadrian's Wall in the early 5th century. As a youth he was captured by Irish raiders and spent six years as a slave. He escaped, became a priest and at the age of about 30 returned to Ireland as a bishop around the year 432.

After founding his first church at Saul in County Down, he travelled throughout Ireland, converting the Celtic chieftains to Christianity. His mission had been preceded by that of Palladius, ordained as Ireland's first bishop in 431, but the Roman missionary was eclipsed by Patrick's greater fame.

Although the details of Patrick's life are uncertain, he is known to have preached in Ireland for 30 or 40 years and died before the end of the century.

# HILLSBOROUGH

**ⓘ Hillsborough Tourist Information Office** *The Courthouse, The Square; tel: 028 9268 9717. Open year-round.*

It's worth stopping for a stroll through this graceful Georgian village with its pretty terraced houses, antique shops, pub and restaurants. There are several historic buildings, including the **Courthouse** of 1790, topped by a cupola, in the town square. The **parish church**, rebuilt in 1773, contains striking Gothic woodwork and an 18th-century organ. **Hillsborough Castle**, residence of visiting diplomats and royals to Northern Ireland, is not open to the public, but its wrought-iron gates, dating to 1745, are arguably the country's finest. **Hillsborough Fort**, opposite the Courthouse and adjoining the **forest park**, is a 17th-century artillery fort remodelled with its more picturesque façade in the 18th century.

# LISBURN

**ⓘ Lisburn Tourist Information Office** *15 Lisburn Square; tel: 028 9266 0038. Open year-round.*

Lisburn is an attractive town with fine parks whose main attraction is the **Irish Linen Centre and Lisburn Museum**, where the 'Flax to Fabric' exhibition tells the story of the region's great linen industry. You can watch the weavers plying this ancient trade in the hand-loom

**Irish Linen Centre and Lisburn Museum £** 15 Lisburn Square; tel: 028 9266 3377. Open Mon–Sat 0930–1700.

workshop. The museum also covers the history and culture of the region. Behind the centre is Christ Church Cathedral. Built in 1623, it is a good example of the so-called Planters' Gothic style; the spire was added in the early 19th century. There are many Huguenot graves in the churchyard.

# MOUNT STEWART

**Mount Stewart ££** Portaferry Road, Newtownards; tel: 028 4278 8387. House open mid-Mar–Oct Thur–Tue 1100–1800; lakeside gardens open year-round daily 1000–1800; formal gardens open mid-Mar–Oct daily 1000–1800; Temple of the Winds open mid-Mar–Oct Sun 1400–1700.

Built in the 18th century, with later additions, Mount Stewart was the former seat of the Marquess of Londonderry. It is best known for its formal gardens, some of the finest in the British Isles. Covering 98 acres (40 hectares), they were planted with exotic plants and trees in the 1920s. The Shamrock Garden has a yew hedge in the shape of a shamrock and a topiary Irish harp; the Dodo Terrace has stone statues of dodos and an ark. The **Temple of the Winds**, a banqueting hall overlooking Strangford Lough, was built by James 'Athenian' Stuart, a pioneer of neoclassical architecture, in 1785. Highlights of the house include the dining room, with 22 chairs from the Congress of Vienna (1815) presented to Lord Castlereagh, the British foreign secretary, for his role in the talks; and a painting of the racehorse Hambletonian by George Stubbs.

# NEWCASTLE

**Newcastle Tourist Information Centre** 10–14 Central Promenade; tel: 028 4372 2222. Open year-round.

Newcastle is one of County Down's most popular resorts, with its 5-mile (8km) stretch of sandy beach, backed by the commanding Slieve Donard Mountain, rising to 2,795ft (852m). There are several family attractions, including the Tropicana Pleasure Beach with water slides and a heated outdoor pool, and Coco's, an adventure playground. Automobile lovers can visit the **Route 66 American Car Museum**. Nearby is the vast and beautiful **Tyrella Beach**, a Blue Flag beach where the mountains seem to sweep down to the sea.

## Accommodation and food in Newcastle

**Burrendale Hotel & Country Club ££–£££** *51 Castlewellan Road; tel: 028 4372 2599; fax: 028 4372 2328; www.burrendale.com.* The rooms are as luxurious as the views at this splendid hotel, set beneath the Mourne Mountains just outside Newcastle. The spacious rooms and suites have a light, modern décor and all amenities. Service is impressive in the Vine Restaurant, where you can choose from an excellent à la carte or *table d'hôte* menu of fresh Ulster fare and a fine wine list. The casual Cottage Kitchen has a good bistro menu; there are also two bars. Guests can use the pool, whirlpools, saunas and fitness facilities in the Country Club.

# PORTAFERRY

**Portaferry Tourist Information Centre**
*The Stables, Castle Street; tel: 028 4272 9882. Open Easter–Sept.*

**Exploris ££**
*The Rope Walk, Castle Street; tel: 028 4272 8062; www.exploris.org.uk. Open Apr–Aug Mon–Fri 1000–1800, Sat 1100–1800, Sun 1200–1800; Sept–Mar Mon–Fri 1000–1700, Sat 1100–1700, Sun 1300–1700.*

**Strangford Lough Car Ferry**
*Tel: 028 4488 1637; www.roadsni.gov.uk/strangfordferry. Departs Strangford every 30 minutes: Mon–Fri 0730–2230, Sat 0800–2300, Sun 0930–2230. Departs Portaferry: Mon–Fri 0745–2245, Sat 0815–2315, Sun 0945–2245.*

The best time to see this picturesque village on the banks of Strangford Lough is at sunset, a view that will look familiar from many brochure photographs. Its pretty waterfront, lined with terraced cottages, pubs and shops, is backed by rolling green hills. The remains of five tower houses stand on the shores around the slim channel that links the lough to the Irish Sea. Twice a day, 400 million tonnes of water flow in and out of the lough with the tides through 'the Narrows'. The lough area is a haven for marine life, with more than 2,000 species, including corals and sponges. Many can be seen at **Exploris**, Northern Ireland's only aquarium. A car ferry links Portaferry with Strangford on the opposite shore.

## Accommodation and food in Portaferry

**The Portaferry Hotel ££** *10 The Strand; tel: 028 4272 8231; fax: 028 4272 8999; email: info@portaferryhotel.com; www.portaferryhotel.com.* You can pamper yourself without breaking the bank at this charming waterside inn overlooking Strangford Lough. Some of the 14 beautifully appointed guest rooms have four-poster beds; others have lough views. Fresh flowers, *objets d'art* and Irish paintings enhance the hotel's intimate atmosphere. The award-winning restaurant features fresh seafood and local produce such as Mourne lamb, prime Ulster beef and game from nearby estates, and several vegetarian choices. A bar menu is served *from 1230 to 1430*, and there is a light early evening meal as well as the à la carte menu.

# STRANGFORD

**Castle Ward ££**
*Tel: 028 4488 1204. House open mid-Mar–Oct daily 1100–1700; grounds open Apr–Sept daily 1100–2000, Oct–Mar 1000–1600.*

This pretty village lies opposite Portaferry and is the other port for the Strangford Lough car ferry. Just outside town is **Castle Ward**, an 18th-century mansion with a split personality. It sports Palladian classical architecture on the front façade and Gothic on the garden side. This schizophrenic construction is the result of a dispute between Lord and Lady Bangor, who built the mansion in the 1760s. They disagreed about almost everything; the style of their house was no exception and represents a compromise. The interior design is equally mixed. There is also a Victorian laundry, a working corn mill and a pastime centre where children can dress up and play games. The 750-acre (300-hectare) estate, with beautiful walks and equestrian trails, is home to the **Strangford Lough Wildlife Centre**, with interpretive displays on the wildfowl, marine life, fauna and flora that can be seen in the area.

Cloughy Rocks lie south of Strangford, off the A2. You can often see seals here, depending on the tides. Nearby are the ruins of **Kilclief Castle** and the fishing village of **Ardglass**, with no fewer than six castle ruins around the harbour.

# ULSTER FOLK AND TRANSPORT MUSEUM

**Ulster Folk and Transport Museum ££** *Cultra, Holywood; tel: 028 9042 8428; www.uftm.org.uk. Open Mar–Sept Tue–Sun 1000–1700; Oct–Feb Tue–Fri 1000–1600, Sat & Sun 1100–1600. Last admission 1 hour before closing.*

Set in the grounds of Cultra Manor, this open-air museum – one of the best in Ireland – traces Ulster's past through a variety of reconstructed buildings. A thatched weaver's cottage, Victorian terraced houses, a rectory, a parish church, a village school and a flax mill are among the buildings that portray ways of life down the ages. There are also demonstrations of traditional crafts. The indoor transport galleries present every method of transport imaginable, from donkeys to modern aircraft. Top exhibits include the De Lorean automobile, produced in Belfast in 1982; the Irish Railway and Road Transport collections; and the exhibit on the *Titanic*, the fated luxury liner built in Belfast which sank in 1912.

# Suggested tour

**Total distance:** The main route is 68 miles (110km). The detour to the eastern side of the Ards Peninsula will add an extra 12 miles (19km). The drive around the Mourne Mountains will add an additional 65 miles (105km).

**Time:** The main route can be driven in 2–3 hours, depending on traffic, which can cause significant delays. The detour around the Mourne Mountains is similar in length, though you may want to break your journey with an overnight stay at Newcastle.

**Links:** This route connects with the Boyne Valley tour (*see page 66*) via Newry and Dundalk.

Leave Belfast on the A2 heading northeast along Belfast Lough (signposted Bangor). After 7 miles (11km) turn right at Cultra for the **ULSTER FOLK AND TRANSPORT MUSEUM ❶**. Continue along the A2 for 4 miles (6km), and turn right for **Newtownards**, with its octagonal 17th-century market cross that once served as a watchtower and gaol. **Scrabo Tower**, a 135ft (41m) Scottish baronial folly, built as a memorial to the 3rd Marquess of Londonderry in 1858, stands on a hill above the town. There are great views over the lake from the top. Head south on the A20, signposted to Portaferry, which runs along the banks of Strangford Lough to **MOUNT STEWART ❷**. Just south of the estate is the village of **Greyabbey**, named after a Cistercian abbey founded here in the 12th century. Continue south on the A20 to **PORTAFERRY ❸**.

**Detour:** To explore the eastern side of the Ards Peninsula, turn left off the A20 at Kircubbin on to the B173, which cuts across the peninsula. Turn left on to the A2 for **Portavogie**, a fishing village with an attractive harbour. If you're here when the boats are being unloaded, you may see seals who come in to scavenge for an easy meal in the harbour. Take the A2 south for 2 miles (3km) to Cloghy; turn left and follow the signposts

**ⓘ Kilkeel Tourist Information Centre**
*Nautilus Centre, Rooney Road; tel: 028 4176 2525. Open Easter–Dec.*

to **Kearney**, 4 miles (6km) further south along minor roads. This former fishing village has neat whitewashed houses that have been restored by the National Trust. There are good walks along the shore, with views across the Irish Sea to the Isle of Man, Scotland and England, and a sandy beach nearby. South of the village, there is an ancient burial site, the Millin Bay cairn, and a holy well and penance stone dating from the 7th century at Temple Cowey. Follow the road around the tip of the peninsula to rejoin the main tour at Portaferry.

Take the car ferry across Strangford Lough to **STRANGFORD ❹**. Take the A25 for 9 miles (14km) to **DOWNPATRICK ❺**, then the A7 north towards Belfast, and turn left on to the B2 for Ballynahinch. From here take the B177 northwest to **HILLSBOROUGH ❻**, then take the A1 north to **LISBURN ❼**. Continue on the A1/M1 back into Belfast.

**Detour:** For a longer route that explores the lovely **Mourne Mountains**, take the A25 south from Downpatrick; at Clough, take the A2 south to **NEWCASTLE ❽**. Continue south along the coast. Just before the fishing village of **Annalong**, watch for signs on your right leading to the **Silent Valley**. The valley, which encompasses reservoirs providing water for the greater Belfast area, is closed to traffic beyond the visitor centre, but there are fine walks or a shuttle bus to the top of Ben Crom Mountain. Follow signposts back to the coast at **Kilkeel**. The B27 cuts north through the mountains to Hilltown, but the road may be closed at **Spelga Dam**; ask locally before starting out. There are splendid views from the high point north of the dam. Alternatively, continue around the coast on the A2 (signposted Warrenpoint) to **Rostrevor**, a pretty village whose sheltered position between the mountains and Carlingford Lough allows lush vegetation to flourish. There is a forest park nearby. Take the B25 north to Hilltown (the viewpoint above Spelga Dam can be reached from this side as well). Continue north on the B25 through **Rathfriland**. Patrick Brontë, father of the Brontë sisters, was born in this area, and fans of the novelists can follow a signposted Brontë Homeland route (10 miles/16km) from the Drumballyroney school where he taught before moving to England. Carry on along the B25 to Katesbridge; turn left on the A50 (signposted Banbridge) and then right after about a mile (1.6km) to continue north on the B25 to the junction with the A1. Turn right and continue through Dromore to rejoin the main tour at Hillsborough.

**Irish linen**

With the arrival of Huguenot weavers at the end of the 17th century, Ulster became a major linen producer, particularly in the 'linen triangle' that stretched from Belfast southwest to Armagh and Dungannon. The industry flourished for over 200 years, but the costly production process eventually led to a decline in demand. Today, only small quantities are produced for the luxury goods market. Dozens of abandoned mills – often called 'beetling mills', after the final stage of the process in which the cloth was hammered to create a sheen – are dotted around the area.

## Also worth exploring

The western side of Strangford Lough, along the A22, is also scenic and has several attractions, including the castle at **Killyleagh**, the **Nendrum** monastic site and the **Castle Espie** Wetlands and Wildlife Centre.

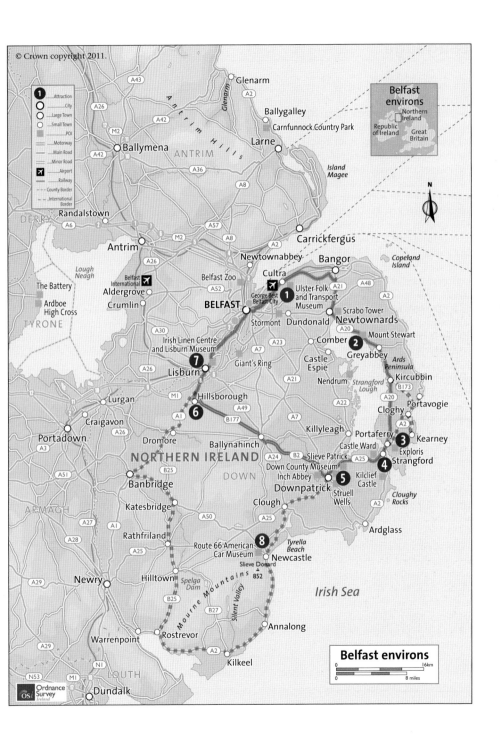

# Language

Ireland is officially bilingual. Everybody speaks English, although Irish prevails in the Gaeltacht regions (*see page 201*). Irish is a Gaelic language, though it is not called 'Gaelic' as such, and it differs from the Gaelic spoken in Scotland. It is the purest of the Celtic languages that were once spoken throughout much of Europe. The Norman gentry adopted Irish as their chosen tongue, and the country remained Irish speaking until the 16th century, but with the English Plantation and ascendancy of Crown control, the native language became a victim of the cultural genocide inflicted on the Irish in the 18th century. The potato famine and subsequent death and emigration of tens of thousands of Irish speakers took a further toll, and the use of Irish was relegated to the remote rural areas of the west coast.

A revival of the Irish language began in the late 19th century, spurred both by the nationalist movement and by the literary renaissance launched by writers such as W B Yeats, J M Synge and Lady Gregory, who plumbed the richness of Ireland's ancient storytelling tradition. Douglas Hyde initiated a campaign to promote the Irish language, and the Gaelic League was established in 1893. For the first time, Irish was taught in primary schools. After independence, the move to make Irish compulsory in schools was initially met with the usual Irish resistance to edicts of any form; yet many people willingly paid fees to give their children private lessons. Today, knowledge of Irish is a requirement for attending university. Although surveys vary, it is estimated that 11 per cent of the population are fluent Irish speakers. And although only 3–5 per cent use Irish as their everyday language – primarily in Gaeltacht regions – interest in learning it remains strong and people from around the country send their children to summer schools or to board with Irish-speaking families.

The English spoken in Ireland today still has traces of its Irish roots, as well as of the old English spoken in the Plantation days, in its structure and vocabulary. And the English language is all the richer for the Irish eloquence and turn of phrase. Almost all place names in Ireland are anglicised versions of Irish names, many of which describe the ancient landscape: for example, Glenbeigh (Gleann Beithe, or 'birch glen'), Derry (Doire or 'oak grove') and Adare (Ath Dara, or 'the ford of the oak tree'). American visitors will recognise words and phrases long a part of their own vernacular, and in this sense the language represents a preservation of Irish culture by those who were forced to leave, and their contribution to a new land.

Spoken Irish often bears little relation to the written word and visitors find it difficult to pronounce. There are few long vowels and many silent letters, such as the combination of *dh* (*sidhe*, for example, is pronounced 'shee'). Spellings of many place names, in both Irish and their English translations, vary from map to map and road sign to road sign.

Here are a few useful words, or words you will come across often in place names:

| | |
|---|---|
| **leithreas** | toilet |
| **fir** | men |
| **mná** | women |
| **an lár** | town centre |
| **bealach amach** | exit |
| **bealach isteach** | entrance |
| **dúnta** | closed |
| **oscailte** | open |
| **tra, trá** | a strand or beach |
| **knock, cnoc** | a hill |
| **baile** | a town |
| **clon, cluain** | a meadow |
| **mór, mor** | big or great |
| **kill, cill** | a church |
| **dun, dún** | a fort |

# Index

# Acknowledgements

**Project management:** Cambridge Publishing Management Limited
**Project editor:** Ed Robinson
**Series design:** Fox Design
**Cover design:** Liz Lyons Design
**Layout:** Cambridge Publishing Management Limited
**Mapwork:** PCGraphics (UK) Ltd
**Repro and image setting:** Cambridge Publishing Management Limited

We would like to thank **Donna Dailey** for the photographs in this book,
to whom the copyright belongs, except for the following images:

**Dreamstime.com:** pages 1A, 14 (Eireanna), 85 (Jeannel), 133 (Steve Dunn), 166 (Walshphotos), 176 (Krylon 80), 188 (Richardzz), and 258 (Andy2673); **Larry Dunmire:** pages 4–5, 11, 12, 23, 34, 38, 41, 44, 47, 50, 52, 54, 60, 62, 64, 65, 70A, 70B, 92A, 92B, 95, 101, 116, 121, 123, 134, 139, 142, 147, 158, 161 and 178; **Pictures Colour Library:** pages 24, 78 and 137; **Tourism Ireland Imagery:** page 18; **World Pictures/Photoshot:** pages 32, 168 and 174.

# Feedback form

We're committed to providing the very best up-to-date information in our travel guides and constantly strive to make them as useful as they can be. You can help us to improve future editions by letting us have your feedback. Just take a few minutes to complete and return this form to us.

**When did you buy this book?** ...........................................................................................................
..........................................................................................................................................................................

**Where did you buy it? (Please give town/city and, if possible, name of retailer)**
..........................................................................................................................................................................
..........................................................................................................................................................................

**When did you/do you intend to travel in Ireland?** ...............................................................
..........................................................................................................................................................................

**For how long (approx)?** ................................................................................................................

**How many people in your party?** ............................................................................................

**Which cities, national parks and other locations did you/do you intend mainly to visit?**
..........................................................................................................................................................................
..........................................................................................................................................................................
..........................................................................................................................................................................
..........................................................................................................................................................................

**Did you/will you:**
❏ Make all your travel arrangements independently?
❏ Travel on a fly-drive package?
Please give brief details: .............................................................................................................
..........................................................................................................................................................................

**Did you/do you intend to use this book:**
❏ For planning your trip?          ❏ Both?
❏ During the trip itself?

**Did you/do you intend also to purchase any of the following travel publications for your trip?**
Thomas Cook traveller guides: Ireland or Dublin ........................................................................
A road map/atlas (please specify) ................................................................................................
Other guidebooks (please specify) ...............................................................................................

**Have you used any other Thomas Cook guidebooks in the past? If so, which?**

..............................................................................................................................................................

..............................................................................................................................................................

Please rate the following features of *driving guides Ireland* for their value to you (Circle VU for 'very useful', U for 'useful', NU for 'little or no use'):

| | |
|---|---|
| The *Travel facts* section on pages 12–25 | VU    U    NU |
| The *Driver's guide* section on pages 26–31 | VU    U    NU |
| The *Highlights* on pages 42–3 | VU    U    NU |
| The recommended driving routes throughout the book | VU    U    NU |
| Information on towns and cities, national parks, etc | VU    U    NU |
| The maps of towns and cities, parks, etc | VU    U    NU |

Please use this space to tell us about any features that in your opinion could be changed, improved, or added in future editions of the book, or any other comments you would like to make concerning the book:

..............................................................................................................................................................

..............................................................................................................................................................

..............................................................................................................................................................

..............................................................................................................................................................

..............................................................................................................................................................

..............................................................................................................................................................

..............................................................................................................................................................

..............................................................................................................................................................

**Your age category:**    ❏ 21–30   ❏ 31–40   ❏ 41–50   ❏ over 50

Your name: Mr/Mrs/Miss/Ms ...............................................................................................

(First name or initials) .........................................................................................................

(Last name) ........................................................................................................................

Your full address (please include postal or zip code):

..............................................................................................................................................................

..............................................................................................................................................................

..............................................................................................................................................................

..............................................................................................................................................................

..............................................................................................................................................................

Your daytime telephone number: ......................................................................................

**Please detach this page and send it to: driving guides Series Editor, Thomas Cook Publishing, PO Box 227, The Thomas Cook Business Park, 9 Coningsby Road, Peterborough PE3 8SB**

**Alternatively, you can email us at: *books@thomascook.com***